KRISTAL

CW00961084

28/10

by
Siegfried Haenisch

AGS Publishing
Circle Pines, Minnesota 55014-1796
800-328-2560

About the Author

Siegfried Haenisch, Ed.D., holds a master's degree in mathematics and has taught mathematics at every level, from elementary to graduate school, most recently as Professor in the Department of Mathematics and Statistics at the College of New Jersey. The Mathematical Association of America granted him the 1995 Award for Distinguished Teaching of Mathematics. Dr. Haenisch was the site director for the training of teachers in the New Jersey Algebra Project. He was a member of the National Science Foundation Institutes in Mathematics at Rutgers University, Oberlin College, and Princeton University. At Yale University, he was a member of the Seminar in the History of Mathematics, sponsored by the National Endowment in the Humanities. Dr. Haenisch currently serves as a mathematics curriculum consultant to school districts.

Photo credits for this textbook can be found on page 494.

The publisher wishes to thank the following educators for their helpful comments during the review process for *Pre-Algebra*. Their assistance has been invaluable.

David Arnold, SLD Teacher, Winter Park Ninth Grade Center, Winter Park, Florida; **Tamara Bell,** Special Education Teacher, Muncie Community Schools, Southside High School, Muncie, Indiana; **Jacqueline DeWitt,** Cooperative Consultant, Umatilla High School, Sorrento, Florida; **Tina Dobson,** Special Education Math Resource Specialist, Sandridge Junior High School; Roy, Utah; **Connie Eichhorn,** Career Center and Adult Education Program, Omaha Public Schools, Omaha, Nebraska; **Dr. Rita Giles,** Program Director, Fairfax County Public Schools, Alexandria, Virginia; **Anne Hobbs,** Special Education Secondary Coordinator, Hobbs Municipal Schools, Hobbs, New Mexico; **Deborah Horn,** Wayne City High School, Wayne City, Illinois; **Rosanne Hudok,** Learning Support Teacher, Keystone Oaks High School, Pittsburgh, Pennsylvania; **Robert Jones,** Mathematics Supervisor, Cleveland Public Schools, Cleveland, Ohio; **Lee Kucera,** Math Teacher, Capistrano Valley High School, Mission Viejo, California; **Anne Lally,** Algebra Teacher, Eli Whitney School, Chicago, Illinois; **Christine Lansford,** Coordinator of Special Education, Melville Comprehensive School, Melville, Saskatchewan, Canada; **Robert Maydak,** Math Specialist, Pittsburgh Mt. Oliver Intermediate Unit, Pittsburgh, Pennsylvania; **Kathe Neighbor,** Math Chair, Crawford High School, San Diego, California; **Rachelle Powell,** Department Chair, Dr. Ralph H. Poteet High School, Mesquite, Texas; **Jacqueline Smith,** Resource Department Chair, Sterling High School, Baytown, Texas; **Carol Warren,** Math Teacher, Crockett County High School, Alamo, Tennessee; **William Wible,** Math Resource Teacher, San Diego Unified, San Diego, California

Publisher's Project Staff

Vice President, Product Development: Kathleen T. Williams, Ph.D., NCSP; Associate Director, Product Development: Teri Mathews; Managing Editor; Patrick Keithahn; Assistant Editor: Karen Anderson; Development Assistant: Bev Johnson; Senior Designer: Tony Perleberg; Creative Services Manager: Nancy Condon; Desktop Publishing Artist: Jack Ross; Purchasing Agent: Mary Kaye Kuzma; Senior Marketing Manager/Secondary Curriculum: Brian Holl

© 2004 AGS Publishing
4201 Woodland Road
Circle Pines, MN 55014-1796
800-328-2560 • www.agsnet.com

AGS Publishing is a trademark and trade name of American Guidance Service, Inc.

All rights reserved, including translation. No part of this publication may be reproduced or transmitted in any form or by any means without written permission from the publisher.

Printed in the United States of America

ISBN 0-7854-3555-7

Product Number 93800

A 0 9 8 7 6 5

Contents

How to Use This Book: A Study Guide

Welcome to *Pre-Algebra.* This book includes the basic concepts of mathematics and introduces you to algebra concepts. Why do you need these skills? There are many jobs that use mathematics and algebra. People who work in food service, banking, printing, electronics, construction, surveying, and insurance all use these skills on the job. You will also use these skills at home and in school.

As you read this book, notice how each lesson is organized. Information will appear at the beginning of each lesson. Read this information carefully. A sample problem with step-by-step instructions will follow. Use the instructions to learn how to solve a certain kind of problem. Once you know how to solve this kind of problem, you will have the chance to solve similar problems on your own. If you have trouble with a lesson, try reading it again.

Before you start to read this book, it is important that you understand how to use it. It is also important to know how to be successful in this course. This first section of the book is here to help you achieve these things.

How to Study

These tips can help you study more effectively:

◆ Plan a regular time to study.
◆ Choose a quiet desk or table where you will not be distracted. Find a spot that has good lighting.
◆ Gather all the books, pencils, paper, and other equipment you will need to complete your assignments.
◆ Decide on a goal. For example: "I will finish reading and taking notes on Chapter 1, Lesson 1, by 8:00."
◆ Take a five- to ten-minute break every hour to keep alert.
◆ If you start to feel sleepy, take a break and get some fresh air.

Chapter

1 Algebra and Whole Numbers

If you picked a peck of pickled peppers (or maybe peaches), how many would you pick? A peck is a measurement, like pint or bushel. There are four pecks in a bushel. You could count all the peaches in those bushel baskets. You would use the ten numerals from our decimal system: 0, 1, 2, 3, 4, 5, 6, 7, 8, and 9. You use these numerals every day when you tell your age, remember a phone number, or count the number of music CDs you have. In math, you use these numerals to show whole numbers and parts of whole numbers—fractions and decimals.

In Chapter 1, you will review basic operations of arithmetic and be introduced to simple algebraic expressions.

Goals for Learning

◆ To review addition and subtraction using whole numbers
◆ To learn to estimate sums and differences
◆ To review multiplication and division using whole numbers
◆ To learn to estimate products and quotients
◆ To recognize true, false, and open statements
◆ To recognize algebraic and numerical expressions
◆ To evaluate algebraic expressions

1

Before Beginning Each Chapter

◆ Read the chapter title and study the photograph. What does the photo tell you about the chapter title?
◆ Read the opening paragraphs.
◆ Study the Goals for Learning. The Chapter Review and tests will ask questions related to these goals.
◆ Look at the Chapter Review. The questions cover the most important information in the chapter.

Note the Chapter Features

Application
A look at how a topic in the chapter relates to real life

Notes
Hints or reminders that point out important information

Look for this box for helpful tips!

Technology Connection
Use technology to
apply math skills

Try This
New ways to think about
problems and solve them

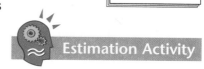

Writing About Mathematics
Opportunities to write about
problems and alternate solutions

Estimation Activity
Use estimation as a way to
check reasonableness of
an answer

Calculator Practice
How to solve problems using
a calculator

Algebra in Your Life
Relates algebra to the "real world"

Before Beginning Each Lesson

Read the lesson title and
restate it in the form of
a question.

For example, write: *How do
you add whole numbers?*

Look over the entire lesson,
noting the following:
◆ bold words
◆ text organization
◆ exercises
◆ notes in the margins
◆ photos

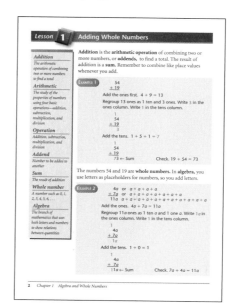

As You Read the Lesson

◆ Read the major headings.

◆ Read the subheads and paragraphs that follow.

◆ Read the content in the example boxes.

◆ Before moving on to the next lesson, see if you understand the concepts you read. If you do not, reread the lesson. If you are still unsure, ask for help.

◆ Practice what you have learned by doing the exercises in each lesson.

Using the Bold Words

Knowing the meaning of all the boxed words in the left column will help you understand what you read.

These words appear in **bold type** the first time they appear in the text and are often defined in the paragraph.

> Interest is stated in **percents,** or parts per hundred.

All of the words in the left column are also defined in the **glossary**.

> **Percent** (pər sent′) Parts per one hundred, hundredth (p. 50)

Bold type
Words seen for the first time will appear in bold type
Glossary
Words listed in this column are also found in the glossary

What to Do with a Word You Do Not Know

When you come to a word you do not know, ask yourself:

◆ **Is the word a compound word?**
Can you find two words within the word? This could help you understand the meaning. For example: *rainfall.*

◆ **Does the word have a prefix at the beginning?**
For example: *improper.* The prefix *im-* means "not," so this word refers to something that is not proper.

◆ **Does the word have a suffix at the end?**
For example: *variable, -able.* This means "able to vary."

◆ **Can you identify the root word?**
Can you sound it out in parts?
For example: *un known.*

◆ **Are there any clues in the sentence that will help you understand the word?**

Look for the word in the margin box, glossary, or dictionary.

If you are still having trouble with a word, ask for help.

Using Tables to Solve Problems

Four tables can be found in the back of this book. There is one for each of the four main math operations: addition, subtraction, multiplication, and division. You are encouraged to memorize these tables or refer to them as needed. If you are allowed to use a calculator, you may choose to use one instead of these tables.

Using the Chapter Reviews

◆ For each Chapter Review, answer the multiple choice questions first.

◆ Answer the questions under the other parts of the Chapter Review.

◆ To help you take tests, read the Test-Taking Tips at the end of each Chapter Review.

Test-Taking Tip

Drawing pictures or diagrams is one way to help you understand and solve problems.

Preparing for Tests

◆ Complete the exercises in each lesson. Make up similar problems to practice what you have learned. You may want to do this with a classmate and share your questions.

◆ Review your answers to lesson exercises and Chapter Reviews.

◆ Test yourself on vocabulary words and key ideas.

◆ Practice problem-solving strategies.

Using the Answer Key

Pages 392–426 of this book show answers and solutions to selected problems. The problems with black numbers show answers. The problems with red numbers also show step-by-step solutions. Use the answers and solutions to check your work.

Using a Calculator

An electronic calculator can help you with many algebra problems. There are many different kinds of calculators available. Some calculators have a few keys and perform only a few simple operations. Other calculators have many keys and do many advanced calculations. It is important to know what your calculator can do and how to use it. Here are some tips for using the keys on most calculators. To learn more about your own calculator, read the instructions that come with it.

The diagram shows an example of a scientific calculator. It describes the keys that you will most likely use in algebra.

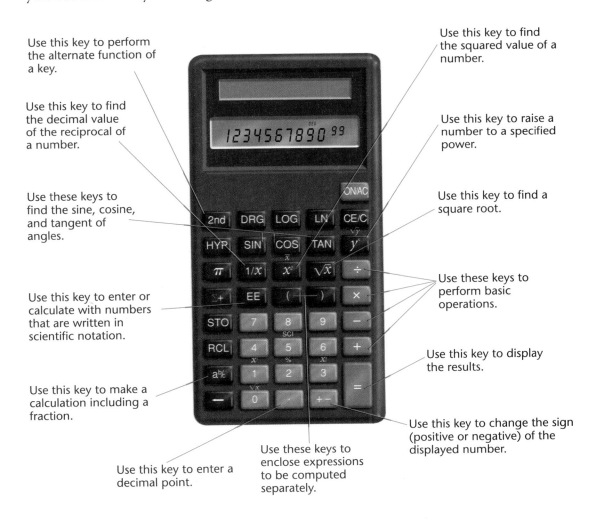

Use this key to perform the alternate function of a key.

Use this key to find the squared value of a number.

Use this key to find the decimal value of the reciprocal of a number.

Use this key to raise a number to a specified power.

Use these keys to find the sine, cosine, and tangent of angles.

Use this key to find a square root.

Use this key to enter or calculate with numbers that are written in scientific notation.

Use these keys to perform basic operations.

Use this key to display the results.

Use this key to make a calculation including a fraction.

Use this key to enter a decimal point.

Use these keys to enclose expressions to be computed separately.

Use this key to change the sign (positive or negative) of the displayed number.

Problem-Solving Strategies

The main reason for learning math skills is to help us use math to solve everyday problems. You will notice sets of problem-solving exercises throughout your text. When you learn a new math skill, you will have a chance to apply this skill to a real-life problem.

Following these steps will help you to solve the problems.

1 Read

Read the problem to discover what information you are to gather. Study the problem to decide if you have all the information you need or if you need more data. Also study the problem to decide if it includes information you do not need to solve the problem. Begin thinking about the steps needed to solve the problem.

Ask yourself:

◆ Am I looking for a part of a number?
◆ Am I looking for a larger number?
◆ Am I looking for more than one number?
◆ Will solving the problem require multiple steps?

For example, read this problem:

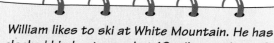

William likes to ski at White Mountain. He has clocked his best speed at 16 miles per hour. On his first run, William's time is 42 seconds. He completes his second run in 54 seconds. What is William's best time? What is his average time for the two runs?

This problem asks you to figure out William's best time and his average time. The problem gives you information about each of the run times. It also gives unnecessary information about his clocked speed in miles per hour.

In order to answer the questions, you see that you need to compare the two run times, then calculate an average. You will solve for two numbers.

2   Plan

Think about the steps you will need to do to solve the problem. Decide if you are going to calculate this mentally, on paper, or with a calculator. Will you need to add, subtract, multiply, or divide? Will you need to do more than one step? If possible, estimate your answer.

These strategies may help you to find a solution:

◆ Simplify or reword the problem
◆ Draw a picture
◆ Make a chart or graph to illustrate the problem

◆ Divide the problem into smaller parts
◆ Look for a pattern
◆ Use a formula or write an equation

Divide the example problem into two parts.

◆ First, compare the two run times to decide which is William's best time.
◆ Second, find the average of the two numbers. Use the formula for finding the average or *mean* of a set of values.

3   Solve

Follow your plan and do the calculations. Check your work. Make sure to label your answer correctly.

Best Run Time
Compare the numbers 42 and 54. 42 < 54. 42 seconds is William's best time.
Average Time
Add the values. $42 + 54 = 96$
Count the number of pieces of data.   2 values
Divide the sum of the values by the number of pieces of data. $96 \div 2 = 48$

The average of 42 seconds and 54 seconds is 48 seconds.

4   Reflect

Reread the problem and ask yourself if your answer makes sense. Did you answer the questions? You can also check your work to see if your answers are correct.

William's best time is 42 seconds, because 42 is less than 54. His average time for the two runs is 48 seconds. The answer makes sense because 48 is exactly halfway between 42 and 54.

Algebra and Whole Numbers

I f you picked a peck of pickled peppers (or maybe peaches), how many would you pick? A peck is a measurement, like pint or bushel. There are four pecks in a bushel. You could count all the peaches in those bushel baskets. You would use the ten numerals from our decimal system: 0, 1, 2, 3, 4, 5, 6, 7, 8, and 9. You use these numerals every day when you tell your age, remember a phone number, or count the number of music CDs you have. In math, you use these numerals to show whole numbers and parts of whole numbers—fractions and decimals.

In Chapter 1, you will review basic operations of arithmetic and be introduced to simple algebraic expressions.

Goals for Learning

◆ To review addition and subtraction using whole numbers

◆ To learn to estimate sums and differences

◆ To review multiplication and division using whole numbers

◆ To learn to estimate products and quotients

◆ To recognize true, false, and open statements

◆ To recognize algebraic and numerical expressions

◆ To evaluate algebraic expressions

Addition is the **arithmetic operation** of combining two or more numbers, or **addends,** to find a total. The result of addition is a **sum.** Remember to combine like place values whenever you add.

Addition

The arithmetic operation of combining two or more numbers to find a total

Arithmetic

The study of the properties of numbers using four basic operations—addition, subtraction, multiplication, and division

Operation

Addition, subtraction, multiplication, and division

Addend

Number to be added to another

Sum

The result of addition

Whole number

A number such as 0, 1, 2, 3, 4, 5, 6, . . .

Algebra

The branch of mathematics that uses both letters and numbers to show relations between quantities

EXAMPLE 1

$$54$$
$$+\ 19$$

Add the ones first. $4 + 9 = 13$

Regroup 13 ones as 1 ten and 3 ones. Write 3 in the ones column. Write 1 in the tens column.

$$1$$
$$54$$
$$+\ 19$$
$$\overline{3}$$

Add the tens. $1 + 5 + 1 = 7$

$$1$$
$$54$$
$$+\ 19$$
$$\overline{73} \leftarrow \text{Sum}$$ Check. $19 + 54 = 73$

The numbers 54 and 19 are **whole numbers.** In **algebra,** you use letters as placeholders for numbers, so you add letters.

EXAMPLE 2

$$4a \quad \text{or} \quad a + a + a + a$$
$$+\ 7a \quad \text{or} \quad a + a + a + a + a + a + a$$
$$11a \quad a + a + a + a + a + a + a + a + a + a + a$$

Add the ones. $4a + 7a = 11a$

Regroup 11a ones as 1 ten a and 1 one a. Write 1a in the ones column. Write 1 in the tens column.

$$1$$
$$4a$$
$$+\ 7a$$
$$\overline{1a}$$

Add the tens. $1 + 0 = 1$

$$1$$
$$4a$$
$$+\ 7a$$
$$\overline{11a} \leftarrow \text{Sum}$$ Check. $7a + 4a = 11a$

The order in which you add numbers does not change the answer.
For example,
$2 + 6 = 8$ and
$6 + 2 = 8$.

EXAMPLE 3 Add $267 + 1{,}342 + 68$.

Write the problem in vertical form. Add the ones. Regroup 17 ones as 1 ten and 7 ones. Write 7 in the ones column. Write 1 in the tens column.

$$
\begin{array}{r}
1 \\
267 \\
1{,}342 \\
+\quad 68 \\
\hline
7
\end{array}
$$

Add the tens. Regroup 17 tens as 1 hundred and 7 tens. Write 7 in the tens column. Write 1 in the hundreds column.

$$
\begin{array}{r}
1 \\
267 \\
1{,}342 \\
+\quad 68 \\
\hline
77
\end{array}
$$

Add the hundreds. Write 6 in the hundreds column.

$$
\begin{array}{r}
1 \\
267 \\
1{,}342 \\
+\quad 68 \\
\hline
677
\end{array}
$$

Add the thousands. Write 1 in the thousands column.

$$
\begin{array}{r}
267 \\
1{,}342 \\
+\quad 68 \\
\hline
1{,}677
\end{array}
$$

Exercise A Add the following addends.

1. 23
    $+\ 9$

6. 27
    $+\ 54$

11.   919
     $+\ 1{,}884$

2. 38
    $+\ 13$

7. 18
    $+\ 45$

12. $4a$
     $+\ 8a$

3. 58
    $+\ 5$

8. 186
    $+\ 458$

13. $92x$
     $+\ 68x$

4. 97
    $+\ 7$

9. 906
    $+\ 87$

14. $453x$
     $+\ 94x$

5. 68
    $+\ 3$

10. 553
     $+\ 699$

15. $49a$
     $+\ 27a$

Exercise B Write each problem in vertical form. Then add.

16. $41 + 329 + 7$

17. $754 + 62 + 276$

18. $18 + 62 + 121$

19. $158 + 64 + 352$

20. $91 + 56 + 165$

21. $1{,}269 + 789 + 56$

22. $503a + 17a + 407a$

23. $7a + 29a + 232a$

24. $25x + 429x + 654x$

Calculator Practice

You can use a calculator to solve addition problems and to check your answers.

EXAMPLE 4 Add 243 + 475.

Enter *243*.

Press ☐ + ☐.

Enter *475*.

Press ☐ = ☐.

The display reads *718*.

Exercise C Use a calculator to find the answers.

25. 135 + 89

26. 268 + 352

27. 471 + 625

28. 144 + 62 + 361

29. 550 + 332 + 663

30. 895 + 752 + 402

 PROBLEM SOLVING

Exercise D Solve each problem.

31. Natawa has $85 in her savings account. She deposits $55 that she received for her birthday. How much money is in her account now?

32. Brett has 324 sports cards. His sister, Mariette, has 1,232 sports cards. How many cards do they have altogether?

33. On Tuesday Leon drove 412 miles. On Wednesday he drove 463 miles. How many miles did he drive altogether?

34. Ana has 32 CDs, Gina has 51 CDs, and Callie has 46 CDs. How many CDs do they have altogether?

35. Ann earned $121 the first week, $132 the second week, and $128 the third week at her cashier's job. How much money did she make in the three weeks?

Subtraction is the arithmetic operation of taking one number away from another. The result of subtraction is a **difference.**

Subtraction

The arithmetic operation of taking one number away from another

Difference

The result of subtraction

Inverse

Exactly opposite

Rename

To give a new form that is equal to the original

EXAMPLE 1

$$\begin{array}{r} 18 \\ -\ 6 \\ \hline 12 \end{array} \leftarrow \text{Difference}$$

Check.
$$\begin{array}{r} 12 \\ +\ 6 \\ \hline 18 \end{array}$$

In algebra, you use letters for numbers, so a subtraction problem could look like this.

EXAMPLE 2

$$\begin{array}{lll} 4x & \text{or} & x + x + \cancel{x} + \cancel{x} \\ -\ 2x & \text{or} & -\ \qquad \cancel{x} + \cancel{x} \\ \hline 2x & \text{or} & x + x \end{array}$$

Since subtraction and addition are **inverse,** or opposite, operations, you can check a subtraction problem using addition.

$$\begin{array}{r} 4x \\ -\ 2x \\ \hline 2x \end{array} \qquad \text{Check.} \qquad \begin{array}{r} 2x \\ +\ 2x \\ \hline 4x \end{array}$$

Just as you can check the answer to a subtraction problem by adding, you can check the answer to an addition problem by subtracting. For example,
610 + 22 = 632.
Check:
632 − 22 = 610.

Sometimes when you subtract, you need to **rename.**

EXAMPLE 3

53 − 9 = ■

You cannot subtract 9 from 3. Rename 5 tens 3 ones as 4 tens 13 ones.

$$\begin{array}{r} 53 \\ -\ 9 \end{array} \qquad \text{Rename:} \qquad \begin{array}{r} \overset{4\ 13}{\cancel{5}\ \cancel{3}} \\ -\ 9 \end{array}$$

Then subtract.

$$\begin{array}{r} \overset{4\ 13}{5\ 3} \\ -\ \ 9 \\ \hline 4\ 4 \end{array}$$

Check. 44 + 9 = 53

EXAMPLE 4 $4,321 - 586 = \blacksquare$

Write the problem in vertical form.

$$\begin{array}{r} 4,321 \\ -\ \ 586 \end{array}$$

You cannot subtract 6 from 1. Rename 2 tens 1 one as 1 ten 11 ones. Subtract. Then rename the hundreds and thousands and subtract.

$$\begin{array}{r} {\scriptstyle 3\ 12\ 11\ 11} \\ 4,3\ 2\ 1 \\ -\ 5\ 8\ 6 \\ \hline 3,7\ 3\ 5 \end{array}$$

Check.
$$\begin{array}{r} 3,735 \\ +\ \ 586 \\ \hline 4,321 \end{array}$$

Addition problems have *addends* and *sums.* Subtraction problems have *minuends, subtrahends,* and *differences.*

$$\begin{array}{r} 18 \leftarrow \text{minuend} \\ -6 \leftarrow \text{subtrahend} \\ \hline 12 \leftarrow \text{difference} \end{array}$$

Exercise A Subtract. Find the difference.

1. $\begin{array}{r} 74 \\ -\ 68 \end{array}$

4. $\begin{array}{r} 41 \\ -\ \ 8 \end{array}$

7. $\begin{array}{r} 36a \\ -\ 7a \end{array}$

2. $\begin{array}{r} 90 \\ -\ 32 \end{array}$

5. $\begin{array}{r} 47 \\ -\ 18 \end{array}$

8. $\begin{array}{r} 54a \\ -\ 29a \end{array}$

3. $\begin{array}{r} 55 \\ -\ \ 6 \end{array}$

6. $\begin{array}{r} 62x \\ -\ 9x \end{array}$

9. $\begin{array}{r} 23x \\ -\ 5x \end{array}$

Technology Connection

Using a Calculator to Budget Your Money
Calculators are so small that you can take them everywhere. They're handy tools. Carry one with you to a ball game or a shopping mall. You can use the calculator to help you make the most of your spending money. Think about the snacks and items you want to buy. Use the calculator to subtract their cost from the cash you have. You'll be able to see whether or not you can afford them all—before you actually spend your money.

10. $1,400 - 379$

11. $5,000 - 748$

12. $24,115 - 4,246$

13. $26,388 - 1,699$

14. $53,404 - 898$

15. $167,124y - 18,246y$

16. $7,125x - 836x$

17. $152,647a - 36,458a$

18. $34,472k - 14,854k$

Calculator Practice

You can use a calculator to solve subtraction problems and to check your answers.

EXAMPLE 5   Subtract $13,456 - 798$.
Enter *13456*.
Press $\boxed{-}$.
Enter *798*.
Press $\boxed{=}$.
The display reads *12658*.

Exercise C Use a calculator to find the answers.

19. $135 - 89$

20. $352 - 168$

21. $1,638 - 942$

22. $9,978 - 45$

23. $13,413 - 332$

24. $1,765 - 752$

25. $48,987 - 43,444$

26. $16,540 - 8,324$

PROBLEM SOLVING

Exercise D Solve each problem.

27. Tasty Apple Orchard has 385 bushels of apples for sale. The orchard sells 223 bushels in one week. How many bushels are left?

28. At the local supermarket, a loaf of bread usually costs $2.15. This week, bread is on sale for $1.59. How much can you save by buying one loaf of bread this week?

29. The library has 2,530 children's books. If 335 children's books have been checked out, how many remain in the library?

30. The Lincoln High School team won the basketball game with 123 points. Washington High School's team scored fifteen fewer points. What was the Washington team's final score?

Writing About Mathematics

Write a short paragraph expressing your opinion about whether using coupons is worthwhile. Be sure to give reasons to support your opinion.

TRY THIS ➧ Newspapers often have coupons for products. Cut out a coupon for one item. Find out how much the item costs without the coupon. How much will you pay if you redeem the coupon when you buy the item?

Estimate

A careful guess; a close or nearly correct answer

When rounding a number to its greatest place value, look at the numeral next to the greatest place value. If the numeral is 5 or more, round up. If it is less than 5, round down. For example, round 591 up to 600 and 531 down to 500.

You can use **estimation** to check whether a sum or difference makes sense.

EXAMPLE 1   Estimate 3,243 + 262 + 1,894.

Round each number to its greatest place value.

$$3,243 \rightarrow 3,000$$
$$262 \rightarrow 300$$
$$1,894 \rightarrow 2,000$$

Add the rounded numbers.

$$
\begin{array}{r}
3,000 \\
300 \\
+\ 2,000 \\
\hline
5,300
\end{array}
$$

An estimate of the sum
3,243 + 262 + 1,894 is 5,300.

EXAMPLE 2   Estimate 1,984 − 632.

Round each number to its greatest place value.

$$1,984 \rightarrow 2,000$$
$$632 \rightarrow 600$$

Subtract the rounded numbers.

$$
\begin{array}{r}
2,000 \\
-\ \ \ 600 \\
\hline
1,400
\end{array}
$$

An estimate of the difference
1,984 − 632 is 1,400.

Whenever you add or subtract to find exact sums and differences, estimate first. Then compare your exact answer to your estimate and decide whether your answer makes sense.

Exercise A Estimate each sum.

1. 643 + 821

2. 3,916 + 542

3. 21,647 + 912 + 385

4. 40,429 + 6,950 + 532

5. 105,990 + 67,192 + 8,915 + 78

Exercise B Estimate each difference.

6. 875 − 397

7. 1,980 − 529

8. 18,401 − 8,640

9. 101,600 − 36,970

10. 214,401 − 67,801

Exercise C Estimate. Then find the exact answer.

11. 28 + 73

12. 643 + 825

13. 912 + 556

14. 85 − 47

15. 864 + 544

16. 753 − 364

17. 10,642 + 2,652

18. 63,467 + 88,926

19. 95,110 − 65,257

20. 100,354 − 29,689

Multiplication

The arithmetic operation that adds a number a given amount of times

Factor

The numbers in a multiplication statement

Product

The result of multiplication

Multiplication gives the same result as repeated addition.

$$
\begin{array}{r}
4 \\
4 \\
+\ 4 \\
\end{array} \quad \text{4 three times}
$$

$$
\underbrace{4 \quad \times \quad 3}_{\text{factors}} \quad = \quad \underset{\text{product}}{12}
$$

EXAMPLE 1 $42 \times 7 = \blacksquare$

$$
\begin{array}{r}
42 \\
\times\ 7 \\
\hline
14 \\
+\ 280 \\
\hline
294 \\
\end{array}
$$

      14   Multiply the ones, 2×7.
  + 280   Multiply the tens, 40×7.
     294   Add.

Different symbols are used to indicate multiplication. $\times$ means "multiply," so $6 \times 2 = 12$. • means "multiply," so $6 \cdot 2 = 12$. Parentheses can mean "multiply," so $6(2) = 12$.

In algebra, you multiply numbers with letters, such as $3x$ times 3. You multiply in the same way as in arithmetic.

EXAMPLE 2

$$
\begin{array}{r}
3x \cdot 3 \\
\\
3x \\
\times\ 3 \\
\hline
9x \\
\end{array}
$$

or

$$
\begin{array}{l}
3x \cdot 3 \\
x + x + x \\
x + x + x \\
x + x + x \\
9x \\
\end{array}
$$

$3x$ three times

When the product of the ones is greater than 9, you must rename the tens and ones.

EXAMPLE 3 $54 \times 38 = \blacksquare$

Step 1	Step 2	Step 3
$\begin{array}{r} 3 \\ 54 \\ \times\ 38 \\ \hline 432 \end{array}$	$\begin{array}{r} 1 \\ 54 \\ \times\ 38 \\ \hline 432 \\ 1{,}620 \end{array}$	$\begin{array}{r} 54 \\ \times\ 38 \\ \hline 432 \\ +\ 1{,}620 \\ \hline 2{,}052 \end{array}$
Multiply the ones.	Multiply the tens.	Add.

You multiply the same way in algebra, but you also must include the letter as part of the answer.

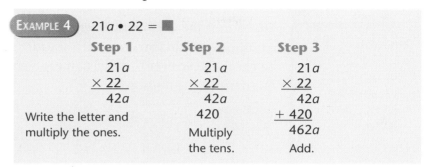

EXAMPLE 4 $21a \cdot 22 = \blacksquare$

Step 1	Step 2	Step 3
$21a$	$21a$	$21a$
$\times\ 22$	$\times\ 22$	$\times\ 22$
$42a$	$42a$	$42a$
	420	$+\ 420$
		$462a$
Write the letter and multiply the ones.	Multiply the tens.	Add.

Exercise A Multiply the following problems.

1.	4 ×6	**5.**	8 ×4	**9.**	96 ×63	**13.**	5 ×9	**17.**	$9a$ ×6
2.	24 ×4	**6.**	85 ×34	**10.**	64 ×64	**14.**	86 ×6	**18.**	73 ×$8x$
3.	54 ×46	**7.**	93 ×87	**11.**	7 ×8	**15.**	88 ×41	**19.**	64 ×$9x$
4.	65 ×45	**8.**	56 ×7	**12.**	74 ×82	**16.**	37 ×84	**20.**	$24a$ ×78

Exercise B Rewrite these problems in vertical form. Then multiply.

21. 237×456 **22.** 971×365 **23.** 147×447

PROBLEM SOLVING

Exercise C Solve each problem.

24. A complex has 4 office buildings. Each building has 26 offices. How many offices are there in the complex?

25. Jessica bought 3 reams of paper. Each ream has 500 sheets of paper. How many sheets of paper did Jessica buy?

Division

The arithmetic operation of finding how many times a number goes into another number

Divisor

The number that is used to divide

Dividend

The number that is divided

Quotient

The result of division

Remainder

Amount left over when dividing

Division is the arithmetic operation of finding how many times a number, the **divisor,** goes into another number, the **dividend.** To check the answer to a division problem, multiply the **quotient** by the divisor.

EXAMPLE 1 $42 \div 7 = \blacksquare$

$$\begin{array}{r} 6 \\ 7\overline{)42} \end{array}$$
Divisor → $7\overline{)42}$ ← Dividend
 $\qquad\qquad$ ← Quotient

Check.   6 ← Quotient
      $\underline{\times\ 7}$ ← Divisor
      42 ← Dividend

Division is the same in algebra as in arithmetic.

EXAMPLE 2 $8a \div 2 = \blacksquare$ or $8a \div 2 = \blacksquare$

$a + a + a + a | a + a + a + a$ $(8 \div 2)a =$

$\qquad 4a \qquad\qquad\quad 4a$ $\dfrac{8}{2}a = 4a$

$\qquad 8a \div 2 = 4a$

Check. $4a$
         $\underline{\times\ 2}$
          $8a$

When dividing, place the numbers correctly in each step.

EXAMPLE 3 $144 \div 6 = \blacksquare$

$$\begin{array}{r} 24 \\ 6\overline{)144} \\ -\ 12 \\ \hline 24 \\ -\ 24 \\ \hline 0 \end{array}$$

6 goes into 14 two times. Multiply 6 by 2.
Subtract 12 from 14. Bring down the 4.
6 goes into 24 four times. Multiply 6 by 4.
Subtract 24 from 24. The **remainder** is 0.

Check. $24 \times 6 = 144$

A remainder is always written as part of the quotient.

EXAMPLE 4 $300 \div 8 = \blacksquare$

$$
\begin{array}{r}
37 \text{ r4} \\
8\overline{)300} \\
-24 \\
60 \\
-56 \\
4
\end{array}
$$

8 does not go into 3.
8 goes into 30 three times. Multiply 8 by 3.
Subtract 24 from 30. Bring down the 0.
8 goes into 60 seven times. Multiply 8 by 7.
Subtract 56 from 60. Write the remainder 4 as part of the quotient.

Check. $(37 \times 8) + 4 = 296 + 4 = 300$

Exercise A Divide these problems.

1. $5\overline{)45}$

2. $8\overline{)96}$

3. $3\overline{)27}$

4. $5\overline{)120}$

5. $9\overline{)72}$

6. $6\overline{)378}$

7. $6\overline{)48c}$

8. $4\overline{)116b}$

9. $8\overline{)64a}$

10. $9\overline{)621x}$

Exercise B Divide. Check your work.

11. $5\overline{)412}$

12. $9\overline{)566}$

13. $2\overline{)347}$

14. $8\overline{)659}$

15. $7\overline{)589}$

16. $7\overline{)499}$

17. $8\overline{)489}$

18. $6\overline{)623}$

19. $6\overline{)827}$

20. $5\overline{)403}$

Exercise C Divide. Be sure to show your work.

21. $4,650 \div 8$

22. $27,542 \div 9$

23. $7,652 \div 13$

24. $5,625 \div 24$

25. $61,923 \div 64$

26. $42,450 \div 89$

Calculator Practice

You can use a calculator to solve division and multiplication problems and to check your answers.

EXAMPLE 5 | Divide 630 ÷ 45.
Enter *630*.
Press ÷ .
Enter *45*.
Press = .
The display reads *14*.

Use multiplication to check your work.
Multiply 14 × 45.
Enter *14*.
Press × .
Enter *45*.
Press = .
The display reads *630*.

Exercise D Use a calculator to find the answers.

27. 910 ÷ 35

28. 2,673 ÷ 3

29. 7,560 ÷ 168

30. 14,444 ÷ 92

31. 3,256 ÷ 88

32. 582 × 246

33. 731 × 601

34. 987 × 99

35. 149 × 89

36. 203 × 203

TRY THIS Identify the inverse, or opposite, operation of division. Provide examples that illustrate the inverse relationship.

PROBLEM SOLVING

Exercise E Solve each problem.

37. A restaurant orders 320 packages of crackers in cartons. If 20 packages are in each carton, how many cartons of crackers does the restaurant receive?

38. A local movie critic sees 3 movies every week that she works. If she has seen 141 movies this year, how many weeks has she worked this year?

39. All the seats of the main cabin of Flight 204 are filled. There are 192 passengers in this section. There are 8 seats in each row. How many rows of seats are there?

40. The new hotel purchased uniforms for its 420 employees. Each employee needs 2 uniforms. The uniforms are packaged 6 to a carton. How many cartons were shipped to the hotel?

Algebra in Your Life

Using Division on the Job
Next time you're shopping, talk to some people who work at an ice cream shop or a pizza stand. Ask them how many scoops of ice cream they get from one container. Ask how many slices they get from one pizza. Think about what happens if they don't divide a container of ice cream into the correct number of scoops. Ask what happens if they don't divide a pizza into the correct number of slices. What happens if the pieces are too big or too small?

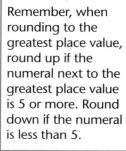

Compatible numbers

Two numbers that form a basic division fact

Remember, when rounding to the greatest place value, round up if the numeral next to the greatest place value is 5 or more. Round down if the numeral is less than 5.

You can use estimation to check whether a product or quotient makes sense.

EXAMPLE 1 $54 \times 62 = \blacksquare$

Round each factor to its greatest place value.

$54 \rightarrow 50$
$62 \rightarrow 60$

Multiply the rounded factors.

$50 \times 60 = 3,000$

An estimate of the product 54×62 is 3,000.

Two numbers that form a basic division fact are **compatible numbers.** Compatible numbers can be used to estimate quotients.

EXAMPLE 2 $1,515 \div 42 = n$

The numbers 15 and 4 are not compatible.

$1,515 \div 42$

Write compatible numbers for the dividend and divisor.

$1,515 \div 42$
$\downarrow \qquad \downarrow$
$1,600 \div 40 \qquad 16 \div 4$ is a basic fact.

Divide.

$1,600 \div 40 = 40$

An estimate of the quotient $1,515 \div 42$ is 40.

EXAMPLE 3   4,639 ÷ 89 = ■
Write the compatible numbers.
4,639 ÷ 89
↓   ↓
4,500 ÷ 90
Divide.
4,500 ÷ 90 = 50
An estimate of the quotient 4,639 ÷ 89 is 50.

Exercise A Estimate each product.

1. 92 × 64

2. 65 × 95

3. 72 × 46

4. 476 × 39

5. 872 × 404

6. 76 × 88

7. 28 × 32

8. 234 × 61

9. 1,654 × 24

10. 5,176 × 486

Exercise B Estimate each quotient.

11. 375 ÷ 6

12. 826 ÷ 9

13. 2,386 ÷ 24

14. 19,995 ÷ 54

15. 16,115 ÷ 41

16. 712 ÷ 8

17. 335 ÷ 4

18. 6,428 ÷ 33

19. 65,454 ÷ 63

20. 41,118 ÷ 38

Exercise C Estimate. Then find the exact answer.

21. 3,412 × 653

22. 62,338 ÷ 31

23. 41,392 ÷ 13

24. 986 × 744

25. 9,800 ÷ 46

TRY THIS ▷ Write 10 division problems, some with compatible numbers and some with numbers that are not compatible. Read each problem to a partner and challenge him or her to identify whether the numbers in the problem are compatible.

These exercises show the four basic operations.

$$15 + 6 = \blacksquare$$
$$15 - 8 = \blacksquare$$
$$4 \times 5 = \blacksquare$$
$$15 \div 3 = \blacksquare$$

If you perform each operation correctly, the statements are *true*. If you make a mistake, the statements are *false*.

Open statement

A sentence that is neither true nor false

Terms

Parts of an expression separated by operation signs such as $+$, $-$, $\bullet$, $\times$, or $\div$

Expression

A mathematical statement that usually includes numbers, variables, and symbols

EXAMPLE 1	True Statements	False Statements
	$15 + 6 = 21$	$15 + 6 = 23$
	$15 - 8 = 7$	$15 - 8 = 9$
	$4 \times 5 = 20$	$4 \times 5 = 25$
	$15 \div 3 = 5$	$15 \div 3 = 8$

In algebra, statements include letters as well as numbers. Letters are used as placeholders for numbers. Suppose n is a placeholder for an unknown number.

$4n$ means 4 times n. In algebra, the multiplication sign can be confused with the letter x. This is how you show multiplication in algebra: $4n$ or $4 \bullet n$ or $4(n)$.

- $15 + n$ means 15 plus *some number.*
- $15 - n$ means 15 minus *some number.*
- $4n$ means 4 times *some number.*
- $15 \div n$ means 15 divided by *some number.*

The statement $4n = 20$ is neither true nor false. It is an **open statement.**

EXAMPLE 2	Open Statements
	$15 + n = 21$
	$15 - n = 7$
	$4n = 20$
	$15 \div n = 5$

In these examples, 15 and n are called **terms.** Terms are the parts of an **expression** separated by an operation sign.

Exercise A Write *true* or *false* for each statement.

1. $5 + 4 = 9$

2. $12 - 8 = 3$

3. $6 \times 9 = 54$

4. $81 \div 9 = 9$

5. $5 \times 5 = 30$

6. $16 + 6 = 22$

7. $35 - 11 = 14$

8. $8 \times 8 = 56$

9. $21 \div 7 = 3$

10. $14 - 4 = 9$

Exercise B Tell whether each statement is *true, false,* or *open.*

11. $7 + 5 = 12$

12. $5n = 45$

13. $17 - n = 10$

14. $36 \div 12 = 2$

15. $15 + 14 = 30$

16. $14 + n = 32$

17. $15 \div n = 5$

18. $10n = 100$

19. $31 - 18 = 13$

20. $15 + 8 = 22$

Exercise C Use words to write the meaning of each of the following.

21. $34 \div n$

22. $14n$

23. $16 - n$

24. $24 + n$

25. $n \div 8$

Estimation Activity

Estimate: A gallon of gasoline costs $\$1.49\frac{9}{10}$. How many gallons can you buy for $10?

Solution: Round price to $1.50

Think: $1.50 for 1 gal
$3.00 for 2 gal
$6.00 for 4 gal
} add: $9.00 for 6 gallons

You get a little more than 6 gallons for $10.

$10 \div 1.50 = 6.67$ gallons or $6\frac{2}{3}$ gallons

Variable

A letter that represents an unknown number

Algebraic expression

A mathematical statement that includes at least one operation and variable

Numerical expression

A mathematical sentence that uses operations and numbers

Recall that a letter can be used as a placeholder for a number. This letter is known as a **variable.**

An expression with at least one variable and one operation is called an **algebraic expression.**

An expression that includes only numbers is called a **numerical expression.**

EXAMPLE 1

Numerical Expressions	Algebraic Expressions
$6 + 5$	$6 + n$
$16 - 3$	$n - 3$
14×5	$14 \times a$
$24 \div 4$	$y \div 4$

Remember that any letter can be used as the variable in an algebraic expression.

When describing an expression, you decide whether it is a numerical or algebraic expression. You identify the operations and name any variable.

EXAMPLE 2 Classify the expression, name the operation(s), and identify any variables.

$$4n + 5$$

The expression $4n + 5$ is an algebraic expression.

There are two operations in the expression—multiplication and addition.

There is one variable—the letter n.

Writing About Mathematics

Suppose someone asks you to explain the difference between a numerical expression and an algebraic expression. Write a short explanation.

Exercise A Name the variable in each expression.

1. $18 + x$
2. $2n$
3. $6a + 15$
4. $15 - y$
5. $36 \div t$

6. $5 + b$
7. $40h$
8. $k - 11$
9. $n \div 16$
10. $2d + 3$

Exercise B Identify the operation(s) in each expression.

11. $n + 10$
12. $4n - 3$
13. $x \div 7$
14. $7n$
15. $6x + 14$

16. $8m \div 2$
17. $2y + 5$
18. $6y - 3$
19. $d - 10$
20. $5n$

Exercise C Classify each expression as numeric or algebraic, name the operation(s), and identify any variables.

21. $15 + 22$
22. $14 - 8$
23. $y \div 10$
24. $11 - x$
25. $2y + 5$

26. $14 \cdot 12$
27. $3m + 6$
28. $18 + 4$
29. $25n$
30. $12 \div 6$

Substitute

To put a number in place of a variable

Evaluate

To find the numerical value of an algebraic expression

Recall that statements such as $4n = 20$ are open statements. An open statement becomes a true or false statement when you substitute a number for the variable. When you **substitute** a number for the variable, follow these steps to **evaluate** the expression.

Step 1 First, substitute a number.

Step 2 Perform the operations from left to right.

EXAMPLE 1 Evaluate $8 + m$ when $m = 3$.

Step 1 Substitute the number for the variable.

$8 + 3$

Step 2 Perform the operation.

$8 + 3 = 11$

The statement $8 + 3 = 11$ is a true statement.

EXAMPLE 2 Is $4n = 12$ a true or false statement
when $n = 1, 2,$ or 3?

When $n = 1$,
$4n = 12 \rightarrow 4 \bullet 1 = 4$, or $4 = 12 \rightarrow$ false statement

When $n = 2$,
$4n = 12 \rightarrow 4 \bullet 2 = 8$, or $8 = 12 \rightarrow$ false statement

When $n = 3$,
$4n = 12 \rightarrow 4 \bullet 3 = 12$, or $12 = 12 \rightarrow$ true statement

Exercise A Write an algebraic expression.

1. add 5 to some number

2. some number times 3

3. 15 divided by some number

4. some number minus 8

5. 2 times some number plus 5

6. subtract 46 from some number

7. 10 minus some number

8. some number plus 16

9. some number divided by 9

10. 23 times some number

Writing About Mathematics

Write a short paragraph comparing true, false, and open statements. Provide an example of each type of sentence in your paragraph.

Exercise B Evaluate each expression.

11. $m + 15$ when $m = 14$

12. $n - 17$ when $n = 30$

13. $4n$ when $n = 21$

14. $100 \div n$ when $n = 20$

15. $2m + 7$ when $m = 3$

16. $4m - 8$ when $m = 2$

17. $16 - 3y$ when $y = 3$

18. $42 - n$ when $n = 27$

19. $n \div 12$ when $n = 60$

20. $5 + 3m$ when $m = 8$

Exercise C Write *true* or *false*.

Is $5 + n = 12$ a true or false statement when

21. $n = 3$?

22. $n = 5$?

23. $n = 7$?

Calculator Practice

You can use the calculator to help you evaluate algebraic expressions easily.

EXAMPLE 3 $49 \div x = 7$ when $x = 7$.
Press 49 $\div$ 7 $=$. The display reads 7.
The statement $49 \div x = 7$ when $x = 7$ is true.

EXAMPLE 4 $8x = 56$ when $x = 6$.
Press 8 $\times$ 6 $=$. The display reads 48.
The statement $8x = 56$ when $x = 6$ is false.

Exercise D Use your calculator to evaluate each expression. Then identify the expression as *true* or *false*.

24. $35 \div x = 5$ when $x = 7$.

25. $182 + x = 186$ when $x = 3$.

26. $184 - x = 134$ when $x = 50$.

27. $25 \div x = 5$ when $x = 5$.

28. $49 \div x = 8$ when $x = 9$.

29. $x + 22 = 30$ when $x = 7$.

30. $22x = 132$ when $x = 6$.

Using Formulas Perimeter is the distance around the outside of a figure. Area is the amount of surface inside a figure.

EXAMPLE 1 Find the perimeter of the figure shown.

Add the lengths of the sides.

$10 + 5 + 7 + 8 + 3 + 7 = 40$ in.

The perimeter is 40 inches.

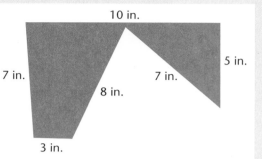

10 in.

7 in.   5 in.

7 in.

8 in.

3 in.

EXAMPLE 2 The area of a rectangle can be found by using the formula $A = lw$, where l is the length and w is the width.

Find the **area** of the rectangle shown.

Substitute the numbers into the expression lw.

$A = lw$

$\quad = (15)(4)$

$\quad = 60$

The area of the rectangle is 60 square inches.

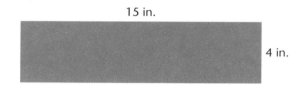

15 in.

4 in.

Exercise Solve each problem.

1. Keesha has a garden 12 feet by 9 feet. What is the area of her garden?

2. Keesha wants to put up a fence around the perimeter of her garden. (See problem 1.) What is the perimeter?

3. Kate is going to carpet a floor that has a length of 14 feet and a width of 12 feet. How many square feet of carpeting will Kate need?

Chapter 1   R E V I E W

Write the letter of the correct answer.

1. Find the sum of 9,273 + 291
   A 9,464
   B 8,982
   C 9,564
   D 12,183

2. Find the difference of 111 − 99
   A 11
   B 22
   C 200
   D 12

3. Find the product of 42 × 53
   A 2,226
   B 2,136
   C 95
   D 126

4. Find the quotient of 23,670 ÷ 31
   A 789
   B 763
   C 763 r17
   D 673 r11

5. Evaluate the expression $n + 7$ when $n = 8$
   A 16
   B 1
   C 15
   D 14

6. Evaluate the expression $60 \div y$ when $y = 5$
   A 300
   B 12
   C 15
   D 65

Find each sum.

Example: 2,158 + 1,682

Solution: 2,158
           + 1,682
           3,840

7. 32,105 + 4,999   **9.** 295 + 638

8. 105,213 + 6,897   **10.** 12,683 + 75,922

Find each difference.

Example: 3,422 − 2,193

Solution: 3,422
           − 2,193
           1,229

11. 42,647 − 3,859   **13.** 131,050 − 29,682

12. 2,218 − 517   **14.** 486,982 − 321,518

Find each product.

Example: 28 × 16

Solution: 28
            × 16
             168
           + 280
             448

15. 363 × 249   **17.** 16 × 8

16. 42 × 39   **18.** 760 × 5

Find each quotient. Remember to write any remainder as part of the quotient.

Example: 434 ÷ 7

Solution: 62
           7) 434
             − 42
               14
             − 14
                0

19. 1,438 ÷ 42   **21.** 158 ÷ 30

20. 625 ÷ 25   **22.** 9,696 ÷ 8

Estimate each answer.

Example: $1{,}921 - 473$ Solution:
$$\begin{array}{r} 2{,}000 \\ -\ 500 \\ \hline 1{,}500 \end{array}$$

23. $65{,}402 + 54{,}410$ **25.** $103{,}412 - 49{,}205$

24. 321×856 **26.** $33{,}464 \div 74$

Tell whether each statement is true, false, or open.

Example: $6 + 7 = 12$ Solution: $6 + 7 = 13$, so $6 + 7 = 12$ is false.

27. $15 - n = 8$ **29.** $14 + 6 = 21$

28. $7 \times 4 = 28$ **30.** $30 \div 5 = n$

Classify each expression, name the operation(s), and identify any variables.

Example: $4 - x$ Solution: algebraic expression, subtraction, x

31. $2m + 9$ **34.** $15 - x$

32. $5 \times 6 + 3$ **35.** $3x$

33. $g \div 58$ **36.** $918 + 413$

Write true or false.

Example: $21 \div n = 7$ when $n = 3$.   Solution: $3\overline{)21}$ with 7 above   True

37. $5y = 80$ when $y = 14$.

38. $q \div 16 = 8$ when $q = 128$.

39. $14 + n = 22$ when $n = 8$.

40. $19 - n = 14$ when $n = 4$.

Test-Taking Tip

When you review your notes to prepare for an exam, use a marker to highlight key words and example problems.

2 Using Decimals

There are almost as many kinds of money as there are countries in the world. But it is interesting to know that almost every country uses a similar system for counting its money. One U.S. or Canadian dollar is worth 100 cents, and the Egyptian pound is worth 100 piastres. The Euro is worth 100 cents, and the Chinese yuan renminbi is worth 100 fen. These countries (and many more) divide these 100 units in some way by 50, 20, or 10. When numbers are based on tens, it is called a decimal system. The world is using a decimal system that can be traced back thousands of years.

In Chapter 2, you will perform basic operations with decimals.

Goals for Learning

- ◆ To identify the place value of digits
- ◆ To compare and round decimals
- ◆ To add and subtract decimals
- ◆ To multiply and divide decimals
- ◆ To change decimals to fractions and fractions to decimals
- ◆ To use a bar to identify a repeating decimal
- ◆ To rename percents as decimals
- ◆ To evaluate algebraic expressions with decimals

You use **decimals** every day when you handle money. In money, the **digits** to the left of the decimal point represent dollars, or numbers greater than or equal to 1. The digits to the right of the **decimal point** represent cents, or parts of a dollar.

$2.35

- dollars
- values greater than or equal to 1

- cents
- values that are part of a whole

The chart of **place values** shows the value of each digit based on its position in a numeral.

Millions	Hundred-thousands	Ten-thousands	Thousands	Hundreds	Tens	Ones	.	Tenths	Hundredths	Thousandths	Ten-thousandths	Hundred-thousandths	Millionths
					8	6	.	2	3	4	7		

Decimal

A number that has a decimal point in it

Digit

Any one of the symbols 0, 1, 2, 3, 4, 5, 6, 7, 8, or 9

Decimal point

A period that separates digits representing numbers that are one or more from digits representing numbers that are less than one

Place value

Worth of a digit based on its position in a numeral

Places to the right of the decimal point end in *th* to indicate that they are part of a whole. For example, 0.2 is read "two tenths," 0.03 is read "three hundredths," and 0.004 is read "four thousandths."

EXAMPLE 1 Write the place of the underlined digit in 86.234̲7.

The digit 4 is three places to the right of the decimal point.

The digit 4 is in the thousandths place, so its value is 4×0.001, or 0.004.

EXAMPLE 2 What is the value of the digit 2 in the numeral 2̲,345.167?

The digit 2 is in the thousands place, so its value is $2 \times 1,000$, or 2,000.

Exercise A Write the place of each underlined digit.

1. 164.1<u>3</u>
2. 2<u>4</u>.267
3. 624.55<u>5</u>
4. 0.432<u>6</u>
5. <u>7</u>65.92
6. 6,423.9<u>2</u>5
7. <u>6</u>4.021
8. <u>1</u>,234.567
9. 4<u>0</u>.12

Exercise B Write the value of each underlined digit.

10. 786.<u>3</u>4
11. 2.635<u>9</u>
12. <u>4</u>81.73
13. <u>8</u>7.665
14. 6.795<u>6</u>
15. 84<u>2</u>.167
16. 0.6<u>5</u>78
17. <u>1</u>,482
18. 8.<u>2</u>9
19. <u>3</u>,675.8
20. 95.7<u>7</u>28
21. 0.64<u>7</u>
22. <u>9</u>7.84
23. 3.267<u>9</u>8
24. 346.88<u>7</u>

Exercise C Write the value of the last digit in each numeral.

25. 42.361
26. 0.25
27. 98.5623
28. 0.5
29. 365.066
30. 5.00004

When reading a number with a decimal out loud, say "and" or "point" for the decimal point. So 40.12 would be read "forty and twelve hundredths" or "forty point one two."

TRY THIS Write instructions for placing a digit in a specific place; for example, place 3 in the tenths place. Ask a partner to follow your instructions. Check his or her answer.

Lesson 2 — Comparing and Rounding Decimals

One of the reasons it's easy to compare $2.45 and $2.50 is because both decimals have the same number of places to the right of the decimal point.

Remember, you can use signs to show how one number is related to another. For example, = means equals; < means less than; > means greater than; ≤ means less than or equal to; ≥ means greater than or equal to.

EXAMPLE 1 Compare 14.256 and 14.26.

First, add one zero to 14.26 so that each decimal has the same number of places to the right of the decimal point.

14.256   14.260   (add one zero)

Next, compare the decimals.

14.256 *is less than* 14.260 because 256 *is less than 260.*

14.256 < 14.260

EXAMPLE 2 Compare 0.0576 and 0.05.

Add two zeros to 0.05.

0.0576   0.0500   (add two zeros)

Compare the two decimals.

0.0576 *is greater than* 0.0500 because 576 *is greater than 500.*

0.0576 > 0.0500

Sometimes, when working with decimals, you may need to round.

EXAMPLE 3 Round 13.036 to the nearest hundredth.

Step 1 Find the place to be rounded.

13.036   The place to be rounded is the hundredths place.

Step 2 Find the digit to the right of the place you are rounding to.

13.036   If the digit is 5 or greater, add 1 to the digit in the place you are rounding to. If the digit is less than 5, do not change the digit in the place you are rounding to.

Step 3 13.04   Since 6 is greater than 5, add 1 to the digit in the hundredths place. Drop the digits to the right of the place you are rounding to.

So, 13.036 rounded to the nearest hundredth is 13.04.

Exercise A Compare each pair of decimals. Write < or >.

1. 5.403 ■ 5.03   6. 7.0 ■ 0.77

2. 8.43 ■ 8.340   7. 403.079 ■ 403.07

3. 91.8 ■ 91.8135   8. 0.653924 ■ 0.65394

4. 2.2210 ■ 2.223   9. 30.19 ■ 300.19

5. 2.04 ■ 2.044   10. 634.5 ■ 634.203

Exercise B Make a chart. Then round these decimals to the nearest tenth, hundredth, and thousandth.

	Tenth	Hundredth	Thousandth
11. 2.6345			
12. 1.8092			
13. 0.9024			
14. 37.2099			
15. 6.4625			
16. 0.6502			
17. 2.7995			
18. 88.0092			
19. 14.0365			
20. 53.4798			
21. 5.6541			
22. 1.2349			
23. 19.9873			
24. 0.3397			
25. 523.6745			

TRY THIS Find numerals with decimal points in a newspaper or magazine. Cut the numbers out. In a group, round the numerals you found to the digit left of the last digit.

Adding and subtracting decimals is like adding and subtracting money or whole numbers. To add or subtract decimals, line up the decimal points. Then add or subtract each place value.

Perimeter

The distance around the outside of a shape

Formula

A combination of symbols used to state a rule

EXAMPLE 1 Find the **perimeter** of the triangle at the right.

14.25 cm

6.5 cm

9.755 cm

To find the perimeter of a triangle, you can use the **formula** $P = a + b + c$, where a, b, and c are the lengths of the sides of the triangle and P is the perimeter.

First, substitute the lengths of the sides into the formula.
$$P = 6.5 \text{ cm} + 9.755 \text{ cm} + 14.25 \text{ cm}$$

Next, line up the decimal points.

```
    6.5
    9.755
 + 14.25
       .        Bring down the decimal point.
```

Then add.

```
    6.5
    9.755
 + 14.25
   30.505
```

EXAMPLE 2 Suppose you pay $13.99 for a CD (including sales tax). You give the clerk $20. How much change do you receive?

First, include zeros to help you subtract.
$20 = $20.00

Next, line up the decimal points.

```
  $20.00
 - 13.99
       .        Bring down the decimal point.
```

Then subtract.

```
  $20.00
 - 13.99
  $ 6.01
```

You receive $6.01 in change.

Exercise A Add or subtract.

1. 3.2 + 0.91 + 6

2. 4.3 + 0.455 + 0.6

3. 4.13 − 2.6

4. 0.34 − 0.023

5. 32.1 − 0.8

6. 0.9 − 0.099

7. 23.5 + 5 + 96.9

8. 9.5 + 3.52 + 0.004

9. 16 + 0.72 + 3.2 + 3

10. 1 − 0.674

11. 38.5 − 21.392

12. 74.4 + 0.3904 + 5.04

Calculator Practice You can use a calculator to add or subtract decimals.

EXAMPLE 3   34.543 − 28.698 = ▇
Press *34* ⋅ *543* − *28* ⋅ *698* =.
The display reads *5.845*.

Exercise B Use a calculator to find each sum or difference.

13. 1.5 + 0.21 + 0.35 + 0.611

14. 9 + 2.1 + 0.62 + 0.1711

15. 6 − 0.04321

16. 246.62 − 18.7346

17. 891.289 + 42.6758

18. 0.9325 − 0.7439

19. $50 − $32.46

20. $5.62 + $10.30 + $6.40 + $0.32

21. $0.34 + $2.50 + $13.18 + $113.54

PROBLEM SOLVING

Exercise C Solve these problems.

22. Troy jogs 5 miles on Monday, 6.05 miles on Tuesday, and 8.7 miles on Wednesday. How many total miles does Troy jog in the three days?

23. Amar's school supplies cost $15.95 with tax. If he gives the clerk $20, how much change does he receive?

24. Anna has a pet-sitting service. She earns $8.50 for walking a dog, $6.50 for sitting a cat, and $12.75 for overnight care. How much does she earn for walking one dog, sitting for one cat, and taking care of a bird for a night?

25. Station A charges $1.312 for a gallon of gasoline. Station B charges $1.295. How much more does Station A charge per gallon of gasoline?

Power of ten

A product of multiplying 10 by itself one or more times

Exponent

Number that tells the times another number is a factor

The power of a number, or the number of times it should be multiplied by itself, is shown by a small number written on the upper right side. This number is called an exponent. For example, in 10^2, the raised 2 indicates that 10 should be multiplied by itself 2 times. 2 is the exponent. $10 \times 10 = 100$.

There are an infinite number of **powers of 10.**

$$10^1 = 10$$
$$10^2 = 10 \times 10 = 100$$
$$10^3 = 10 \times 10 \times 10 = 1,000$$
$$10^4 = 10 \times 10 \times 10 \times 10 = 10,000$$
$$10^5 = 10 \times 10 \times 10 \times 10 \times 10 = 100,000$$
$$10^6 = 10 \times 10 \times 10 \times 10 \times 10 \times 10 = 1,000,000$$
$$\vdots$$
$$10^n = \underbrace{10 \times 10 \times 10 \ldots 10}_{n \text{ times}}$$

The small number next to the 10s above are called **exponents.** An exponent tells the number of times another number is a factor.

To multiply any number by a power of 10, count the number of zeros in the power of 10 and move the decimal point that many places to the right. If the number does not have a decimal point, add one after the last digit. Then move it to the right to multiply by a power of 10.

EXAMPLE 1 4.34×100

In 100, there are two zeros. Move the decimal point two places to the right.

$$4.34 \rightarrow 4.34 \rightarrow 434$$

So, $4.34 \times 100 = 434$.

EXAMPLE 2 645×10^3

$645 \times 10^3 = 645 \times 1,000$

Add a decimal point. In 1,000, there are three zeros. Move the decimal point three places to the right. You need to add zeros.

$$645. \rightarrow 645000 \rightarrow 645,000$$

So, $645 \times 10^3 = 645,000$.

Writing About Mathematics

The definition of a *power of ten* is "a product of multiplying 10 by itself one or more times." Using this definition, write a definition for the power of any number. Include examples.

Exercise A Multiply.

1. 2.36×10^2

2. 0.05×10

3. 2.7×10^3

4. 5.36×100

5. $1.441 \times 1,000$

6. 0.00276×100

7. 7.710×10^5

8. $18.8 \times 10,000$

9. 7.3×10^4

10. $5.02 \times 100,000$

11. 8.4104×10^1

12. $0.0565 \times 1,000$

13. $0.769 \times 10,000$

14. 2.2×10^6

15. 4.044×10^3

16. $0.25 \times 100,000$

17. $1.0112 \times 1,000,000$

18. $0.0063 \times 10,000$

19. 8.907×10^2

20. $162.5 \times 1,000$

Exercise B Write *true, false,* or *open* for each statement.

21. $3.3 \times 10^1 = 33$

22. $35.04 \times 1,000 = 3,504$

23. $0.204 \times 100 = 2.04$

24. $8.9 \times n = 89$

25. $60.4 \times 100 = n$

26. $2.87 \times 10^2 = 287$

27. $0.64 \times 10 = 6.4$

28. $0.94 \times 1,000 = 94$

29. $n \times 10^3 = 5,140$

30. $1.15 \times 100 = 1,150$

Technology Connection

Microscopes Multiply Size
An electron microscope lets you look at things that are very small. Suppose an object measures 0.05 inches long. That's too small for your eye to see it clearly. But an electron microscope will multiply the size by as much as 10^5. How big does the object appear now? At this size, you can see even the smallest details easily. Even at 10^1, you can see some of the details. How big does an object that is 0.005 inches long appear at 10^3?

Circumference

Distance around a circle

Pi (π)

Ratio of the circumference of a circle to its diameter

Diameter

Distance across a circle through the center

Circumference is the distance around a circle. The formula for finding the circumference of a circle is $C = \pi d$, where

C = circumference
π = **pi** π is about 3.14
d = **diameter**

EXAMPLE 1 Find the circumference of a circle with a diameter of 8 inches.

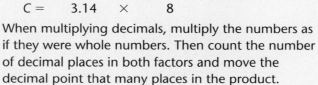

circumference

diameter

Substitute the numbers into the formula. Let π be equal to 3.14. Then multiply.

$C =$ π $\times$ d
$C =$ 3.14 $\times$ 8

When multiplying decimals, multiply the numbers as if they were whole numbers. Then count the number of decimal places in both factors and move the decimal point that many places in the product.

```
    3.14   two decimal places
 ×     8   zero decimal places
  25.12    two decimal places
```

The circumference is 25.12 inches.

EXAMPLE 2 Find the circumference of a circle with a diameter of 3.5 centimeters.

$C =$ π $\times$ d
$C =$ 3.14 $\times$ 3.5

```
    3.14   two decimal places
 ×   3.5   one decimal place
   1570
 + 942
  10.990   three decimal places
```

The circumference is 10.990 cm.

Exercise A Multiply.

1. 2.36
 × 9

3. 7.82
 × 5

5. 2.9
 × 7.1

7. 8.31
 × 0.8

9. 3.18
 × 0.09

11. 23.14
 × 3.7

2. 4.5
 × 7

4. 3.2
 × 6.4

6. 4.7
 × 2.6

8. 2.65
 × 2.4

10. 0.26
 × 0.8

12. 3.14
 × 3.14

Exercise B Find the circumference of each circle. Use 3.14 for π.

13. Diameter = 10 inches

14. Diameter = 15 inches

15. Diameter = 50 inches

Calculator Practice

A calculator can be used to multiply decimals.

EXAMPLE 3   4.321 × 63.7 = ■
Press 4 · 321 × 63 · 7 = .
The display reads 275.2477.

Exercise C Use a calculator to find each product.

16. 3.2 × 6.4 × 0.018

19. 8.9 × 0.33 × 5.2

17. 0.423 × 7.6 × 0.05

20. 65.9 × 0.08 × 0.004

18. 6.19 × 0.53 × 23

21. 0.03 × 0.04 × 0.05

PROBLEM SOLVING

Exercise D Solve these problems.

22. Brian works 35.5 hours a week. If he earns $15.75 an hour, how much does Brian make in a week? Round your answer to the nearest cent.

23. At the supermarket, bananas cost $0.59 per pound. How much do 3.5 pounds of bananas cost? Round your answer to the nearest cent.

24. Venus buys 13 CDs at $18.99 each. How much does she spend on CDs?

25. Vang drives for 3.5 hours at an average speed of 45.5 miles per hour. How far does he drive?

Recall that when you multiply a decimal by a power of 10, you move the decimal point to the right. When dividing by a power of 10, move the decimal point to the left.

EXAMPLE 1

$35 \div 10 = \blacksquare$

In 10, there is one zero. To divide by 10, move the decimal point one place to the left.

$3\,5\,. \ \rightarrow \ 3\,.\,5 \ \rightarrow \ 3.5$

So, $35 \div 10 = 3.5$.

EXAMPLE 2

$20.4 \div 1{,}000 = \blacksquare$

In 1,000, there are three zeros. To divide by 1,000, move the decimal point three places to the left. You may need to insert zeros.

$2\,0\,.\,4 \ \rightarrow \ .0\,2\,0\,4 \ \rightarrow \ 0.0204$

So, $20.4 \div 1{,}000 = 0.0204$.

EXAMPLE 3

$9.4 \div 10^2 = \blacksquare$

$9.4 \div 10^2 = 9.4 \div 100$

In 100, there are two zeros. To divide by 100, move the decimal point two places to the left.

$9\,.\,4 \ \rightarrow \ .0\,9\,4 \ \rightarrow \ 0.094$

So, $9.4 \div 10^2 = 0.094$.

Exercise A Divide.

1. 6.6 ÷ 10

2. 0.08 ÷ 100

3. 93 ÷ 1,000

4. 47.6 ÷ 10^1

5. 2.03 ÷ 100

6. 4.8 ÷ 1,000

7. 11.5 ÷ 1,000

8. 0.45 ÷ 10

9. 24.4 ÷ 10^2

10. 0.004 ÷ 100

11. 243.2 ÷ 1,000

12. 0.56 ÷ 1,000

13. 73.6 ÷ 10^2

14. 125.3 ÷ 10,000

15. 0.0005 ÷ 1,000

16. 48.84 ÷ 10^3

17. 0.03 ÷ 10,000

18. 123.4 ÷ 100,000

19. 300.05 ÷ 10^1

20. 324 ÷ 10^4

Exercise B Write *true, false,* or *open* for each statement.

21. 6.5 ÷ 10 = 0.65

22. 55.1 ÷ 10,000 = 0.0551

23. 0.007 ÷ 100 = 0.00007

24. 75.4 ÷ n = 0.0754

25. 3.91 ÷ 10^2 = 0.0391

26. 3.63 ÷ 10^1 = n

27. 9.94 ÷ 1,000 = 0.0994

28. n ÷ 10^3 = 0.001

29. 35.6 ÷ 100 = 0.356

30. 135.79 ÷ 1,000 = 0.13579

Algebra in Your Life

Working with Tiny Things
Microbiologists work in almost every area of life: in the food industry, in agriculture, in the medical field, and in pollution control. In their jobs, microbiologists work with very small things, so they are used to dividing decimals. Some microbiologists work with bacteria. They try to find out how bacteria can harm us or help us. Some microbiologists track down outbreaks of disease. Some of them travel the world looking for the tiny germs that cause diseases.

When dividing with decimals, the divisor must be a whole number.

Remember, the divisor is the number by which you divide, the dividend is the number that you divide, and the quotient is the result of the division.

EXAMPLE 1

Ricky earns $16.50 in 3 hours. How much does he earn in 1 hour?

Write the division.

$$3 \overline{)\$16.50}$$

Since the divisor is a whole number, write a decimal point in the quotient.

$$3 \overline{)\$16.50}^{\,.}$$

Divide.

$$
\begin{array}{r}
\$5.50 \\
3 \overline{)\$16.50} \\
-\underline{15} \\
15 \\
-\underline{15} \\
00
\end{array}
$$

Ricky earns $5.50 in 1 hour.

Sometimes you must make the divisor a whole number before you divide.

EXAMPLE 2

$$0.5 \overline{)1.86}$$

Move the decimal point in the divisor and in the dividend one place to the right.

$$0.5 \overline{)1.86}$$

Place a decimal point in the quotient.

$$5 \overline{)18.6}^{\,.}$$

Divide.

$$
\begin{array}{r}
3.72 \\
5 \overline{)18.6} \\
-\underline{15} \\
36 \\
-\underline{35} \\
10 \\
-\underline{10} \\
0
\end{array}
$$

So, $1.86 \div 0.5 = 3.72$

Exercise A Divide. Round your answer to the nearest hundredth.

1. 5.21 ÷ 4

2. 142.51 ÷ 53

3. 8.65 ÷ 0.6

4. 1.7571 ÷ 0.21

5. 0.2360 ÷ 0.05

6. 2 ÷ 0.83

7. 221 ÷ 0.14

8. 0.285 ÷ 0.012

9. 9.63 ÷ 0.036

10. 512.68 ÷ 0.009

Calculator Practice

You can use a calculator to divide decimals.

EXAMPLE 3   0.55543 ÷ 0.67 = ■
Press ⟨·⟩ ⟨55543⟩ ⟨÷⟩ ⟨·⟩ ⟨67⟩ ⟨=⟩.
The display reads *0.829*.

Exercise B Use a calculator to find each quotient. Round your answer to the nearest thousandth.

11. 16.5 ÷ 27.58

12. 207.7 ÷ 538.92

13. 609 ÷ 4,710.5

14. 58.493 ÷ 237.6

15. 2 ÷ 4.5 ÷ 0.198

16. 8.6 ÷ 77.1 ÷ 41.9

PROBLEM SOLVING

Exercise C Solve these problems.

17. Carlos buys 8 pounds of dog food for $8.45. What is the price per pound? Round your answer to the nearest cent.

18. Carrie drives 262.85 miles in 4.5 hours. What is her average speed in miles per hour? Round your answer to the nearest hundredth.

19. Vernon earns $558.25 a week. If he works 38.5 hours each week, how much does Vernon earn an hour?

20. Megan spent $54.18 on food for her dinner party. If she is having five friends over for dinner, what is the average amount of money she spent for food per person? (Hint: Include Megan.)

Fraction

Part of a whole number such as $\frac{1}{2}$

Denominator

The number below the fraction bar

Numerator

The number above the fraction bar

Simplify

State as a fraction whose only common factor of the numerator and denominator is 1

Equivalent fraction

A fraction that has the same value as another fraction

To change a decimal to a **fraction,** follow these steps.

Step 1 Find the place of the last digit. The place value for this digit becomes the **denominator.**

Step 2 Use the numeral in the decimal for the **numerator.**

Step 3 **Simplify** the fraction.

> **EXAMPLE 1** Write 0.75 as a fraction.
>
> **Step 1** Find the place value of the last digit.
>
> 5 is in the hundredths place
>
> The denominator of the fraction is 100.
>
> **Step 2** Use the numeral in the decimal for the numerator.
>
> $0.75 \rightarrow \frac{75}{100}$
>
> **Step 3** Simplify the fraction.
>
> $\frac{75}{100} = \frac{75 \div 25}{100 \div 25} = \frac{3}{4}$

Sometimes you may need to change a fraction to a decimal.

> **EXAMPLE 2** Write $\frac{17}{100}$ as a decimal.
>
> When the denominator is a power of 10, identify the place value of the denominator.
>
> $\frac{17}{100}$ Place value is hundredths.
>
> Write the decimal using the numeral in the numerator.
>
> $\frac{17}{100} = 0.17$

> **EXAMPLE 3** Write $\frac{8}{25}$ as a decimal.
>
> Since the denominator is not a power of 10, write an **equivalent fraction** whose denominator is a power of 10.
>
> $\frac{8}{25} = \frac{8 \times 4}{25 \times 4} = \frac{32}{100}$
>
> Write the decimal for $\frac{32}{100}$. 0.32
>
> $\frac{8}{25} = 0.32$

Remember that another way to rewrite a fraction as a decimal is to divide the numerator of the fraction by the denominator of the fraction.

Exercise A Write each decimal as a fraction. Simplify your answer.

1. 0.28   **5.** 0.004   **9.** 0.0075   **13.** 0.0011

2. 0.05   **6.** 8.4   **10.** 0.875   **14.** 2.5

3. 0.54   **7.** 0.29   **11.** 5.05   **15.** 0.045

4. 0.60   **8.** 0.625   **12.** 0.202   **16.** 0.0032

Exercise B Write each fraction as a decimal.

17. $\frac{3}{10}$ **21.** $\frac{15}{25}$ **25.** $\frac{12}{40}$ **29.** $\frac{63}{125}$

18. $\frac{23}{100}$ **22.** $2\frac{3}{5}$ **26.** $\frac{175}{10,000}$ **30.** $\frac{21}{200}$

19. $\frac{250}{1,000}$ **23.** $\frac{62}{500}$ **27.** $6\frac{1}{2}$ **31.** $\frac{9}{16}$

20. $\frac{4}{5}$ **24.** $\frac{11}{20}$ **28.** $\frac{124}{250}$ **32.** $\frac{15}{80}$

PROBLEM SOLVING

Exercise C Solve these problems.

33. Elena bought $3\frac{1}{2}$ yards of fabric for $32.75. What was the cost of the fabric per yard to the nearest cent?

34. Julia has a length of string that measures $15\frac{3}{4}$ feet. If she cuts a piece 6.5 feet long, how much of the string will she have left?

35. Alex earns $15 an hour for writing insurance reports. If he works for $5\frac{2}{5}$ hours, how much will Alex earn?

Repeating decimal

A decimal in which one or more digits repeat

The formula for changing degrees Fahrenheit to degrees Celsius is

$$C = \frac{5}{9}(F - 32),$$

where F is degrees Fahrenheit and C is degrees Celsius.

EXAMPLE 1   If it is 35°F outside, what is the Celsius temperature?

First, substitute 35° Fahrenheit into the formula.

$$C = \frac{5}{9}(F - 32)$$
$$C = \frac{5}{9}(35 - 32)$$

Then simplify.

$$C = \frac{5}{9}(3)$$
$$C = \frac{15}{9}$$

Temperature is usually given as a decimal, not as a fraction. So change $\frac{15}{9}$ to a decimal.

```
        1.666
    9 ) 15.0
      −  9
         6 0
       − 5 4
           60
         − 54
```

In the quotient, the digit 6 repeats. The quotient is a **repeating decimal.**

To write a repeating decimal, place a bar over the repeating digit(s).

$$1.666 = 1.\overline{6}$$

If you are asked to write $1.\overline{6}$°C as a whole number, round $1.\overline{6}$°C to 2°C.

The Celsius scale is used in most of the world, while the United States generally uses the Fahrenheit scale.

Exercise A Write each fraction as a repeating decimal.

1. $\frac{1}{3}$

2. $\frac{1}{11}$

3. $\frac{5}{6}$

4. $\frac{1}{9}$

5. $\frac{2}{3}$

6. $\frac{4}{11}$

7. $\frac{9}{11}$

8. $\frac{4}{9}$

9. $\frac{8}{9}$

Exercise B Use the formula $C = \frac{5}{9}(F - 32)$ to find the Celsius temperature for each Fahrenheit temperature. Round your answer to the nearest whole degree.

10. $F = 62°$

11. $F = 54°$

12. $F = 73°$

13. $F = 88°$

14. $F = 49°$

15. $F = 95°$

16. $F = 55°$

17. $F = 39°$

18. $F = 102°$

19. $F = 78°$

20. $F = 115°$

Estimation Activity

Estimate: Compare these fractions. Which statement is true?

$\frac{3}{5} < \frac{3}{4}$

$\frac{3}{5} = \frac{3}{4}$

$\frac{3}{5} > \frac{3}{4}$

Solution:

Draw a scale from 0 to 1.

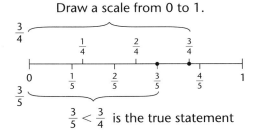

$\frac{3}{5} < \frac{3}{4}$ is the true statement

(shorter distance) (longer distance)

TRY THIS The formula for changing degrees Celsius to degrees Fahrenheit is $F = \frac{9}{5}(C) + 32$. Change 25° Celsius to degrees Fahrenheit.

Interest

The amount of money paid or received for the use of money

Percent

Part per one hundred; hundredth

When you deposit money in a bank, your money earns **interest.** Interest is stated in **percents,** or parts per hundred. The formula for simple interest is one way to determine the amount of money you will earn.

The simple interest formula is $I = p \times r \times t$ or $I = prt$ where I is the interest in dollars, p is the principal in dollars, r is the rate in percent, and t is the time in years.

EXAMPLE 1   Suppose you deposit $500 into an account that earns 6% for 1 year. How much interest will you be paid?

First, you need to change 6% to a decimal. $6\% = \frac{6}{100}$. Write 6% as 0.06.

   6%   →   0.06

Next, substitute the values into the formula and solve.

$p = \$500$ $I = prt$
$r = 6\% = 0.06$ $= (500)(0.06)(1)$
$t = 1$ year $I = 30$

The interest you will be paid is $30.

Sometimes the amount of time is not a whole number of years.

EXAMPLE 2   Sara borrows $1,000 at a rate of $9\frac{1}{2}\%$ for 6 months. How much interest will she pay?

First, write $9\frac{1}{2}\%$ as a decimal. To change the percent to a decimal, move the decimal point two places to the left.

$9\frac{1}{2}\%$ →   9.5%   →   09.5   →   0.095

Because 6 months represents $\frac{1}{2}$ of a year, and $\frac{1}{2} = 0.5$, use 0.5 for t.

$p = \$1,000$ $I = prt$
$r = 9\frac{1}{2}\% = 0.095$ $= (1,000)(0.095)(0.5)$
$t = 6$ months or 0.5 year $I = \$47.50$

The interest Sara will pay is $47.50.

Exercise A Change each percent to a decimal.

1. 5% **3.** $4\frac{1}{2}$% **5.** 0.6% **7.** 0.8%

2. 32% **4.** 150% **6.** $\frac{7}{8}$% **8.** $\frac{1}{2}$%

Exercise B Find the interest each principal will earn. If necessary, round your answer to the nearest cent.

9. Principal: $3,000
Rate: 5.5% per year
Time: 1 year

11. Principal: $5,000
Rate: 11.5% per year
Time: 6 months

10. Principal: $8,000
Rate: 8% per year
Time: 3 months

PROBLEM SOLVING

Exercise C Solve each problem.

12. Gail opens a savings account with a deposit of $2,000 at 5.5% annual interest. How much interest will she receive after 2 years?

13. Suppose you lend a relative $800 for 1 year. You loan the money at a rate of 4.75%. How much will your relative pay you in interest at the end of 1 year?

14. Chen wants to know which would earn more interest: $10,000 earning $6\frac{3}{4}$% for a year or $100,000 earning $3\frac{1}{2}$% for a year. Tell him which deposit would earn more interest.

15. Credit cards usually have high interest rates. Cathy has a credit card bill of $1,350. The annual interest rate is 16.25%. How much interest would she pay at the end of 1 month? (Hint: one month is $\frac{1}{12}$ of a year.)

When you evaluate expressions, you substitute a number for the variable and then perform arithmetic operations from left to right.

Remember, different symbols are used in mathematics to indicate multiplication.
$\times$ means multiply, so $6 \times 2 = 12$.
• means multiply, so $6 \cdot 2 = 12$.
Parentheses can mean multiply, so $6(2) = 12$.

EXAMPLE 1   Evaluate $8.25 + m$ when $m = 6.008$.
In the expression, substitute 6.008 for m.
$$8.25 + 6.008$$
Perform the arithmetic operation.
$$8.25 + 6.008 = 14.258$$

EXAMPLE 2   Evaluate $1.3m + 2.5n$ when $m = 6$ and $n = 3.14$.
In the expression, substitute 6 for m and 3.14 for n.
$$1.3(6) + 2.5(3.14)$$
Multiply. Then add.
$$7.8 + 7.85 = 15.65$$

When you evaluate an open statement, you determine whether the number that is substituted for the variable makes the statement true or false.

EXAMPLE 3   Is $4.5n = 13.5$ a true or false statement when $n = 1$, 2, or 3?
When $n = 1$, $4.5n = 13.5 \rightarrow 4.5 \times 1 = 4.5$, or
$4.5 = 13.5 \rightarrow$ false statement
When $n = 2$, $4.5n = 13.5 \rightarrow 4.5 \times 2 = 9.0$, or
$9.0 = 13.5 \rightarrow$ false statement
When $n = 3$, $4.5n = 13.5 \rightarrow 4.5 \times 3 = 13.5$, or
$13.5 = 13.5 \rightarrow$ true statement

Exercise A Evaluate each expression.

   1. $m + 2.07$ when $m = 3.085$

   2. $n - 6.257$ when $n = 20$

   3. $3.14d$ when $d = 2.6$

   4. $n \div 100$ when $n = 0.572$

   5. $4m + 7.26$ when $m = 3.479$

   6. $2l + 2w$ when $l = 10.75$ and $w = 5.5$

   7. $l \times w$ when $l = 16.29$ and $w = 3.4$

   8. $16 - n$ when $n = 0.0825$

   9. $n \div 1.23$ when $n = 6.42$

   10. $2.4a + 2.67b$ when $a = 6.8$ and $b = 0.02$

Exercise B Write true or false.

Is $4s = 18$ a true or false statement when

   11. $s = 3.5$?   **12.** $s = 4.5$?   **13.** $s = 5.5$?

Is $\$1,200 \times n \times 3 = \$216$ a true or false statement when

   14. $n = 4\%$?   **15.** $n = 5\%$?   **16.** $n = 6\%$?

Is $8.5n = 8.585$ a true or false statement when

   17. $n = 1.01$?   **18.** $n = 1.1$?   **19.** $n = 1.001$?

   20. $n = 1.0085$?

Converting Measurements Sometimes you may need to convert measures from one measurement system to another. Most of the everyday measurements use the following four base units of the metric system. The meter is used for length and distance, the kilogram for weight of an object, the liter for capacity, and Celsius for temperature.

EXAMPLE 1 If 1 foot = 0.3048 meters, 15 feet equals how many meters?

Step 1 Use the decimal to convert the measurement.

Step 2 Multiply: (0.3048)(15) = 4.572

$$15 \text{ feet} = 4.572 \text{ meters}$$

EXAMPLE 2 If 1 pound = 0.4536 kilograms, 15 pounds equals how many kilograms?

Step 1 Use the decimal to convert the measurement.

Step 2 Multiply: (0.4536)(15) = 6.804

$$15 \text{ pounds} = 6.804 \text{ kilograms}$$

Exercise Solve each problem.

1. One gallon is equal to 3.7853 liters. How many liters are in 22 gallons?

2. One inch equals 2.54 centimeters. How many centimeters does a standard 12-inch ruler have?

3. In competition swimming, the long-course pool is 164 feet long and the short-course pool is about 82 feet long. How many meters long is each pool? One foot equals 0.3048 m. Round to the nearest whole number.

Chapter 2 REVIEW

Write the letter of the correct answer.

1. Add: 22.56 + 0.385.
    A 23.0   **C** 22.175
    B 22.945   **D** 22.96

2. Subtract: 3.658 − 2.31.
    A 3.427   **C** 1.348
    B 5.968   **D** 1.34

3. Multiply: 4.1804 × 100.
    A 418.04   **C** 4180.4
    B 41.804   **D** 0.041804

4. Multiply: $9.20 × 40.5.
    A $3726   **C** $3.726
    B $37.26   **D** $372.60

5. Divide: $62.85 \div 10^2$. Round the answer to the nearest thousandth.
    A 6.285   **C** 62.900
    B 0.629   **D** 0.063

6. Write the fraction $\frac{19}{100}$ as a decimal.
    A 0.19   **C** 19
    B 1.9   **D** 0.02

7. Evaluate the expression $2l + 2w$ when $l = 6.3$ and $w = 5.75$.
    A 17.8   **C** 12.05
    B 18.35   **D** 24.1

Identify place or value.

Example: the place of 6 in 5.062   Solution: 6 is in the hundredths place.

8. the value of 3 in the decimal 324.15

9. the place of 5 in the decimal 26.9875

10. the value of 2 in 1,204.5

11. the place of 8 in 75.832

Add or subtract.

Example: 1.23 − 0.45   Solution:

$$\begin{array}{r} 1.23 \\ -\ 0.45 \\ \hline 0.78 \end{array}$$

12. 0.963 + 1.58   **14.** $60 − $24.63

13. 3 − 0.746   **15.** 5.9 + 5.32 + 0.496

Multiply. Round to the nearest thousandth when necessary.

Example: 2.48 × 3.1   Solution:

$$\begin{array}{r} 2.48 \\ \times\ \ 3.1 \\ \hline 248 \\ +\ 7440 \\ \hline 7.688 \end{array}$$

16. 0.568 × 23.3   **18.** 32.41 × 7.3

17. 6.872 × 9.18   **19.** 8.72×10^3

Divide. If necessary, round your answer to the nearest thousandth.

Example: 2.829 ÷ 1.23   Solution:

$$\begin{array}{r} 2.3 \\ 1.23\,\overline{)\,2.829} \\ -\ 2\,46 \\ \hline 369 \\ -\ 369 \\ \hline 0 \end{array}$$

20. 8.4 ÷ 1,000   **22.** 72.85 ÷ 5.3

21. 68.5 ÷ 0.6   **23.** $63.7 \div 10^2$

Write each decimal as a fraction. Simplify your answer.

Example: 0.50   Solution: $0.50 = \frac{50}{100} = \frac{1}{2}$

24. 0.625   **26.** 0.045

25. 0.250   **27.** 0.875

Write each fraction as a decimal. Round to the nearest hundredth if necessary.

Example: $\frac{1}{4}$ Solution: $\frac{1}{4} \times \frac{25}{25} = \frac{25}{100} = 0.25$

28. $\frac{2}{7}$ **30.** $\frac{5}{9}$

29. $\frac{7}{8}$

Find the interest earned.

Example: What is the interest earned on $500 at 8% for 1 year?

Solution: I (interest) = p (principal) r (rate) t (time) $500 × .08(1) = $40

31. What is the interest earned on $24,000 at $8\frac{1}{2}$% for 2 years?

32. What is the interest earned on $1,500 at 5.2% for 3 years?

Evaluate each expression. Round to the nearest hundredth if necessary.

Example: $y + 18$ when $y = 2.1$ Solution: $\begin{array}{r} 2.1 \\ + 18.0 \\ \hline 20.1 \end{array}$

33. $x - 6.25$ when $x = 11.99$

34. $6.3a - 5.2b$ when $a = 2.3$ and $b = 2$

35. $n \div 4.5$ when $n = 125.25$

Test-Taking Tip

When studying for a test, write your own test problems with a partner. Then complete each other's test. Double-check your answers.

Number Theory

Did you know that computers use a language of numbers? Circuit boards and microchips like the one in the picture are a computer's "brain." They contain millions of bits of information. They work in special patterns of ones and zeros. This is called *binary code*. Binary code is a mathematical pattern. It allows computers to process information. The number pattern of binary code is very useful. Mathematicians have worked for centuries to discover other useful patterns in the way numbers work together. These patterns are called properties. Once you learn those properties, you can use them to succeed at math.

In Chapter 3, you will identify and use properties of numbers.

Goals for Learning

◆ To identify divisible numbers

◆ To tell prime numbers from composite numbers

◆ To find the greatest common divisor

◆ To use the distributive property to multiply or factor expressions

◆ To find the least common multiple

◆ To use scientific notation for large and small numbers

Divisible

Able to be divided by a whole number with no remainder

Divisibility is a useful property of whole numbers. For example, 4 divides 8, and 5 divides 25. The symbol | is used to represent the word *divides*.

EXAMPLE 1   Which of these statements are true?
Which are false?

2|16   9|19   7|40   3|21

2|16 is true because 2 • 8 = 16.

9|19 is false because 9 • NO WHOLE NUMBER = 19.

7|40 is false because 7 • NO WHOLE NUMBER = 40.

3|21 is true because 3 • 7 = 21.

Divisibility Rule

In general, a whole number *a* divides a whole number *b* if and only if there is a whole number *n* so that *a* • *n* = *b*.

a|*b* if and only if there is a whole number *n* so that *a* • *n* = *b*.

Another way to think about divisibility is to think about remainders. If a division produces a remainder other than zero, then the numbers are not divisible.

EXAMPLE 2   Which of these statements are true?
Which are false?

5|32   8|8   4|36   2|9

5|32 is false because 32 ÷ 5 = 6 r2.

8|8 is true because 8 ÷ 8 = 1 r0.

4|36 is true because 36 ÷ 4 = 9 r0.

2|9 is false because 9 ÷ 2 = 4 r1.

To test larger numbers for divisibility, use these rules:

Rule—Divisibility by 2

A number is divisible by 2 if its last digit is 0, 2, 4, 6, or 8.

EXAMPLE 3 Is 4,320 divisible by 2?

4,320 is divisible by 2 because its last digit is 0.

Rule—Divisibility by 3

A number is divisible by 3 if the sum of its digits is divisible by 3.

EXAMPLE 4 Is 4,320 divisible by 3?

4,320 is divisible by 3 because the sum of its digits
(4 + 3 + 2 + 0 = 9) is divisible by 3. (9 ÷ 3 = 3)

Rule—Divisibility by 4

A number is divisible by 4 if the number represented by its last two digits is divisible by 4.

EXAMPLE 5 Is 4,320 divisible by 4?

4,320 is divisible by 4 because the number represented by its last two digits (20) is divisible by 4. (20 ÷ 4 = 5)

Estimation Activity

Estimate: Find the value of n to the nearest whole number when $3n = 17.8$

Solution: 3 times what whole number = 17 or 18.

Answer: 5 is too small, $3 \cdot 5 = 15$
              6 is good, $3 \cdot 6 = 18$
              7 is too large, $3 \cdot 7 = 21$
              The best estimate is 6.

Rule—Divisibility by 5

A number is divisible by 5 if its last digit is 0 or 5.

EXAMPLE 6   Is 4,320 divisible by 5?

4,320 is divisible by 5 because its last digit is 0.

Rule—Divisibility by 6

A number is divisible by 6 if it is divisible by 2 and by 3.

EXAMPLE 7   Is 4,320 divisible by 6?

4,320 is divisible by 6 because it is divisible by 2 and by 3.

Rule—Divisibility by 8

A number is divisible by 8 if the number represented by its last three digits is divisible by 8.

EXAMPLE 8   Is 4,320 divisible by 8?

4,320 is divisible by 8 because the number represented by its last three digits (320) is divisible by 8. (320 ÷ 8 = 40)

Rule—Divisibility by 9

A number is divisible by 9 if the sum of its digits is divisible by 9.

EXAMPLE 9   Is 4,320 divisible by 9?

4,320 is divisible by 9 because the sum of its digits (4 + 3 + 2 + 0 = 9) is divisible by 9. (9 ÷ 9 = 1)

> **Rule—Divisibility by 10**
> A number is divisible by 10 if its last digit is 0.

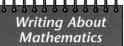 **Is 4,320 divisible by 10?**
4,320 is divisible by 10 because its last digit is 0.

Writing About Mathematics

There is no rule given for divisibility by 7. Describe some numbers you know are divisible by 7.

Exercise A Evaluate each statement. Write *true* or *false*.

1. 2|12

2. 5|48

3. 9|81

4. 3|154

5. 10|375

6. 4|228

7. 6|742

8. 8|400

9. 5|850

10. 3|907

11. 4|1,116

12. 9|2,649

Exercise B Is each number divisible by 2? by 3? by 4? by 5? by 6? by 8? by 9? by 10?

13. 90

14. 812

15. 5,760

16. 51,840

17. 248,121

18. 1,036,800

PROBLEM SOLVING

Exercise C Answer each question.

19. Write a whole number greater than ten million that is divisible by 2, 3, 4, 5, 6, 8, 9, and 10.

20. If you know that 2,388 is divisible by 6, what other numbers do you know also divide 2,388? Why?

Prime number

A whole number greater than one that has only 1 and itself as factors

Composite number

A whole number that is not a prime number

Some whole numbers have only two factors. For example, $5 = 1 \cdot 5, 7 = 1 \cdot 7, 13 = 1 \cdot 13$. Any whole number greater than one that has only 1 and itself as factors is called a **prime number.**

EXAMPLE 1   Is 29 a prime number?

Since $1 \cdot 29 = 29$, and there are no other ways to make a product of 29 using two whole numbers as factors, 29 is a prime number.

A whole number may have factors other than 1 and itself. For example, 12 has six different factors—1, 2, 3, 4, 6, and 12. Any whole number that has factors other than 1 and itself is called a **composite number.** A composite number cannot be prime.

EXAMPLE 2   Is 14 a composite number?

Since $2 \cdot 7 = 14$, 14 is a composite number.

Eratosthenes (ehr uh TAHS thuh neez) was a Greek mathematician who lived more than 2,000 years ago. He developed an organized way to find prime numbers. This organized way is known as the Sieve of Eratosthenes. (A *sieve* is something that is used to separate one thing from another.)

TRY THIS

The numbers 2, 3, and 5 represent the prime factors of a person's age. How old is that person?

EXAMPLE 3   Find all of the prime numbers greater than 0 and less than 50.

Step 1   Create a table of positive numbers from 1 to 50.

Step 2   Cross out 1; 1 is not a prime number.

Step 3   Circle 2; 2 is a prime number. Then cross out every multiple of 2 because every multiple of 2 is a composite number.

Step 4   Circle 3; 3 is a prime number. Then cross out every multiple of 3.

Step 5   Circle 5. Then cross out every multiple of 5.

Step 6   Circle 7. Then cross out every multiple of 7.

EXAMPLE 3 *(continued)*

Step 7 Circle the remaining numbers.
The circled numbers —2, 3, 5, 7, 11, 13, 17, 19, 23, 29, 31, 37, 41, 43, 47—are the prime numbers that are greater than 0 and less than 50.

1̸	②	③	4̸	⑤	6̸	⑦	8̸	9̸	1̸0̸
⑪	1̸2̸	⑬	1̸4̸	1̸5̸	1̸6̸	⑰	1̸8̸	⑲	2̸0̸
2̸1̸	2̸2̸	㉓	2̸4̸	2̸5̸	2̸6̸	2̸7̸	2̸8̸	㉙	3̸0̸
㉛	3̸2̸	3̸3̸	3̸4̸	3̸5̸	3̸6̸	㊲	3̸8̸	3̸9̸	4̸0̸
㊶	4̸2̸	㊸	4̸4̸	4̸5̸	4̸6̸	㊼	4̸8̸	4̸9̸	5̸0̸

In Lesson 1, you learned how to test a number for divisibility by 2, 3, 4, 5, 6, 8, 9, and 10. You can use these tests to help you decide whether a number is prime or composite.

Writing About Mathematics

Read about the Greek mathematician Eratosthenes and write about his contributions to mathematics.

Exercise A

1. On grid paper, copy the example table of numbers from 1 to 50 and extend it to 100. Use the Sieve of Eratosthenes method to find all of the prime numbers from 1 to 100.

Exercise B Decide whether each number is prime or composite.

2. 108

3. 109

4. 119

5. 121

6. 137

7. 142

8. 149

9. 177

10. 221

11. 239

12. 691

PROBLEM SOLVING

Exercise C Answer each question.

13. The numbers 2 and 3 are consecutive and prime. Is there another pair of numbers between 1 and 100 that are consecutive and prime? Tell why or why not.

14. Prime numbers like 5 and 7, 11 and 13, and 17 and 19 are called *twin*

primes because they differ by 2. List all twin primes between 1 and 100. Use your table from Exercise A.

15. Find a number that is greater than 150 and has exactly three different factors.

Simplest form

A fraction in which the only common factor of the numerator and denominator is 1

Greatest common divisor (GCD)

The largest factor that two or more numbers or terms have in common

Common factor

A number that will divide each of two or more numbers with no remainder

A factor of a number is also a divisor of the number. You can use either word.

To write a fraction in **simplest form,** divide the numerator and denominator of the fraction by the **greatest common divisor** of the numerator and denominator. The greatest common divisor (GCD) of two or more numbers is the largest **common factor** of two or more numbers.

EXAMPLE 1 Express $\frac{20}{48}$ in simplest form.

$$\frac{20 \div 4}{48 \div 4} = \frac{5}{12}$$

In this example, the greatest common divisor of 20 and 48 is 4.

Step 1 To find a greatest common divisor, first list all of the factors of each number.

20: 1 2 4 5 10 20

48: 1 2 3 4 6 8 12 16 24 48

Step 2 Then circle the factors that are common to, or shared by, each number.

20: ① ② ④ 5 10 20

48: ① ② 3 ④ 6 8 12 16 24 48

Step 3 Choose the greatest common divisor or factor.

The greatest common divisor of 20 and 48 is 4 and can be written GCD (20, 48) = 4.

You can also find the greatest common divisor of algebraic terms.

EXAMPLE 2 Find GCD (6*x*, 21).

Step 1 List all of the factors of each term.

6*x*: 1 2 3 6 *x*

21: 1 3 7 21

Step 2 Circle the factors that are common to, or shared by, each term.

6*x*: ① 2 ③ 6 *x*

21: ① ③ 7 21

Step 3 Choose the greatest common divisor:
GCD (6*x*, 21) = 3.

Greatest common factor (GCF)

The largest factor of two or more numbers or terms

EXAMPLE 3 Find GCD (5*a*, 17*a*).

Step 1 List all of the factors of each term.

5*a*: 1   5   *a*

17*a*: 1   17   *a*

Step 2 Circle the factors that are common to, or shared by, each number.

5*a*: (1)   5   (*a*)

17*a*: (1) 17   (*a*)

Step 3 Choose the greatest common divisor:

GCD (5*a*, 17*a*) = *a*.

The greatest common divisor, or GCD, is sometimes called the **greatest common factor,** or GCF.

Exercise A Find the greatest common divisor.

1. (10, 50)

2. (16, 30)

3. (9, 24)

4. (72, 18)

5. (12, 32)

6. (54, 1)

7. (4*x*, 8)

8. (7, 28*c*)

9. (6*a*, 12)

10. (45*r*, 15)

11. (14, 6*e*)

12. (36, 42*q*)

13. (49*y*, 21)

14. (3*b*, 9*b*)

15. (20*h*, 5*h*)

16. (18*m*, 24*m*)

17. (45*d*, 27*d*)

18. (84*n*, 54*n*)

19. (26*v*, 65*v*)

20. (56*p*, 72*p*)

TRY THIS Find two whole numbers in a newspaper or a magazine. Find their greatest common divisor.

Distributive property

Numbers within parentheses that can be multiplied by the same factor

The **distributive property** can be used to multiply or to factor expressions. When you *multiply* using the distributive property, the product will have no parentheses.

EXAMPLE 1 $2(3 + 5)$

$2(3 + 5)$ means $(3 + 5) + (3 + 5) = 8 + 8 = 16$. You can use the distributive property as a shortcut to get the same answer.

Apply the distributive property. $2(3 + 5)$

$(2 \bullet 3) + (2 \bullet 5)$

$\quad 6 \quad + \quad 10$

$\quad\quad\quad 16$

EXAMPLE 2 $3(r + 4)$

$3(r + 4)$ means $(r + 4) + (r + 4) + (r + 4) =$ $(r + r + r) + (4 + 4 + 4) = 3r + 12$

Apply the distributive property. $3(r + 4)$

$(3 \bullet r) + (3 \bullet 4)$

$\quad 3r \quad + \quad 12$

EXAMPLE 3 $2(a + 6b + 1)$

$2(a + 6b + 1)$ means $(a + 6b + 1) + (a + 6b + 1) =$ $(a + a) + (6b + 6b) + (1 + 1) = 2a + 12b + 2$

Apply the distributive property. $2(a + 6b + 1)$

$(2 \bullet a) + (2 \bullet 6b) + (2 \bullet 1)$

$\quad 2a \quad + \quad 12b \quad + \quad 2$

The distributive property is also useful whenever you factor expressions. To factor an expression, first find the greatest common divisor. Then use the distributive property to place parentheses between the factors.

EXAMPLE 4   Factor $4x + 6$.

Step 1   First find the greatest common divisor, or GCD, of each term.

$4x$: ① ② 4 x

6:   ① ② 3 6

The GCD of $4x$ and 6 is 2.

Step 2   Write the GCD outside parentheses.

2( )

Step 3   To complete the factoring, use the distributive property in reverse.

$2(2x + 3)$

Step 4   Check your work using the distributive property.

$2(2x + 3) = (2 \cdot 2x) + (2 \cdot 3) = 4x + 6$

EXAMPLE 5   Factor $3x + 3y$.

Step 1   First find the GCD of each term.

$3x$: ① ③ x

$3y$: ① ③ y

The GCD of $3x$ and $3y$ is 3.

Step 2   Write the GCD outside parentheses.

3( )

Step 3   To complete the factoring, use the distributive property in reverse.

$3(x + y)$

Step 4   Check your work using the distributive property.

$3(x + y) = (3 \cdot x) + (3 \cdot y) = 3x + 3y$

Technology Connection

Spell Check This!

A spell-check program on a computer works something like factoring. Suppose you've written the word "algebra." First, it factors out all the words that have the same number of letters as *algebra*. Then it works through the alphabet. It looks at all words that begin with *a*. Then it looks at all the words that begin with the letters *al,* and so on, until it has made sure that the word "algebra" that you wrote matches the word *algebra* in the computer's dictionary.

EXAMPLE 6 Factor $ab + ac$.

Step 1 First find the GCD of each term.

ab: ⓐ b

ac: ⓐ c

The GCD of ab and ac is a.

Step 2 Write the GCD outside parentheses.

$a(\quad)$

Step 3 To complete the factoring, use the distributive property in reverse.

$a(b + c)$

Step 4 Check your work using the distributive property.

$a(b + c) = (a \bullet b) + (a \bullet c) = ab + ac$

Some expressions cannot be factored.

The greatest common divisor, or GCD, is sometimes called the greatest common factor, or GCF. A factor is also a divisor.

EXAMPLE 7 Factor $4x + 7y$.

First find the GCD of each term.

$4x$: ① 4 x

$7y$: ① 7 y

The GCD of $4x$ and $7y$ is 1. When the GCD of any group of numbers or terms is 1, the expression cannot be factored.

Whenever you factor an expression, you are rewriting the expression as the product of two or more factors.

Exercise A Use the distributive property to multiply each expression.

1. $3(2 + 6)$

2. $15(3 + 4)$

3. $2(a + 5)$

4. $7(8 + w)$

5. $20(m + 1)$

6. $9(q + 11)$

7. $4(n + 3p + 2)$

8. $8(6k + h + 10)$

9. $2(v + 13 + 2x)$

10. $25(9 + b + 5d)$

Exercise B Find the GCD of each term.

11. $2x + 10$ **13.** $4m + 4n$ **15.** $3z + 8y$

12. $28 + 7p$ **14.** $15c + 5d$ **16.** $6x + 8$

Exercise C Use the distributive property to factor each expression.

17. $2d + 9$ **22.** $13g + 39h$

18. $10s + 20$ **23.** $23b + 4n$

19. $9j + 3$ **24.** $6h + 27f$

20. $12t + 18$ **25.** $22x + 2y$

21. $15w + 6y$ **26.** $bc + cd$

PROBLEM SOLVING

Exercise D Use the distributive property to solve each problem.

27. Jarrod has 6 CDs and his sister Nadine has 5. If they both double the number of CDs they have, how many do they have altogether?

28. Carmen has written 3 letters to each of 2 people this month. Last month she wrote 3 letters to each of 4 people. How many letters has she written in the past two months?

29. Megan earns $18 baby-sitting on Friday night and $24 baby-sitting on Saturday night. The amount she earns in an hour is the GCD of $18 and $24. Find the GCD and factor the expression to show the number of hours she baby-sits each night.

30. Justin collects sports cards. He says that he has 9 times 25 baseball cards and 9 times 14 basketball cards. How many sports cards does he have?

Least Common Multiple

Least common multiple (LCM)

The smallest number divisible by all numbers in a group

Prime factorization

An expression showing a composite number as a product of its prime factors

The **least common multiple,** or LCM, is useful in working with fractions. The least common multiple is the smallest number that is a common multiple of two or more numbers. You find a LCM whenever you add or subtract fractions with unlike denominators.

EXAMPLE 1 Find $\frac{1}{3} + \frac{3}{5}$.

Step 1 Find the LCM of the denominators by first writing several multiples (M) of each denominator.

$M_3 = \{3, 6, 9, 12, 15, 18, 21, 24, 27, 30, 33, ...\}$

$M_5 = \{5, 10, 15, 20, 25, 30, 35, ...\}$

Step 2 Determine common multiples.

$M_3 = \{3, 6, 9, 12, ⟨15⟩ 18, 21, 24, 27, ⟨30⟩ 33, ...\}$

$M_5 = \{5, 10, ⟨15⟩ 20, 25, ⟨30⟩ 35, ...\}$

Step 3 Choose the least (smallest) common multiple.

LCM (3, 5) = 15

Step 4 Write equivalent fractions using 15 as the denominator. Then add.

$$\frac{1}{3} + \frac{3}{5} =$$

$$\frac{1}{3} \cdot \frac{5}{5} + \frac{3}{5} \cdot \frac{3}{3} =$$

$$\frac{5}{15} + \frac{9}{15} =$$

$$\frac{14}{15}$$

In this example, the method of writing multiples of a number works well if the numbers are small. If, however, the numbers are large, this method will take too much time. To find the LCM of greater numbers, use **prime factorization.**

EXAMPLE 2 Find LCM (54, 120).

Step 1 Write the prime factorization of each number.

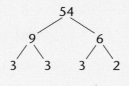 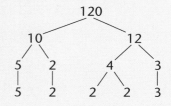

$2 \cdot 3 \cdot 3 \cdot 3$ or $2 \cdot 3^3$ $2 \cdot 2 \cdot 2 \cdot 3 \cdot 5$ or $2^3 \cdot 3 \cdot 5$

Step 2 Identify the greatest power of each prime factor.

The greatest power of the prime factor 2 is 2^3.

The greatest power of the prime factor 3 is 3^3.

The greatest power of the prime factor 5 is 5.

Step 3 Find the product of the greatest power of each prime factor.

$2^3 \cdot 3^3 \cdot 5 = 8 \cdot 27 \cdot 5 = 1{,}080$

LCM (54, 120) = 1,080

Find the LCM of three numbers the same way you find the LCM of two numbers.

EXAMPLE 3 Find LCM (18, 55, 125).

Step 1 Write the prime factorization of each number.

$18 = 2 \cdot 3^2$

$55 = 5 \cdot 11$

$125 = 5^3$

Step 2 Identify the greatest power of each prime factor.

The greatest power of the prime factor 2 is 2.

The greatest power of the prime factor 3 is 3^2.

The greatest power of the prime factor 5 is 5^3.

The greatest power of the prime factor 11 is 11.

Step 3 Find the product of the greatest power of each prime factor.

$2 \cdot 3^2 \cdot 5^3 \cdot 11 = 2 \cdot 9 \cdot 125 \cdot 11 = 24{,}750$

LCM (18, 55, 125) = 24,750

Exercise A Find each LCM.

1. LCM (8,12)

2. LCM (10, 18)

3. LCM (13, 3)

4. LCM (15, 25)

5. LCM (16, 22)

6. LCM (48, 54)

7. LCM (72, 32)

8. LCM (21, 25)

9. LCM (64, 42)

10. LCM (5, 14, 18)

11. LCM (45, 30, 9)

12. LCM (100, 144, 250)

Calculator Practice

You can use a calculator to check the prime factorization of any number.

EXAMPLE 4 Suppose you determine that the prime factorization of 48 is $2^4 \cdot 3$.

To check with a calculator, use the $\boxed{y^x}$ or $\boxed{x^y}$ key on your calculator.

Press 2 $\boxed{y^x}$ 4 $\boxed{\times}$ 3 $\boxed{=}$.

The calculator display reads 48.

Writing About Mathematics

Is the least common multiple of two different positive numbers always greater than the greatest common divisor of those numbers? Do some examples. Explain.

Exercise B Use a calculator and find the value of each expression.

13. 5 $\boxed{y^x}$ 3 $\boxed{\times}$ 2 $\boxed{=}$

14. 7 $\boxed{y^x}$ 2 $\boxed{\times}$ 2 $\boxed{y^x}$ 3 $\boxed{=}$

15. $3^3 \cdot 2^2$

16. $11^3 \cdot 5 \cdot 3^2$

17. $7^2 \cdot 13 \cdot 19^2$

PROBLEM SOLVING

Exercise C Solve these problems.

18. Kayla and Tia work at the same business. Kayla has every sixth and seventh day off. Tia has every fourth and fifth day off. If both Kayla and Tia are off work today, what is the minimum number of days until both will be off again on the same day?

19. Marcus and Dan decide to ride their bicycles around a circular track. At the start/finish line, both riders begin riding at the same time. If Marcus completes a lap every 42 seconds, and Dan completes a lap every 48 seconds, in how many minutes will Marcus and Dan cross the start/finish line at the same time?

20. Tiffany earns 8¢ for every newspaper she delivers. Last week she used all of the money she saved from delivering newspapers to give a gift of $10.00 to each of her 2 brothers and 2 sisters. What is the least number of newspapers Tiffany could have delivered to give the gifts?

Did you know that Earth has a weight of about 6.6×10^{21} tons? The number 6.6×10^{21} is written in **scientific notation.** Scientific notation is a way of writing very large numbers.

$$6.6 \times 10^{21}$$

a number from 1 to 10   exponent   power of 10

Scientific notation

A number written as the product of a number between 1 and 10 and a power of 10

Any number in scientific notation =
$(1 \le x < 10)(10^n)$

Recall that you learned about the power of ten in Chapter 2.

10^1 equals 10.

10^2 equals 100.

10^3 equals 1,000 and so on.

EXAMPLE 1   Write 43,000,000 in scientific notation.

There is a decimal point at the end of every whole number. The decimal point is usually not written. Move the decimal point so that 43,000,000 becomes a number between 1 and 10.

     43,000,000.   →   4.3

Count the number of place values the decimal point was moved.

          43,000,000

The decimal point was moved seven places to the left. Seven places to the left means 10^7.

In scientific notation, 43,000,000 becomes 4.3×10^7.

EXAMPLE 2   Write 234,000,000,000 in scientific notation.

Move the decimal point eleven places to the left.

     234,000,000,000   →   2.34

In scientific notation, 234,000,000,000 becomes 2.34×10^{11}.

You can also write decimals in scientific notation.

EXAMPLE 3   Write 0.643 in scientific notation.

Move the decimal point so that 0.643 becomes a number between 1 and 10.

     0.643   →   6.43

The decimal point was moved one place to the right. When you move the decimal point to the right, the exponent is negative. One place to the right means 10^{-1}.

In scientific notation, 0.643 becomes 6.43×10^{-1}.

Writing About Mathematics

Write about planet Earth, using scientific notation. Earth's total surface area is about 509,700,000 square kilometers. About 139,500,000 of this area is covered by water.

Exercise A Write each number in scientific notation.

1. 62,000

2. 524,000

3. 306,000,000

4. 32,000,000

5. 12,000

6. 312,000

7. 6,221,000

8. 800,000,000

9. 33,400

10. 51,000,000,000

11. 119,400,000,000

12. 445,000,000,000,000

Exercise B Write each decimal in scientific notation.

13. 0.005

14. 0.03

15. 0.4402

16. 0.00002089

17. 0.000666

18. 0.00000506

19. 0.0000000004

20. 0.000000000062

Exercise C Write *true* or *false* for each statement.

21. $2.4 \times 10^4 = 24,000$

22. $8.416 \times 10^3 = 84,160$

23. $7.83 \times 10^5 = 78,300$

24. $4.75 \times 10^{-3} = 0.0475$

25. $9.3 \times 10^{-1} = 0.93$

TRY THIS Work with a partner to solve this problem. The closest Jupiter's orbit gets to the Sun is 4.602×10^8 miles. The closest Earth's orbit gets to the Sun is 9.14×10^7. Find the difference between these two numbers.

Algebra in Your Life

A Good Way to Write Big Numbers
Why do people use scientific notation? Well, suppose you're a scientist. You need to describe the mass of the Sun to a group of students. You write the number on the board. It is 1,989,000,000,000,000,000,000,000,000,000 kilograms! Imagine how easy it would be to make a mistake writing such a huge number! Instead, you can describe the star's size this way: 1.989×10^{30} kilograms. It's a whole lot less writing and a whole lot less chance of error!

Making Conjectures A conjecture is a statement that has not been proven to be true, but has not been proven to be false. Mathematician Christian Goldbach (1690–1764) conjectured that every even whole number greater than 2 can be represented as a sum of two prime numbers.

EXAMPLE 1 Represent 10 as the sum of two prime numbers.

3 and 7 are prime numbers. $3 + 7 = 10$
Another possibility is 5 and 5. $5 + 5 = 10$

EXAMPLE 2 Represent 16 as the sum of two prime numbers.

3 and 13 are prime numbers. $3 + 13 = 16$
Another possibility is 5 and 11. $5 + 11 = 16$

EXAMPLE 3 Represent 50 as the sum of two prime numbers.

19 and 31 are prime numbers. $19 + 31 = 50$
Another possibility is 7 and 43. $7 + 43 = 50$

In the more than 250 years that have passed since Goldbach first made this conjecture, no one has proved that he was correct. But no one has proved him wrong!

Exercise Represent each of these numbers as the sum of two prime numbers. There may be more than one pair of prime numbers for each number.

1. 8

2. 14

3. 20

4. 28

5. 32

6. 36

7. 40

8. 48

9. 58

10. 70

Chapter 3 REVIEW

Write the letter of the correct answer.

1. Find the greatest common divisor of 15 and 28.

   A 5   **C** 1

   B 3   **D** 7

2. Find the greatest common divisor of 9 and $27c$.

   A c **C** $3c$

   B 3   **D** 9

3. Find the GCD of $12z + 32y$.

   A 4   **C** $6zy$

   B $4zy$ **D** 8

4. Factor $5s + 15$.

   A $3(s + 5)$ **C** $s(1 + 3)$

   B $5(s + 3)$ **D** $s(5 + 15)$

5. Factor $19b + 7n$.

   A $19b + 7n$ **C** $4(5b + 2n)$

   B $7(3b + n)$ **D** $bn(19 + 7)$

6. Find the LCM of 24 and 36.

   A 60   **C** 36

   B 72   **D** 3

7. Find the LCM of 8 and 16.

   A 32   **C** 2

   B 24   **D** 16

Evaluate each statement. Write true or false.

Example: 5|15   Solution: 5 • 3 = 15   True

8. 3|19   **10.** 7|91

9. 4|40   **11.** 2|103

Is each number divisible by 2? by 3? by 4? by 5? by 6? by 8? by 9? by 10?

Example: 20   Solution: 20 is divisible by 2, 4, 5, and 10.

12. 52   **14.** 1,080

13. 624   **15.** 90,200

Decide whether each number is prime or composite.

Example: 123   Solution: 123 is composite because it is divisible by 3 and 41 as well as itself and 1.

16. 113   **18.** 135

17. 124   **19.** 147

Use the distributive property to find the product of each expression.

Example: 2(14 + 3)   Solution: 2 • 14 + 2 • 3 = 28 + 6 = 34

20. $6(3 + 1)$ **22.** $18(3 + 2h)$

21. $2(12 + 5)$ **23.** $3(b + 10 + 5x)$

Find the GCD of each term.

Example: $6b + 8ab$ Solution: 6b: ① ② 3 6 ⓑ
8ab: ① ② 4 a ⓑ   GCD = 2b

24. $4d + 12$ **26.** $9c + 3b$

25. $14 + 7p$ **27.** $3g + 11p$

Factor.

Example: $9b + 6$ Solution: $9b$: ① ③ 9 b
6: ① 2 ③ 6   GCD = 3
$3(3b + 2)$

28. $2x + 8$

29. $8j + 4$

30. $10t + 32$

31. $18w + 6k$

32. $12g + 36t$

33. $9f + 24m$

Find each LCM.

Example: $(12, 24)$ Solution: 12: 12 ㉔ 36 ㊽ 60 ㊲
24: ㉔ ㊽ ㊲   LCM $(12, 24) = 24$

34. LCM $(14, 35)$

35. LCM $(15, 40)$

36. LCM $(7, 29)$

37. LCM $(12, 50)$

Use a calculator and find the value of each expression.

Example: $3^3 \cdot 5^3$ Solution: 3 $\boxed{y^x}$ 3 $\boxed{\times}$ 5 $\boxed{y^x}$ 3 $\boxed{=}$ 3,375

38. $5 \cdot 7^2$

39. $2^6 \cdot 3^3$

40. $7 \cdot 17 \cdot 19^3$

41. $2^3 \cdot 3^3 \cdot 4^3$

Write in scientific notation.

Example: 18,000 Solution: 1.8×10^4

42. 26,160,000

43. 8,900,000,000

44. 0.0002402

45. 0.0428

Test-Taking Tip

If you are having trouble solving a problem on a test, go on to the next problem and come back to any skipped problems.

4 Rational Numbers and Fractions

How many chocolate chip cookies would you have to bake to feed your whole school? It would depend on how many students are in your school and how many cookies each student got. One recipe makes two or three dozen. That is about the enough for one classroom. To make enough for the whole school, you would have to equally increase the amount of every ingredient in the recipe. It is likely some amounts would be fractions of whole numbers. Knowing how to work with fractions can help you cook up a recipe for success.

In Chapter 4, you will identify and use fractions and mixed numbers.

Goals for Learning

◆ To identify proper and improper fractions and mixed numbers
◆ To write equivalent fractions
◆ To express fractions in their simplest form
◆ To compare and order fractions
◆ To add and subtract fractions and mixed numbers with like or unlike denominators
◆ To multiply and divide fractions and mixed numbers

Fractions can be used to represent part of a whole or part of a set.

Proper fraction

A fraction in which the numerator is less than the denominator

In this whole circle, three of four equal parts are yellow. The fraction $\frac{3}{4}$ can be used to describe the number of parts that are yellow.

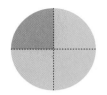

$$\frac{3}{4} \leftarrow \text{number of yellow parts} \atop \leftarrow \text{total number of parts}$$

Remember that the numerator of a fraction is the number above the fraction bar, and the denominator is the number below the fraction bar.

In this set of shapes, two out of five shapes are squares. The fraction $\frac{2}{5}$ can be used to describe the part of the set that is made up of squares.

$$\frac{2}{5} \leftarrow \text{number of squares in set} \atop \leftarrow \text{total number of shapes in set}$$

In any fraction, the number above the fraction bar is the numerator of the fraction. The number below the fraction bar is the denominator of the fraction.

$$\frac{3}{4} \begin{array}{l} \leftarrow\text{numerator} \\ \leftarrow\text{denominator} \end{array} \qquad \frac{2}{5} \begin{array}{l} \leftarrow\text{numerator} \\ \leftarrow\text{denominator} \end{array}$$

The fraction $\frac{3}{4}$ is read "three-fourths," and the fraction $\frac{2}{5}$ is read "two-fifths."

A fraction of the form $\frac{a}{b}$ where $0 \leq a < b$ is a **proper fraction.** In other words, a proper fraction is a fraction in which the numerator is less than the denominator.

EXAMPLE 1 Which proper fractions are named by this number line?

$$\frac{0}{3} \quad \frac{1}{3} \quad \frac{2}{3} \quad \frac{3}{3}$$

Step 1 Recall that in any proper fraction, the numerator is less than the denominator.

Step 2 Choose the fractions in which the numerator is less than the denominator. The proper fractions

$$\frac{0}{3} \quad \frac{1}{3} \quad \frac{2}{3}$$

are named by the number line.

Exercise A Write the proper fraction that represents the shaded part of each whole or set.

1.   **2.**

3.

Exercise B Which proper fractions are named by these number lines?

4. 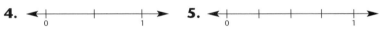   **5.**

Exercise C

6. Write five different proper fractions that have a denominator of 8.

7. Draw a picture or diagram in which $\frac{7}{10}$ of a set is shaded.

8. Draw a picture or diagram in which $\frac{3}{4}$ of a whole is *not* shaded.

PROBLEM SOLVING

Exercise D Solve each problem.

9. Jamal lives 6 blocks from school. He has walked five blocks. What part of the total distance has he walked?

10. Cathy wants to read all 20 of her favorite author's books. So far she has read 13 of them. What part of the total number has she read?

Improper fraction

A fraction in which the numerator is greater than or equal to the denominator

Mixed number

A whole number and a proper fraction

Rational number

Any number that can be represented by $\frac{a}{b}$ where a and b are integers and $b \neq 0$

A fraction of the form $\frac{a}{b}$ where $0 < b \leq a$ is an **improper fraction.** In other words, an improper fraction is a fraction in which the numerator is greater than or equal to the denominator.

EXAMPLE 1 What improper fractions are named by this number line?

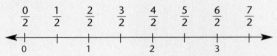

Step 1 Recall that in any improper fraction, the numerator is greater than or equal to the denominator.

Step 2 Choose the fractions in which the numerator is greater than or equal to the denominator.

The improper fractions

$$\frac{2}{2} \quad \frac{3}{2} \quad \frac{4}{2} \quad \frac{5}{2} \quad \frac{6}{2} \quad \frac{7}{2}$$

are named by the number line.

Improper fractions, and proper fractions that you studied earlier, are examples of **rational numbers.** A rational number is any number that can be represented by $\frac{a}{b}$ where a and b are integers and $b \neq 0$.

The following are examples of rational numbers.

$$\frac{0}{4} \quad \frac{5}{6} \quad \frac{14}{14} \quad \frac{32}{20} \quad \frac{-5}{10} \quad \frac{10}{-11} \quad -\frac{1}{2}$$

Mixed numbers are also examples of rational numbers. A mixed number is the sum of a whole number and a proper fraction. Mixed numbers belong to the set of rational numbers because mixed numbers can be expressed as improper fractions.

EXAMPLE 2 Express $\frac{11}{2}$ as a mixed number.

Step 1 In any fraction, the fraction bar (or line segment) that separates the numerator from the denominator means "divide." To express an improper fraction as a mixed number, divide the numerator by the denominator.

Step 2 Divide.

$$\frac{11}{2} = 11 \div 2 = 2\overline{)11} \begin{array}{r} 5 \\ \hline -10 \\ \hline 1 \end{array}$$

Step 3 List the remainder as a fraction of the divisor 2.

$$\frac{11}{2} = 11 \div 2 = 2\overline{)11} \begin{array}{r} 5 \\ \hline -10 \\ \hline 1 \end{array} = 5\frac{1}{2}$$

Sometimes when you change an improper fraction to a mixed number, the remainder will be zero. When this happens, the answer is a whole number.

EXAMPLE 3 Express $\frac{45}{5}$ as a mixed number.

Step 1 To express an improper fraction as a mixed number, divide the numerator by the denominator.

Step 2 Divide.

$$\frac{45}{5} = 45 \div 5 = 5\overline{)45} \begin{array}{r} 9 \\ \hline -45 \\ \hline 0 \end{array}$$

Step 3 Since the remainder is zero, the answer is a whole number.

$$\frac{45}{5} = 45 \div 5 = 5\overline{)45} \begin{array}{r} 9 \\ \hline -45 \\ \hline 0 \end{array} = 9$$

It is also possible to express a mixed number as an improper fraction.

EXAMPLE 4 Express $13\frac{1}{2}$ as an improper fraction.

Step 1 To express a mixed number as an improper fraction, multiply the whole number by the denominator of the fraction.

$$13\frac{1}{2} \qquad 13 \cdot 2 = 26$$

Step 2 Add the numerator to the product you found in Step 1.

$$26 + 1 = 27$$

Step 3 Write the sum from Step 2 as the numerator of an improper fraction. Write the denominator of the mixed number as the denominator of your improper fraction.

$$13\frac{1}{2} = \frac{27}{2}$$

Exercise A Use the number line below for problems 1 and 2.

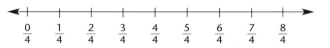

$$\frac{0}{4} \quad \frac{1}{4} \quad \frac{2}{4} \quad \frac{3}{4} \quad \frac{4}{4} \quad \frac{5}{4} \quad \frac{6}{4} \quad \frac{7}{4} \quad \frac{8}{4}$$

1. Name the improper fractions shown by the number line.

2. Name the rational numbers shown by the number line.

Exercise B Label each fraction *proper* or *improper*.

3. $\frac{3}{8}$

4. $\frac{4}{1}$

5. $\frac{5}{12}$

6. $\frac{38}{32}$

7. $\frac{13}{16}$

8. $\frac{0}{3}$

9. $\frac{23}{6}$

10. $\frac{7}{10}$

Writing About Mathematics

Can the sum of a proper fraction and an improper fraction ever be exactly 1? Explain.

Exercise C Express each improper fraction as a mixed or whole number.

11. $\frac{2}{2}$

12. $\frac{15}{2}$

13. $\frac{11}{4}$

14. $\frac{14}{9}$

15. $\frac{29}{10}$

16. $\frac{8}{3}$

17. $\frac{19}{12}$

18. $\frac{24}{5}$

19. $\frac{31}{8}$

20. $\frac{19}{6}$

Exercise D Express each mixed number as an improper fraction.

21. $4\frac{1}{3}$

22. $7\frac{1}{4}$

23. $12\frac{1}{2}$

24. $2\frac{5}{6}$

25. $9\frac{3}{8}$

26. $15\frac{7}{10}$

27. $8\frac{5}{16}$

28. $20\frac{4}{5}$

29. $100\frac{1}{20}$

30. $2\frac{4}{9}$

PROBLEM SOLVING

Exercise E Solve each problem. Give each answer as a whole or mixed number.

31. Eric has 31 golf balls that he bought in sets of 9. How many sets of golf balls does Eric still have?

32. Maria has 15 sets of earrings. Each set has two earrings. How many earrings does she have?

33. Lali is adding 29 photographs to her photo album. How many sheets of the album will she use if each sheet holds 6 photographs?

34. Leroy is making word cards for Spanish class. He needs 35 cards. If he cuts eight cards from each sheet of paper, how many sheets will he use?

35. Anton pours 17 ounces of juice into three glasses. If he pours the same amount of juice into each glass, how many ounces of juice will be in each glass?

Fundamental Law of Fractions

The value of a fraction does not change if its numerator and its denominator are multiplied by the same number

Study these figures.

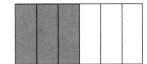 

In the figure at the left, three of six congruent parts (or $\frac{3}{6}$) of the figure are shaded. In the figure at the right, four of eight congruent parts (or $\frac{4}{8}$) of the figure are shaded. Although the fractions $\frac{3}{6}$ and $\frac{4}{8}$ do not look alike, both fractions represent the same rational number. Fractions that name the same rational number are equivalent fractions.

For any rational number, there are an infinite number of equivalent fractions. You can create equivalent fractions by applying the **Fundamental Law of Fractions.**

Remember that an equivalent fraction is a fraction that has the same value as another fraction.

Fundamental Law of Fractions

For any rational number $\frac{a}{b}$ and any whole number $c \neq 0$,

$$\frac{a}{b} = \frac{ac}{bc}.$$

This is true because $\frac{c}{c} = 1$, which is the same as multiplying by 1.

The Fundamental Law of Fractions states that the value of a fraction does not change if its numerator and its denominator are multiplied by the same number.

 EXAMPLE 1 Write an equivalent fraction for $\frac{2}{3}$.

Apply the Fundamental Law of Fractions—choose a number, then multiply the numerator and the denominator of $\frac{2}{3}$ by that number.

$$\frac{2}{3} \cdot \frac{5}{5} = \frac{10}{15}$$

The fractions $\frac{2}{3}$ and $\frac{10}{15}$ are equivalent fractions. In this example, the numerator and denominator were multiplied by 5. You could have chosen a different number.

EXAMPLE 2   Write an equivalent fraction for $\frac{2}{3}$.

Multiply the numerator and the denominator of $\frac{2}{3}$ by 4.

$$\frac{2}{3} \bullet \frac{4}{4} = \frac{8}{12}$$

The following fractions are equivalent fractions.

$$\frac{2}{3} \quad \frac{10}{15} \quad \frac{8}{12}$$

Whenever you must write equivalent fractions, choose any number you want to multiply by. Just remember to multiply the numerator and the denominator by the number you chose.

Exercise A Write two equivalent fractions for each fraction.

1. $\frac{1}{3}$

2. $\frac{5}{6}$

3. $\frac{7}{8}$

4. $\frac{2}{5}$

5. $\frac{3}{10}$

6. $\frac{5}{16}$

7. $\frac{3}{8}$

8. $\frac{1}{6}$

9. $\frac{9}{10}$

10. $\frac{11}{16}$

Exercise B Write two equivalent fractions for each pair of figures.

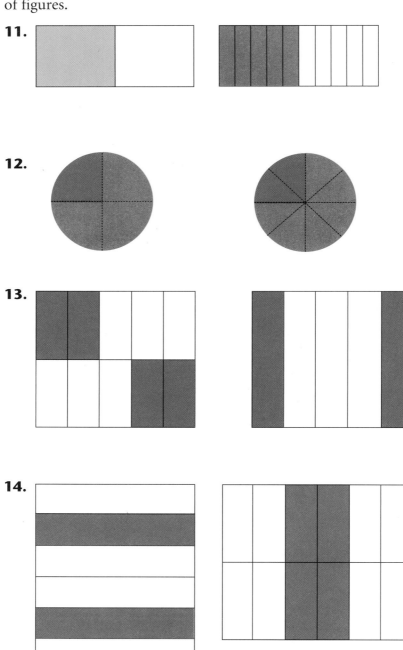

11.

12.

13.

14.

Calculator Practice

You can use a calculator to check if two or more fractions are equivalent fractions.

EXAMPLE 3   Are $\frac{3}{4}$ and $\frac{6}{8}$ equivalent fractions?

Since a fraction bar (the line segment that separates the numerator from the denominator) in any fraction means "divide," use a calculator to divide each fraction.

$\frac{3}{4}$ Press 3 ÷ 4 = . The display reads 0.75.

$\frac{6}{8}$ Press 6 ÷ 8 = . The display reads 0.75.

Since the fractions name the same decimal value, the fractions are equivalent.

Exercise C Use a calculator to decide if each pair of fractions are equivalent. Write *yes* or *no*.

15. $\frac{1}{5}$ $\frac{10}{50}$

16. $\frac{4}{20}$ $\frac{1}{4}$

17. $\frac{7}{9}$ $\frac{2}{3}$

18. $\frac{1}{6}$ $\frac{8}{48}$

19. $\frac{7}{19}$ $\frac{14}{39}$

20. $\frac{4}{7}$ $\frac{20}{35}$

TRY THIS Write three fractions on a sheet of paper. Exchange papers with a partner. Write five equivalent fractions for each fraction your partner wrote.

Lesson 4 — Simplest Form

Recall that the greatest common divisor (GCD) of two or more numbers is the greatest factor the numbers have in common.

EXAMPLE 1 Find GCD (9, 21).

Step 1 List all of the factors of each number.

9:    1   3   9

21:   1   3   7   21

Step 2 Circle the factors that are common, or shared by, each number.

9:    ①   ③   9

21:   ①   ③   7   21

Step 3 Choose the greatest common divisor.

GCD (9, 21) = 3.

The GCD is used to express a fraction in simplest form. A fraction is said to be in simplest form when the greatest common divisor of its numerator and denominator is 1.

Expressing a fraction in simplest form means the same as reducing the fraction to lowest terms.

EXAMPLE 2 Express $\frac{9}{21}$ in simplest form.

Step 1 Find the GCD of the numerator and the denominator. (Look again at the previous example.)

GCD (9, 21) = 3.

Step 2 Divide the numerator and denominator of $\frac{9}{21}$ by 3, the GCD.

$$\frac{9 \div 3}{21 \div 3} = \frac{3}{7}$$

The fraction $\frac{3}{7}$ is in simplest form because the GCD of its numerator and denominator is 1.

Recall that the greatest common divisor (GCD) is the same as the greatest common factor (GCF).

EXAMPLE 3 Express $\frac{15}{60}$ in simplest form.

Step 1 Find the GCD of 15 and 60. GCD (15, 60) = 15.

Step 2 Divide the numerator and denominator of $\frac{15}{60}$ by 15, the GCD.

$$\frac{15 \div 15}{60 \div 15} = \frac{1}{4}$$

Exercise A Find the greatest common divisor (GCD) of each pair of numbers.

1. $(8, 16)$ **4.** $(8, 20)$

2. $(10, 35)$ **5.** $(16, 42)$

3. $(12, 18)$ **6.** $(6, 27)$

Exercise B Express each fraction in simplest form.

7. $\frac{10}{16}$ **13.** $\frac{15}{18}$ **19.** $\frac{56}{64}$

8. $\frac{4}{8}$ **14.** $\frac{7}{42}$ **20.** $\frac{78}{96}$

9. $\frac{5}{15}$ **15.** $\frac{28}{35}$ **21.** $\frac{60}{144}$

10. $\frac{4}{6}$ **16.** $\frac{30}{80}$ **22.** $\frac{72}{108}$

11. $\frac{9}{15}$ **17.** $\frac{55}{60}$

12. $\frac{12}{40}$ **18.** $\frac{42}{60}$

PROBLEM SOLVING

Exercise C Answer each question. In a mathematics class, $\frac{5}{8}$ of the students are female. In another mathematics class, $\frac{3}{8}$ of the students are male.

23. Is it possible for both classes to have the same numbers of female and male students? Explain.

24. Is it possible for both classes to have different numbers of female and male students? Explain.

25. How many students are in each class? Tell how you know.

A number line can be used to compare fractions. To compare fractions means to decide which fraction is greater or smaller.

EXAMPLE 1 Which is greater, $\frac{3}{4}$ or $\frac{5}{4}$?

Step 1 The number line below is divided into fourths. Find each fraction on the number line.

Step 2 On the line, the fraction farther to the right is the greater fraction.

$\frac{5}{4}$ is greater than $\frac{3}{4}$ or $\frac{5}{4} > \frac{3}{4}$

Number lines can also be used to compare fractions with different, or unlike, denominators.

EXAMPLE 2 Which is smaller, $\frac{2}{3}$ or $\frac{2}{5}$?

Step 1 One number line below is divided into thirds. The other is divided into fifths. Find each fraction.

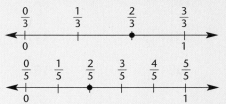

Step 2 The fraction farther to the left is the smaller fraction.

$\frac{2}{5}$ is less than $\frac{2}{3}$ or $\frac{2}{5} < \frac{2}{3}$

Using a number line to compare fractions is not always practical, especially when the denominators of the fractions to be compared are unlike.

EXAMPLE 3 Suppose that $\frac{5}{8}$ of the students in a mathematics class earned a perfect score on the first quiz of the year. On the second quiz of the year, $\frac{3}{5}$ of the students earned a perfect score. On which quiz did a greater number of students earn a perfect score?

EXAMPLE 3   *(continued)*

Compare $\frac{5}{8}$ and $\frac{3}{5}$ to find the greater fraction.

Step 1   Find the least common multiple (LCM) of the denominators of the fractions.

8 → 8   16   24   32   ⑷40   48   56   64   72
5 → 5   10   15   20   25   30   35   ⑷40   45

The LCM of 8 and 5 is 40.

Step 2   Write equivalent fractions for $\frac{5}{8}$ and $\frac{3}{5}$ using the LCM (40) as the denominator.

$$\frac{5}{8} \bullet \frac{5}{5} = \frac{25}{40}$$

$$\frac{3}{5} \bullet \frac{8}{8} = \frac{24}{40}$$

Step 3   Compare $\frac{25}{40}$ and $\frac{24}{40}$. $\frac{25}{40} > \frac{24}{40}$ and $\frac{5}{8} > \frac{3}{5}$

A greater number of students earned a perfect score on the first quiz.

It is also possible to compare improper fractions and mixed numbers.

EXAMPLE 4   Compare $2\frac{1}{5}$ and $\frac{9}{4}$. Which is smaller?

Step 1   Change $2\frac{1}{5}$ to an improper fraction.

$$2\frac{1}{5} = \frac{11}{5}$$

Step 2   Find the LCM of the denominators of the fractions $\frac{11}{5}$ and $\frac{9}{4}$.

5 → 5   10   15   ⑵20   25   30   35
4 → 4   8   12   16   ⑵20   24   28

Step 3   Write equivalent fractions for $\frac{11}{5}$ and $\frac{9}{4}$ using the LCM (20) as the denominator.

$$\frac{11}{5} \bullet \frac{4}{4} = \frac{44}{20}$$

$$\frac{9}{4} \bullet \frac{5}{5} = \frac{45}{20}$$

Step 4   Compare $\frac{44}{20}$ and $\frac{45}{20}$. $\frac{44}{20}$ is less than $\frac{45}{20}$ and $2\frac{1}{5} < \frac{9}{4}$.

Comparing fractions is the first step in ordering two or more fractions or mixed numbers.

The value of a fraction does not change if its numerator and its denominator are multiplied by the same number.

EXAMPLE 5 Order the following from least to greatest.

$$1\frac{2}{3} \qquad \frac{3}{4} \qquad 1\frac{1}{2}$$

Step 1 Change $1\frac{2}{3}$ and $1\frac{1}{2}$ to improper fractions.

$$1\frac{2}{3} = \frac{5}{3}$$

$$1\frac{1}{2} = \frac{3}{2}$$

Step 2 Find the LCM of the denominators of these fractions.

$$\frac{5}{3} \qquad \frac{3}{4} \qquad \frac{3}{2}$$

$3 \rightarrow$	3	6	9	⑫	15	18	21
$4 \rightarrow$	4	8	⑫	16	20	24	28
$2 \rightarrow$	2	4	6	8	10	⑫	14

Step 3 Write equivalent fractions for the following using the LCM (12) as the denominator. $\frac{5}{3} \quad \frac{3}{4} \quad \frac{3}{2}$

$$\frac{5}{3} \bullet \frac{4}{4} = \frac{20}{12}$$

$$\frac{3}{4} \bullet \frac{3}{3} = \frac{9}{12}$$

$$\frac{3}{2} \bullet \frac{6}{6} = \frac{18}{12}$$

Step 4 Compare these fractions. $\frac{20}{12} \quad \frac{9}{12} \quad \frac{18}{12}$

$\frac{9}{12}$ is less than $\frac{18}{12}$ and $\frac{18}{12}$ is less than $\frac{20}{12}$.

The order from least to greatest is $\frac{3}{4} \quad 1\frac{1}{2} \quad 1\frac{2}{3}$.

Exercise A Use the number lines below for problems 1–2.

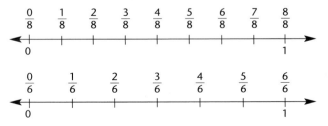

1. Which is greater, $\frac{3}{8}$ or $\frac{1}{6}$?

2. Which is smaller, $\frac{5}{6}$ or $\frac{5}{8}$?

TRY THIS ⬇

Using only the ÷ and = keys on a calculator, describe a way to use a calculator to order fractions from greatest to least or from least to greatest.

Exercise B Compare the fractions. Write > or <.

3. $\frac{4}{5}$ ■ $\frac{3}{5}$ **7.** $\frac{3}{10}$ ■ $\frac{2}{5}$ **11.** $\frac{4}{7}$ ■ $\frac{9}{14}$

4. $\frac{3}{10}$ ■ $\frac{7}{10}$ **8.** $\frac{2}{3}$ ■ $\frac{7}{12}$ **12.** $\frac{1}{6}$ ■ $\frac{2}{9}$

5. $\frac{1}{2}$ ■ $\frac{1}{3}$ **9.** $\frac{11}{16}$ ■ $\frac{5}{8}$ **13.** $1\frac{1}{3}$ ■ $1\frac{4}{15}$

6. $\frac{5}{8}$ ■ $\frac{1}{2}$ **10.** $\frac{3}{5}$ ■ $\frac{3}{4}$ **14.** $4\frac{11}{12}$ ■ $4\frac{4}{5}$

Exercise C Order from greatest to least.

15. $\frac{1}{2}$ $\frac{2}{3}$ $\frac{3}{4}$ **17.** $\frac{11}{12}$ $\frac{5}{6}$ $\frac{7}{8}$

16. $\frac{1}{4}$ $\frac{1}{3}$ $\frac{1}{5}$ **18.** $\frac{3}{10}$ $\frac{2}{5}$ $\frac{1}{3}$

Exercise D Order from least to greatest.

19. $\frac{3}{4}$ $\frac{5}{8}$ $\frac{1}{2}$ **21.** $\frac{4}{7}$ $\frac{9}{14}$ $\frac{1}{2}$

20. $\frac{2}{5}$ $\frac{1}{3}$ $\frac{7}{15}$ **22.** $\frac{7}{12}$ $\frac{2}{3}$ $\frac{5}{8}$

PROBLEM SOLVING

Exercise E Compare fractions to solve each problem.

23. On a test, Gina got $\frac{5}{6}$ of the answers correct, and Terrence got $\frac{7}{8}$ of the answers correct. Who had more correct answers?

24. Jacob can mow $\frac{4}{5}$ of Mr. Abert's lawn in an hour. Julio can mow $\frac{7}{9}$ of the same lawn in an hour. Who mows more of the lawn in an hour?

25. James lives $\frac{7}{10}$ of a mile from school, and Matt lives $\frac{13}{18}$ of a mile from school. Who lives closer to school?

Some of the work you will perform in algebra involves computations. Some of these computations include adding fractions with like denominators. You perform computations in algebra in the same way you do in arithmetic.

EXAMPLE 1 Add $\frac{2}{5} + \frac{1}{5}$.

Step 1 Add the numerators of the fractions.

$$\frac{2}{5} + \frac{1}{5} = \frac{2+1}{5} = \frac{3}{\_}$$

Step 2 Write the denominator of the fractions.

$$\frac{2}{5} + \frac{1}{5} = \frac{3}{5}$$

EXAMPLE 2 Add $\frac{2x}{5} + \frac{1x}{5}$.

Step 1 Add the numerators of the fractions.

$$\frac{2x}{5} + \frac{1x}{5} = \frac{2x+1x}{5} = \frac{3x}{\_}$$

Step 2 Write the denominator of the fractions.

$$\frac{2x}{5} + \frac{1x}{5} = \frac{3x}{5}$$

You can also add fractions that have like variables as denominators.

EXAMPLE 3 Add $\frac{b}{x} + \frac{c}{x}$.   Add $\frac{2}{y} + \frac{d}{y}$.

Step 1 Add the numerators of the fractions.

$$\frac{b}{x} + \frac{c}{x} = \frac{b+c}{\_}\qquad\qquad \frac{2}{y} + \frac{d}{y} = \frac{2+d}{\_}$$

Step 2 Write the denominator of the fractions.

$$\frac{b}{x} + \frac{c}{x} = \frac{b+c}{x}\qquad\qquad \frac{2}{y} + \frac{d}{y} = \frac{2+d}{y}$$

Some of the computations you will perform in algebra include subtracting fractions with like denominators.

In algebra, $1x$ is simply written as x.

<table>
</table>

EXAMPLE 4 Subtract $\frac{2}{3} - \frac{1}{3}$. Subtract $\frac{2x}{3} - \frac{x}{3}$.

Step 1 Subtract the numerators of the fractions.

$$\frac{2}{3} - \frac{1}{3} = \frac{2-1}{\_} = \frac{1}{\_} \qquad \frac{2x}{3} - \frac{1x}{3} = \frac{2x-1x}{\_} = \frac{1x}{\_} = \frac{x}{\_}$$

Step 2 Write the denominator of the fractions.

$$\frac{2}{3} - \frac{1}{3} = \frac{1}{3} \qquad \frac{2x}{3} - \frac{x}{3} = \frac{x}{3}$$

Whenever you add or subtract fractions, write your answer in simplest form.

Recall that the fraction bar that separates a numerator from a denominator means "divide."

EXAMPLE 5 Add $\frac{3}{8} + \frac{7}{8}$. Add $\frac{3x}{8} + \frac{7x}{8}$.

Step 1 Add the fractions.

$$\frac{3}{8} + \frac{7}{8} = \frac{3+7}{8} = \frac{10}{8} \qquad \frac{3x}{8} + \frac{7x}{8} = \frac{3x+7x}{8} = \frac{10x}{8}$$

Step 2 Simplify.

$$\frac{10}{8} = 8\overline{)10} = 1\frac{2}{8} = 1\frac{1}{4} \qquad \frac{10x}{8} = 8\overline{)10x} = 1\frac{2}{8}x = 1\frac{1}{4}x$$

You can also subtract fractions with like variables as denominators.

EXAMPLE 6 Subtract $\frac{b}{x} - \frac{c}{x}$. Subtract $\frac{d}{y} - \frac{3}{y}$.

Step 1 Subtract the numerators of the fractions.

$$\frac{b}{x} - \frac{c}{x} = \frac{b-c}{\_} \qquad \frac{d}{y} - \frac{3}{y} = \frac{d-3}{\_}$$

Step 2 Write the denominator of the fractions.

$$\frac{b}{x} - \frac{c}{x} = \frac{b-c}{x} \qquad \frac{d}{y} - \frac{3}{y} = \frac{d-3}{y}$$

Estimation Activity

Estimate: $9\frac{1}{5} - 1\frac{3}{5}$

Solution: Round to the nearest whole number.

$9\frac{1}{5}$ to 9

$1\frac{3}{5}$ to 2

Subtract whole numbers: $9 - 2 = 7$

Some of the computations you will perform in algebra will also include adding and subtracting mixed numbers with like denominators.

EXAMPLE 7 Find $(2\frac{1}{10} + 5\frac{7}{10}) - 3\frac{3}{10}$.   Find $(2\frac{x}{10} + 5\frac{7x}{10}) - 3\frac{3x}{10}$.

Step 1 Perform the computation inside ( ) first.

$(2\frac{1}{10} + 5\frac{7}{10}) - 3\frac{3}{10}$ $(2\frac{x}{10} + 5\frac{7x}{10}) - 3\frac{3x}{10}$
$\downarrow$ $\downarrow$
$7\frac{8}{10}$ $7\frac{8x}{10}$

Step 2 Perform the remaining computation.

$(2\frac{1}{10} + 5\frac{7}{10}) - 3\frac{3}{10}$ $(2\frac{x}{10} + 5\frac{7x}{10}) - 3\frac{3x}{10}$
$\downarrow$ $\downarrow$
$7\frac{8}{10} - 3\frac{3}{10}$ $7\frac{8x}{10} - 3\frac{3x}{10}$
$\downarrow$ $\downarrow$
$4\frac{5}{10}$ $4\frac{5x}{10}$

Step 3 Simplify if possible.

$4\frac{5}{10} = 4\frac{1}{2}$ $4\frac{5x}{10} = 4\frac{x}{2}$

Exercise A Add or subtract. Write your answer in simplest form.

1. $\frac{3}{4} - \frac{1}{4}$

2. $\frac{2}{3} + \frac{2}{3}$

3. $\frac{4}{5} - \frac{2}{5}$

4. $2\frac{13}{16} + 1\frac{11}{16}$

5. $10\frac{7}{12} - 4\frac{5}{12}$

6. $5\frac{9}{10} - 3\frac{3}{10}$

7. $6\frac{7}{12} + 9\frac{11}{12}$

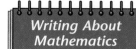

Writing About Mathematics

Explain how to subtract $7\frac{3}{4}$ from $15\frac{1}{4}$.

Exercise B Add or subtract. Write your answer in simplest form.

8. $\frac{7x}{8} - \frac{x}{8}$

9. $\frac{5x}{6} - \frac{x}{6}$

10. $\frac{5}{x} + \frac{3}{x}$

11. $\frac{x}{y} - \frac{1}{y}$

12. $\frac{2x}{6} - \frac{x}{6}$

13. $\frac{y}{x} - \frac{3}{x}$

14. $\frac{5}{6} + \frac{x}{6}$

15. $\frac{3x}{5} + \frac{2x}{5}$

Exercise C Perform each computation inside the ( ) first. Write your answer in lowest terms.

16. $(\frac{4}{5} - \frac{1}{5}) + \frac{2}{5}$

17. $\frac{2}{3} + (\frac{2}{3} - \frac{1}{3})$

18. $\frac{3}{4} - (\frac{1}{4} + \frac{1}{4})$

19. $(\frac{5}{6} - \frac{1}{6}) + \frac{5}{6}$

20. $(\frac{5}{8} - \frac{3}{8}) + \frac{7}{8}$

21. $\frac{1}{12} + (\frac{11}{12} - \frac{5}{12})$

22. $(\frac{13}{16} - \frac{7}{16}) + \frac{9}{16}$

23. $(\frac{x}{8} + \frac{7x}{8}) - \frac{5x}{8}$

24. $\frac{2x}{5} + (\frac{3x}{5} - \frac{3x}{5})$

25. $\frac{3x}{10} + (\frac{9x}{10} - \frac{7x}{10})$

Algebra in Your Life

A Little Here and a Little There
Visit a fabric store, and you will see fractions in action. Imagine you're making some decorations. Each decoration uses a different kind of fabric. You need $\frac{1}{3}$ yard of one kind of fabric, $\frac{1}{3}$ yard of another one, and so on. Now suppose the store is running a special. You get a free gift for every yard of fabric you buy. You would want to know how to add up your pieces of fabric to make sure you received your gift!

Sometimes your work in algebra will include subtracting fractions with unlike denominators.

EXAMPLE 1 Subtract $\frac{5}{8} - \frac{1}{3}$.   Subtract $\frac{5x}{8} - \frac{x}{3}$.

Step 1 Find the LCM of the denominators.

LCM $(8, 3) = 24$ LCM $(8, 3) = 24$

Step 2 Write an equivalent fraction for each fraction using the LCM (24) as the denominator.

$$\frac{5}{8} \cdot \frac{3}{3} = \frac{15}{24} \qquad\qquad \frac{5x}{8} \cdot \frac{3}{3} = \frac{15x}{24}$$

$$\frac{1}{3} \cdot \frac{8}{8} = \frac{8}{24} \qquad\qquad \frac{x}{3} \cdot \frac{8}{8} = \frac{8x}{24}$$

Step 3 Subtract.

$$\frac{15}{24} - \frac{8}{24} = \frac{15 - 8}{24} = \frac{7}{24} \qquad \frac{15x}{24} - \frac{8x}{24} = \frac{15x - 8x}{24} = \frac{7x}{24}$$

In the examples, it is not necessary to simplify because $\frac{7}{24}$ and $\frac{7x}{24}$ are in simplest form.

You can also subtract fractions that have unlike variables as denominators.

EXAMPLE 2 Subtract $\frac{3}{k} - \frac{2}{m}$.

Step 1 Find equivalent fractions by multiplying each fraction's numerator and denominator by the other fraction's denominator.

$$\frac{3}{k} \qquad\qquad \frac{3}{k} \cdot \frac{m}{m} = \frac{3m}{km}$$

$$\frac{2}{m} \qquad\qquad \frac{2}{m} \cdot \frac{k}{k} = \frac{2k}{km}$$

Step 2 Write the equivalent fractions into the equation.

$$\frac{3}{k} - \frac{2}{m} \qquad\qquad \frac{3m}{km} - \frac{2k}{km}$$

Step 3 Subtract.

$$\frac{3m}{km} - \frac{2k}{km} = \frac{3m - 2k}{km}$$

Sometimes your work in algebra will include adding fractions with unlike denominators.

EXAMPLE 3   Add $\frac{3}{4} + \frac{2}{3}$.   Add $\frac{3x}{4} + \frac{2x}{3}$.

Step 1   Find the LCM of the denominators.
LCM (4, 3) = 12   LCM (4, 3) = 12

Step 2   Write an equivalent fraction for each fraction using the LCM (12) as the denominator.

$\frac{3}{4} \cdot \frac{3}{3} = \frac{9}{12}$ $\frac{3x}{4} \cdot \frac{3}{3} = \frac{9x}{12}$

$\frac{2}{3} \cdot \frac{4}{4} = \frac{8}{12}$ $\frac{2x}{3} \cdot \frac{4}{4} = \frac{8x}{12}$

Step 3   Add.

$\frac{9}{12} + \frac{8}{12} = \frac{9+8}{12} = \frac{17}{12}$ $\frac{9x}{12} + \frac{8x}{12} = \frac{9x+8x}{12} = \frac{17x}{12}$

Step 4   Simplify.

$\frac{17}{12} = 1\frac{5}{12}$ $\frac{17x}{12} = \frac{17}{12}x = 1\frac{5}{12}x$

You can also add fractions that have unlike variables as denominators.

EXAMPLE 4   Add $\frac{5}{x} + \frac{2}{y}$.

Step 1   Find equivalent fractions by multiplying each fraction's numerator and denominator by the other fraction's denominator.

$\frac{5}{x}$ $\frac{5}{x} \cdot \frac{y}{y} = \frac{5y}{xy}$

$\frac{2}{y}$ $\frac{2}{y} \cdot \frac{x}{x} = \frac{2x}{xy}$

Step 2   Write the equivalent fractions into the equation.

$\frac{5}{x} + \frac{2}{y}$ $\frac{5y}{xy} + \frac{2x}{xy}$

Step 3   Add.

$\frac{5y}{xy} + \frac{2x}{xy} = \frac{5y+2x}{xy}$

Your work in algebra will also include computing with mixed numbers.

EXAMPLE 5   Add $6\frac{4}{5} + 1\frac{7}{10}$.   Add $6\frac{4}{5}x + 1\frac{7}{10}x$.

Step 1   Find the LCM of the denominators.

LCM (5, 10) = 10   LCM (5, 10) = 10

Step 2   Write an equivalent mixed number for each fraction using the LCM (10) as the denominator.

$$\frac{4}{5} \cdot \frac{2}{2} = \frac{8}{10}$$ $$\frac{4}{5}x \cdot \frac{2}{2} = \frac{8}{10}x$$

$$6\frac{4}{5} = 6\frac{8}{10}$$ $$6\frac{4}{5}x = 6\frac{8}{10}x$$

Step 3   Add.

$$6\frac{8}{10} + 1\frac{7}{10} = 7\frac{15}{10}$$ $$6\frac{8}{10}x + 1\frac{7}{10}x = 7\frac{15}{10}x$$

Step 4   Simplify.

$$7\frac{15}{10} = 8\frac{1}{2}$$ $$7\frac{15}{10}x = 8\frac{1}{2}x$$

Exercise A Add or subtract. Write your answer in simplest form.

1. $\frac{1}{3} + \frac{3}{4}$ **6.** $\frac{3}{4} - \frac{2}{3}$

2. $\frac{7}{8} - \frac{2}{3}$ **7.** $\frac{3}{16} + \frac{4}{5}$

3. $\frac{1}{4} + \frac{2}{5}$ **8.** $\frac{3}{5} - \frac{1}{8}$

4. $\frac{5}{8} - \frac{1}{4}$ **9.** $\frac{4}{9} + \frac{4}{7}$

5. $\frac{3}{10} - \frac{1}{6}$ **10.** $\frac{7}{12} + \frac{13}{16}$

Exercise B Add or subtract. Write your answer in simplest form.

11. $\frac{5}{6}x - \frac{1}{2}x$

14. $\frac{3}{x} - \frac{1}{y}$

12. $\frac{1}{x} + \frac{5}{y}$

15. $\frac{9x}{10} - \frac{7x}{8}$

13. $\frac{7x}{12} + \frac{3x}{8}$

Exercise C Add or subtract. Write your answer in simplest form.

16. $2\frac{3}{4} - 1\frac{1}{2}$

21. $34\frac{3}{8} - 11\frac{1}{12}$

17. $7\frac{7}{8} + 3\frac{1}{4}$

22. $15\frac{15}{16} - 5\frac{1}{3}$

18. $8\frac{9}{10} + 6\frac{2}{5}$

23. $27\frac{5}{12} + 19\frac{3}{10}$

19. $9\frac{4}{5} - 8\frac{1}{8}$

24. $5\frac{1}{4}x + 4\frac{2}{3}x$

20. $1\frac{5}{12} + 12\frac{3}{4}$

25. $7\frac{9}{16}x - 2\frac{1}{5}x$

Technology Connection

Changing Crude Oil into Fractions
You may have seen a movie or TV show where oil rushes out of the ground. How does that thick, black liquid change into the thin, golden liquid we pump into our cars' gasoline tanks? A process called *fractional distillation* separates crude oil into different products. The crude oil is heated up. At different temperatures, the vapor is collected and cooled down so that it becomes a liquid again. The liquid is then refined into gasoline, kerosene, or diesel fuel.

Sometimes it is necessary to rename before you can subtract. Renaming is sometimes called *regrouping* or *borrowing*.

EXAMPLE 1   Subtract $9\frac{1}{5} - 1\frac{3}{5}$.

Step 1   Since you cannot subtract $\frac{3}{5}$ from $\frac{1}{5}$, you must rename.

$$9\frac{1}{5} = 8\frac{6}{5}$$

Think: $9\frac{1}{5} = 9 + \frac{1}{5} = \boxed{8} + \boxed{1} + \boxed{\frac{1}{5}}$

$$- 1\frac{3}{5}$$

$$\boxed{8} + \boxed{\frac{5}{5}} + \boxed{\frac{1}{5}} = 8\frac{6}{5}$$

Step 2   Subtract.

$$8\frac{6}{5}$$
$$- 1\frac{3}{5}$$
$$\overline{7\frac{3}{5}}$$

In this example, the whole number 1 was renamed as $\frac{5}{5}$. There are an infinite number of ways to rename the whole number 1. These are some of the ways.

$$\frac{2}{2} \quad \frac{3}{3} \quad \frac{4}{4} \quad \frac{6}{6} \quad \frac{8}{8} \quad \frac{10}{10}$$

When subtracting fractions with unlike denominators, you must write equivalent fractions using the LCM before you perform any other operations.

EXAMPLE 2   Subtract $4\frac{2}{5} - 2\frac{7}{12}$.

Step 1   Find the LCM of the denominators.

LCM (5, 12) = 60

Step 2   Write equivalent mixed numbers for $\frac{2}{5}$ and $\frac{7}{12}$ using the LCM (60) as the denominator.

$$\frac{2}{5} \cdot \frac{12}{12} = \frac{24}{60}$$

$$\frac{7}{12} \cdot \frac{5}{5} = \frac{35}{60}$$

EXAMPLE 2 (continued)

Step 3 Since you cannot subtract $\frac{35}{60}$ from $\frac{24}{60}$, you must rename.

$4\frac{24}{60} = 3\frac{84}{60}$ Think: $4\frac{24}{60} = 4 + \frac{24}{60} = \boxed{3} + \boxed{1} + \boxed{\frac{24}{60}}$

$- 2\frac{35}{60}$

$\boxed{3} + \boxed{\frac{60}{60}} + \boxed{\frac{24}{60}} = 3\frac{84}{60}$

Step 4 Subtract.

$3\frac{84}{60}$
$- 2\frac{35}{60}$
$\overline{1\frac{49}{60}}$

Always check to make sure your answer is in simplest form.

Exercise A Subtract. Write your answer in simplest form.

1. $3\frac{1}{4} - 1\frac{3}{4}$ **5.** $6\frac{1}{3} - 3\frac{2}{3}$ **9.** $18\frac{3}{8} - 4\frac{7}{16}$ **13.** $8\frac{3}{10} - 7\frac{1}{3}$

2. $7\frac{2}{5} - 4\frac{4}{5}$ **6.** $5\frac{1}{6} - 2\frac{5}{6}$ **10.** $9\frac{1}{4} - 6\frac{1}{3}$ **14.** $19\frac{9}{16} - 12\frac{2}{5}$

3. $8\frac{3}{10} - 2\frac{7}{10}$ **7.** $9\frac{7}{12} - 8\frac{11}{12}$ **11.** $10\frac{5}{8} - 1\frac{1}{5}$ **15.** $31\frac{5}{12} - 9\frac{5}{7}$

4. $11\frac{1}{8} - 10\frac{5}{8}$ **8.** $17\frac{1}{10} - 14\frac{1}{2}$ **12.** $21\frac{3}{4} - 17\frac{5}{6}$

PROBLEM SOLVING

Exercise B Add or subtract.

16. Yesterday Lin worked $3\frac{3}{4}$ hours. She has worked $5\frac{1}{2}$ hours today. How many hours has she worked altogether?

17. Justin weighs $188\frac{3}{16}$ pounds. He wants to lose $9\frac{7}{8}$ pounds. How much will he weigh if he loses the weight?

18. Tisha studies $3\frac{1}{2}$ hours after school. If she has studied for $2\frac{5}{8}$ hours, how much longer will she study?

19. Rafael lives $18\frac{3}{4}$ miles from the amusement park. His friend lives $53\frac{2}{3}$ miles from the park. How much closer to the park does Rafael live?

20. For a project, Tracy needs $5\frac{1}{2}$ yards of blue yarn, $8\frac{3}{4}$ yards of yellow yarn, and $2\frac{1}{3}$ yards of green yarn. How many yards of yarn does she need altogether?

Computations sometimes involve multiplying fractions. To multiply two or more fractions, multiply the numerators and multiply the denominators. Then simplify your answer if possible.

EXAMPLE 1   Multiply $\frac{5}{6} \cdot \frac{2}{3}$.   Multiply $\frac{5x}{6y} \cdot \frac{2}{3}$.

Step 1   Multiply the numerators.

$$\frac{5}{6} \cdot \frac{2}{3} = \frac{5 \cdot 2}{} = \frac{10}{} \qquad \frac{5x}{6y} \cdot \frac{2}{3} = \frac{5x \cdot 2}{} = \frac{10x}{}$$

Step 2   Multiply the denominators.

$$\frac{5}{6} \cdot \frac{2}{3} = \frac{10}{6 \cdot 3} = \frac{10}{18} \qquad \frac{5x}{6y} \cdot \frac{2}{3} = \frac{10x}{6y \cdot 3} = \frac{10x}{18y}$$

Step 3   If possible, simplify by dividing the numerator and denominator by the GCD.

$$\frac{10}{18} \div \frac{2}{2} = \frac{5}{9} \qquad \frac{10x}{18y} \div \frac{2}{2} = \frac{5x}{9y}$$

Multiplication computations sometimes include a mixed number.

EXAMPLE 2   Multiply $1\frac{3}{4} \cdot \frac{3}{8}$.   Multiply $1\frac{3}{4}x \cdot \frac{3}{8}$.

Step 1   Change the mixed number to an improper fraction.

$$1\frac{3}{4} = \frac{7}{4} \qquad 1\frac{3}{4}x = \frac{7}{4}x$$

Step 2   Multiply the numerators.

$$\frac{7}{4} \cdot \frac{3}{8} = \frac{7 \cdot 3}{} = \frac{21}{} \qquad \frac{7}{4}x \cdot \frac{3}{8} = \frac{7 \cdot 3}{}x = \frac{21}{}x$$

Step 3   Multiply the denominators.

$$\frac{7}{4} \cdot \frac{3}{8} = \frac{21}{32} \qquad \frac{7}{4}x \cdot \frac{3}{8} = \frac{21}{32}x$$

The fractions cannot be simplified.

Writing About Mathematics

Write a short explanation about how you might use a calculator to check a multiplication problem that includes mixed numbers.

Exercise A Multiply. Write your answer in simplest form.

1. $\frac{1}{4} \cdot \frac{1}{3}$

2. $\frac{2}{5} \cdot \frac{1}{8}$

3. $\frac{2}{3} \cdot \frac{1}{5}$

4. $\frac{3}{8} \cdot \frac{4}{5}$

5. $\frac{5}{6} \cdot \frac{1}{8}$

6. $\frac{3}{5} \cdot \frac{3}{10}$

7. $\frac{1}{12} \cdot \frac{3}{16}$

8. $\frac{1}{6} \cdot \frac{3}{4}x$

9. $\frac{5}{8y} \cdot \frac{1}{10}$

10. $\frac{5}{7}x \cdot \frac{1}{20}y$

Exercise B Multiply. Write your answer in simplest form.

11. $1\frac{1}{2} \cdot 1\frac{1}{2}$

12. $2\frac{1}{4} \cdot 2\frac{1}{4}$

13. $3\frac{1}{3} \cdot 1\frac{1}{6}$

14. $2\frac{2}{5} \cdot 3\frac{1}{5}$

15. $5\frac{2}{3} \cdot 1\frac{1}{3}$

16. $3\frac{3}{4} \cdot 4\frac{1}{2}$

17. $1\frac{3}{10} \cdot 1\frac{2}{5}$

18. $2\frac{5}{8} \cdot 2\frac{1}{16}$

19. $1\frac{1}{2}x \cdot 2\frac{1}{4}$

20. $2\frac{3}{8}y \cdot 1\frac{1}{4}$

Calculator Practice

Suppose you use pencil and paper to determine that $\frac{1}{2} \cdot \frac{2}{5} = \frac{1}{5}$. To check your answer using a calculator, follow these steps.

EXAMPLE 3 Find the decimal equivalent for your answer.
Press $1 \div 5 =$. The calculator display reads 0.2.
Perform the computation using a calculator.
Press $1 \div 2 \times 2 \div 5 =$. The calculator display reads 0.2.
Compare your first answer to your second answer. If the answers are different, use pencil and paper to perform the computation again.

Exercise C Use a calculator to perform these computations. If the answer is correct, write *correct*. If the answer is not correct, write *not correct*.

21. $\frac{1}{4} \cdot \frac{7}{8} = 0.583$

22. $\frac{4}{5} \cdot \frac{1}{2} = 0.4$

23. $\frac{3}{8} \cdot \frac{1}{6} = 0.0625$

24. $\frac{7}{16} \cdot \frac{3}{16} = 0.1346$

25. $\frac{9}{17} \cdot \frac{2}{5} = 0.2117647$

Dividing Fractions and Mixed Numbers

Reciprocal

The reciprocal of any non-zero number x is $\frac{1}{x}$, sometimes called the multiplicative inverse of that number

Computations sometimes involve dividing fractions or mixed numbers. Whenever you are asked to divide fractions or mixed numbers, use a **reciprocal.** The reciprocal of any non-zero number x is $\frac{1}{x}$.

EXAMPLE 1 What is the reciprocal of $\frac{1}{2}$?

The reciprocal of $\frac{1}{2}$ is $\frac{2}{1}$.

What is the reciprocal of $\frac{y}{3}$?

The reciprocal of $\frac{y}{3}$ is $\frac{3}{y}$.

You can also write the reciprocal of a mixed number.

EXAMPLE 2 What is the reciprocal of $2\frac{3}{4}$ and of $2\frac{3}{4}x$?

Step 1 Express the mixed number as an improper fraction.

$$2\frac{3}{4} = \frac{11}{4} \qquad\qquad 2\frac{3}{4}x = \frac{11}{4}x = \frac{11x}{4}$$

Step 2 Write the reciprocal of the improper fraction.

The reciprocal of $\frac{11}{4}$ is $\frac{4}{11}$.

The reciprocal of $\frac{11x}{4}$ is $\frac{4}{11x}$.

The product of any number (x) and its reciprocal $(\frac{1}{x})$ is 1.

EXAMPLE 3 5 and $\frac{1}{5}$ are reciprocals. $\qquad$ $5x$ and $\frac{1}{5x}$ are reciprocals.

$$5 \bullet \frac{1}{5} = \frac{5}{1} \bullet \frac{1}{5} = \frac{5}{5} = 1 \qquad 5x \bullet \frac{1}{5x} = \frac{5x}{1} \bullet \frac{1}{5x} = \frac{5x}{5x} = 1$$

When simplifying fractions, the value of a fraction is not changed if both the numerator and denominator are divided by the same number.

The reciprocal of a number is sometimes called the *multiplicative inverse* of that number. Use the reciprocal or multiplicative inverse to divide fractions or mixed numbers.

EXAMPLE 4   Divide $\frac{3}{4} \div \frac{3}{8}$.   Divide $\frac{3}{4} \div \frac{3}{8x}$.

Step 1   Find the reciprocal of the divisor.

The reciprocal of $\frac{3}{8}$ is $\frac{8}{3}$.   The reciprocal of $\frac{3}{8x}$ is $\frac{8x}{3}$.

Step 2   Multiply the dividend by the reciprocal of the divisor.

$$\frac{3}{4} \div \frac{3}{8} = \frac{3}{4} \cdot \frac{8}{3} = \frac{24}{12} \qquad \frac{3}{4} \div \frac{3}{8x} = \frac{3}{4} \cdot \frac{8x}{3} = \frac{24x}{12}$$

Step 3   If possible, simplify.

$$\frac{24}{12} = 2 \qquad\qquad \frac{24x}{12} = 2x$$

Rule

To divide two fractions, multiply by the reciprocal of the second fraction, which is the divisor.

$$\frac{a}{b} \div \frac{c}{d} = \frac{a}{b} \cdot \frac{d}{c}$$

Also use a reciprocal whenever you divide one or more mixed numbers.

EXAMPLE 5   Divide $1\frac{1}{2} \div 2\frac{3}{8}$.   Divide $1\frac{1}{2}y \div 2\frac{3}{8}$.

Step 1   Express each mixed number as an improper fraction.

$$1\frac{1}{2} = \frac{3}{2} \qquad\qquad 1\frac{1}{2}y = \frac{3}{2}y$$

$$2\frac{3}{8} = \frac{19}{8} \qquad\qquad 2\frac{3}{8} = \frac{19}{8}$$

Step 2   Multiply the dividend by the reciprocal of the divisor.

$$1\frac{1}{2} \div 2\frac{3}{8} \qquad\qquad 1\frac{1}{2}y \div 2\frac{3}{8}$$
$$\downarrow \qquad \downarrow \qquad\qquad\qquad \downarrow \qquad \downarrow$$
$$\frac{3}{2} \div \frac{19}{8} = \frac{3}{2} \cdot \frac{8}{19} = \frac{24}{38} \qquad \frac{3}{2}y \div \frac{19}{8} = \frac{3}{2}y \cdot \frac{8}{19} = \frac{24}{38}y$$

Step 3   If possible, simplify.

$$\frac{24}{38} = \frac{12}{19} \qquad\qquad \frac{24}{38}y = \frac{12}{19}y$$

Writing About Mathematics

Write one or more sentences to answer this question. How can you check your work when finding the reciprocal of a number or fraction?

Exercise A Divide. Write your answer in simplest form.

1. $\frac{3}{4} \div \frac{5}{8}$

2. $\frac{7}{10} \div \frac{3}{4}$

3. $\frac{1}{4} \div \frac{2}{3}$

4. $\frac{5}{16} \div \frac{5}{8}$

5. $\frac{1}{2} \div \frac{3}{10}$

6. $\frac{7}{8}b \div \frac{1}{3}$

7. $\frac{1}{3} \div \frac{1}{2m}$

8. $\frac{11}{12} \div \frac{3x}{4}$

Exercise B Divide. Write your answer in simplest form.

9. $2\frac{1}{2} \div 1\frac{1}{5}$

10. $3\frac{3}{4} \div 1\frac{1}{4}$

11. $1\frac{1}{3} \div 4\frac{1}{6}$

12. $2\frac{7}{8} \div 5\frac{1}{2}$

13. $1\frac{1}{2} \div 1\frac{3}{4}$

14. $4\frac{2}{3} \div 2\frac{1}{10}$

15. $2\frac{1}{4}h \div 1\frac{5}{8}$

16. $2\frac{5}{12} \div 6\frac{2}{3}y$

17. $3\frac{3}{8}k \div 5\frac{1}{4}$

Exercise C Solve each problem.

18. A tennis court is 36 feet wide. The half-court playing width for singles is $13\frac{1}{2}$ feet. What part of the full width does each half-court take up?

20. The national park has $19\frac{1}{3}$ miles of road. If Claire skates the entire length of the road in $3\frac{3}{4}$ hours, how many miles per hour does she skate?

19. Shanelle has a bolt of material that is $17\frac{1}{2}$ feet long. She cuts the material into pieces $\frac{2}{5}$ foot long. How many $\frac{2}{5}$-foot long pieces does she have?

TRY THIS Find the quotient $\frac{1}{2} \div \frac{2}{3} \div \frac{3}{4} \div \frac{4}{5}$.

Hint: Do the operations from left to right in the order they appear.

Cooking with Fractions Open any cookbook and you will find many fractions. A recipe may call for $\frac{1}{2}$ cup milk, $\frac{1}{3}$ teaspoon ground sage, and so on. Sometimes you want to make more or less than the amount called for in the recipe. To do so, you need to know how to compute with fractions.

EXAMPLE 1 Derek is making a rice and beans dish. The recipe says to cook $\frac{3}{4}$ cups of rice in $1\frac{1}{2}$ cups of water. Derek is doubling the recipe. How much rice does he use? How much water?

Step 1 Set up the expression.

$$2 \bullet \frac{3}{4} = \text{cups of rice} \qquad 2 \bullet 1\frac{1}{2} = \text{cups of water}$$

Step 2 Change the mixed number to an improper fraction and substitute it in the expression.

$$1\frac{1}{2} = \frac{3}{2} \qquad 2 \bullet 1\frac{1}{2} = 2 \bullet \frac{3}{2}$$

Step 3 Multiply the expression.

$$2 \bullet \frac{3}{4} = \frac{6}{4} \text{ cups of rice} \qquad \frac{2}{1} \bullet \frac{3}{2} = \frac{6}{2} \text{ cups of water}$$

Step 4 Simplify if possible.

$$\frac{6}{4} = 1\frac{1}{2} \text{ cups of rice} \qquad \frac{6}{2} = 3 \text{ cups of water}$$

Derek uses $1\frac{1}{2}$ cups of rice and 3 cups of water.

Exercise Solve each problem.

1. Emmet is making three recipes that use flour. One recipe uses $\frac{1}{3}$ cup of flour, one uses $3\frac{1}{2}$ cups of flour, and one uses $\frac{1}{4}$ cup of flour. How much flour does Emmet use?

2. The recipe Lee Ann is making calls for $\frac{2}{3}$ teaspoons of salt, but she uses only $\frac{1}{2}$ that amount. How much salt does she use?

3. Maura uses $\frac{1}{4}$ of the berries a recipe calls for. If the recipe calls for 7 cups of berries, how many cups does Maura use?

Chapter 4 R E V I E W

Write the letter of the correct answer.

1. How would $1\frac{2}{3}$ be expressed as an improper fraction?

 A $\frac{3}{3}$ **C** $\frac{7}{3}$

 B $\frac{5}{3}$ **D** $\frac{3}{5}$

2. How would $\frac{15}{2}$ be expressed as a mixed number?

 A $7\frac{1}{2}$ **C** $8\frac{1}{2}$

 B $2\frac{1}{7}$ **D** $6\frac{1}{2}$

Add, subtract, multiply, or divide.

3. $2\frac{1}{5} \cdot 2\frac{1}{5} =$

 A $1\frac{1}{5}$ **B** $4\frac{2}{5}$ **C** $4\frac{21}{25}$ **D** 1

4. $\frac{5}{8} - \frac{3}{8} =$

 A $\frac{1}{4}$ **B** $\frac{2}{0}$ **C** $\frac{25}{64}$ **D** $\frac{8}{8}$

5. $\frac{1}{3} \div \frac{2}{3} =$

 A $\frac{3}{2}$ **B** 1 **C** $\frac{1}{2}$ **D** $\frac{1}{6}$

6. $1\frac{1}{2} \cdot 4\frac{1}{2} =$

 A 6 **B** $6\frac{3}{4}$ **C** $5\frac{3}{4}$ **D** $5\frac{1}{2}$

7. $\frac{1}{2}x + \frac{1}{4}x =$

 A $\frac{2}{8}x$ **B** $\frac{1}{6}x$ **C** $\frac{1}{8}x$ **D** $\frac{3}{4}x$

Express each improper fraction as a mixed number and express each mixed number as an improper fraction.

Example: $\frac{11}{6}$ and $3\frac{1}{8}$

Solution: $\frac{11}{6} = 1\frac{5}{6}$ and $3\frac{1}{8} = \frac{3 \cdot 8 + 1}{8} = \frac{25}{8}$

$$6\overline{)11}$$
$$\underline{-6}$$
$$5$$

8. $\frac{5}{4}$

9. $\frac{10}{3}$

10. $4\frac{5}{6}$

11. $2\frac{2}{5}$

12. $\frac{24}{7}$

13. $3\frac{1}{3}$

Write two equivalent fractions for each fraction.

Example: $\frac{5}{8}$

Solution: $\frac{5}{8} \cdot \frac{2}{2} = \frac{10}{16}$ $\qquad$ $\frac{5}{8} \cdot \frac{3}{3} = \frac{15}{24}$

14. $\frac{2}{3}$

15. $\frac{1}{4}$

16. $\frac{3}{5}$

17. $\frac{7}{10}$

18. $\frac{1}{16}$

19. $\frac{5}{12}$

Express each fraction in simplest form.

Example: $\frac{10}{16}$ $\qquad$ Solution: GCD(10, 16) = 2 $\qquad$ $\frac{10}{16} \div \frac{2}{2} = \frac{5}{8}$

20. $\frac{6}{8}$

21. $\frac{4}{6}$

22. $\frac{8}{10}$

23. $\frac{2}{8}$

24. $\frac{3}{15}$

25. $\frac{14}{30}$

Order from least to greatest.

Example: $\frac{1}{2}$ $\frac{2}{5}$ $\frac{3}{4}$ Solution: $\frac{1}{2} = \frac{10}{20}$ $\frac{2}{5} = \frac{8}{20}$ $\frac{3}{4} = \frac{15}{20}$

$\frac{8}{20} < \frac{10}{20} < \frac{15}{20}$ so $\frac{2}{5}$ $\frac{1}{2}$ $\frac{3}{4}$

26. $\frac{1}{5}$ $\frac{1}{3}$ $\frac{4}{15}$ **28.** $\frac{7}{10}$ $\frac{3}{5}$ $\frac{1}{2}$

27. $\frac{11}{12}$ $\frac{5}{6}$ $\frac{2}{3}$ **29.** $\frac{5}{8}$ $\frac{13}{24}$ $\frac{9}{16}$

Add, subtract, multiply, or divide. Simplify your answer if possible.

Example: Add $\frac{1}{3} + \frac{1}{12}$.   Solution: $\frac{1}{3} + \frac{1}{12} = \frac{4}{12} + \frac{1}{12} = \frac{5}{12}$

30. $\frac{2}{5} + \frac{1}{5}$ **38.** $2\frac{5}{8} - 1\frac{1}{6}$

31. $\frac{3}{4} \cdot \frac{3}{4}$ **39.** $5\frac{1}{8} - 2\frac{7}{12}$

32. $\frac{3}{16} + \frac{7}{8}$ **40.** $8\frac{1}{3} \div 4\frac{1}{6}$

33. $\frac{4}{5} \div \frac{9}{10}$ **41.** $3\frac{1}{2} \cdot 1\frac{11}{16}$

34. $3\frac{1}{8} - 1\frac{3}{4}$ **42.** $4\frac{1}{4} \div 2\frac{1}{8}$

35. $6\frac{5}{12} + 10\frac{2}{3}$ **43.** $6\frac{2}{3}h + 6\frac{3}{4}h$

36. $1\frac{1}{6} \div 3\frac{1}{2}$ **44.** $2\frac{1}{6}y \cdot 3\frac{2}{5}$

37. $5\frac{3}{8} + 8\frac{1}{3}$ **45.** $\frac{5a}{6} - \frac{2a}{3}$

Test-Taking Tip

When you read a mathematics problem, decide whether multiple steps are required to solve the problem.

Chapter

5

Basic Operations and Rational Expressions

S uspension bridges are the longest and strongest of all bridges. The roadway hangs from cables. The cables are connected to towers at each end of the bridge. Besides the weight of the roadway, the towers and cables must support weight of cars driving across the bridge. Architects and engineers figure out how much weight the cables and towers can hold. Their calculations must be correct, or the bridge will fall. They use rational numbers to calculate the height of the towers and the number of cables holding the roadway. Learning how to use rational numbers can be your bridge to more advanced mathematics.

In Chapter 5, you will use basic operations to solve problems with rational numbers.

Goals for Learning

◆ To use the order of operations to solve problems correctly
◆ To evaluate algebraic expressions
◆ To solve algebraic equations through substitution
◆ To solve equations by adding and subtracting
◆ To simplify complex fractions
◆ To add and subtract to simplify rational expressions
◆ To multiply rational expressions

Order of operations

Rules that describe the order that addition, subtraction, multiplication, and division must be performed

Examples of operations include addition, subtraction, multiplication, and division. Number sentences and expressions often contain more than one operation.

When expressions and number sentences contain two or more operations, the order in which you perform those operations is very important.

EXAMPLE 1 Find $2 + 8 \div 2$.

By looking at the problem, you may think you could do the problem in two ways—add then divide, or divide then add. But there is only one correct solution. According to the rules for the **order of operations**, you must divide first.

Step 1 Divide first. $2 + 8 \div 2$
$\downarrow$
4

Step 2 Then add. $2 + 4$
$\downarrow$
6

The solution $2 + 8 \div 2 = 6$ is correct. Whenever a number sentence or expression contains more than one operation, the operations must be performed in a specific order.

Order of Operations

1. If grouping symbols such as parentheses are used, perform the operations inside the grouping symbols first.
2. Evaluate powers.
3. Multiply and divide in order from left to right.
4. Add and subtract in order from left to right.

These rules are known as the order of operations. Follow the order of operations whenever an expression or number sentence contains two or more operations.

Expressions and number sentences sometimes contain three or more operations.

EXAMPLE 2 $4 \div 2 + 16 \bullet 2$

Step 1   Since the number sentence does not contain grouping symbols, multiply and divide in order from left to right.

$$4 \div 2 + 16 \bullet 2$$
$$\downarrow \qquad \downarrow$$
$$2 \quad + \quad 32$$

Step 2   Add and subtract in order from left to right.

$$4 \div 2 + 16 \bullet 2$$
$$\downarrow \qquad \downarrow$$
$$2 \quad + \quad 32$$
$$\downarrow$$
$$34$$

EXAMPLE 3 $2(7 - 4) - 9 \div 3$

Follow the order of operations.

$2(7 - 4) - 9 \div 3$ Perform the operations inside
$\qquad \downarrow$ the grouping symbols.

$2(3) \quad - 9 \div 3$ Multiply and divide from left
$\downarrow \qquad \downarrow$ to right.

$6 \quad - \quad 3$ Add and subtract from left
$\downarrow$ to right.
3

Exercise A Simplify each expression by applying the rules for the order of operations.

1. $24 - 8 \div 4$

2. $11 + 9 \cdot 3$

3. $3(6 - 2)$

4. $9(12 \div 3)$

5. $1 + 17(7 - 5)$

6. $(6 \cdot 6) \div 12 + 6$

7. $11 + 4(5 - 1)$

8. $2 + 4 \cdot 6 - 8 \div 4$

9. $3 \cdot 5 + 10 \div 5$

10. $8 - 4 \div 2 - 2 \cdot 1$

11. $10(2 + 8) + 3 \cdot 2$

12. $28 \div (4 \cdot 7) - 0$

13. $20(2 + 6) - 10(32 \div 4)$

14. $(10 \div 2) \div 5 + 1$

15. $7 + 12 \div 3$

Calculator Practice

You can use a scientific calculator to find the solution to a numerical expression. Input the expression exactly as it appears. Include the ⊠ to multiply the amount within the parentheses.

EXAMPLE 4 $(15 \div 4 - 1) + 4(3 - 2)$

Press $(\ 15\ \div\ 4\ -\ 1\ )\ \ +\ 4\ \times$

$(\ 3\ -\ 2\ )\ =$.

The display reads 6.75.

If you have a standard calculator, it may not follow the order of operations. Before relying on the calculator, work one problem with paper and pencil to verify the answer on your calculator. Follow these steps and the order of operations to work the problem with a standard calculator.

EXAMPLE 5 $(15 \div 4 - 1) + 4(3 - 2)$

Press $15\ \div\ 4\ =\ -\ 1\ =$.

The display reads 2.75.

Press M+.

Press $3\ -\ 2\ =\ \times\ 4\ =$.

Press M+.

The display reads 4.

Press MRC.

The display reads 6.75.

Writing About Mathematics

When you apply the order of operations, can addition and/or subtraction sometimes be performed first? Write one or two sentences explaining when this can happen.

Exercise B Use a scientific calculator to simplify each expression. Input each expression exactly as it appears.

16. $10 - 2 \cdot 4 + 1$

17. $5(4 - \frac{1}{5})$

18. $16 \div 4(3 - 1)$

19. $5 + 2(12 - 4) + 20 \div 4$

20. $2 + 3 \cdot 4 - 6 \div 2 + 9 - 18 \div 3$

Estimation Activity

Estimate: A bag of dry dog food weighs $8\frac{1}{2}$ pounds. If a dog eats $\frac{1}{2}$ pound each day, how many days will a bag last?

Solution: $2(\frac{1}{2}$ lb) = 1 lb lasts 2 days

8 lb lasts 16 days

$8\frac{1}{2}$ lb lasts 17 days

TRY THIS Write a numerical expression that contains $+$, $-$, $\bullet$, and $\div$. Simplify the expression incorrectly. Then show the expression and its incorrect solution to a classmate and challenge him or her to find the error that you made.

Lesson 2 Evaluating Algebraic Expressions

Constant

A number in an expression that does not change such as 2, −6, and $\frac{1}{3}$ in an expression such as $2x - 6y + \frac{1}{3}z$.

Enclosing a number in parentheses does not change its value. For example, $2 = (2)$ and $3 \cdot 5 = (3) \cdot (5)$.

Recall that an algebraic expression is made up of one or more variables and usually includes one or more **constants** and one or more operations.

It is possible to evaluate an expression. To evaluate means to substitute given values for the variable(s), then simplify by following the order of operations.

EXAMPLE 1 Evaluate $3x + 5$ when $x = 1, 2,$ and 3.

Step 1 For each variable x in the expression, substitute a given number. Write the number inside parentheses.

Step 2 Simplify the expression by following the order of operations.

$$3x + 5 \text{ when } x = 1.$$
$$\downarrow$$
$$3(1) + 5$$
$$\downarrow \quad \text{Multiply.}$$
$$3 + 5$$
$$\downarrow \quad \text{Add.}$$
$$8$$

$$3x + 5 \text{ when } x = 2.$$
$$\downarrow$$
$$3(2) + 5$$
$$\downarrow \quad \text{Multiply.}$$
$$6 + 5$$
$$\downarrow \quad \text{Add.}$$
$$11$$

$$3x + 5 \text{ when } x = 3.$$
$$\downarrow$$
$$3(3) + 5$$
$$\downarrow \quad \text{Multiply.}$$
$$9 + 5$$
$$\downarrow \quad \text{Add.}$$
$$14$$

EXAMPLE 2 Evaluate $\frac{3}{x} + x$ when $x = 1, 2,$ and 3.

Step 1 For each variable x in the expression, substitute a given number.

Step 2 Simplify the expression by following the order of operations.

$\frac{3}{x} + x$ when $x = 1$.
↓
$\frac{3}{1} + 1$
↓   Divide.
$3 + 1$
  ↓ Add.
4

$\frac{3}{x} + x$ when $x = 2$.
↓
$\frac{3}{2} + 2$
↓   Divide.
$1\frac{1}{2} + 2$
  ↓ Add.
$3\frac{1}{2}$

$\frac{3}{x} + x$ when $x = 3$.
↓
$\frac{3}{3} + 3$
↓   Divide.
$1 + 3$
  ↓ Add.
4

EXAMPLE 3   Evaluate $4 - \dfrac{2}{y}$ when $y = 1, 2,$ and 3.

Step 1   For each variable y in the expression, substitute a given number.

Step 2   Simplify the expression by following the order of operations.

$$4 - \frac{2}{y} \text{ when } y = 1.$$
$$\downarrow$$
$$4 - \frac{2}{1}$$
$$\downarrow \text{ Divide.}$$
$$4 - 2$$
$$\downarrow \text{ Subtract.}$$
$$2$$

$$4 - \frac{2}{y} \text{ when } y = 2.$$
$$\downarrow$$
$$4 - \frac{2}{2}$$
$$\downarrow \text{ Divide.}$$
$$4 - 1$$
$$\downarrow \text{ Subtract.}$$
$$3$$

$$4 - \frac{2}{y} \text{ when } y = 3.$$
$$\downarrow$$
$$4 - \frac{2}{3}$$
$$\downarrow \text{ Divide.}$$
$$4 - \frac{2}{3}$$
$$\downarrow \text{ Subtract.}$$
$$3\frac{1}{3}$$

Exercise A Evaluate each expression.

1. $a - \frac{2}{3}$ when $a = 9$

2. $a + \frac{3}{4}$ when $a = 13$

3. $3a - 1$ when $a = 5$

4. $15 - 7a$ when $a = 2$

5. $\frac{a}{2} - 4$ when $a = 10$

6. $17 + \frac{a}{2}$ when $a = 5$

7. $8 + 9a$ when $a = 3$

8. $2a + \frac{1}{a}$ when $a = 4$

9. $\frac{a}{4} + \frac{a}{4}$ when $a = 3$

10. $30a - 32 \div 2a$ when $a = 4$

Exercise B Evaluate each expression for $x = 12$.

11. $x + 2(x)$

12. $\frac{x}{6} + 3 - \frac{1}{2}$

13. $18(\frac{9}{x}) \div x$

14. $3(x - 2)$

15. $\frac{1}{x} + (\frac{10}{5} - \frac{1}{2})$

16. $4x - (15 \div 3)$

17. $38 \div 19 \cdot x$

PROBLEM SOLVING

Exercise C Write and solve an equation.

18. Kareem is one year younger than his sister. The sum of their ages is 29. How old is Kareem? How old is his sister? (Hint: Let x = Kareem's age and $x + 1$ = his sister's age.)

19. Sherry is two years younger than Sara. The sum of their ages is 46. How old is Sherry? How old is Sara? (Hint: Let x = Sherry's age and $x + 2$ = Sara's age.)

20. The Shore Building is two feet taller than the Everly Building. The sum of their heights is 1,424 feet. How tall is each building? (Hint: Let x = the Everly Building and $x + 2$ = the Shore Building.)

One way to solve an **equation** is to substitute numbers for the variable. You continue substituting other numbers until you have an equation with sides equal to one another.

Equation

A mathematical sentence stating that two quantities are equal and written as two expressions separated by an equal sign

Root of the equation

The number substituted for a variable that makes the equation a true statement

EXAMPLE 1 Evaluate $3x + 2 = 14$. Substitute 0 for the variable.

Step 1 Write the equation.

$$3x + 2 = 14$$

Step 2 Choose a number to substitute for the variable.

$$3(0) + 2 = 14$$

Step 3 Solve the one side of the equation to see if it matches the other side.

$$0 + 2 = 14$$

$$2 = 14 \quad \text{False. So } x \text{ is not 0.}$$

Continue substituting other numbers until you have an equation with both sides equal to one another.

Evaluate $3x + 2 = 14$ when $x = 1$.

$$3x + 2 = 14$$
$$3(1) + 2 = 14$$
$$3 + 2 = 14$$
$$5 = 14 \quad \text{False}$$

Evaluate $3x + 2 = 14$ when $x = 2$.

$$3x + 2 = 14$$
$$3(2) + 2 = 14$$
$$6 + 2 = 14$$
$$8 = 14 \quad \text{False}$$

Evaluate $3x + 2 = 14$ when $x = 3$.

$$3x + 2 = 14$$
$$3(3) + 2 = 14$$
$$9 + 2 = 14$$
$$11 = 14 \quad \text{False}$$

Evaluate $3x + 2 = 14$ when $x = 4$.

$$3x + 2 = 14$$
$$3(4) + 2 = 14$$
$$12 + 2 = 14$$
$$14 = 14 \quad \text{True}$$

When $x = 4$, $3x + 2 = 14$ is true. Therefore, $x = 4$ is called a solution, or **root of the equation** $3x + 2 = 14$.

Exercise A Tell whether each equation is true or false when the given number is substituted for x.

1. $4x - 3 = 13$ when $x = 2$

2. $35 - 2x = 15$ when $x = 10$

3. $\frac{3}{4}x = 36$ when $x = 48$

4. $2x + 14 = 26$ when $x = 5$

5. $12 - 3x = 9$ when $x = 4$

Exercise B Substitute numbers into each equation to find the root of the equation.

6. $17 - 3x = 11$

7. $22x + 5 = 93$

8. $\frac{1}{2}x + 15 = 20$

9. $7 + 14x = 7$

10. $6 \cdot x = 12$

11. $7 + 4x = 11$

12. $4x - 10 = 26$

13. $x \cdot 4 = 12$

14. $3 + 6x = 21$

15. $x + x = 14$

Algebra in Your Life

Don't Give Up!
Scientists often use the substitution method when they do research. If one solution doesn't work, they try another and then another until they find a solution. Benjamin Franklin once wrote, "I haven't failed; I've found 10,000 ways that don't work." Here's another quotation from the writer Thomas H. Palmer that you've probably heard before. It seems especially relevant to learning something new like algebra: "'Tis a lesson you should heed, / Try, try again. / If at first you don't succeed, / Try, try again."

Inverse operation

An operation that undoes another operation

In Lesson 3, you solved equations by substituting numbers for the variable. You can also solve equations by using mathematics operations. In this lesson, you will solve addition problems by using subtraction.

> **EXAMPLE 1** Solve $x + 1 = 3$ for x.
>
> **Step 1** Subtract 1 from each side of the equation.
>
> $$x + 1 = 3$$
> $$x + 1 - 1 = 3 - 1$$
>
> **Step 2** Perform the operation.
>
> $$x + 1 - 1 = 3 - 1$$
> $$x = 2$$
>
> **Step 3** Check by substituting your answer into the equation.
>
> $$x + 1 = 3$$
> $$2 + 1 = 3 \quad \text{True}$$

Whenever you apply an inverse operation to solve an equation, always remember to apply that operation to both sides of the equation.

In this example, you subtracted from each side of the equation so that the variable x would be by itself on one side of the equation. This is called isolating the variable. To isolate a variable, you perform an **inverse operation.** Subtraction is the inverse operation of addition.

> **EXAMPLE 2** Solve $x + \frac{1}{4} = \frac{3}{4}$ for x.
>
> **Step 1** Isolate the variable x by subtracting $\frac{1}{4}$ from each side of the equation.
>
> $$x + \frac{1}{4} = \frac{3}{4}$$
> $$x + \frac{1}{4} - \frac{1}{4} = \frac{3}{4} - \frac{1}{4}$$
>
> **Step 2** Perform each operation.
>
> $$x + \frac{1}{4} - \frac{1}{4} = \frac{3}{4} - \frac{1}{4}$$
> $$x = \frac{2}{4}$$

EXAMPLE 2 *(continued)*
Step 3 Simplify.
$$x = \frac{2}{4} \div \frac{2}{2} = \frac{1}{2}$$

Step 4 Check by substituting your answer (before it was simplified) into the original equation.
$$x + \frac{1}{4} = \frac{3}{4}$$
$$\frac{2}{4} + \frac{1}{4} = \frac{3}{4}$$
$$\frac{3}{4} = \frac{3}{4} \quad \text{True}$$

Exercise A Write what you would subtract to isolate the variable in each expression.

1. $x + \frac{2}{3}$

2. $x + \frac{9}{10}$

3. $y + 4$

4. $y + 12$

Exercise B Solve for each variable. Write your answer in simplest form. Check each solution.

5. $a + 3 = 17$

6. $h + 15 = 38$

7. $32 + q = 49$

8. $s + 18 = 25$

9. $x + \frac{1}{5} = \frac{3}{5}$

10. $\frac{1}{6} + y = \frac{5}{6}$

11. $\frac{5}{12} + k = \frac{11}{12}$

12. $1\frac{3}{5} = w + \frac{2}{5}$

13. $\frac{3}{8} = d + \frac{1}{8}$

14. $\frac{9}{16} = x + \frac{7}{16}$

15. $\frac{3}{4} = \frac{3}{8} + m$

In Lesson 4, you solved addition equations by using the mathematics operation of subtraction. In this lesson, you will solve subtraction problems by using addition.

Remember to apply the operation to both sides of the equation whenever you use the inverse operation of addition or subtraction to solve an equation.

EXAMPLE 1   Solve $x - \frac{1}{4} = \frac{3}{4}$ for x.

Step 1   Isolate the variable x by adding $\frac{1}{4}$ to each side of the equation.

$$x - \frac{1}{4} = \frac{3}{4}$$

$$x - \frac{1}{4} + \frac{1}{4} = \frac{3}{4} + \frac{1}{4}$$

Step 2   Perform each operation.

$$x - \frac{1}{4} + \frac{1}{4} = \frac{3}{4} + \frac{1}{4}$$

$$x = \frac{4}{4}$$

Step 3   Simplify.

$$x = \frac{4}{4} = 1$$

Step 4   Check by substituting your answer (before it was simplified) into the original equation.

$$x - \frac{1}{4} = \frac{3}{4}$$

$$\frac{4}{4} - \frac{1}{4} = \frac{3}{4}$$

$$\frac{3}{4} = \frac{3}{4} \quad \text{True}$$

In this example, you added to each side of the equation so that the variable x would be by itself on one side of the equation. To isolate the variable, you used addition as the inverse operation of subtraction.

TRY THIS

Read these problems to a partner. Ask your partner to use mental math to solve them. Use paper and pencil to check your partner's answer to the problems.

$x - 5 = 14$

$x + 42 = 45$

$x + 7 = 21$

$x - 11 = 9$

Exercise A Solve for each variable. Write your answer in simplest form. Check each solution.

1. $x - 14 = 22$

2. $c - 6 = 36$

3. $p - 52 = 13$

4. $c - \frac{3}{8} = \frac{1}{8}$

5. $h - \frac{5}{10} = \frac{3}{10}$

6. $n - \frac{2}{3} = \frac{1}{3}$

7. $1 = q - \frac{1}{4}$

8. $\frac{3}{8} = d - \frac{1}{8}$

PROBLEM SOLVING

Exercise B Use addition and subtraction to solve these problems.

9. Mars is about 48 million miles farther away from the Sun than the Earth. Earth is about 93 million miles from the Sun. How far is Mars from the Sun?

(Hint: $x - 48 = 93$ million miles)

10. Mercury is about 57 million miles closer to the Sun than the Earth. How far is Mercury from the Sun?

(Hint: $x + 57 = 93$ million miles)

Complex fraction

A fraction in which the numerator, the denominator, or both the numerator and the denominator are fractions

Recall that to divide two fractions, you multiply the dividend by the reciprocal of the divisor.

$$\frac{2}{3} \div \frac{7}{8} = \frac{2}{3} \cdot \frac{8}{7} = \frac{16}{21}$$

This idea—to multiply the dividend by the reciprocal of the divisor—can also be used to simplify **complex fractions.** A complex fraction is a fraction in which the numerator, the denominator, or both the numerator and the denominator are fractions.

The following fractions are examples of complex fractions.

$$\frac{2}{\frac{1}{3}} \qquad \frac{\frac{4}{5}}{8} \qquad \frac{\frac{3}{4}}{\frac{1}{2}}$$

Recall that the fraction bar separating the numerator from the denominator means "divide."

The complex fraction $\dfrac{2}{\frac{1}{3}}$ means "two divided by one-third."

The complex fraction $\dfrac{\frac{4}{5}}{8}$ means "four-fifths divided by eight."

The complex fraction $\dfrac{\frac{3}{4}}{\frac{1}{2}}$ means "three-fourths divided by one-half."

Look again at the example $\frac{2}{3} \div \frac{7}{8}$. It shows division of two fractions, written horizontally.

The complex fraction $\dfrac{\frac{2}{3}}{\frac{7}{8}}$ shows division of the same two fractions, written vertically.

Expressions involving complex fractions can be simplified.

EXAMPLE 1 Simplify $\dfrac{\frac{1}{2}}{\frac{3}{4}}$.

Step 1 Rewrite the complex fraction horizontally.

$$\frac{\frac{1}{2}}{\frac{3}{4}} = \frac{1}{2} \div \frac{3}{4}$$ Think: $\dfrac{\frac{1}{2}}{\frac{3}{4}}$ means "one-half divided by three-fourths."

Step 2 To divide two fractions, multiply the dividend by the reciprocal of the divisor.

$$\frac{1}{2} \div \frac{3}{4} = \frac{1}{2} \bullet \frac{4}{3} = \frac{4}{6}$$

Step 3 Simplify.

$$\frac{4}{6} = \frac{2}{3}$$

The numerator of a complex fraction is sometimes a whole number.

EXAMPLE 2 Simplify $\dfrac{2}{\frac{1}{3}}$.

Step 1 Rewrite the complex fraction horizontally.

$$\frac{2}{\frac{1}{3}} = 2 \div \frac{1}{3}$$ Think: $\dfrac{2}{\frac{1}{3}}$ means "two divided by one-third."

Step 2 Write 2 as an improper fraction, then multiply the dividend by the reciprocal of the divisor.

$$2 \div \frac{1}{3} = \frac{2}{1} \div \frac{1}{3} = \frac{2}{1} \bullet \frac{3}{1} = \frac{6}{1}$$

Step 3 Simplify.

$$\frac{6}{1} = 6$$

The denominator of a complex fraction is sometimes a whole number.

EXAMPLE 3 Simplify $\dfrac{\frac{4}{5}}{8}$.

Step 1 Rewrite the complex fraction horizontally.

$$\dfrac{\frac{4}{5}}{8} = \frac{4}{5} \div 8 \qquad \text{Think: } \dfrac{\frac{4}{5}}{8} \text{ means "four-fifths divided by eight."}$$

Step 2 Write 8 as an improper fraction, then multiply the dividend by the reciprocal of the divisor.

$$\frac{4}{5} \div 8 = \frac{4}{5} \div \frac{8}{1} = \frac{4}{5} \cdot \frac{1}{8} = \frac{4}{40}$$

Step 3 Simplify.

$$\frac{4}{40} = \frac{1}{10}$$

Writing About Mathematics

Write a brief description of how you might use a calculator to check a complex fraction that includes mixed numbers.

Exercise A Simplify each complex fraction.

1. $\dfrac{\frac{1}{2}}{\frac{2}{3}}$

2. $\dfrac{\frac{1}{5}}{\frac{3}{4}}$

3. $\dfrac{\frac{3}{1}}{\frac{1}{3}}$

4. $\dfrac{\frac{4}{5}}{4}$

5. $\dfrac{\frac{5}{8}}{\frac{1}{6}}$

6. $\dfrac{\frac{1}{16}}{2}$

7. $\dfrac{5}{\frac{1}{2}}$

8. $\dfrac{\frac{7}{12}}{3}$

9. $\dfrac{\frac{5}{6}}{\frac{1}{5}}$

10. $\dfrac{8}{\frac{2}{3}}$

11. $\dfrac{\frac{1}{8}}{\frac{3}{16}}$

12. $\dfrac{\frac{4}{5}}{10}$

13. $\dfrac{12}{\frac{5}{12}}$

14. $\dfrac{9}{\frac{1}{3}}$

15. $\dfrac{\frac{7}{8}}{16}$

16. $\dfrac{\frac{3}{4}}{\frac{7}{12}}$

17. $\dfrac{20}{\frac{7}{10}}$

18. $\dfrac{15}{\frac{3}{5}}$

Suppose you use pencil and paper to determine that $\dfrac{\frac{1}{2}}{\frac{5}{8}} = \dfrac{4}{5}$.

To check your answer using a calculator, follow these steps.

EXAMPLE 4

Step 1 Find the decimal equivalent for your answer.

Press $\boxed{4}\ \boxed{\div}\ \boxed{5}\ \boxed{=}$.

The display reads *0.8*.

Step 2 Use the calculator to find the decimal equivalent of $\dfrac{\frac{1}{2}}{\frac{5}{8}}$.

Press $\boxed{(}\ \boxed{1}\ \boxed{\div}\ \boxed{2}\ \boxed{)}\ \boxed{\div}\ \boxed{(}\ \boxed{5}\ \boxed{\div}\ \boxed{8}\ \boxed{)}\ \boxed{=}$.

The display reads *0.8*.

If the decimal answer you found in Step 1 does not match the decimal answer you found in Step 2, use pencil and paper to simplify the fraction again.

If you have a calculator with a fraction key $\boxed{a^{b/c}}$, follow these steps:

Press $1\ \boxed{a^{b/c}}\ 2\ \boxed{\div}\ 5\ \boxed{a^{b/c}}\ 8\ \boxed{=}$.

The display will read $\dfrac{4}{5}$.

Exercise B Use a calculator to perform these computations. If the answer is correct, write *correct*. If the answer is not correct, write *not correct*.

19. $\dfrac{1}{4} \div \dfrac{1}{8} = 0.002$

20. $\dfrac{3}{10} \div \dfrac{1}{5} = 0.15$

21. $\dfrac{1}{8} \div \dfrac{4}{5} = 0.15625$

22. $\dfrac{1}{4} \div \dfrac{1}{16} = 2$

23. $\dfrac{2}{5} \div \dfrac{4}{5} = 0.05$

24. $\dfrac{5}{12} \div \dfrac{1}{3} = 1.25$

25. $\dfrac{3}{4} \div \dfrac{1}{4} = 0.3$

Rational expression

An algebraic expression that can be written like a fraction.

Rational expressions often contain operation signs such as $+, -, \cdot,$ or $\div$. The parts of an expression that are separated by operation signs are known as the terms of the expression.

$$\frac{1}{2}x + \frac{1}{4}x \qquad 10 + \frac{7}{8}c - d$$

$$\uparrow \quad \uparrow \qquad \uparrow \quad \uparrow \quad \uparrow$$

terms   terms

You can simplify some rational expressions by collecting like terms and adding them. Like terms have the same variable.

EXAMPLE 1 Simplify $\frac{a}{2} + \frac{a}{2}$. Simplify $\frac{2x}{3} + \frac{x}{3}$.

Step 1 Add the fractions.

$$\frac{a}{2} + \frac{a}{2} = \frac{2a}{2} \qquad \frac{2x}{3} + \frac{x}{3} = \frac{3x}{3}$$

Step 2 If possible, simplify your answer.

$$\frac{2a}{2} = a \qquad \frac{3x}{3} = x$$

Remember when you add or subtract a fraction with the same denominator, you add or subtract the numerator only. You do not add or subtract the denominator.

Before you can add rational expressions with unlike denominators, you must convert the fractions to equivalent fractions with like denominators.

EXAMPLE 2 Simplify $\frac{a}{2} + \frac{a}{3}$.

Step 1 Find the least common multiple of the denominators.

LCM = 6

Step 2 Multiply both the numerators and denominators by numbers to make the denominator of both fractions alike.

$$\frac{a \cdot 3}{2 \cdot 3} + \frac{a \cdot 2}{3 \cdot 2} = \frac{3a}{6} + \frac{2a}{6}$$

Step 3 Add the equivalent fractions.

$$\frac{3a}{6} + \frac{2a}{6} = \frac{5a}{6}$$

Step 4 If possible, simplify your answer.

$\frac{5a}{6}$ is in simplest form.

Writing About Mathematics

How is adding and subtracting expressions that do not contain variables like adding and subtracting expressions that do contain variables? How is it different?

Exercise A Simplify. Write your answer in simplest form.

1. $\frac{1}{8a} + \frac{5}{8a}$

2. $\frac{2x}{4} + \frac{x}{4}$

3. $\frac{2}{5c} + \frac{4}{5c}$

4. $\frac{4}{6m} + \frac{1}{6m}$

5. $\frac{3y}{8} + \frac{7y}{8}$

6. $\frac{4x}{7} + \frac{6x}{7}$

7. $\frac{6}{9t} + \frac{1}{9t}$

8. $\frac{14x}{17} + \frac{3x}{17}$

9. $\frac{1}{8b} + \frac{3}{8b}$

10. $\frac{7g}{10} + \frac{5g}{10}$

Exercise B Simplify by collecting like terms. Write your answer in simplest form.

11. $\frac{7}{10n} + \frac{5}{10n}$

12. $\frac{1}{4r} + \frac{9}{16r}$

13. $\frac{11d}{12} + \frac{d}{3}$

14. $\frac{3z}{5} + \frac{z}{6}$

15. $\frac{2}{3b} + \frac{3}{4b}$

Technology Connection

Technology Simplifies Your Life

Imagine writing a term paper on a typewriter instead of a computer. Every time you wanted to rewrite a sentence or delete a paragraph, you'd have to start over. Word processing has simplified that problem.

Imagine hauling your water from a well in a bucket instead of turning on a faucet. Whenever you washed clothes or did the dishes, you'd have to refill the bucket. Modern plumbing technology has simplified your life.

Technology has simplified almost every area of our lives.

You can simplify some rational expressions by collecting like terms and subtracting them.

> **EXAMPLE 1** Simplify $\frac{5y}{4} - \frac{2y}{4}$.
>
> **Step 1** Subtract the fractions.
> $$\frac{5y}{4} - \frac{2y}{4} = \frac{3y}{4}$$
>
> **Step 2** If possible, simplify your answer.
> $\frac{3y}{4}$ is in simplest form.

Before you can subtract rational expressions with unlike denominators, you must convert the fractions to equivalent fractions with like denominators.

> **EXAMPLE 2** Simplify $\frac{a}{2} - \frac{a}{3}$.
>
> **Step 1** Find the least common multiple of the denominators.
> LCM = 6
>
> **Step 2** Multiply both the numerators and denominators by numbers to make the denominator of both fractions alike.
> $$\frac{a \bullet 3}{2 \bullet 3} - \frac{a \bullet 2}{3 \bullet 2} = \frac{3a}{6} - \frac{2a}{6}$$
>
> **Step 3** Subtract the equivalent fractions.
> $$\frac{3a}{6} - \frac{2a}{6} = \frac{1a}{6} = \frac{a}{6}$$
>
> **Step 4** If possible, simplify your answer.
> $\frac{a}{6}$ is in simplest form.

Exercise A Simplify. Write your answer in simplest form.

1. $\dfrac{5}{8a} - \dfrac{1}{8a}$

2. $\dfrac{3x}{4} - \dfrac{x}{4}$

3. $\dfrac{4}{5c} - \dfrac{2}{5c}$

4. $\dfrac{5}{6m} - \dfrac{1}{6m}$

5. $\dfrac{7y}{8} - \dfrac{3y}{8}$

6. $\dfrac{6x}{7} - \dfrac{4x}{7}$

7. $\dfrac{6}{9t} - \dfrac{1}{9t}$

8. $\dfrac{14x}{17} - \dfrac{3x}{17}$

9. $\dfrac{3}{8b} - \dfrac{1}{8b}$

10. $\dfrac{7g}{10} - \dfrac{5g}{10}$

Exercise B Simplify by collecting like terms. Write your answer in simplest form.

11. $\dfrac{7}{10n} - \dfrac{1}{2n}$

12. $\dfrac{9r}{16} - \dfrac{r}{4}$

13. $\dfrac{11}{12d} - \dfrac{1}{3d}$

14. $\dfrac{3x}{5} - \dfrac{x}{6}$

15. $\dfrac{2}{3b} - \dfrac{1}{4b}$

16. $\dfrac{7}{8y} - \dfrac{5}{16y}$

17. $\dfrac{8q}{9} - \dfrac{q}{6}$

PROBLEM SOLVING

Exercise C Solve these problems.

18. Henry has $\frac{1}{2}$ dollar and Kari had $\frac{1}{4}$ dollar. How much more money does Henry have?

19. Ron spends $\frac{1}{3}$ of his allowance on pet supplies. How much of his allowance does he have left?

20. Ling has $\frac{2}{3}$ yards of material. She uses $\frac{1}{4}$ of the material. How much material does she have left?

Just as you can add and subtract the terms of a rational expression, you can multiply the terms of rational expressions.

When you multiply fractions, you multiply the numerators and the denominators.

Recall that to divide a fraction, you multiply the dividend by the reciprocal of the divisor.

$$\frac{a}{b} \div \frac{c}{d} = \frac{a}{b} \bullet \frac{d}{c}$$

EXAMPLE 1 Multiply $\frac{3}{5} \bullet \frac{2}{3}$.

Step 1 Multiply the numerators and the denominators.

$$\frac{3}{5} \bullet \frac{2}{3} = \frac{3 \bullet 2}{5 \bullet 3} = \frac{6}{15}$$

Step 2 If possible, simplify the fraction.

$$\frac{6}{15} = \frac{2}{5}$$

Step 3 Check by dividing your answer by one of the terms to find the other term.

$$\frac{2}{5} \div \frac{2}{3} = \frac{2}{5} \bullet \frac{3}{2} = \frac{2 \bullet 3}{5 \bullet 2} = \frac{6}{10} = \frac{3}{5}$$

$\frac{3}{5}$ is the other term in your rational expression, so $\frac{3}{5} \bullet \frac{2}{3} = \frac{2}{5}$ is true.

EXAMPLE 2 Multiply $\frac{3}{5} \bullet \frac{2a}{3}$.

Step 1 Multiply the numerators and the denominators.

$$\frac{3}{5} \bullet \frac{2a}{3} = \frac{3 \bullet 2a}{5 \bullet 3} = \frac{6a}{15}$$

Step 2 If possible, simplify the fraction.

$$\frac{6a}{15} = \frac{2a}{5}$$

Step 3 Check by dividing your answer by one of the terms to find the other term.

$$\frac{2a}{5} \div \frac{2a}{3} = \frac{2a}{5} \bullet \frac{3}{2a} = \frac{2a \bullet 3}{5 \bullet 2a} = \frac{3}{5}$$

$\frac{3}{5}$ is the other term in your rational expression, so $\frac{3}{5} \bullet \frac{2a}{3} = \frac{2a}{5}$ is true.

Exercise A Multiply. Write your answer in simplest form.

1. $\frac{1}{4} \cdot \frac{2}{3}$

2. $\frac{5}{6} \cdot \frac{1}{8}$

3. $\frac{3}{10} \cdot \frac{9}{11}$

4. $\frac{2}{5} \cdot \frac{2}{7}$

5. $\frac{4}{15} \cdot \frac{4}{9}$

6. $\frac{1}{12} \cdot \frac{3}{8}$

7. $\frac{4}{15} \cdot \frac{2}{9}$

8. $\frac{3}{5} \cdot \frac{9}{13}$

9. $\frac{8}{9a} \cdot \frac{4}{7}$

10. $\frac{3}{13} \cdot \frac{7b}{9}$

11. $\frac{2}{3x} \cdot \frac{5x}{8}$

12. $\frac{12}{17h} \cdot \frac{2}{5}$

13. $\frac{7}{9y} \cdot \frac{6}{7}$

14. $\frac{4}{11s} \cdot \frac{11s}{12}$

15. $\frac{15}{16} \cdot \frac{5p}{7}$

PROBLEM SOLVING

Exercise B Solve each problem. Write your answer in simplest form.

16. Libby is $\frac{3}{5}$ Rachel's age. Rachel is 35 years old. How old is Libby? (Hint: Remember to make the whole number a fraction by placing it over 1 before multiplying.)

17. $\frac{2}{3}$ of the cereal that was in a box is left. After Tyrone pours $\frac{1}{3}$ of the remaining cereal out of the box, how much will be left in the box?

18. Stacy drove $\frac{1}{4}$ of the way to Atlanta in one day. The next day she drove $\frac{3}{5}$ of the remaining distance. How much farther does she have to drive?

19. Justin has $\frac{5}{8}$ of a casserole left over. If he eats $\frac{1}{4}$ of that, how much of the casserole is left?

20. The Statue of Liberty is about $\frac{15}{28}$ the height of the Washington Monument. The Washington Monument is almost 560 feet tall. How tall is the Statue of Liberty?

Converting Measurements Sometimes when working with measurements, you want to convert larger measurements into smaller ones or smaller measurements into larger ones. You can use simple formulas to help you make these conversions.

EXAMPLE 1 Convert 39 inches into feet.

Formula: 1 inch = $\frac{1}{12}$ foot

Step 1 Set up the equation.
To change inches to feet, you multiply.

$$\frac{1}{12} \bullet 39$$

Step 2 Multiply to find the number of feet.

$$\frac{1}{12} \bullet \frac{39}{1} = \frac{1 \bullet 39}{12 \bullet 1} = \frac{39}{12}$$

Step 3 Simplify the fraction.

$$\frac{39}{12} = 3\frac{3}{12} = 3\frac{1}{4}$$

$$39 \text{ inches} = 3\frac{1}{4} \text{ feet}$$

Exercise Solve the problems using formulas.

1. The doctor told Karen she was 66 inches tall. How tall is she in feet?

2. Olivia is making a recipe that calls for 5 cups of milk. She has 1 quart of milk. Does she have enough milk for the recipe? Explain your answer.
    Formula: 1 cup = $\frac{1}{4}$ quart

3. David ran $2\frac{1}{2}$ kilometers. How many meters did he run?
    Formula: 1 kilometer = 1,000 meters

4. Franz used 6 quarts of oil when he changed the oil in his car. How many gallons of oil did he use? Formula:
    1 quart = $\frac{1}{4}$ gallon

Chapter 5   REVIEW

Write the letter of the correct answer.
Simplify each expression by following the order of operations.

1. $2(7 - 3) - 12 \div 6$

   A $\frac{1}{6}$ **C** 3

   B 6   **D** 10

2. $10(15 \div 5)$

   A 30   **C** 3

   B 6   **D** 10

3. $18 \div 6 + 3(7 - 2)$

   A 40   **C** 7

   B 11   **D** 18

Evaluate each expression for $m = 5$.

4. $m - 4$

   A 9   **C** 0

   B 1   **D** 20

5. $3m + 1$

   A 14   **C** 9

   B 20   **D** 16

6. $2 + \frac{1}{m}$

   A $\frac{1}{7}$ **C** $\frac{1}{10}$

   B $1\frac{4}{5}$ **D** $2\frac{1}{5}$

7. $5m + 2m$

   A 7   **C** 35

   B 25   **D** 250

Tell whether each equation is true or false when the given number is substituted for x.

Example: $2x - 3 = 13$ when $x = 8$ Solution: $2x - 3 = 13$
$$2(8) - 3 = 13$$
$$16 - 3 = 13 \quad \text{True}$$

8. $4(9) - x = 27$ when $x = 9$ **12.** $22 + 3x = 34$ when $x = 4$

9. $3(x) + x = 18$ when $x = 6$ **13.** $6x \cdot 4 = 48$ when $x = 2$

10. $x + 31 = 38$ when $x = 7$ **14.** $7 + 8x = 54$ when $x = 6$

11. $29 - 5x = 4$ when $x = 5$ **15.** $2x \div 3 = 9$ when $x = 8$

Solve for x. Write your answer in simplest form.

Example: $3 + x = 25$ Solution: $3 + x = 25$
$$3 + x - 3 = 25 - 3$$
$$x = 22$$

16. $x + 13 = 17$ **20.** $2\frac{5}{8} - x = \frac{1}{8}$

17. $25 - x = 19$ **21.** $\frac{2}{3}x - \frac{1}{3} = 3\frac{2}{3}$

18. $\frac{3}{4}x + \frac{3}{4} = 6\frac{3}{4}$ **22.** $\frac{3}{4} + \frac{1}{4}x = 3\frac{3}{4}$

19. $\frac{1}{9} + 4x = 44\frac{1}{9}$

Simplify each complex fraction.

Example: Simplify $\dfrac{\frac{1}{2}}{\frac{2}{3}}$ Solution: $\dfrac{\frac{1}{2}}{\frac{2}{3}} = \frac{1}{2} \div \frac{2}{3} = \frac{1}{2} \bullet \frac{3}{2} = \frac{3}{4}$

23. $\dfrac{\frac{1}{3}}{\frac{1}{2}}$ **26.** $\dfrac{\frac{5}{6}}{3}$ **29.** $\dfrac{8}{\frac{5}{8}}$

24. $\dfrac{\frac{3}{4}}{\frac{3}{5}}$ **27.** $\dfrac{\frac{1}{8}}{\frac{1}{16}}$ **30.** $\dfrac{\frac{11}{12}}{6}$

25. $\dfrac{2}{\frac{1}{4}}$ **28.** $\dfrac{\frac{2}{3}}{9}$

Simplify. Write your answer in simplest form.

Example: Simplify $\frac{5}{12a} + \frac{19}{12a}$ Solution: $\frac{5}{12a} + \frac{19}{12a} = \frac{24}{12a} = \frac{2}{a}$

31. $\frac{1}{8c} + \frac{3}{8c}$

32. $\frac{11}{12m} - \frac{1}{2m}$

33. $\frac{9}{16r} + \frac{3}{4r}$

34. $\frac{7}{8b} - \frac{2}{3b}$

35. $\frac{5}{6z} - \frac{1}{5z}$

36. $\frac{3}{16h} + \frac{7}{16h} + \frac{5}{16h}$

37. $\frac{11}{12w} - \frac{1}{12w} + \frac{7}{12w}$

38. $\frac{2}{3z} - \frac{1}{6z} + \frac{3}{4z}$

Multiply. Write your answer in simplest form.

Example: $\frac{3r}{5} \cdot \frac{3}{4}$ Solution: $\frac{3r}{5} \cdot \frac{3}{4} = \frac{3r \cdot 3}{5 \cdot 4} = \frac{9r}{20}$

39. $\frac{4}{9x} \cdot \frac{1}{4}$

40. $\frac{3q}{16} \cdot \frac{3}{10}$

41. $\frac{9}{11w} \cdot \frac{1}{8}$

42. $\frac{14}{19h} \cdot \frac{5}{6}$

43. $\frac{4}{9} \cdot \frac{7p}{10}$

44. $\frac{3}{5y} \cdot \frac{2}{15}$

45. $\frac{2}{3a} \cdot \frac{5}{12}$

Test-Taking Tip

Before you begin an exam, skim through the whole test to find out what is expected of you.

Ratios, Proportions, and Percents

Why is it so hard to pedal when you start out in tenth gear? The gear on the pedal is larger than the gear on the rear wheel. When the pedal turns one rotation, the rear wheel might turn three rotations. That is a gear ratio of three to one. The larger the ratio, the more effort it takes to pedal. In a lower gear, you might have a ratio of one-and-a-half to one, which takes less effort. You can calculate gear ratios. Count the teeth on each gear. Then divide the larger number by the smaller one. Is it a high or a low gear ratio?

In Chapter 6, you will work with ratios, proportions and percents.

Goals for Learning

◆ To express ratios in different forms

◆ To solve problems using proportions

◆ To change fractions and decimals to percents

◆ To solve problems using percents

Lesson 1 — Ratios

Ratio

A comparison of two like quantities using a fraction

Recall that examples of fractions include proper fractions such as $\frac{3}{4}$ and improper fractions such as $\frac{5}{2}$. Proper and improper fractions are examples of **ratios.** A ratio is a comparison of two quantities using a fraction.

EXAMPLE 1   In a class of 15 students, 7 students are female and 8 students are male. The following ratios can be written to describe that class.

$\frac{7}{8}$ The ratio of female students to male students

$\frac{8}{7}$ The ratio of male students to female students

$\frac{7}{15}$ The ratio of female students to the total number of students

$\frac{8}{15}$ The ratio of male students to the total number of students

$\frac{15}{7}$ The ratio of the total number of students to the number of female students

$\frac{15}{8}$ The ratio of the total number of students to the number of male students

The word *to* and the symbol : can also be used to express a ratio.

To find the simplest form of a fraction, find the GCD of the numerator and denominator, then divide both the numerator and denominator by the GCD.

EXAMPLE 2   In a collection of 32 books, 13 books are fiction and 19 books are nonfiction. Write the ratio of nonfiction books to the total number of books three different ways.

1. Write the ratio as a fraction $\frac{19}{32}$

2. Write the ratio using the word *to*   19 to 32

3. Write the ratio using the symbol :   19:32

EXAMPLE 3 Express the ratios 10:2 and 24 to 16 in simplest form.

Write each ratio as a fraction. Use division to find the simplest form of each fraction. Then rewrite each fraction.

$$10:2 = \frac{10}{2} = \frac{10 \div 2}{2 \div 2} = \frac{5}{1} = 5:1$$

$$24 \text{ to } 16 = \frac{24}{16} = \frac{24 \div 8}{16 \div 8} = \frac{3}{2} = 3 \text{ to } 2$$

Exercise A Express each ratio two different ways.

1. 4 to 3

2. 1:8

3. $\frac{7}{2}$

4. 100:9

5. $\frac{5}{11}$

6. 29 to 41

Exercise B Express each ratio as a fraction in simplest form.

7. 9:18

8. 26 to 13

9. $\frac{34}{4}$

10. 10 to 42

11. 64:18

12. $\frac{6}{16}$

13. 7 to 42

14. 17:24

PROBLEM SOLVING

Exercise C Solve these problems. Give the answers in simplest form.

15. In a class of 14 students, 6 students are male. What is the ratio of female students to the total number of students in the class?

16. Of the 120 compact discs in a music collection, 45 compact discs contain jazz music. What is the ratio of non-jazz compact discs to the total number of compact discs in the collection?

17. The ratio of girls to boys in a family is 1 to 2. If there are two girls in the family, how many boys are in the family?

18. If the ratio of males to females in each of two different mathematics classes is 5 to 4, is the ratio of males to females still 5 to 4 if the classes were considered as one large class instead of two smaller classes?

19. In a coin collection, the ratio of coins minted before 1940 to those minted in 1940 or after is 3 to 1. Is there an odd or even number of coins in the collection? Explain.

20. Suppose one person describes the number of sunny days to cloudy days in June as 18 to 12, and another person describes the number of sunny days to cloudy days in June as 3 to 2. Can each person be describing the same month in the same year? Explain.

Proportion

An equation made up of two equal ratios

Cross product

The result of multiplying the denominator of one fraction with the numerator of another

For any ratio, you can write an infinite number of equivalent ratios. The following are examples of equivalent ratios for $\frac{1}{2}$.

$$\frac{2}{4} \quad \frac{3}{6} \quad \frac{4}{8} \quad \frac{5}{10} \quad \text{and so on}$$

Any ratio (such as $\frac{1}{2}$) and an equivalent ratio (such as $\frac{2}{4}$) can be combined to form a **proportion**. A proportion is a statement of the form $\frac{a}{b} = \frac{c}{d}$. Examples of proportions include

$$\frac{1}{2} = \frac{2}{4} \qquad \frac{5}{7} = \frac{15}{21} \qquad \frac{6}{10} = \frac{24}{40}$$

In any true proportion written in the form $\frac{a}{b} = \frac{c}{d}$, a, b, c, and d are terms of the proportion, and $ad = bc$.

EXAMPLE 1   Is $\frac{3}{4} = \frac{6}{8}$ a true proportion?

Decide if $ad = bc$.

$$\frac{a}{b} = \frac{c}{d} \quad \rightarrow \quad a \bullet d = b \bullet c$$

$$\downarrow \qquad \qquad \downarrow \quad \downarrow \quad \downarrow \quad \downarrow \quad \downarrow$$

$$\frac{3}{4} = \frac{6}{8} \quad \rightarrow \quad 3 \bullet 8 \; \blacksquare \; 4 \bullet 6$$

$$24 = 24$$

Because $ad = bc$, $\frac{3}{4} = \frac{6}{8}$ is a true proportion.

The terms ad and bc are sometimes called the **cross products** of a proportion. You can use cross products to find the missing value in a proportion.

EXAMPLE 2   Solve $\frac{24}{15} = \frac{8}{n}$ for n.

Step 1   Set the cross products of the proportion equal to each other.
$$(24)(n) = (15)(8)$$

Step 2   Multiply.
$$24n = 120$$

Step 3   Divide each side of the equation by 24.
$$\frac{24n}{24} = \frac{120}{24}$$

Step 4   Simplify.
$$n = 5$$

The variable can appear anywhere in a proportion.

Because of the commutative property of multiplication, $(x)(6)$ can be rewritten as $(6)(x)$ or $6x$.

EXAMPLE 3 Solve $\frac{2}{x} = \frac{6}{30}$ for x.

Step 1 Set the cross products of the proportion equal to each other.
$$(2)(30) = (x)(6)$$

Step 2 Multiply.
$$60 = 6x$$

Step 3 Divide each side of the equation by 6.
$$\frac{60}{6} = \frac{6x}{6}$$

Step 4 Simplify.
$$x = 10$$

Each time you solve for the variable in a proportion, check your work by finding the cross products of the proportion. If the cross products are equal to each other, your answer is correct.

Exercise A Is each proportion a true proportion? Write *yes* or *no*.

1. $\frac{3}{10} = \frac{10}{30}$ **3.** $\frac{1}{4} = \frac{6}{27}$ **5.** $\frac{4}{5} = \frac{16}{20}$

2. $\frac{16}{24} = \frac{2}{3}$ **4.** $\frac{9}{12} = \frac{12}{15}$ **6.** $\frac{10}{28} = \frac{2}{7}$

Exercise B Solve for the variable in each proportion.

7. $\frac{2}{n} = \frac{8}{12}$ **10.** $\frac{m}{10} = \frac{2}{5}$ **13.** $\frac{g}{16} = \frac{3}{4}$

8. $\frac{3}{7} = \frac{c}{28}$ **11.** $\frac{8}{56} = \frac{1}{b}$ **14.** $\frac{1}{7} = \frac{9}{r}$

9. $\frac{4}{h} = \frac{1}{4}$ **12.** $\frac{3}{d} = \frac{18}{24}$ **15.** $\frac{5}{h} = \frac{25}{30}$

Technology Connection

Making Microchips Takes a Toll
Microchips are small, but they require a huge amount of fossil fuels to make. Compare making one chip to making one car. A single microchip takes about 3.5 pounds of fossil fuel. Making a car requires more than 3,300 pounds of fossil fuel. If you look at the ratio of fossil fuel to weight, the ratio to make a car is about 2 to 1. For a microchip, it is about 630 to 1. Proportionally, it takes a lot more energy to make a microchip.

Equivalent

The same in value

A proportion is made up of two equal ratios. In some problems, one ratio and part of an **equivalent** ratio are given. One way to solve these problems is to make a table.

EXAMPLE 1   The ratio of computers to students in a classroom is 1 to 3. If there are 15 students in the class, how many computers are in the classroom?

Step 1   Make a table that displays the data in the problem. In the table, write the proportion that is given.

Number of computers	1	
Number of students	3	

Step 2   Complete the table using the remaining data in the problem.

Number of computers	1	n
Number of students	3	15

Step 3   Solve the proportion shown in the table.

$$\frac{1}{3} = \frac{n}{15}$$

$(1)(15) = (3)(n)$ Set the cross products equal to each other.

$15 = 3n$ Divide each side of the equation by 3.

$5 = n$

There are 5 computers in the classroom.

You can also solve proportion problems by just writing and solving a proportion.

EXAMPLE 2   In one hour, a bicyclist pedaled 16 miles. At that rate, how far can the bicyclist pedal in 4 hours?

Step 1   Write a proportion.
$$\frac{1 \text{ hour}}{16 \text{ miles}} = \frac{4 \text{ hours}}{x \text{ miles}}$$

Step 2   Set the cross products equal to each other.

$(1)(x) = (16)(4)$

$1x = 64$

$x = 64$

The bicyclist can pedal 64 miles in 4 hours.

Each time you solve a proportion, remember to check your work by making sure the cross products in your completed proportion are equal to each other.

PROBLEM SOLVING

Exercise A Solve each problem.

1. A baseball player averages one hit in every three at bats. If the player bats 480 times during a season, how many hits can the player be expected to get?

2. On a basketball team, the ratio of players less than six feet tall to players six feet or taller is 2 to 5. If 10 players on the team are six feet or taller, how many players are less than six feet tall?

3. Last year during league bowling, Jeremy averaged one strike for every five frames he bowled. If he bowled 84 strikes last season, how many frames did he bowl?

4. In a 72-hole golf tournament, Pat scored under par every 2 out of 9 holes. For the tournament, how many times did Pat score under par?

5. In a gymnastics meet, a gymnast earned a perfect score of ten from one out of every four judges. If there were eight judges altogether at the meet, how many perfect scores did the gymnast earn?

6. In a track-and-field meet, a runner ran the first 200 meters of an 800-meter race in 24 seconds. If the runner runs the remainder of the race at that speed, how many minutes and seconds will it take the runner to complete the race?

7. On a football team, 7 out of every 9 players weigh 190 pounds or more. If 42 players weigh more than 190 pounds, how many players are on the team?

8. At a swim meet, a swimmer completes the first 50 meters of the 800-meter freestyle race in 34 seconds. If the swimmer does not swim faster or slower for the remainder of the race, will the swimmer complete the race in more than or less than 9 minutes? Explain.

9. Twelve hundred fans are attending a tennis match. If the ratio of adult fans to children is 73 to 7, how many children are attending the match?

10. The ratio of goals scored by a soccer team to the goals scored by opponents is 3:2. If 55 goals were scored altogether last season by the team and its opponents, how many goals were scored by the opponents?

A great deal of data is given as percents. For example, a weather forecaster might say that the chance of rain is 40%, and the state might charge a sales tax of 7%.

The word *percent* comes from the Latin phrase *per centum*, which means "per hundred." In general, a percent is the numerator of a fraction whose denominator is 100.

> Remember, percent means part per one hundred.

A hundreds grid is a grid that measures 10 units by 10 units and contains 100 unit squares.

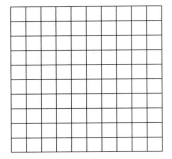

A hundreds grid can be used to show percents.

EXAMPLE 1   What is the ratio of the number of shaded squares to the total number of squares in this figure?

Step 1   Determine the number of shaded squares.

The figure contains 29 shaded squares.

Step 2   Determine the total number of squares.

The figure contains 100 squares altogether.

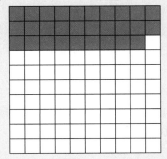

Step 3   Write the ratio. The ratio of the number of shaded squares to the total number of squares in the figure is 29 to 100.

Recall that any ratio written in the form *a* to *b* can also be written in the form $\frac{a}{b}$.

EXAMPLE 2 What fraction of this figure is shaded?

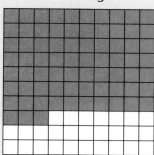

Step 1 Determine the number of shaded squares.
The figure contains 73 shaded squares.

Step 2 Determine the total number of squares.
The figure contains 100 squares altogether.

Step 3 Write the fraction: $\frac{73}{100}$ of the figure is shaded.

To write a fraction whose denominator is 100 as a percent, write the numerator and use the % symbol.

EXAMPLE 3 What percent of this figure is shaded?

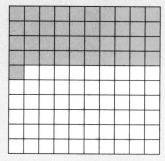

Since 41 out of 100 or $\frac{41}{100}$ of the figure is shaded,
41% of the figure is shaded.

Exercise A Write a fraction to describe the percent of each figure that is shaded.

1.

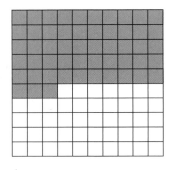

2.

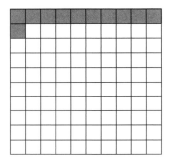

3.

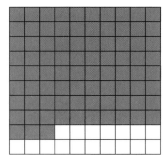

Exercise B What percent of each figure is shaded?

4.

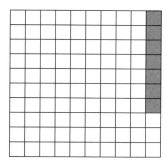

5.

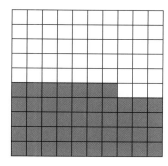

6.

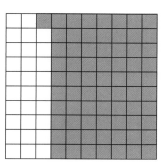

7.

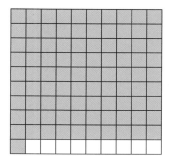

Writing About Mathematics

Suppose 25 squares in a 10 by 10 grid are shaded and 12 squares in a 6 by 8 grid are shaded. Is the same percent of each grid shaded? Explain.

Exercise C Write each fraction as a percent.

8. $\frac{22}{100}$

9. $\frac{95}{100}$

10. $\frac{40}{100}$

11. $\frac{53}{100}$

12. $\frac{82}{100}$

13. $\frac{33}{100}$

14. $\frac{67}{100}$

15. $\frac{9}{100}$

TRY THIS In a figure measuring 100 by 100 units, 4,000 units are shaded. In simplest form, what fraction of the figure is shaded? What fraction of the figure is not shaded? What is the sum of the shaded and not shaded regions?

Recall that percent is the numerator of a fraction whose denominator is 100. You can express any decimal as a percent by first writing the decimal as a fraction that has a denominator of 100.

EXAMPLE 1   Express 0.5 as a percent.

Step 1   Write the decimal as a fraction that has 100 as its denominator.

$$0.5 = \frac{0.5}{1} \cdot \frac{100}{100} = \frac{(0.5)(100)}{1 \cdot 100}$$

Step 2   Multiply.

$$\frac{0.5 \cdot 100}{100} = \frac{50}{100}$$

Step 3   Write the fraction as a percent.

$$\frac{50}{100} = 50\%$$

The decimal 0.5 is equivalent to 50%.

You can use a shortcut to change the decimal to a percent.

EXAMPLE 2   Write 0.12 as a percent.

Step 1   Move the decimal two places to the right. This is the same as multiplying by 100.

$$0.12 \cdot 100 = 0.12 \rightarrow 12$$

Step 2   Write the decimal as a percent by adding the percent symbol.

$$0.12 = 12\%$$

Multiplying by 100 and then adding the percent symbol is the same as multiplying by $\frac{100}{100}$.

To express a percent as a decimal, write the percent as a fraction with a denominator of 100. Then write it as a decimal.

EXAMPLE 3   Write 46% as a decimal.

Step 1   Write the percent as a fraction. Since percent means "per one hundred," write $46\% = \frac{46}{100}$.

$$46\% = \frac{46}{100}$$

Step 2   Write the fraction as a decimal.

$$\frac{46}{100} = 0.46$$

Recall that to express a fraction whose denominator is 100 as a percent, you write the numerator of the fraction and use the % symbol. To express a fraction whose denominator is not 100 as a percent, first express the fraction as a decimal. Then express the decimal as a percent.

Remember, moving the decimal point two places to the right is the same as multiplying by 100. Adding the percent symbol is the same as dividing by 100.

EXAMPLE 4   Express $\frac{3}{8}$ as a percent.

Step 1   First change the fraction to a decimal. Remember, a fraction bar means "divide."

$$\frac{3}{8} = 3 \div 8 = 0.375$$

Step 2   Write the decimal as a percent by moving the decimal point two places to the right. Then add the percent symbol.

$$0.375 = 37.5\%$$

Algebra in Your Life

Smart Shoppers Figure Percents
Knowing how to find percents helps you every time you shop. When there is a sale, it is sometimes a percentage off the original price. There are signs like "15% off!" or "Buy One and Get a Second One for 50% off." Most times the price tag doesn't show the sale price for that new sweater or CD. So, before you get to the cash register, you can figure out just exactly what you'll have to pay. That's being a math-smart shopper.

Writing About Mathematics

Suppose you double in weight between your ninth and fifteenth birthdays. Express the change in percent. Do you need to know the actual weight? Why or why not?

Exercise A Express each decimal as a percent.

1. 0.75

2. 0.80

3. 0.18

4. 0.42

5. 0.78

6. 0.24

7. 0.88

8. 0.04

9. 0.1

Exercise B Express each fraction as a percent.

10. $\frac{1}{2}$

11. $\frac{1}{4}$

12. $\frac{7}{8}$

13. $\frac{2}{5}$

14. $\frac{3}{4}$

15. $\frac{7}{10}$

16. $\frac{15}{16}$

17. $\frac{19}{25}$

18. $\frac{64}{100}$

Exercise C Express each percent as a decimal.

19. 11%

20. 46%

21. 68%

22. 3%

23. 17%

24. 27%

25. 5%

26. 91%

27. 83%

PROBLEM SOLVING

Exercise D Solve these problems.

28. Can a percent ever be greater than 100? Explain.

29. Jessica purchased $2,000 worth of stocks. The stocks value increased by $\frac{1}{5}$ each month. What is the percent of increase per month?

30. At the beginning of a day, a floppy computer disk contains 840 kilobytes of data. By the end of the day, the disk contains 630 kilobytes of data. The disk is $\frac{3}{4}$ full. What percent of the disk is full of data?

31. Between 9 A.M. and 11 A.M., a cafe expects to serve 40 meals. The number of meals served increases 3 and a half times between 11 A.M. and 1 P.M. What percent does the number increase?

32. Alex is scheduled to work 37.5 hours each week. Last week he was only able to work 33.75 hours. He worked 10% less. Write a fraction to show the decrease in number of hours.

33. Two hundred people attended the first performance of a school play. The second performance was attended by 220 people. The attendance increased by $\frac{1}{10}$. What is the percent of increase?

34. When asked to describe the soccer team's winning rate, Jan said 60%, Allison said 0.6, and Jesse said $\frac{3}{5}$. Is it possible that each person is describing the same winning rate? Tell why or why not.

35. Suppose Marc is receiving an allowance increase. If he could choose the amount of the increase, should he choose an increase of $\frac{1}{5}$ or an increase of 15%? Why?

As you work with percents, you sometimes will be asked to find the percent of a number. To find a percent of a number, you can use a proportion.

EXAMPLE 1 40% of 72 is what number?

Step 1 Use a proportion. Express the percent as a ratio.

$$40\% = \frac{40}{100}$$

Step 2 Let x represent the part of 72 you are trying to find.

$$\frac{40}{100} = \frac{x}{72}$$

Step 3 Solve the proportion by setting the cross products equal to each other. Then solve for x.

$$\frac{40}{100} = \frac{x}{72} \quad \rightarrow \quad (40)(72) = (100)(x)$$
$$2{,}880 = 100x$$

Divide both sides by 100. $28.80 = x$

40% of 72 is 28.8.

Another way to find a portion of a number is using the 1% solution method.

EXAMPLE 2 25% of 200 is what number?

Step 1 Write an equation for 100%.

$$100\% = 200$$

Step 2 Divide both sides of the equation by 100 to find 1% of the number.

$$\frac{100\%}{100} = \frac{200}{100}$$
$$1\% = 2$$

Step 3 Multiply both sides by 25 to find the number.

$$1\% \cdot 25 = 2 \cdot 25$$
$$25\% = 50$$

25% of 200 is 50.

You can also write and solve an equation to find what number is a percent of another number.

EXAMPLE 3 80% of 48 is what number?

Step 1 Write an equation.

80% of 48 is what number?
↓ ↓ ↓ ↓
(80%)(48) = n

Step 2 Change the percent to a decimal, then solve for n.

(80%)(48) = n
↓
(0.80)(48) = n
38.4 = n

80% of 48 is 38.4.

Exercise A Solve to answer each question.

1. 12% of 12 is what number?

2. 30% of 18 is what number?

3. 150% of 320 is what number?

4. 60% of 125 is what number?

5. 39% of 2,400 is what number?

6. 125% of 10 is what number?

7. 67% of 200 is what number?

8. 42% of 442 is what number?

9. 75% of 874 is what number?

10. 200% of 0.5 is what number?

Estimation Activity

Estimate: A gas station owner earns 2% of the price for each gallon of gas sold. If the price of gasoline is $1.63 per gallon, how much does he make on a 10 gallon sale?

Solution: Find the approximate value of 1%, double, multiply by ten.

100% = $1.63
1% = $0.0163   is about 1.6 cents
2% = 3.2 cents is about 3 cents
(10)(3¢) = 30 cents

He earns a little more than 30 cents for 10 gallons.

Sometimes you will be asked to find what percent one number is of another. To find what percent one number is of another, you can use a proportion.

EXAMPLE 1 What percent of 10 is 35?

Step 1 Express the ratio of part to whole as a fraction.
$$\frac{part}{whole} = \frac{35}{10}$$

Step 2 Write the unknown percent as a ratio.
$$\frac{35}{10} = \frac{x}{100}$$

Step 3 Solve the proportion by setting the cross products equal to each other. Then solve for x.
$$\frac{35}{10} = \frac{x}{100} \quad \rightarrow \quad (35)(100) = (10)(x)$$
$$3{,}500 = 10x$$
$$350 = x$$

350% of 10 is 35.

You can use the 1% solution method to find what percent one number is of the total.

EXAMPLE 2 What percent of 300 is 36?

Step 1 Write an equation to show the amount that is equal to 100%.
$$100\% = 300$$

Step 2 Divide both sides by 100.
$$\frac{100\%}{100} = \frac{300}{100}$$
$$1\% = 3$$

Step 3 Divide 36 by the 1% amount to find the percent.
$$\frac{36}{3} = 12\%$$

12% of 300 is 36.

You can also write and solve an equation to find what percent one number is of another.

EXAMPLE 3 What percent of 20 is 8?

Step 1 Write an equation.

What percent of 20 is 8?
  ↓   ↓   ↓
  (n) $(20) = 8$

Step 2 Solve for n.

$$(n)(20) = 8$$
$$20n = 8$$
$$n = \frac{8}{20}$$

Step 3 Rewrite the fraction as a decimal, then as a percent.

$$n = \frac{8}{20} = 0.4 = 40\%$$

40% of 20 is 8.

These examples help show that you can solve percent problems in different ways.

Exercise A Solve to answer each question.

1. What percent of 4 is 10?

2. What percent of 72 is 18?

3. What percent of 40 is 15?

4. What percent of 65 is 195?

5. What percent of 900 is 45?

Calculator Practice

Some calculators have a percent key. You can use these calculators to solve percent problems.

EXAMPLE 4 Use a calculator to find 15% of 60.

To find a percent of a number, multiply.

Press 60 $\times$ 15 $\%$ $=$.

The display reads 9.

Exercise B Find the given percent of the given number.

6. Find 18% of 75.

7. Find 6% of 2.5.

8. Find 300% of 800.

9. Find 28% of 1,400.

10. Find 95% of 9.

Percent problems sometimes ask you to find the percent of increase or decrease. To find the percent of increase or decrease, first find the amount of increase or decrease. Then write and solve a proportion, the 1% solution, or an equation.

EXAMPLE 1   On his fourth birthday, Lon was 40 inches tall. On his fifth birthday, he was 43 inches tall. By what percent did his height increase between his fourth and fifth birthdays?

Step 1   Find the amount of increase.

$$43 \text{ inches} - 40 \text{ inches} = 3 \text{ inches}$$

Step 2   Write an equation.

3 inches is what percent of 40 inches?
$$\downarrow \qquad \downarrow \quad \downarrow \qquad\qquad \downarrow$$
$$(3) \qquad = \quad (x) \qquad\quad 40$$

Step 3   Solve the equation for x.

$$3 = (x)(40)$$
$$\frac{3}{40} = x$$

Step 4   Change the fraction to a decimal, then to a percent.

$$\frac{3}{40} = 3 \div 40 = 0.075 = 7.5\%$$

Lon's height increased by 7.5%.

Some percent problems ask you to find the percent of decrease.

EXAMPLE 2   The price of a pair of shoes has been reduced from $60 to $48. By what percent has the price been reduced?

Step 1   Find the amount of decrease.

$$\$60 - \$48 = \$12$$

Step 2   Write a proportion.

$$\frac{\text{amount of decrease}}{\text{original price}} = \frac{x}{100} \rightarrow \frac{12}{60} = \frac{x}{100}$$

EXAMPLE 2 *(continued)*

Step 3 Set the cross products of the proportion equal to each other, then solve for *x*.

$$\frac{12}{60} = \frac{x}{100}$$

$$(12)(100) = (60)(x)$$

$$1{,}200 = 60x$$

$$20 = x$$

The percent of decrease was 20%.

If a percent problem asks you to solve for the percent of increase or decrease, remember to first find the amount of the increase or decrease.

A proportion, the 1% solution, or an equation can be used to solve a percent problem.

Exercise A What is the amount of increase or decrease in each situation?

1. Each Wednesday, the cost of museum admission for senior citizens is $4.00. On days other than Wednesday, the cost for senior citizens is $7.50.

2. In 1996, the amount of precipitation during the month of June totaled 4.2 inches. In 1997, the amount of precipitation during the month of June totaled 5.1 inches.

PROBLEM SOLVING

Exercise B Solve each problem.

3. Suppose an investment in the stock market cost $1,600 to purchase and was worth $1,850 one year later. Did the value of the investment increase or decrease during that year? By what percent?

4. On the first quiz of the year, Roberto answered 6 of 10 questions correctly. On the second quiz, he answered 8 of 10 questions correctly. By what percent did the number of questions he answered correctly increase?

5. Leslie's old car had an average fuel economy of 30 miles per gallon of gasoline. Her new car has an average fuel economy of 27.6 miles per gallon of gasoline. By what percent did the fuel economy decrease?

Compound interest

Interest paid on both the original amount of money plus any interest added to date; compound interest is usually computed on deposits placed into savings accounts

Compounding period

The amount of time that the interest rate is calculated

The **compound interest** formula is an example of a formula that includes a percent. The compound interest formula is used to find the amount of money earned after a given number of **compounding periods.**

> **The Compound Interest Formula**
>
> $A = P(1 + i)^n$ where A = the amount of money in the account, P = the principal or original deposit, i = the interest rate per period expressed as a decimal, and n = the number of compounding periods.

To use the formula, substitute values for P, i, and n.

EXAMPLE 1 $2,000 is deposited in a savings account that pays 6% interest compounded annually. Find the amount of money in the account after 2 years.

Step 1   Determine the values that represent P, i, and n. In this example:

P is $2,000, the amount of the deposit.

i is 0.06, the interest rate per period (6%) expressed as a decimal.

n is 2, the number of compounding periods. (In this example, compounding occurs annually. Annually means once at the end of each year. The number of compounding periods in this example is 2—once at the end of each year for two years.)

Step 2   Substitute P, i, and n into the compound interest formula. Then solve for A.

$$A = P(1 + i)^n$$
$$A = 2,000(1 + 0.06)^2$$
$$A = 2,000(1.06)^2$$
$$A = 2,000(1.1236)$$
$$A = 2,247.20$$

After two years, the value of the account will be $2,247.20.

Calculator Practice

A calculator is a very helpful tool to use whenever you need to find compound interest.

EXAMPLE 2 $5,000 is deposited in a savings account that pays $4\frac{1}{2}\%$ interest compounded annually. Find the amount of money in the account after 5 years.

Step 1   Determine the values that represent *P*, *i*, and *n*.

P is $5,000, the amount of the deposit.

i is 0.045, the interest rate per period ($4\frac{1}{2}\%$) expressed as a decimal.

n is 5, the number of compounding periods. (You need to find the amount of money in the account after 5 years. The number of compounding periods is 5—once at the end of each year for five years.)

Step 2   Substitute *P*, *i*, and *n* into the compound interest formula. Then use a calculator to solve for *A*.

$$A = P(1 + i)^n$$
$$A = 5,000(1 + 0.045)^5$$
$$A = \boxed{5000}\ \boxed{\times}\ \boxed{(}\ \boxed{1}\ \boxed{+}\ \boxed{0.045}\ \boxed{)}\ \boxed{y^x}\ \boxed{5}\ \boxed{=}$$
$$A = \boxed{6230.90968827}$$

After five years, the value of the account will be $6,230.91.

TRY THIS

How many years will it take an account to double in value at 10% interest compounded annually? Round your answer to the nearest whole number of years.

Exercise A In problems 1–4, the interest is compounded annually. Find the value of each account at the end of each period of time.

1. $P = \$500$; $i = 5\%$; $t = 2$ years

2. $P = \$10,000$; $i = 8\%$; $t = 4$ years

3. $P = \$2,500$; $i = 7.5\%$; $t = 5$ years

4. $P = \$1,000$; $i = 5\%$; $t = 3$ years

5. Suppose that on your tenth birthday, you deposit $108 into an account that pays an average of 12% interest compounded annually. If you do not make additional deposits to that account and you do not withdraw money from that account, what will be the value of the account on your fiftieth birthday?

Calculating Taxes Many states and communities charge a sales tax on goods you buy. When you buy goods in these states and communities, you pay the purchase price of the goods plus the tax.

Suppose your state has a 10% sales tax. To find 10% of a price, you can multiply tax rate by the price.

EXAMPLE 1 Find 10% of $500.

$$
\begin{array}{ccc}
10\% & \rightarrow & 0.10 \\
\times\ \$500 & & \times\ \$500 \\
\hline
& & \$50.00
\end{array}
$$

You can also find the tax rate when you know the purchase price of a good and the total amount charged.

What is the tax rate when an item costs $35 and you pay $36.75?

First subtract the purchase price from the total cost to find the amount of tax.

$36.75 - \$35 = \$1.75$

Then divide the tax amount by the purchase price to find the percent of tax, or tax rate.

$\$1.75 \div \$35.00 = 0.05$ or 5%

Exercise Solve each problem.

1. If the tax rate is 8%, what would be the total cost of a CD that has a purchase price of $17.00?

2. The tax rate is 5.25%. What amount of tax will Jason pay when he buys a $500.00 video player?

3. Gloria paid $3.00 in taxes on a $50.00 purchase. What is the tax rate in her community?

Chapter 6   R E V I E W

Write the letter of the correct answer.

1. Express the ratio 3:15 as a fraction in simplest form.

   A $\frac{3}{15}$ **C** $\frac{15}{3}$

   B 5   **D** $\frac{1}{5}$

2. Choose the true proportion to $\frac{3}{8}$.

   A $\frac{9}{28}$ **C** $\frac{8}{3}$

   B $\frac{9}{24}$ **D** $\frac{6}{24}$

3. Solve for d. $\frac{6}{d} = \frac{18}{39}$

   A $d = 13$ **C** $d = 3$

   B $d = 236$ **D** $d = 24$

4. Solve for v. $\frac{5}{6} = \frac{v}{12}$

   A $v = 30$ **C** $v = 5$

   B $v = 10$ **D** $v = 11$

5. Express 0.94 as a percent.

   A 9.4%   **C** 94%

   B 0.94%   **D** 940%

6. Express $\frac{3}{5}$ as a percent.

   A $\frac{3}{5}$%   **C** 30%

   B 60%   **D** 8%

7. Express 83% as a decimal.

   A 0.83   **C** 830

   B 83   **D** 8.3

Express each decimal as a percent.

Example: 0.60   Solution: 0.60 = 60%

8. 0.40

9. 0.12

10. 0.09

11. 0.55

12. 0.03

13. 0.5

14. 0.81

Express each fraction as a percent.

Example: $\frac{3}{4}$ Solution: $\frac{3}{4}$ = 3 ÷ 4 = 0.75 = 75%

15. $\frac{1}{10}$

16. $\frac{5}{16}$

17. $\frac{1}{4}$

18. $\frac{3}{10}$

19. $\frac{4}{25}$

20. $\frac{11}{25}$

21. $\frac{29}{50}$

22. $\frac{77}{100}$

Express each percent as a decimal.

Example: 12%   Solution: 12% = 0.12

23. 21%

24. 54%

25. 19%

26. 6%

27. 11%

28. 95%

29. 79%

30. 61%

Solve each problem.

Example: The tax in Lake County is 7%. How much tax will you pay if you buy a T-shirt for $14.00?   Solution: 7% = 0.07

0.07 • $14 = $0.98   7% of $14 is $0.98.

31. Robert buys a sweater that originally cost $60 for $30. What is his percent of savings on the sweater purchase?

32. Kara is buying a round-trip airplane ticket to Paris for $2,580. The tax on the ticket is 11%. How much is the total cost of the ticket with tax?

33. Mike deposits $1,500 in a savings account that pays 7% interest compounded annually. How much money will he have in the account after 3 years? Remember, the compound interest formula is $A = P(1 + i)^n$.

34. Rosa works in the local library. On Wednesday, she checked out 50 books. On Thursday, she checked out 65 books. What was the percent of increase in the number of books she checked out?

35. Chan is a camera operator for the late-night news program. He works 4 of 7 days a week. What percent of the week does he work? Round your answer to the nearest tenth of a percent.

Test-Taking Tip

Whenever you solve problems that involve money, remember to check the placement of the decimal point in your answer.

Chapter

7 Integers

Galileo lived in Italy in the 1500s. He studied how to measure temperature. Galileo found that a liquid would rise or fall in a glass tube, depending on the temperature. The liquid rose or dropped, and the temperature was marked on the glass. Sound familiar? Glass and alcohol or mercury thermometers are really number lines, just like you use in math. They're marked by degrees of temperature. Alcohol or mercury expands and moves up into the positive numbers when heated. It shrinks and moves into the negative numbers when cooled. Those positive and negative numbers are called integers. In math, integers can be a really hot topic.

In Chapter 7, you will work with integers.

Goals for Learning

◆ To identify the absolute value of integers
◆ To compare the values of negative and positive whole numbers
◆ To add and subtract integers
◆ To multiply and divide integers

Integer

Any positive or negative whole number including zero

Real number

Any number on the number line

Negative integer

A whole number less than zero

Positive integer

A whole number greater than zero

In arithmetic, you learned to add, subtract, multiply, and divide whole numbers greater than zero. In algebra, you also use whole numbers less than zero.

You can use a number line to show the relation between positive and negative whole numbers, also called **integers.**

Every point on the number line corresponds to a specific **real number.** A real number can be used to describe one and only one point on the number line. The arrows at the ends of the number line show that the line continues.

Numbers to the left of zero are **negative integers.** They are read as "negative 1, negative 2," and so on.

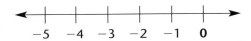

Numbers to the right of zero are **positive integers.** They are read as "positive 1, positive 2," and so on.

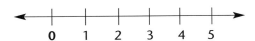

Zero is neither positive nor negative.

A negative integer is always indicated by the use of a minus $(-)$ sign. A positive integer may be indicated by a plus $(+)$ sign or no sign at all.

Absolute value

The distance from zero of a number on a number line

Opposites

Numbers the same distance from zero but on different sides of zero on the number line

Whole numbers are the counting numbers 1, 2, 3, 4, ... and zero.

The **absolute value** of an integer is the distance between the integer and zero on the number line. The integer can be either to the left or to the right of zero. The symbol for absolute value is | |.

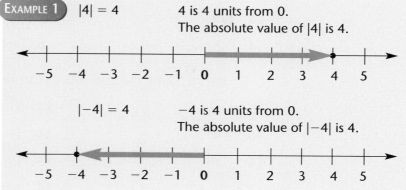

EXAMPLE 1 |4| = 4   4 is 4 units from 0.
The absolute value of |4| is 4.

|−4| = 4   −4 is 4 units from 0.
The absolute value of |−4| is 4.

Every number other than 0 has an **opposite number.** Opposites are the same distance from zero.

EXAMPLE 2   9 is the opposite of −9.
−9 is the opposite of 9.
9 is 9 units from 0.
Both 9 and −9 are 9 units from 0.

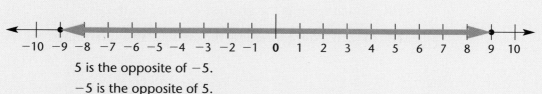

5 is the opposite of −5.
−5 is the opposite of 5.
5 is 5 units from 0.
Both 5 and −5 are 5 units from 0.

Exercise A Find each absolute value.

1. $|3|$ **5.** $|-12|$

2. $|-3|$ **6.** $|24|$

3. $|10|$ **7.** $|-73|$

4. $|-6|$ **8.** $|-4|$

Exercise B Name the opposite of each integer.

9. 4   **13.** 8

10. -7 **14.** -12

11. -73 **15.** 1

12. 73   **16.** -9

Exercise C Solve these problems using the number line.

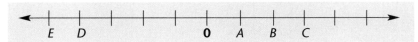

17. Which letters represent positive real numbers?

18. Which letters represent negative real numbers?

19. Which letter is the greatest distance from zero?

20. Which letter represents the greatest absolute value?

Exercise D Give an integer that describes each situation.

21. A gain of 3 yards in a football game

22. A loss of 15 yards in a football game

23. A withdrawal of $40 from a bank account

24. A deposit of $100 in a bank account

25. A temperature of 13°F below zero

26. A temperature of 32°F above zero

27. Ten seconds before space shuttle launch time

28. Thirty seconds after launch time

29. An altitude of 2,500 feet above sea level

30. An ocean depth of 900 feet below sea level

Consecutive

Following one after the other in order

Integers can be arranged in an increasing or decreasing order. **Consecutive** integers are integers arranged from least to greatest or greatest to least without any missing integers. The integers on a number line are consecutive integers.

You can use a number line to compare two integers. On a number line, the greater of two numbers is the number farthest to the right.

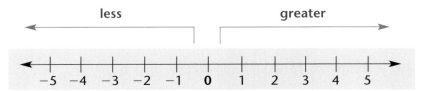

EXAMPLE 1   Compare 2 and −3.

2 is to the right of −3 on the number line.

2 is greater than −3.

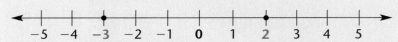

EXAMPLE 2   Compare −1 and −5.

−1 is to the right of −5 on the number line.

−1 is greater than −5.

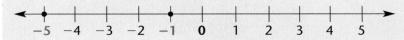

The symbol $>$, read "is greater than," is used to show that one integer is greater than another.

$2 > -3, -1 > -5$

EXAMPLE 3 Compare $|-5|$ and $|-3|$.

-5 is 5 units from zero, so $|-5| = 5$.

-3 is 3 units from zero, so $|-3| = 3$.

5 is farther to the right than 3, so $|-5| > |-3|$.

Exercise A Compare each pair. Use $>$ or $=$.

1. $5 \blacksquare 2$

2. $11 \blacksquare 11$

3. $12 \blacksquare 11$

4. $8 \blacksquare 3$

5. $4 \blacksquare 0$

6. $8 \blacksquare |8|$

7. $|4| \blacksquare 4$

8. $3 \blacksquare -11$

9. $22 \blacksquare -1$

10. $2 \blacksquare 0$

11. $|-2| \blacksquare 2$

12. $1 \blacksquare -11$

13. $2 \blacksquare -4$

14. $4 \blacksquare -2$

15. $|8| \blacksquare -3$

16. $|-8| \blacksquare |-3|$

17. $-11 \blacksquare -15$

18. $10 \blacksquare |-1|$

19. $|-13| \blacksquare 13$

20. $|-12| \blacksquare 12$

Algebra in Your Life

On the Road Again

Suppose your family wants to go on a driving vacation. Maybe you have several places in mind—Yosemite National Park, the Grand Canyon, or Washington D.C. Because you're driving, you know you can't go everywhere. However, you can use a road atlas to figure out how far away each place is from your home. Then, you can compare the distances and figure out which place makes the most sense to visit. It's another way you can use algebra in your life!

You can use a number line to compare two integers. On a number line, the lesser of two numbers is the number farthest to the left.

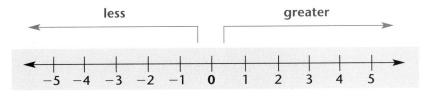

EXAMPLE 1 Compare −3 and 1.

−3 is to the left of 1 on the number line.

−3 is less than 1.

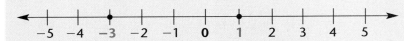

EXAMPLE 2 Compare −5 and −3.

−5 is to the left of −3 on the number line.

−5 is less than −3.

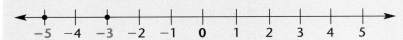

The symbol <, read "is less than," is used to show that one integer is less than another.

$-3 < 1, -5 < -3$

EXAMPLE 3   Compare −5 and |−3|.

−3 is 3 units from zero, so |−3| = 3

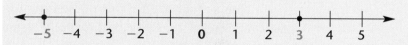

−5 is farther to the left than 3, so −5 < |−3|.

Exercise A Compare each pair. Use < or =.

1. 2 ■ 5

2. 3 ■ 11

3. 12 ■ |−12|

4. 3 ■ 8

5. 4 ■ 4

6. −5 ■ −2

7. 8 ■ |8|

8. −11 ■ −3

9. −22 ■ −1

10. −2 ■ 0

11. −2 ■ 1

12. −11 ■ 2

13. −4 ■ 3

14. −3 ■ |2|

15. −8 ■ −3

16. −8 ■ |−3|

17. −9 ■ 1

18. |−1| ■ 10

19. −15 ■ 10

20. |−6| ■ 6

PROBLEM SOLVING

Exercise B Solve these problems.

21. Marlene lists these five numbers and says that they are consecutive integers: −2, −1, 0, 1, 2, 3. Is she right? Tell why or why not.

22. Kito is drawing and labeling a number line. Where would she place −9 in relation to +3? Why?

23. Aaron wants to know which is less, −3 or −5. Draw a number line to show him which number is less.

24. The temperature was 0°F on Saturday and −11°F today. Which temperature is higher? Explain.

25. Cory says that he is thinking of an integer that is 8 units from 0. Can you be sure that the integer he is thinking of is greater than 0? Explain.

Lesson 4   Even and Odd Integers

Integers that have a factor of 2 without leaving a remainder are even integers. $-6, -4, -2, 0, +2, +4,$ and $+6$ are examples of even integers.

Integers that do not have a factor of 2 are odd integers. $-5, -3, -1, +1, +3,$ and $+5$ are examples of odd integers.

Zero is an even integer.

You can tell whether a number is even or odd by checking the digit in the ones position. If the digit in the ones position is odd, the number is odd; if the digit in the ones position is even, the number is even.

In 7,893, the digit 7 is in the thousands place, the digit 8 is in the hundreds place, the digit 9 is in the tens place, and the digit 3 is in the ones place.

EXAMPLE 1   2,987,654,321 is an odd integer because 1 is odd.

12,345,678 is an even integer because 8 is even.

Consecutive even integers are even integers arranged in order without any missing even integers. For example, $-10, -8, -6, -4, -2, 0, +2, +4, +6, +8, +10$ are consecutive even integers. Consecutive odd integers are odd integers arranged in order without any missing integers. For example, $-9, -7, -5, -3, -1, +1, +3, +5, +7, +9$ are consecutive odd integers. In both of these examples, the integers are ordered from least to greatest.

When you add or subtract integers, you can predict whether the sum or difference will be odd or even.

Adding Integers	Subtracting Integers
even + even = even	even − even = even
even + odd = odd	even − odd = odd
odd + odd = even	odd − odd = even

EXAMPLE 2

4 + 6 = 10	6 − 4 = 2
4 + 5 = 9	6 − 1 = 5
5 + 3 = 8	5 − 3 = 2

You can also predict whether or not a product will be even.

Multiplying Integers
even • even = even
even • odd = even
odd • odd = odd

EXAMPLE 3

$4 • 6 = 24$

$4 • 5 = 20$

$3 • 5 = 15$

TRY THIS

Make a table showing the result of dividing even by even, even by odd, and odd by odd numbers.

Exercise A Tell whether the following numbers are odd or even.

1. 24,004

2. 35,793

3. 15,378

4. 210,244,663

5. 13,459,235,743,221

Exercise B Find each sum or difference. Tell whether it is even or odd.

6. 432 + 444

7. 523 − 352

8. 134 + 235

9. 793 + 583

10. 669 − 571

11. 1,224 + 3,468

12. 554 + 33

13. 221 − 123

14. 334 − 55

15. 664 − 334

Exercise C Find each product. Tell whether it is even or odd.

16. 24 • 36

17. 39 • 36

18. 27 • 23

19. 22 • 43

20. 59 • 73

Exercise D Tell which operation will give the desired even or odd integer. Then solve each problem. There may be more than one correct answer.

21. 4 ☐ 5 = ■ (even)

22. 6 ☐ 3 = ■ (even)

23. 6 ☐ 3 = ■ (odd)

24. 9 ☐ 3 = ■ (even)

25. 9 ☐ 3 = ■ (odd)

You can use the number line to help you find and understand
how to add positive integers to other positive or negative integers.

EXAMPLE 1 Find the sum of 3 + 5.

Begin at 3.
Then move to the right 5 units.
3 + 5 = 8

Rule

Adding a positive to a positive gives a result farther to the right
on the number line.

EXAMPLE 2 Find the sum of −3 + 5.

Begin at −3.
Then move to the right 5 units.
−3 + 5 = 2

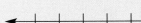

Rule

Adding a positive to a negative gives a result farther to the right
on the number line.

Exercise A Find each sum.

1. $3 + 8$	**9.** $-7 + 2$
2. $4 + 6$	**10.** $6 + 9$
3. $-2 + 7$	**11.** $-12 + 4$
4. $-6 + 4$	**12.** $10 + 9$
5. $-6 + 6$	**13.** $0 + 5$
6. $-2 + 9$	**14.** $-7 + 7$
7. $-4 + 7$	**15.** $-6 + 8$
8. $-7 + 3$	

Remember that a sum is the answer to an addition problem.

Calculator Practice

You can use the $\boxed{+/-}$ key on a calculator to add positive and negative integers.

EXAMPLE 3 Find the sum $-3 + 5$.
Press 3 $\boxed{+/-}$ $\boxed{+}$ 5 $\boxed{=}$.
The display reads 2.

Exercise B Find each sum using a calculator.

16. $652 + 978$	**19.** $-57 + 784$
17. $-441 + 239$	**20.** $888 + 424$
18. $485 + 332$	

Lesson 6 — Adding Negative Integers

You can use the number line to help you find and understand how to add negative integers to other positive or negative integers.

 **Find the sum of 3 + (−5).**

Begin at 3.
Then move to the left 5 units.
3 + (−5) = −2

Rule
Adding a negative to a positive gives a result farther to the left on the number line.

EXAMPLE 2 Find the sum of −3 + (−5).

Begin at −3.
Then move to the left 5 units.
−3 + (−5) = −8

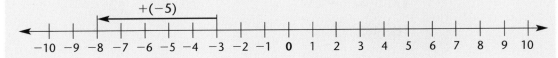

Rule
Adding a negative to a negative gives a result farther to the left on the number line.

Exercise A Find each sum.

1. $-2 + (-7)$ **4.** $4 + (-8)$

2. $-6 + (-6)$ **5.** $12 + (-4)$

3. $-2 + (-9)$ **6.** $28 + (-32)$

Calculator Practice

You can use the $+/-$ key on a calculator to add positive and negative integers.

EXAMPLE 3 Find the sum of $5 + (-7)$.
Press 5 $+$ 7 $+/-$ $=$.
The display reads -2.

Writing About Mathematics

Will you always get a negative number if you add a negative number to another number? Explain.

Exercise B Find each sum using a calculator.

7. $-359 + (-243)$ **10.** $233 + (-873)$

8. $112 + (-444)$ **11.** $975 + (-105)$

9. $-576 + (-495)$ **12.** $-649 + (-573)$

PROBLEM SOLVING

Exercise C Solve each problem by adding integers.

13. An airplane flying at 25,000 feet climbs an additional 2,000 feet. What is the final altitude of the airplane?

14. At midnight the temperature was 29°C. During the day the temperature fell 4 degrees. What was the final temperature?

15. A hot air balloon drifting 2,351 feet above a cornfield suddenly drops 1,334 feet. How far above the cornfield is the balloon?

A number line can be used to show that subtracting a number gives the same result as adding the opposite of the number.

EXAMPLE 1   Find the difference of $3 - (+5)$.

Begin at 3.
Then move to the left 5 units.
$3 - (+5) = -2$

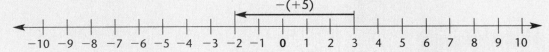

Note that $3 - (+5) = -2$ and $3 + (-5) = -2$ because subtracting 5 is the same as adding -5.

> **Rule**
> Subtracting a positive from a positive gives a result farther to the left on the number line.

EXAMPLE 2   Find the difference of $-3 - (-5)$.

Begin at -3.
Then move to the right 5 units.
$-3 - (-5) = 2$

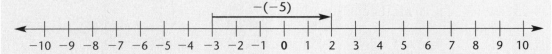

Note that $-3 - (-5) = 2$ and $-3 + 5 = 2$ because 5 and -5 are opposites.
Subtracting is the same as adding the opposite.

> **Rule**
> Subtracting a negative from a negative gives a result farther to the right on the number line.

EXAMPLE 3 Find the difference of $3 - (-5)$.

Begin at 3.
Then move to the right 5 units.
$3 - (-5) = 8$
This is the same as $3 + 5 = 8$.

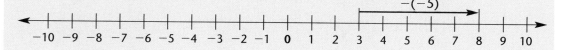

Rule

Subtracting a negative from a positive gives a result farther to the right on the number line.

EXAMPLE 4 Find the difference of $-3 - (+5)$.

Begin at -3.
Then move to the left 5 units.
$-3 - (+5) = -8$

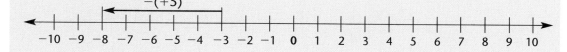

Rule

Subtracting a positive from a negative gives a result farther to the left on the number line.

Look again at addition of positive and negative integers. Compare the results with subtraction of integers.

Subtraction		Addition
$3 - (+5) = -2$	is the same as	$3 + (-5) = -2$
$-3 - (-5) = 2$	is the same as	$-3 + 5 = 2$
$3 - (-5) = 8$	is the same as	$3 + 5 = 8$
$-3 - (+5) = -8$	is the same as	$-3 + (-5) = -8$
Subtraction	is the same as	adding the opposite.

Rule

To subtract a positive or negative integer, add the opposite of the integer.

Exercise A Rewrite each subtraction expression as an addition expression. Find the sum of the new expression.

1. $4 - (+5)$

2. $8 - 4$

3. $-6 - (-5)$

4. $-9 - (-11)$

5. $7 - (+5)$

6. $-6 - 4$

7. $-2 - (+4)$

8. $10 - (+7)$

9. $7 - (-4)$

10. $5 - 4$

Exercise B Find each difference.

11. $3 - (+7)$

12. $6 - 2$

13. $-7 - (-7)$

14. $-8 - (-13)$

15. $9 - (+2)$

16. $-5 - 2$

17. $-3 - (+5)$

18. $12 - (+5)$

19. $9 - (-3)$

20. $6 - 3$

Technology Connection

Bookkeeper—A Job Title of the Past?
Bookkeepers keep track of business expenses and income. Bookkeepers used to write down the business expenses and income in big books called ledgers. Back then, the name of the job fit the work. Today, most bookkeepers no longer "keep books." They use computer software programs instead. These programs are designed specially to do the bookkeeping. They can automatically and quickly calculate expenses and income that in the past had to be done by hand. Perhaps now bookkeepers need a new name.

Exercise C Solve these problems.

21. The highest point on Earth is Mount Everest, 29,028 feet above sea level. The shore of the Dead Sea, at 1,312 feet below sea level, is the lowest place on Earth's surface. What is the vertical distance from the shore of the Dead Sea to the top of Mount Everest?

22. The average depth of the Arctic Ocean is 3,950 feet below sea level. The average depth of the Pacific Ocean is 12,900 feet below sea level. How much deeper is the Pacific Ocean?

23. The highest recorded temperature in North America was 134°F, recorded at Death Valley, California. The lowest recorded temperature was −87°F, recorded at Northice, Greenland. How many degrees separate the two temperatures?

24. What is the difference between Alaska's record low temperature of −80°F and Utah's record low temperature of −69°F?

25. Astronauts board a space shuttle at T−90 minutes. Actual news coverage begins at T−15 minutes. How long are the astronauts on board before the news coverage begins?

Your study of arithmetic showed you that multiplication is the same as repeated addition. For example, 4 • 3 is the same as 3 + 3 + 3 + 3 = 12. You can use the idea of repeated addition and the number line to learn about multiplying two positive integers and multiplying a negative and a positive integer.

EXAMPLE 1 Find the product of (+4)(+3).

Begin at 0.
Then count by 3s to the right.
You will reach 12.
(+4)(+3) = 12

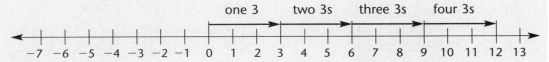

Rule

(Positive) • (Positive) = (Positive)

EXAMPLE 2 Find the product of (−4)(3).

Begin at 0.
Then count by 3s to the left.
− (3) − (3) − (3) − (3) = −12, (−4)(3) = −12

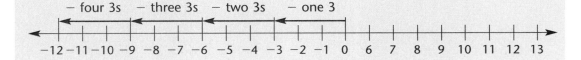

Rule

(Negative) • (Positive) = (Negative)

Remember that a product is the answer to a multiplication problem.

Exercise A Find each product.

1. $(4)(5)$

2. $(-4)(8)$

3. $(-6)(4)$

4. $(-6)(5)$

5. $(9)(11)$

6. $(7)(5)$

7. $(-4)(5)$

8. $(-4)(2)$

9. $(-7)(10)$

10. $(-4)(7)$

11. $(-7)(3)$

12. $(2)(6)$

13. $(7)(7)$

14. $(5)(2)$

15. $(-3)(5)$

16. $(-5)(12)$

17. $(-8)(13)$

18. $(-2)(9)$

19. $(-3)(9)$

20. $(-3)(6)$

Exercise B Tell whether each product is positive or negative.

21. $(167)(192)$

22. $(-19)(421)$

23. $(-8)(58)$

24. $(67)(76)$

25. $(9)(74)$

26. $(-64)(20)$

27. $(-15)(45)$

28. $(102)(10)$

29. $(914)(4)$

30. $(-72)(3)$

Estimation Activity

Estimate: Suppose you owe your friend $12.75. You help your friend with his paper route and get $3.00 deducted per week. How many weeks must you work to pay back your friend?

Solution: $-\$3.00$ per week
$$4(-3) = -12$$

You must work a little longer than 4 weeks.

Remember that multiplication is the same as repeated addition. You can use the idea of repeated addition and the number line to learn about multiplying a negative and a positive integer and multiplying two negative integers.

EXAMPLE 1 Find the product of $(4)(-3)$.

Begin at 0.
Then count by -3s to the left.
$(-3) + (-3) + (-3) + (-3) = -12$, $(4)(-3) = -12$

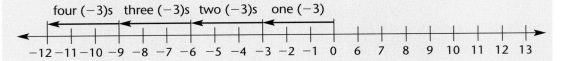

Rule
(Positive) • (Negative) = (Negative)

EXAMPLE 2 Find the product of $(-4)(-3)$.

This case, $(-4)(-3)$ or a negative times a negative, cannot be shown on a number line. The product of $(-4)(-3)$ is $+12$. When you multiply a negative times a negative, use the following rule.

Rule
(Negative) • (Negative) = (Positive)

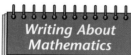

Writing About Mathematics

Explain why
$(-9)(0)$ does not
equal -0.

Exercise A Tell whether each product is positive, negative, or zero.

1. $(-322)(-457)$

2. $(745)(-63)$

3. $(433)(-221)$

4. $(21)(-989)$

5. $(-100)(-13)$

6. $(923)(-576)$

7. $(444)(-333)$

8. $(-197)(-842)$

9. $(-2{,}093)(-22)$

10. $(12)(-294)$

 PROBLEM SOLVING

Exercise B Solve each problem.

11. In each game of a three-game golf tournament, Nathaniel scored 5 under par. How many points under par did he score in the tournament?

12. During one winter day, the temperature fell 4 degrees each hour for 6 hours. How great was the total temperature drop?

13. The price of a stock fell $4 each day for 9 days. What was the total change in price?

14. Every year for the past five years, the forest preserve has lost 16 trees to disease or weather. How many trees have been lost in the past five years?

15. At a local movie theater, senior citizens receive a $2.00 discount. How much less will a senior pay to attend 15 movies in a year?

Recall that multiplication is the same as repeated addition.
Division is the opposite of multiplication—repeated subtraction.

EXAMPLE 1   Find the quotient of 12 ÷ 3.

Begin at 12.
Then count by 3s to the left until you reach zero. You will have four groups of three, 12 ÷ 3 = 4.

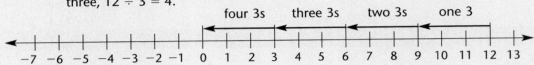

Rule

(Positive) ÷ (Positive) = (Positive)

Because multiplication and division are opposite operations, the rules for multiplying positive and negative integers are similar to the rules for dividing positive and negative integers.

Multiplication		Division
(3)(4) = 12 Rule (+)(+) = (+)	and	12 ÷ 4 = 3 Rule (+) ÷ (+) = (+)
(3)(−4) = −12 Rule (+)(−) = (−)	and	12 ÷ (−4) = −3 Rule (+) ÷ (−) = (−)
(−3)(4) = −12 Rule (−)(+) = (−)	and	(−12) ÷ (4) = −3 Rule (−) ÷ (+) = (−)
(−3)(−4) = 12 Rule (−)(−) = (+)	and	(−12) ÷ (−4) = 3 Rule (−) ÷ (−) = (+)

A general statement can be made that covers all the multiplication and division rules.

Rules

Like signs give positive products and quotients.

Unlike signs give negative products and quotients.

Exercise A Find each quotient.

1. $4 \div 2$

2. $32 \div (-4)$

3. $(-24) \div (4)$

4. $(30) \div (-5)$

5. $(-9) \div (-3)$

6. $(45) \div (5)$

7. $(20) \div (-4)$

8. $(-20) \div (-4)$

9. $(10) \div (-5)$

10. $(-28) \div (-4)$

11. $(-21) \div (-7)$

12. $(-12) \div (-6)$

13. $(-7) \div (7)$

14. $(-50) \div (2)$

15. $(-15) \div (5)$

16. $(-60) \div (-5)$

17. $(-88) \div (11)$

18. $(-18) \div (-2)$

19. $(9) \div (-3)$

20. $(6) \div (-3)$

A quotient is the answer to a division problem.

$$12 \div 4 = 3$$

dividend | divisor | quotient

Exercise B Tell whether each quotient is positive, negative, or zero.

21. $3{,}956 \div 43$

22. $-6{,}324 \div 17$

23. $-221 \div -11$

24. $-989 \div 21$

25. $100 \div 20$

26. $-976 \div -331$

27. $671 \div -13$

28. $-1{,}970 \div 3$

PROBLEM SOLVING

Exercise C Solve each problem.

29. The theater complex has 1,440 seats in six theaters. All theaters have the same number of seats. How many seats does each have?

30. A submarine is moving underwater at -390 meters. It dives to that level in 13 minutes. How many meters does it dive per minute?

TRY THIS ➤ The sum of two integers is -25. The quotient of the integers is 4. What are the integers?

Comparing Elevations Different landforms on Earth can be grouped by their elevation and relief. The elevation of a landform or location is its distance above or below sea level. For instance, the highest point on Mount McKinley in Alaska has an elevation of +20,320 feet.

There are even mountains under the ocean! For example, Mauna Loa in Hawaii stands about 13,700 above sea level. But it also extends beneath the sea. The base of Mauna Loa is about 10,000 feet below sea level, making the actual height of the mountain more than 23,000 feet.

In addition to mountains, there are deep trenches in the oceans that reach far into Earth's surface. The deepest of these is the Mariana Trench, which researchers believe reaches a depth of about 35,840 feet below the surface of the ocean.

Exercise Use the information in the table to answer the questions.

Selected Locations and Their Elevations	
Mount Everest, Nepal–Tibet	+29,028 ft
Mount McKinley, USA	+20,320 ft
Mount Aconcagua, Argentina	+22,834 ft
Death Valley	−282 ft
Dead Sea	−1,292 ft
Ionian Basin, Mediterranean Sea	−16,896 ft
Puerto Rico Trench, Atlantic Ocean	−28,232 ft
Mariana Trench, Pacific Ocean	−35,840 ft

1. Which location is the farthest below sea level?

2. What is the distance from the Dead Sea to the top of Mount McKinley?

3. How much deeper is the Mariana Trench than the Puerto Rico Trench?

Chapter 7   R E V I E W

Write the letter of the correct answer.

1. What is the absolute value of $|-5|$?

    A -5 **C** $-2\frac{1}{2}$

    B 5   **D** -10

2. Name the opposite of the integer -23.

    A -23 **C** -11.5

    B -46 **D** 23

3. Find the sum. $9 + (-2) =$

    A 11   **C** -11

    B -7 **D** 7

4. Find the sum. $-7 + (-3) =$

    A 4   **C** -4

    B -10 **D** 10

5. Find the difference. $7 - (+5) =$

    A 2   **C** -2

    B 12   **D** -12

6. Find the product. $(8)(-3) =$

    A 24   **C** 5

    B -24 **D** 11

7. Find the quotient. $-60 \div 12 =$

    A -72 **C** -5

    B 5   **D** 48

Find each absolute value or distance from zero.

Example: $|-4|$ Solution: $|-4| = 4$

8. $|-9|$ **10.** $|-5|$

9. $|14|$ **11.** $|-71|$

Name the opposite of each integer.

Example: -5 Solution: 5 is the opposite of -5

12. 8

14. 7

13. -4

15. 43

Compare each pair. Use $<$, $>$, or $=$.

Example: 9 ■ -2 Solution: $9 > -2$

16. 7 ■ -7

18. -4 ■ 0

17. 4 ■ 0

19. -2 ■ $|-5|$

Find each sum.

Example: $-8 + 3$ Solution: $-8 + 3 = -5$

20. $8 + 3$

24. $-9 + (-2)$

21. $6 + 4$

25. $-7 + 4$

22. $-6 + (-6)$

26. $8 + (-3)$

23. $6 + (-6)$

27. $-9 + (-9)$

Find each difference.

Example: $-8 - (-5)$ Solution: $-8 - (-5) = -3$

28. $-9 - (-11)$

31. $-7 - (-4)$

29. $-6 - (-4)$

32. $5 - (-4)$

30. $10 - (-7)$

33. $-9 - (-2)$

Find each product.

Example: $(4)(-7)$ Solution: $(4)(-7) = -28$

34. $(3)(5)$

37. $(-8)(-12)$

35. $(-6)(7)$

38. $(9)(5)$

36. $(-6)(-6)$

39. $(5)(-8)$

Find each quotient.

Example: 28 ÷ (−7)   Solution: 28 ÷ (−7) = −4

40. 30 ÷ 5

41. 8 ÷ (−2)

42. −6 ÷ (−6)

43. −120 ÷ (−30)

44. 45 ÷ 5

45. 56 ÷ (−8)

Solve each problem.

Example: The team loses by 84 points in a total of 12 games. They lose by the same number of points in each game. By how many points did they lose per game?

Solution: 84 ÷ 12 = 7 points

46. A submarine dives 96 feet in a minute. At what depth will the submarine be in 15 minutes?

47. What is the difference in elevation of a mountain 22,834 feet tall and an ocean basin floor at −16,896 feet?

48. The temperature was −9°C yesterday and 3°C today. How much did the temperature increase?

49. A pro golf player has these scores for the three games of a tournament: −3, −6, and +2. Find out his score for the tournament by adding the three scores together.

50. Karen walked down 7 flights of stairs. If each flight has 12 steps, how many steps did she walk down?

Test-Taking Tip

To prepare for a test, study in short sessions rather than one long session. In the week before the test, spend time each evening reviewing your notes.

8

Exponents, Square Roots, and the Pythagorean Theorem

When you draw a straight line segment, you make a one-dimensional object. Add three more lines to make a square, which has two dimensions. How do you make something three-dimensional? Well, you could build an ice castle made of cubes, cones, cylinders, and pyramids! Three-dimensional objects have length, width, and depth. In two dimensions, you multiply numbers by themselves to calculate area. A square might have an area of 9 ft^2. A three-dimensional cube might have an volume of 27 m^3. Those small numbers are called exponents or powers. They show if something is squared or cubed. Using exponents can make for some powerful math!

In Chapter 8, you will find the power and roots of numbers and use the Pythagorean theorem.

Goals for Learning

◆ To find the value of numbers raised to a certain power

◆ To multiply and divide terms with exponents

◆ To find area and volume using numbers with exponents

◆ To find the square roots of numbers

◆ To use the Pythagorean theorem to solve problems

Power

The product of multiplying any number by itself once or many times

Exponent

Number that tells how many times another number is a factor

Base

The number being multiplied; a factor

You can use the symbols 3 • 3 to show 3 multiplied by itself. You can also use the symbol 3^2 (read "3 to the second **power**") to show 3 • 3.

3^2 ⟶ 2 is the **exponent**.

⟶ 3 is the **base**.

EXAMPLE 1 2 • 2 • 2 = 2^3

2^3 is read "2 to the third power."

2 is the base.   3 is the exponent.

To write a negative number with an exponent, first place the negative number in parentheses and then write the exponent. For example, the second power of −2 is written $(-2)^2$.

EXAMPLE 2 $(-4)(-4) = (-4)^2$

$(-4)^2$ is read "negative four to the second power."

(−4) is the base.   2 is the exponent.

You can use the same symbols in algebra.

EXAMPLE 3 $a • a • a$ is a to the third power or a^3.

a is the base.   3 is the exponent.

$z • z • z • z • z$ is z to the fifth power or z^5.

z is the base.   5 is the exponent.

Terms such as x^2 or x^3 do not have a numerical value until you substitute numbers for x.

EXAMPLE 4 If $x = 3$, $x^2 = 3 • 3 = 9$ and $x^3 = 3 • 3 • 3 = 27$.

3 to the second power is 9.

3 to the third power is 27.

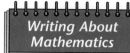

Writing About Mathematics

Can a negative number to the power of 2 be negative? Explain.

Any number to the first power is the number itself.

$$2^1 = 2 \qquad\qquad x^1 = x$$

Any number to the zero power is 1.

$$2^0 = 1 \qquad\qquad y^0 = 1$$

Exercise A Name the exponent in each of the following items.

1. 4^2 **5.** 4^3 **9.** x^1

2. $(-5)^3$ **6.** x^3 **10.** x^n

3. 2^3 **7.** a^5

4. 10^2 **8.** $(-y)^{10}$

Exercise B Rewrite each of the following using exponents.

11. $2 \cdot 2 \cdot 2$ **16.** $(-a)$

12. $3 \cdot 3$ **17.** $x \cdot x \cdot x \cdot x$

13. $4 \cdot 4 \cdot 4$ **18.** $(-y) \cdot (-y) \cdot (-y)$

14. $(-5) \cdot (-5)$ **19.** $m \cdot m \cdot m \cdot m \cdot m \cdot m$

15. $5 \cdot 5 \cdot 5 \cdot 5$ **20.** $p \cdot p \cdot p$

Calculator Practice

Use the y^x or x^y key on your calculator to find the value of expressions with exponents.

EXAMPLE 5   Find 4^5.
Press 4 y^x 5 = .
The display reads *1024*.

Exercise C Use a calculator to find the value of each expression.

21. 2^{10} **24.** $(0.02)^3$

22. $(-5)^3$ **25.** $(-0.5)^2$

23. 16^3

If two terms with exponents have the same base, you can multiply the terms by adding exponents.

EXAMPLE 1

$$2^2 \bullet 2^3 = (2 \bullet 2) \bullet (2 \bullet 2 \bullet 2)$$
$$= 2 \bullet 2 \bullet 2 \bullet 2 \bullet 2$$
$$= 2^5$$
$$\text{or } 2^2 \bullet 2^3 = 2^{2+3} = 2^5$$

$$-5 \bullet (-5)^2 = (-5) \bullet (-5) \bullet (-5)$$
$$= (-5) \bullet (-5) \bullet (-5)$$
$$= (-5)^3$$
$$\text{or } -5 \bullet (-5)^2 = (-5)^{1+2} = (-5)^3$$

$$y^3 \bullet y^3 = (y \bullet y \bullet y) \bullet (y \bullet y \bullet y)$$
$$= y \bullet y \bullet y \bullet y \bullet y \bullet y$$
$$= y^6$$
$$\text{or } y^3 \bullet y^3 = y^{3+3} = y^6$$

$$5^n \bullet 5^n = 5^{n+n}$$
$$= 5^{2n}$$

Rule

To multiply numbers with the same base, add their exponents.

Exercise A Simplify each expression.

1. $4^2 \cdot 4^2$

2. $5^3 \cdot 5^2$

3. $2^4 \cdot 2^3$

4. $10^3 \cdot 10^2$

5. $4^5 \cdot 4^3$

6. $x^7 \cdot x^3$

7. $a^5 \cdot a^3$

8. $y^{10} \cdot y^7$

9. $x^4 \cdot x^3$

10. $p^4 \cdot p^2$

11. $2^n \cdot 2^n$

12. $3^{4x} \cdot 3^x$

TRY THIS

Multiply.

$x^n \cdot x^m$

$a^x \cdot a^y$

Exercise B Tell whether each statement is *true* or *false*. If a statement is false, tell why.

13. $2^3 \cdot 2^5 = 2^8$

14. $3 \cdot 3^2 = 3^3$

15. $4^3 \cdot 5^3 = 9^3$

16. $5^3 \cdot 5^2 = 5^6$

17. $3^3 \cdot 3 = 3^3$

18. $a^3 \cdot a^5 = a^8$

19. $y^5 \cdot y^3 = y^8$

20. $a^5 \cdot a^5 = a^{25}$

21. $n^6 \cdot n^2 = n^{12}$

22. $p^1 \cdot p^1 = p^1$

23. $2^y \cdot 2^y = 2^{2y}$

24. $3^{2n} \cdot 3^{4n} = 3^{8n}$

25. $7^{3x} \cdot 7^x = 7^{4x}$

Algebra in Your Life

It's a Scam!
A pyramid scheme is a kind of business deal where one person receives money from people lower down on the "pyramid." The higher you are on the pyramid, the more money you make. Here's an example: Sammi has four people working for her. Each of those four people has four people working for them. If you do the math, all of a sudden there are 20 people sharing their profits with Sammi. These kinds of deals sound good, but only if you're the person on top.

If two terms with exponents have the same base, you can divide the terms by subtracting exponents.

> Recall that any number to the 0 power is 1, and any number to the first power is the number itself.

EXAMPLE 1

$$3^5 \div 3^3 = \frac{3^5}{3^3}$$

$$= \frac{3 \cdot 3 \cdot 3 \cdot 3 \cdot 3}{3 \cdot 3 \cdot 3}$$

$$= 3^2$$

or $3^5 \div 3^3 = 3^{5-3} = 3^2$

$$5^4 \div 5^3 = \frac{5^4}{5^3}$$

$$= \frac{5 \cdot 5 \cdot 5 \cdot 5}{5 \cdot 5 \cdot 5}$$

$$= 5$$

or $5^4 \div 5^3 = 5^{4-3} = 5$

$$x^4 \div x^3 = \frac{x^4}{x^3}$$

$$= \frac{x \cdot x \cdot x \cdot x}{x \cdot x \cdot x}$$

$$= x^1 = x$$

or $x^4 \div x^3 = x^{4-3} = x^1 = x$

$$5^{2x} \div 5^x = \frac{5^{2x}}{5^x}$$

$$= \frac{5^x \cdot 5^x}{5^x}$$

$$= 5^x$$

or $5^{2x} \div 5^x = 5^{2x-x} = 5^x$

Rule

To divide numbers with the same base, subtract their exponents.

Exercise A Simplify each expression.

1. $7^3 \div 7^2$

2. $6^7 \div 6^3$

3. $2^4 \div 2^3$

4. $10^{18} \div 10^2$

5. $9^4 \div 9^2$

6. $x^8 \div x^4$

7. $h^7 \div h^4$

8. $w^{14} \div w^7$

9. $k^5 \div k^2$

10. $s^4 \div s$

11. $y^2 \div y^1$

12. $8^n \div 8^n$

TRY THIS

Divide.
$19^x \div 19^w$
$m^y \div m^y$

Exercise B Tell whether each statement is *true* or *false*. If a statement is false, tell why.

13. $2^8 \div 2^2 = 2^4$

14. $6^6 \div 6^2 = 6^4$

15. $9^3 \div 9^1 = 9^3$

16. $(-3)^6 \div (-3)^2 = (-3)^4$

17. $3^3 \div 3 = 3^3$

18. $a^{10} \div a^5 = a^5$

19. $x^{12} \div x^3 = x^4$

20. $r^5 \div r^5 = 1$

21. $(-s)^6 \div (-s)^2 = (-s)^3$

22. $b^2 \div b^1 = b$

23. $x^{15} \div x^3 = x^5$

24. $k^{10} \div k^2 = k^8$

25. $7^{3n} \div 7^{2n} = 7^n$

You can use exponents to describe the **area** of a **square.**

Area

The number of square units inside a closed region

Square

A four-sided shape with sides of equal length and four right angles

EXAMPLE 1   Write an expression for the area of the square.

Area of a square = length • width = 3 • 3 = 3^2

You can read 3^2 as "three squared."

The formula for the area of a square can also be written s^2 because the sides of a square are the same length.

You can read s^2 as "side squared."

Area = s^2 = 5 • 5 = 5^2

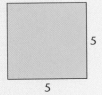

Area = s^2 = a • a = a^2

You can find the area of a square in square units by multiplying.

EXAMPLE 2   Find the area of a square with sides of six inches.

$s^2 = 6^2$
$= 6 • 6 = 36$ square inches

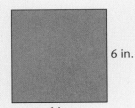

Exercise A Write an expression for the area of each of these squares.

1. 2
2

2.  4
4

3. y
y

4. m
m

5. p
p

Exercise B Multiply to find the area of each square. Use the formula area = s^2.

6. Square with sides 7 centimeters long

7. Square with sides 9 centimeters long

8. Square with sides 2 centimeters long

9. Square with sides 4 centimeters long

10. Square with sides 3 centimeters long

PROBLEM SOLVING

Exercise C Solve each problem.

11. A room is 12 feet wide and 12 feet long. What is the area of a rug that covers the floor?

12. The new classroom measures 35 feet on each side. How many square feet of tile cover the entire floor?

13. Anika buys a fleece blanket that is seven feet long and seven feet wide. What is the area of the blanket?

14. A can of paint covers 100 square feet. Dwayne wants to paint a wall that is 8 feet high and 8 feet long. Will one can of paint be enough for one coat? two coats? Explain.

15. The farmer is harvesting a field that is 800 meters long and 800 meters wide. How many square meters is the field?

Volume

The number of cubic units that fills the interior of a solid

Cube

A solid with six square faces

You can also use exponents to describe the **volume** of a **cube.** The volume of the cube is given in cubic units.

EXAMPLE 1   Write an expression for the volume of the cube.

Volume = length • width • height

$$= 3 • 3 • 3 = 3^3$$

You can read 3^3 as "three cubed."

Volume = length • width • height

$$= 5 • 5 • 5 = 5^3$$

Volume = length • width • height

$$= a • a • a = a^3$$

The formula for the volume of a cube can also be written s^3 because the sides of the cube are the same length.

You can read s^3 as "side cubed."

Volume $= s^3 = 5 • 5 • 5 = 5^3$

Volume $= s^3 = a • a • a = a^3$

You can find the volume of a cube in cubic units by multiplying.

EXAMPLE 2   Find the volume of a cube with sides of six inches.

$$s^3 = 6^3 = 6 • 6 • 6 = 216 \text{ cubic inches}$$

Exercise A Multiply to find the volume of each cube. Use the formula volume $= s^3$.

1. Cube with sides 3 inches long

2. Cube with sides 7 inches long

3. Cube with sides 5 inches long

Exercise B Write an expression for the volume of each of these cubes.

4.

5.

6.

7.

8.

Calculator Practice

You can use a scientific calculator to find the volume of a cube. You will use the y^x or x^y key.

> **EXAMPLE 3** Find the volume of a cube with sides of 4 centimeters. Volume $= s^3 = 4^3$
>
> Press 4 y^x 3 = .
>
> The display reads *64*.
>
> The volume of the cube is 64 cubic centimeters.

Exercise C Use the calculator to find the volume of each cube.

   9. Cube with sides of 8 centimeters

  10. Cube with sides of 15 centimeters

  11. Cube with sides of 2 centimeters

  12. Cube with sides of 12 centimeters

  13. Cube with sides of 18 centimeters

PROBLEM SOLVING

Exercise D Use the formula for volume to solve each problem.

14. Marlene is filling an aquarium that is 1 foot high, 1 foot long, and 1 foot deep. What is the volume of water in cubic feet that will fit in the tank?

15. A television is shipped in a packing box that is a cube. One side is 3 feet long. What is the volume of the packing box?

Root

An equal factor of a number

Square root

A factor of a power of two

The opposite of raising a number to a power is called taking the **root** of a number. The symbol $\sqrt{}$ is used to indicate taking a **square root.**

EXAMPLE 1

Area = 3^2

Area = (3)(3) = 9 square units

3 squared equals 9.

$\sqrt{9} = 3$

The square root of 9 equals 3.

Side of square = $\sqrt{9} = 3$

EXAMPLE 2

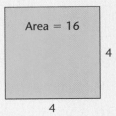

Area = 4^2

Area = (4)(4) = 16 square units

4 squared equals 16.

$\sqrt{16} = 4$

The square root of 16 equals 4.

Side of square = $\sqrt{16} = 4$

EXAMPLE 3

Area = 2^2

Area = $(2)(2)$ = 4 square units

2 squared equals 4.

$\sqrt{4} = 2$

The square root of 4 equals 2.

Side of square = $\sqrt{4} = 2$

EXAMPLE 4

Area = a^2

Area = $(a)(a)$

$\sqrt{a^2} = a$

The square root of a^2 equals a.

Side of square = $\sqrt{a^2} = a$

You can use a number line like the one below to help you estimate the square roots of numbers that are not perfect squares.

1　　　　　**2**　　　　　　　　　　**3**　　　　　　　　　　　　　　**4**

$1 < \ 2 < \ 3 < \ 4 < \ 5 < \ 6 < \ 7 < \ 8 < \ 9 < \ 10 < \ 11 < \ 12 < \ 13 < \ 14 < \ 15 < \ 16$

$\sqrt{1} < \sqrt{2} < \sqrt{3} < \sqrt{4} < \sqrt{5} < \sqrt{6} < \sqrt{7} < \sqrt{8} < \sqrt{9} < \sqrt{10} < \sqrt{11} < \sqrt{12} < \sqrt{13} < \sqrt{14} < \sqrt{15} < \sqrt{16}$

$\sqrt{2}$ is between 1 and 2.　　　$\sqrt{7}$ is between 2 and 3.　　　$\sqrt{13}$ is between 3 and 4.

Calculator Practice

You can use a calculator to find a more accurate decimal value of a square root. You will need a calculator with a $\sqrt{}$ key.

> **EXAMPLE 5** Use a calculator to find the value of $\sqrt{2}$.
>
> First, estimate the value of $\sqrt{2}$: $1 < \sqrt{2} < 2$. You know the value of $\sqrt{2}$ will be between the whole numbers 1 and 2.
>
> Next, use a calculator to find a decimal approximation of $\sqrt{2}$.
>
> Press 2 $\sqrt{}$.
>
> The display reads 1.414213562.

Exercise A Find the positive whole numbers that make each statement true. Then use a calculator to find a decimal value of each square root. Round to the nearest hundredth.

1. $\blacksquare < \sqrt{3} < \blacksquare$

2. $\blacksquare < \sqrt{5} < \blacksquare$

3. $\blacksquare < \sqrt{6} < \blacksquare$

4. $\blacksquare < \sqrt{7} < \blacksquare$

5. $\blacksquare < \sqrt{8} < \blacksquare$

6. $\blacksquare < \sqrt{11} < \blacksquare$

7. $\blacksquare < \sqrt{13} < \blacksquare$

8. $\blacksquare < \sqrt{23} < \blacksquare$

9. $\blacksquare < \sqrt{99} < \blacksquare$

10. $\blacksquare < \sqrt{101} < \blacksquare$

11. $\blacksquare < \sqrt{105} < \blacksquare$

12. $\blacksquare < \sqrt{122} < \blacksquare$

13. $\blacksquare < \sqrt{216} < \blacksquare$

14. $\blacksquare < \sqrt{331} < \blacksquare$

15. $\blacksquare < \sqrt{427} < \blacksquare$

Exercise B Find the length of a side of each square. You may use your calculator. Round to the nearest tenth.

16.

Area = 16

17.

Area = 10

18.

Area = 50

19.

Area = 8

20.
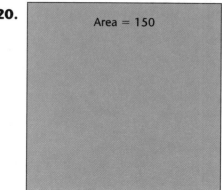
Area = 150

Estimation Activity

Estimate: "Square Roots" to the nearest whole number.

Solution: Try to "squeeze" $\sqrt{16}$, $\sqrt{23}$, $\sqrt{25}$ between perfect square 4 , $\sqrt{23}$, 5

But $\sqrt{23}$ is closer to $\sqrt{25}$ than to $\sqrt{16}$, so 5 is the best estimate.

Irrational number

A real number such as $\sqrt{2}$ that cannot be written in the form $\frac{a}{b}$ in which a and b are whole numbers and b ≠ 0

Graph

A diagram showing how one quantity depends on another

The square roots of some numbers are whole numbers. Often, however, the square root of a number is not a whole number.

Roots of numbers that equal a whole number are called rational numbers. Roots of numbers that do not equal whole numbers are called **irrational numbers.**

EXAMPLE 1 $\sqrt{9}$ is a rational number.

$\sqrt{16}$ is a rational number.

$\sqrt{3}$ is an irrational number.

$\sqrt{7}$ is an irrational number.

It is important to note that not all roots are irrational. For instance, $\sqrt{4} = 2$, and $\sqrt{25} = 5$. In these cases, the root is equal to a rational number, so these roots are *not* irrational.

You can use a **graph** to find the approximate value of an irrational number.

When you draw the line from 45 to the graph, think "45 is closer to 49 than 36." You will graph your point so that it is closer to the point where 49 crosses 7 than the point where 6 crosses 36.

EXAMPLE 2 Find the value of $\sqrt{45}$.

Step 1 Estimate the value of $\sqrt{45}$. 45 is between 36 and 49, so $\sqrt{45}$ is between 6 and 7. $\sqrt{45}$ is an irrational number.

Step 2 Find 45 on the left-hand scale. Draw a straight line from 45 to the graph.

Step 3 Draw a straight line from that point of the graph to the bottom axis. That line will cross the bottom axis at the value $\sqrt{45}$. In this case, the value is approximately 6.7, so $\sqrt{45} \approx 6.7$.

Step 4 Compare this value to the calculator value.

Press 45 √.

The display reads 6.7082039.

So 6.7 from the graph agrees with the calculator value of 6.7082039 rounded to nearest tenth.

The symbol ≈
means "is
approximately
equal to"

EXAMPLE 3 Find the value of $\sqrt{55}$.

Step 1 Estimate the value of $\sqrt{55}$. 55 is between 49 and 64, so $\sqrt{55}$ is between 7 and 8 and is an irrational number.

Step 2 Find 55 on the left-hand scale. Draw a straight line from 55 to the graph.

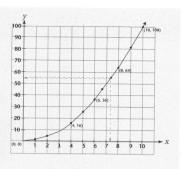

Step 3 Draw a straight line from the point of the graph to the bottom axis. The line will cross the bottom axis at the value $\sqrt{55}$. In this case, the value is approximately 7.5, so $\sqrt{55} \approx 7.5$.

Step 4 Compare this value to the calculator value. Press 55 $\sqrt{\ }$.

The display reads 7.4161984.

So 7.5 from the graph roughly agrees with the calculator value of 7.4161984.

Exercise A Use the graph to estimate these values.

1. $\sqrt{10}$

2. $\sqrt{20}$

3. $\sqrt{30}$

4. $\sqrt{40}$

5. $\sqrt{50}$

6. $\sqrt{60}$

7. $\sqrt{65}$

8. $\sqrt{75}$

9. $\sqrt{85}$

10. $\sqrt{95}$

TRY THIS Use a calculator to find the square roots of these numbers: 81, 91, 111, 121. Tell whether each square root is a rational or an irrational number. If irrational, round to the nearest tenth.

Triangle

A closed figure with three sides

Right triangle

A three-sided figure, or triangle, with one right, or 90°, angle

Angle

A figure made up of two sides or rays with a common endpoint

Right angle

A 90° angle

Hypotenuse

The longest side in a right triangle

Pythagorean theorem

A formula that states that in a right triangle, the length of the hypotenuse c squared is equal to the length of side a squared plus the length of side b squared

You know that $9 + 16 = 25$.

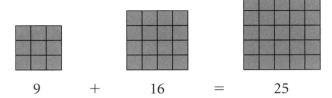

$$9 \quad + \quad 16 \quad = \quad 25$$

You can rearrange the squares to form a **right triangle.** The two legs of the triangle, a and b, form a **right angle.** The side opposite the right angle, c, is called the **hypotenuse.**

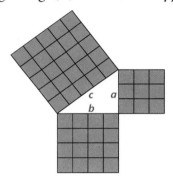

We can let $a^2 = 9$, $b^2 = 16$, and $c^2 = 25$. Since $9 + 16 = 25$, we can say $a^2 + b^2 = c^2$. This is true for any right triangle.

This formula is called the **Pythagorean theorem.**

In a right triangle, the square of the hypotenuse is equal to the sum of the squares of the other two sides.

$$c^2 = a^2 + b^2$$

You can use this formula to find the length of any side of a right triangle.

To find the length of the hypotenuse, take the square root of each side of the equation.

$$c = \sqrt{a^2 + b^2}$$

To find the length of side a, use this formula.

$$a^2 = c^2 - b^2$$

Take the square root of each side of the equation.

$$a = \sqrt{c^2 - b^2}$$

To find the length of side b, use this formula.

$$b^2 = c^2 - a^2$$

Take the square root of each side of the equation.

$$b = \sqrt{c^2 - a^2}$$

EXAMPLE 1   Find the length of the hypotenuse of this right triangle.

Step 1   Substitute the values in the equation $a^2 + b^2 = c^2$ and square the numbers.

$$c^2 = 5^2 + 12^2$$
$$c^2 = 25 + 144$$

Step 2   Take the square root of each side of the equation.

$$c = \sqrt{25 + 144}$$
$$c = \sqrt{169}$$
$$c = 13$$

EXAMPLE 2   Find the length of side a of this right triangle.

Step 1   Substitute the values in the equation $a^2 = c^2 - b^2$.

$$a^2 = 15^2 - 12^2$$
$$a^2 = 225 - 144$$

Step 2   Take the square root of each side of the equation.

$$a = \sqrt{225 - 144}$$
$$a = \sqrt{81}$$
$$a = 9$$

Exercise A Use the Pythagorean theorem to find *x*.

1.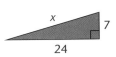

2.

3.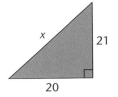

4.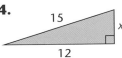

5.

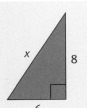

Calculator Practice

You can use a calculator and the Pythagorean theorem to find the length of a side of a right triangle.

EXAMPLE 3 Find the length of the hypotenuse of this right triangle.

Step 1 Press 8 x^2 $+$ 6 x^2 $=$.

The display reads *100*.

Step 2 Press $\sqrt{}$.

The display reads *10*.

The hypotenuse is 10 units long.

Writing About Mathematics

Find out for whom the Pythagorean theorem was named. Write a short paragraph about the person.

TRY THIS

Draw a right triangle. Label two sides of the triangle with the measurements and the third side with an x. Ask a classmate to calculate to find x.

Exercise B Use the Pythagorean theorem and a calculator to find x. Round your answer to the nearest tenth.

6.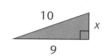

7.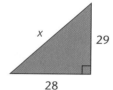

8.

9.

10.

Technology Connection

Designing Buildings on a Computer
Most architects use computer-aided design (CAD) software programs to design buildings. Many of these CAD programs contain basic designs that an architect can change to suit his or her needs. CAD programs can be great time-savers, because the architect doesn't have to start over each time. The program can show a 3-D picture of the building from all sides. This is a great aid to their clients. Some people have a hard time imagining what a building will look like from paper drawings.

<table>
<tr><td>

Scalene triangle

A triangle with no equal sides

Isosceles triangle

A triangle with two sides of equal length

Equilateral triangle

A triangle with three equal sides

</td></tr>
</table>

You know that some triangles, called right triangles, have one angle of 90°. However, there are other ways to identify triangles. One way to name and identify triangles uses the lengths of the sides of the triangle.

If no two sides of a triangle are of equal length, the triangle is a **scalene triangle.**

Scalene

If two sides of a triangle are of equal length, the triangle is an **isosceles triangle.**

Isosceles

If three sides of a triangle are of equal length, the triangle is an **equilateral triangle.**

Equilateral

Can a scalene triangle also be a right triangle? You can use the Pythagorean formula to find out.

> **EXAMPLE 1** The sides of this scalene triangle measure 3, 4, and 5 units.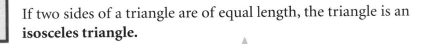
>
> **Step 1** Let $a = 3$, $b = 4$, and $c = 5$.
> **Step 2** In a right triangle, $a^2 + b^2 = c^2$. Substitute values for a, b, and c.
>
> $3^2 + 4^2 = 5^2$
>
> $9 + 16 = 25$ True, so the triangle is a right triangle.
>
>

Use the Pythagorean formula to find out if these triangles are right triangles.

EXAMPLE 2 Two sides of this triangle are $\sqrt{2}$ units long. The third side is 2 units long.

Step 1 Let $a = \sqrt{2}$, $b = \sqrt{2}$, and $c = 2$.

Step 2 In a right triangle, $a^2 + b^2 = c^2$. Substitute values for a, b, and c.

$$\sqrt{2}^2 + \sqrt{2}^2 = 2^2$$

$2 + 2 = 4$ True, so the triangle is a right triangle.

EXAMPLE 3 Each side of this triangle is 4 units long. Is this a right triangle?

Step 1 Let $a = 4$, $b = 4$, and $c = 4$.

Step 2 In a right triangle, $a^2 + b^2 = c^2$. Substitute values for a, b, and c.

$$4^2 + 4^2 = 4^2$$

$16 + 16 = 16$ False, so the triangle is not a right triangle.

Exercise A Use the Pythagorean formula and your knowledge of triangles to complete the following table.

	$a =$	$b =$	$c =$	Right Triangle	Equilateral Triangle	Isosceles Triangle	Scalene Triangle
1.	3 in.	4 in.	____	yes	____	____	____
2.	18	____	30	yes	____	no	____
3.	4 ft	4 ft	4 ft	____	____	no	____
4.	6 m	6 m	____	yes	____	____	____
5.	____	8	10	____	____	no	____

Applying the Pythagorean Theorem   The Pythagorean theorem
is used in construction and surveying work. The distance between
places, the height of a ramp, and the length of a wire can all
be found using the Pythagorean theorem.

EXAMPLE 1   To make a ramp for toy cars, Henrique
placed a board against a wall. The top
of the ramp is 3 feet high on the wall.
The bottom is 4 feet from the wall.
How long is the ramp?

$$c^2 = a^2 + b^2 \qquad c^2 = 3^2 + 4^2 = 9 + 16 \qquad c = \sqrt{9 + 16} = \sqrt{25} = 5 \text{ feet}$$

Exercise   Draw a diagram and use the Pythagorean theorem and your
calculator to solve these problems. Round your answer to the nearest tenth.

1. The park ranger outpost is 22 miles
   north of Bear Ridge. From her
   outpost, the ranger spots a fire 20
   miles west of the outpost. When she
   calls the fire department at Bear
   Ridge, they will need to know how
   far they are from the fire. What
   should she answer?

2. The campers set up their tent 12
   miles east of the entrance to the
   park. They are 3 miles north of the
   boat dock. How far is the boat dock
   from the campsite?

3. The transmitter tower is 10 meters
   high. Each wire brace is anchored 5
   meters from the center of the tower's
   base. How long is each brace?

Chapter 8 R E V I E W

Write the letter of the correct answer.

1. Rewrite $4 \cdot 4 \cdot 4$ using exponents.

    A 64   **C** 12

    B 4^3 **D** 3^4

2. Rewrite $(-a) \cdot (-a) \cdot (-a)$ using exponents.

    A a^3 **C** $3(-a)$

    B a^2 **D** $(-a)^3$

3. Find the value of 16^2.

    A 32   **C** 8

    B 256   **D** 18

4. Find the value of $(-5)^3$.

    A -125 **C** -25

    B -15 **D** 125

5. Simplify the expression $5^2 \cdot 5^2$.

    A 25^4 **C** 125

    B $2(5^2)$ **D** 5^4

6. Simplify the expression $3^5 \div 3^4$.

    A 1^9 **C** 3

    B 3^9 **D** 9^3

7. There is a square with an area of 36. What is the length of a side of the square?

    A 6   **C** 5

    B 36^2 **D** 18

Write an expression for the area of each square. Then find the area.

Example: 2   Solution: $2 \cdot 2 = 2^2 = 4$

8. 4

9. *m*

10. *s*

11.  6

12. 1

Write an expression for the volume of each cube. Then find the volume.

Example: 4   Solution: $4 \cdot 4 \cdot 4 = 4^3 = 64$

13. 6

14. 2

15. *s*

16. 10

17. 5

Estimate the square root of each number.

Example: $\sqrt{12}$ Solution: 3 squared is 9 and 4 squared is 16, so $\sqrt{12}$ is between 3 and 4.

18. $\sqrt{3}$

20. $\sqrt{43}$

19. $\sqrt{69}$

21. $\sqrt{88}$

Find the approximate length of a side of each square.

Example: Area = 4   Solution: $A = s^2 = 4$ $s = 2$

22. Area = 250   **24.** Area = 28

23. Area = 75   **25.** Area = 1,000

Use the Pythagorean formula to find x.

Example: Solution: $a^2 + b^2 = c^2$ $4^2 + 3^2 = x^2$
$16 + 9 = x^2$
$\sqrt{25} = x$ $5 = x$

26.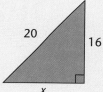

27.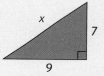

28.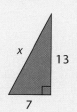

29.

30.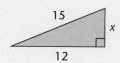

Test-Taking Tip

Before taking a test, find out what tools, such as a calculator, you need to bring with you.

9 Equations from Geometry

There is geometry everywhere you look. Look at all the different shapes in the picture. There are squares, parallel lines, spheres, and arcs of water in the fountain. Just think of all the geometry involved in designing that fountain. The water arcing into the air makes beautiful shapes. How did they know where to place the water spouts? Well, the designer calculated the fountain's circumference, the distance around the round bowl of the fountain. Then, the circumference was divided by the number of spouts to find how far apart they should be. It was all done using geometry.

In Chapter 9, you will use equations to solve geometry problems.

Goals for Learning

◆ To find the perimeters of regular and irregular polygons

◆ To calculate the areas of regular and irregular polygons

◆ To use formulas to find the volumes of cubes, rectangular prisms, and square pyramids

◆ To determine the circumferences and areas of circles

◆ To use formulas to find the volumes of cylinders and spheres

Geometry is the branch of mathematics that studies points, lines, angles, surfaces, and solids. In geometry, you compare and measure figures, including **polygons.**

A polygon is a closed, many-sided figure that is made up of line segments. Each line segment of a polygon is a side of the polygon. Line segments can be **parallel** to one another.

Polygons are named by the number of sides they have. Polygons with three sides are triangles.

Geometry

The study of points, lines, angles, surfaces, and solids

Polygon

A closed, many-sided figure that is made up of line segments

Parallel

Lines that are always the same distance apart; parallel lines never meet

scalene triangle

isosceles triangle

equilateral triangle

Perimeter is a measure of the distance around a figure or shape. The letter *P* is used to indicate perimeter.

scalene triangle

$P = a + b + c$

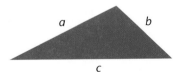

Quadrilateral

A polygon with four sides

Rectangle

A four-sided polygon with four right angles and the opposite sides equal

Rhombus

A four-sided polygon with two pairs of parallel and equal sides

isosceles triangle

$$P = a + a + b$$
$$\text{or}$$
$$P = 2a + b$$

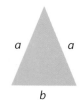

equilateral triangle

$$P = s + s + s$$
$$\text{or}$$
$$P = 3s$$

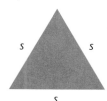

Polygons with four sides are **quadrilaterals.** Examples of quadrilaterals include a **rectangle** and a **rhombus.**

quadrilateral

$$P = a + b + c + d$$

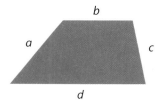

rectangle

$$P = l + l + w + w$$
$$\text{or}$$
$$P = 2l + 2w$$

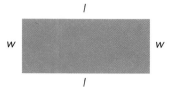

rhombus

$$P = s + s + s + s$$
$$\text{or}$$
$$P = 4s$$

Use a formula to find the perimeter of a polygon.

EXAMPLE 1 Two sides of an isosceles triangle measure 4.5 inches. The remaining side measures 7.5 inches. Find the perimeter of the triangle.

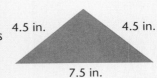

4.5 in.   4.5 in.

7.5 in.

Step 1 Choose a formula. Since the triangle is isosceles, choose $P = a + a + b$ or $P = 2a + b$. If used correctly, either formula will give the correct answer.

$$P = a + a + b \qquad P = 2a + b$$

Step 2 Substitute the given measures into the formula.

$$P = a + a + b \qquad P = 2a + b$$
$$P = 4.5 + 4.5 + 7.5 \qquad P = 2(4.5) + 7.5$$
$$P = 16.5 \qquad P = 9.0 + 7.5$$
$$P = 16.5$$

Step 3 Check to make sure your answer is written in simplest form. Then label your answer. In this example, the unit of measure is inches.
$$P = 16.5 \text{ inches}$$

Exercise A Find the perimeter of each figure.

1.

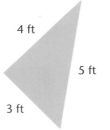

4 ft

5 ft

3 ft

2.   2 in.

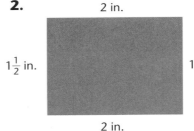

$1\frac{1}{2}$ in. $1\frac{1}{2}$ in.

2 in.

3.

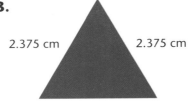

2.375 cm   2.375 cm

2.375 cm

Exercise B Solve each problem to find the perimeter.

4. Two sides of an isosceles triangle measure $3\frac{1}{8}$ inches. The remaining side of the triangle measures $8\frac{1}{2}$ inches. Find the perimeter of the triangle.

5. The sides of a quadrilateral measure 1.15 m, 1.06 m, 1.2 m, and 1.25 m. What is the perimeter of the quadrilateral?

6. Two sides of a rectangle measure 18 cm each and each of the other sides measures 9 cm. Find the perimeter of the rectangle.

7. A scalene triangle has sides measuring 203.25 feet, 197.5 feet, and 211 feet. What is the perimeter of the triangle?

PROBLEM SOLVING

Exercise C Solve each problem.

8. Bell Park is a playground shaped like a rectangle. Two sides of the park are each 42.5 m long. What is the measure of each of the other two sides of the park if the park's perimeter is 257.4 m?

9. Delaney is designing a pin for the Shelby Company in the shape of the company's logo. The logo is an equilateral triangle. Delaney has designed the pin with a 95-mm perimeter. How long is each side of the pin?

10. Jackson is framing a picture he took of swans. It is a rectangle 70 centimeters long and 40 centimeters wide. Will he be able to put the picture in a rectangular frame that is 45 centimeters wide and has a perimeter of 200 centimeters? Why or why not?

TRY THIS ⟩ Write two formulas that can be used to find the perimeter of a square.

Each side and each angle of a **regular polygon** has the same measure.

Regular polygon

A polygon in which each side and each angle has the same measure

equilateral triangle

$$P = s + s + s$$

or

$$P = 3s$$

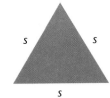

square

$$P = s + s + s + s$$

or

$$P = 4s$$

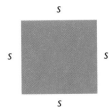

regular pentagon

$$P = s + s + s + s + s$$

or

$$P = 5s$$

regular hexagon

$$P = s + s + s + s + s + s$$

or

$$P = 6s$$

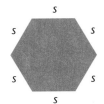

regular heptagon

$$P = s + s + s + s + s + s + s$$
or
$$P = 7s$$

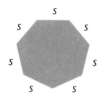

regular octagon

$$P = s + s + s + s + s + s + s + s$$
or
$$P = 8s$$

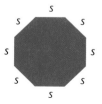

Use a formula to find the perimeter of a regular polygon.

EXAMPLE 1 Each side of a square measures 2.5 feet. Find the perimeter of the square.

2.5 ft

Step 1 Choose a formula. To find the perimeter of a square, use $P = s + s + s + s$ or $P = 4s$. If used correctly, either formula will give the correct answer.

$$P = s + s + s + s \qquad\qquad P = 4s$$

Step 2 Substitute the given measures into the formula.

$$P = s + s + s + s \qquad\qquad P = 4s$$
$$P = 2.5 + 2.5 + 2.5 + 2.5 \qquad P = 4(2.5)$$
$$P = 10.0 \qquad\qquad\qquad P = 10.0$$

Step 3 Check to make sure your answer is written in simplest form. Then label your answer. In this example, the answer can be simplified and the unit of measure is feet.

$$P = 10 \text{ feet}$$

Exercise A Find the perimeter of each regular polygon.

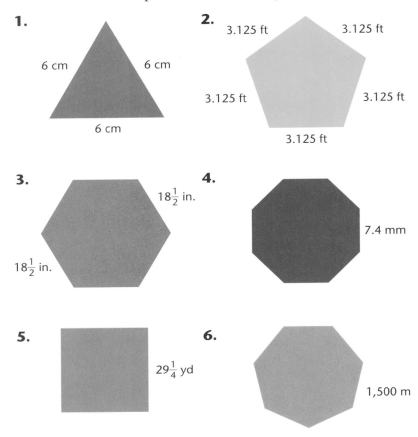

1.

6 cm   6 cm

6 cm

2.

3.125 ft   3.125 ft

3.125 ft   3.125 ft

3.125 ft

3.

$18\frac{1}{2}$ in.

$18\frac{1}{2}$ in.

4.

7.4 mm

5.

$29\frac{1}{4}$ yd

6.

1,500 m

Exercise B Find the number of sides that each shape has.

7. Each side of a regular decagon measures 8.25 inches. The perimeter of the decagon is 82.5 inches. How many sides does a decagon have?

8. The perimeter of a regular dodecagon is 52 cm. Each side of the dodecagon measures $4\frac{1}{3}$ cm. How many sides does a dodecagon have?

Exercise C Solve each problem.

9. Titus is making two drawings of volcanoes. One drawing is on a sheet of square-shaped paper. The other is on a rectangular-shaped paper. The square paper has a side length of 15 inches. The rectangular paper is 20 inches long and 10 inches wide. Titus is decorating the perimeters of his drawings with colored tape. Is it possible that he will use the same amount of tape on both drawings? Explain.

10. The stop sign that a crossing guard uses is an octagon with a perimeter of 64 inches. The handle of the sign is 12 inches long. How much shorter or longer is the handle than each side of the octagon?

TRY THIS

Write a general formula that can be used to find the perimeter of any regular polygon.

> **Irregular polygon**
>
> *A polygon that is not uniform in shape or size*

Recall that a polygon is a closed, many-sided figure that is made up of line segments. In the previous two lessons, you explored how to find the perimeters of ordinary and regular polygons. There are also **irregular polygons.**

You can find the perimeter of an irregular polygon by adding the lengths of all its line segments together.

> Note that a line segment is identified by its endpoints with a line drawn over the letters, such as $\overline{AB}$. This line symbol means "line segment," so $\overline{AB}$ is read "line segment *AB*."

EXAMPLE 1 Find the perimeter of polygon *ABDC*.

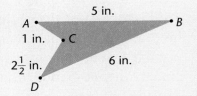

To find the perimeter of an irregular polygon, find the sum of the measures of the sides of the polygon.

$$P = \quad \overline{AB} \quad + \quad \overline{BD} \quad + \quad \overline{DC} \quad + \quad \overline{CA}$$
$$\downarrow \qquad\qquad \downarrow \qquad\qquad \downarrow \qquad\qquad \downarrow$$
$$P = \quad 5 \quad + \quad 6 \quad + \quad 2\frac{1}{2} \quad + \quad 1$$
$$P = 14\frac{1}{2} \text{ in.}$$

Irregular polygons can be many different shapes and sizes.

EXAMPLE 2 Find the perimeter of polygon *UVWXYZ*.

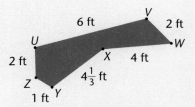

To find the perimeter of an irregular polygon, find the sum of the measures of the sides of the polygon.

$$P = \quad \overline{UV} \quad + \quad \overline{VW} \quad + \quad \overline{WX} \quad + \quad \overline{XY} \quad + \quad \overline{YZ} \quad + \quad \overline{ZU}$$
$$\downarrow \qquad\quad \downarrow \qquad\quad \downarrow \qquad\quad \downarrow \qquad\quad \downarrow \qquad\quad \downarrow$$
$$P = \quad 6 \quad + \quad 2 \quad + \quad 4 \quad + \quad 4\frac{1}{3} \quad + \quad 1 \quad + \quad 2$$
$$P = 19\frac{1}{3} \text{ ft}$$

You can also find the perimeters of some irregular polygons that have a missing measure.

EXAMPLE 3 Find the perimeter of this polygon.

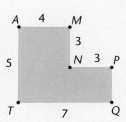

Step 1 Determine the measure of $\overline{PQ}$. Since the measure of $\overline{AT}$ is 5, the measure of $\overline{MN} + \overline{PQ} = 5$. The measure of $\overline{PQ} = 5 - 3$ or 2.

Step 2 Determine the perimeter by finding the sum of the measures of the sides. Begin at a point such as A and move around the figure.

$P = 4 + 3 + 3 + 2 + 7 + 5$

$P = 24$ units

Polygons may sometimes have more than one missing measure.

EXAMPLE 4 Find the perimeter of this polygon.

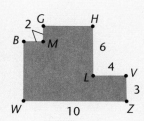

Step 1 Determine the measure of $\overline{GH}$. Since the measure of $\overline{WZ}$ is 10, the measure of $\overline{BM} + \overline{GH} + \overline{LV} = 10$. The measure of $\overline{GH} = 10 - 2 - 4$ or 4.

Step 2 Determine the measure of $\overline{WB}$. Since the measure of $\overline{ZV} + \overline{LH}$ is 3 + 6 or 9, the measure of $\overline{WB} = 9 - 2$ or 7.

Step 3 Determine the perimeter by finding the sum of the measures of the sides. Begin at a point such as G and move around the figure.

$P = 4 + 6 + 4 + 3 + 10 + 7 + 2 + 2 = 38$

$P = 38$ units

Exercise A Find the perimeters.

1.

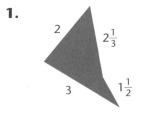

2

$2\frac{1}{3}$

3

$1\frac{1}{2}$

2.

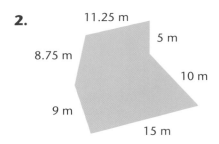

11.25 m

5 m

8.75 m

10 m

9 m

15 m

3.

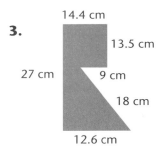

14.4 cm

13.5 cm

27 cm

9 cm

18 cm

12.6 cm

4.

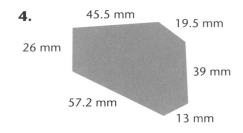

45.5 mm

19.5 mm

26 mm

39 mm

57.2 mm

13 mm

5.

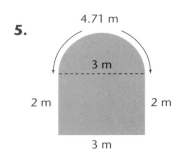

4.71 m

3 m

2 m

2 m

3 m

Technology Connection

Fencing in Fido
  Invisible fencing is a high-tech way to keep a dog in its own yard. The "fence" is a cable, buried around the perimeter of the yard. The dog wears a special collar that picks up radio waves transmitted through the cable. When the dog gets too close to the cable, it hears a beep. If it doesn't move away, the collar gives the dog a mild electric shock. The owner can train the dog to move away as soon as it hears the beep.

Exercise B Find each missing measure x. Then find the perimeter of each colored polygon.

6.

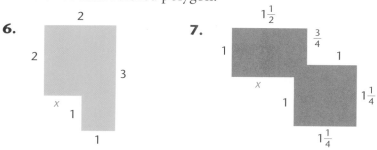

7.

8.

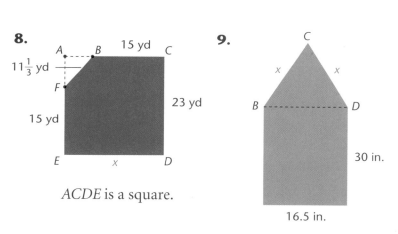

$ACDE$ is a square.

9.

30 in.

16.5 in.

Triangle BCD is an equilateral triangle.

10.

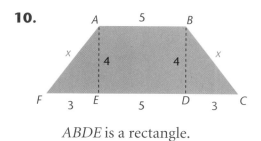

$ABDE$ is a rectangle.

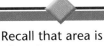

Lesson 4 — Areas of Rectangles and Squares

The area of a figure is a measure of the number of square units in that figure. Each of the smaller squares in the rectangle below measures 1 unit by 1 unit. Altogether, there are 15 unit squares in the rectangle. The rectangle has an area of 15 units^2 or 15 square units.

Recall that area is given in square units, such as square feet. You can use ft^2 to stand for square feet.

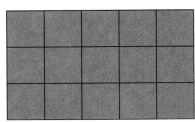

The formula $A = lw$ is used to determine the area of a rectangle. In the formula, l represents the measure of the length of the rectangle and w represents the measure of the width.

For finding the area of a rectangle, the formula $A = bh$ is sometimes used instead of $A = lw$. In the formula $A = bh$, b stands for "base" and h stands for "height." Either formula is correct.

 EXAMPLE 1 Find the area of rectangle *ABCD*.

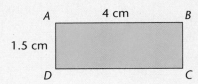

Step 1 Substitute the measures of the length and width of the rectangle into the formula $A = lw$.

$$A = lw$$
$$A = (4)(1.5)$$

Step 2 Simplify and label your answer.

$$A = (4)(1.5)$$
$$A = 6.0$$
$$A = 6 \text{ cm}^2$$

Recall that the formula $A = s^2$ is used to determine the area of a square. In the formula, s represents the measure of any side of the square.

EXAMPLE 2 Find the area of square *JKLM*.

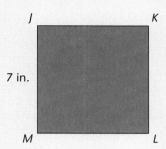

Step 1 Substitute the measure of one side of the square into the formula $A = s^2$.
$$A = s^2$$
$$A = (7)^2$$

Step 2 Simplify. Label your answer.
$$A = 7^2$$
$$A = (7)(7)$$
$$A = 49 \text{ in.}^2$$

Exercise A Find the area of each rectangle.

1. Rectangle *ABCD* with $l = 12$ cm and $w = 7$ cm

2. Rectangle *KLMN* with $l = 10$ in. and $w = 6$ in.

3. Rectangle *WXYZ* with $l = 20.4$ mm and $w = 5$ mm

4. Rectangle *GHPQ* with $l = 8$ ft and $w = 1.25$ ft

5. Rectangle *ABCD* with $l = 2\frac{1}{2}$ yd and $w = 1\frac{1}{2}$ yd

6. Rectangle *JKRS* with $l = 3\frac{1}{4}$ mi and $w = 2\frac{1}{3}$ mi

Exercise B Find the area of each square.

7. Square *RSTU* with $s = 9$ mm

8. Square *DCBA* with $s = 15$ in.

9. Square *QRMS* with $s = 4.4$ m

10. Square *MLKJ* with $s = 12.5$ cm

11. Square *HSYB* with $s = 2\frac{1}{2}$ ft

12. Square *CQDX* with $s = 5\frac{1}{3}$ yd

Calculator Practice

A calculator can be used to find the areas of geometric figures.

EXAMPLE 3   Find the area of this square.

1.04 m

The formula for the area of a square is
  $A = s^2$.
Press 1 · 04 x^2.
The display reads *1.0816*. Round to the nearest tenth.
$A = 1.1$ m^2

Exercise C Use the formula $A = s^2$, a calculator, and the $\boxed{x^2}$ key of the calculator to find the area of each square.

13. $s = 20$ m

14. $s = 14.3$ cm

15. $s = 7.5$ ft

16. $s = 36$ in.

17. $s = 1.12$ mi

18. $s = 11.06$ mi

PROBLEM SOLVING

Exercise D Solve each problem.

19. Grace is a gymnast whose best event is the floor exercise. For the floor exercise, she must stay within the perimeter of the mat, which is a square with sides 12 meters long. What is the area in which Grace performs her floor exercise?

20. The Shipleys' living room is a rectangle 14 feet wide with an area of 224 ft². They are installing floorboards around the perimeter of the room. What is the length of the room? What is its perimeter?

Perpendicular

Two intersecting lines forming right angles

The height of a triangle is measured by a line **perpendicular** to the base of the triangle. Sometimes the line is real and a part of the triangle. Other times it is imaginary and shown as a broken line. But the height of a triangle is never a slant measure.

The height of a right triangle is perpendicular to the base. Therefore, the height line is real and part of the triangle.

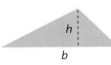

The height of a scalene triangle is an imaginary line that is perpendicular to the base. It is represented by a broken line.

When you know the measures of a triangle's height and base, you can find its area.

$$A = \frac{1}{2}bh \text{ or } A = \frac{bh}{2}$$

In the formula, A equals area, b equals base, and h equals height.

Remember that dividing is the same as multiplying by the inverse of a number.

EXAMPLE 1   Find the area of triangle *ABC*.

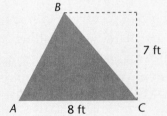

Use the formula $A = \frac{1}{2}bh$ or $A = \frac{bh}{2}$. Substitute the values of b and h into the formula, then simplify. Label your answer with the unit of measurement.

$$A = \frac{1}{2}bh$$

$$A = \frac{1}{2}(8)(7)$$

$$A = \frac{1}{2}(56)$$

$$A = 28 \text{ ft}^2$$

You can use the formula to find the base or height when you know the area and the height or base of a triangle.

> **EXAMPLE 2** Find the base of a triangle with a height of 6 inches and an area of 12 square inches.
>
> $$A = \frac{1}{2}bh$$
> $$12 = \frac{1}{2}b(6)$$
> $$12 = \frac{1}{2}(6)b$$
> $$12 = 3b$$
> $$4 = b \quad \text{The base is 4 inches.}$$

Exercise A Find the area of each figure.

1.

16 in.

10 in.

2.

27 m

11 m

3.

29 ft

18 ft

4.

8 m

5 m

5.

7

6

Exercise B Find the base or height of each triangle.

6. The area of a triangle is 36 in.^{2} and the base is 18 in. What is its height?

7. The area of a triangle is 2 ft^2 and the height is 1 ft. What is its base?

8. The area of a triangle is 42 in.^{2} and its base is 12 in. What is its height?

PROBLEM SOLVING

Exercise C Solve each problem.

9. The Andretti Landscapers are planting flowers in a garden area shaped like a triangle. The base of the triangle is 12 feet and the area is 60 square feet. What is the height of the triangle?

10. Sara is lining the bottom of a triangular box with paper. The base of the triangle is 15 inches and the height is 30 inches. What is the area of the bottom of the box?

Lesson 6 — Areas of Trapezoids and Parallelograms

Parallelogram

A four-sided polygon with two pairs of equal and parallel sides

Trapezoid

A four-sided polygon with one pair of parallel sides and one pair of sides that are not parallel

You have found the areas of rectangles, squares, and triangles. Now you will find the areas of quadrilaterals such as **parallelograms** and **trapezoids.**

The height of a parallelogram or a trapezoid is measured by a line perpendicular to its base. Just as with some triangles, the line is imaginary and shown as a broken line. The height of a parallelogram or a trapezoid is never a slant measure.

parallelogram

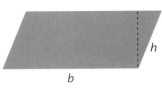

trapezoid

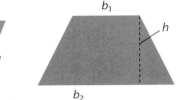

$$A = bh \qquad\qquad A = \frac{b_1 + b_2}{2}h$$

Use $A = bh$ to find the area of a parallelogram.

EXAMPLE 1 Find the area of parallelogram *ABCD*.

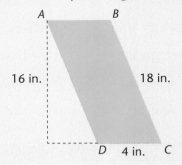

Use the formula $A = bh$. Substitute the values of *b* and *h* into the formula, then simplify.

$$A = bh$$
$$A = (4)(16)$$
$$A = 64 \text{ in.}^2$$

Use $A = \dfrac{b_1 + b_2}{2}h$ to find the area of a trapezoid.

Writing About Mathematics

Are all rectangles parallelograms? Are all parallelograms rectangles? Explain.

EXAMPLE 2 Find the area of trapezoid *WXYZ*.

Use the formula $A = \dfrac{b_1 + b_2}{2}h$. Substitute the values of b_1, b_2, and h into the formula, then simplify. Label your answer.

$$A = \frac{b_1 + b_2}{2}h$$

$$A = \frac{24 + 8}{2}(14)$$

$$A = \frac{32}{2}(14)$$

$$A = (16)(14)$$

$$A = 224 \text{ cm}^2$$

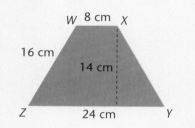

Exercise A Find the area of each quadrilateral.

1.
20 mm
8 mm

2.
8 cm
12 cm
24 cm

3.
15 ft
2 ft

4.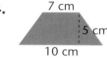
7 cm
5 cm
10 cm

5.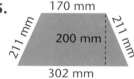
170 mm
211 mm
200 mm
211 mm
302 mm

6.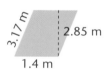
3.17 m
2.85 m
1.4 m

Exercise B Find the base or height of each quadrilateral.

7. A parallelogram has a height of 2 feet and an area of 7 square feet. What is the length of its base?

8. A trapezoid has one base 2 inches long and another base 4 inches long. Its area is 21 square inches. What is its height?

9. With a base of 14 inches and an area of 28 square inches, what is the height of a parallelogram?

10. The bases of a trapezoid equal 10 inches and its area is 35 square inches. What is its height?

Formulas that are used to find the areas of figures such as triangles and rectangles can also be used to find the areas of irregular polygons.

EXAMPLE 1 Find the area of this polygon.

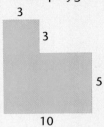

3

3

5

10

Step 1 Since there is no formula that can be used to determine the area of the entire polygon, plan to divide the polygon into smaller regions.

Step 2 Divide the polygon into smaller regions. Note the shape of each region, then use a formula to find the area of that region.

$A = lw$
$A = (10)(5)$
$A = 50$

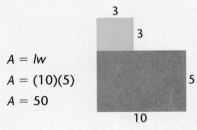

3

3

5

10

$A = s^2$
$A = (3)^2$
$A = 9$

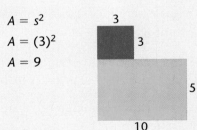

3

3

5

10

Step 3 To find the area of the entire figure, find the sum of the areas of the smaller regions.

$A = \blacksquare + \blacksquare$

$A = 50 + 9 = 59$ square units

Exercise A Find the area of each polygon.

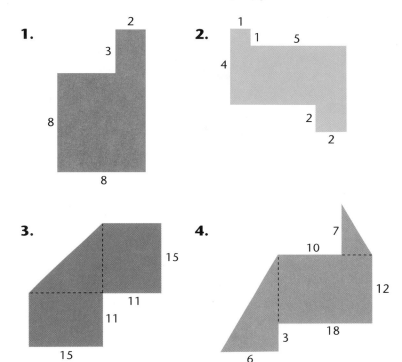

1.

2

3

8

8

2.

1

1   5

4

2

2

3.

15

11

11

15

4.

7

10

12

3   18

6

5.

4   12

28

18

24

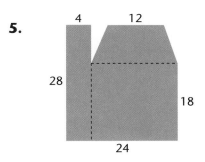

Algebra in Your Life

Irregular Playgrounds
If we couldn't measure areas of irregular polygons, most schools and parks wouldn't have playgrounds! Look at the playground equipment in your neighborhood. Very few of the pieces are perfect squares or circles. More than likely, they look like a lot of rectangles, triangles, and other shapes put together. Next time you go to a playground, think how you might fit more equipment into the same space if you arranged the equipment in a different way.

Prism

A solid figure with two parallel bases that are polygons which have the same shape and size

Rectangular prism

A solid figure with parallel faces and bases that are rectangles

Pyramid

A solid figure with a base that is a polygon and triangular sides

Square pyramid

A solid figure with a square base and triangular sides

Recall that a cube is a solid with six square faces. You can also define a cube as a prism with six square faces.

The area formulas you have explored and used apply to two-dimensional figures such as rectangles and squares. Examples of three-dimensional figures include cubes, **rectangular prisms,** and **square pyramids.**

cube   rectangular prism   square pyramid

Volume is a measure of the number of cubic units contained in a three-dimensional figure. The unit of measure for volume must be a shape that will fill all of the space inside a figure.

The volume of the cube below, for example, can be measured in unit cubes. The cube is made up of 8 unit cubes. A 2 by 2 by 2 cube has a volume of 8 cubic units or 8 units^3.

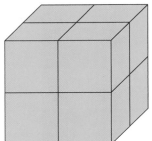

$2 \times 2 \times 2$ cube

The formula $V = e^3$, where V is the volume and e is the measure of any edge of the cube, can be used to find the volume of a cube.

EXAMPLE 1 Find the volume of this cube.

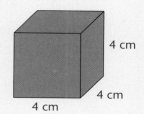

4 cm
4 cm
4 cm

Determine the measure of one edge of the cube.
Then use the formula $V = e^3$.

$V = e^3$
$V = (4)^3$
$V = (4)(4)(4)$
$V = 64 \text{ cm}^3$

The formula $V = lwh$, where l is length, w is width, and h is height, can be used to find the volume of a rectangular prism.

EXAMPLE 2 Find the volume of this rectangular prism.

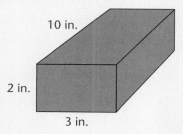

10 in.
2 in.
3 in.

Determine the length, the width, and the height of the prism. Then use the formula $V = lwh$.

$V = lwh$
$V = (10)(3)(2)$
$V = 60$
$V = 60 \text{ in.}^3$

The formula $V = \frac{Bh}{3}$ can also be used to find the volume of a square pyramid. In the formula, B represents the area of the base of the pyramid.

The formula $V = \frac{s^2h}{3}$ (where s is the measure of one side of the square base and h is the height as measured by a line perpendicular to the base) can be used to find the volume of a square pyramid.

EXAMPLE 3 Find the volume of this square pyramid.

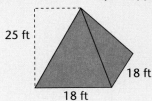

Determine the measure of one side of the square base and the height of the pyramid. Then use the formula $V = \frac{s^2h}{3}$.

$$V = \frac{s^2h}{3}$$
$$V = \frac{(18)^2(25)}{3}$$
$$V = \frac{18 \cdot 18 \cdot 25}{3}$$
$$V = \frac{8,100}{3}$$
$$V = 2,700 \text{ ft}^3$$

Whenever you find volume, remember to label your answer in cubic units.

Exercise A Find the volume of each three-dimensional figure.

1.

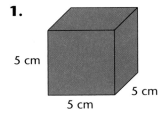

5 cm

5 cm

5 cm

2.

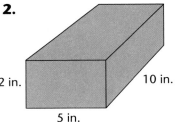

2 in.

10 in.

5 in.

3.

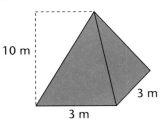

10 m

3 m

3 m

Calculator Practice

A calculator can be used to help find the volume of three-dimensional figures.

EXAMPLE 4   Each edge of a cube measures 12.5 mm. Find the volume of the cube.

Press 12 · 5 y^x 3 $=$.

The display reads 1953.125.

Exercise B Use the formula $V = e^3$ and a calculator to find the volume of each cube.

4. $e = 30$ mm

5. $e = 6.4$ in.

6. $e = 10.7$ cm

7. $e = 124$ in.

8. $e = 1.050$ m

PROBLEM SOLVING

Exercise C Solve each problem.

9. A cube measuring 4 inches by 4 inches by 4 inches has a square hole cut in it. If the hole measures 1 inch by 1 inch and goes all the way through the cube, what is the volume of the cube?

10. The basket of Joel's shopping cart is a rectangular prism 18 inches wide, 30 inches long, and 15 inches high. What is the cart's volume?

Radius

Distance from the center of a circle to the edge of the circle

Recall that circumference is the distance around a circle, diameter is the distance across a circle through the center, and pi (π) is the ratio of the circumference of a circle to the diameter.

Your study of circles will include the terms **radius**, *diameter,* and *circumference.* The length of a diameter is twice the length of a radius.

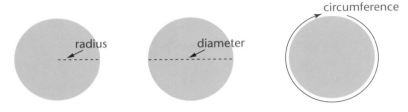

If you would take the time to draw a variety of circles and measure both the diameter and the circumference of each circle, you would find that the circumference of any circle is about three times the length of its diameter.

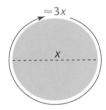

A measure used to describe this relationship is pi—the ratio of the circumference of any circle to the length of its diameter. Because pi is an irrational number, you will use an approximation for it. Three common approximations for pi are 3, 3.14, and $\frac{22}{7}$. The symbol for pi is π. Pi is used in formulas to find the circumference and area of a circle.

To find the circumference of a circle, use the formula $C = \pi d$.

To find the area of a circle, use the formula $A = \pi r^2$.

EXAMPLE 1 Find the circumference of this circle.

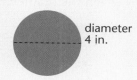

diameter
4 in.

To find the circumference of a circle, use the formula $C = \pi d$. Substitute 3.14 for π and 4 for d. Then simplify and label your answer.

$C = \pi d$

$C = (3.14)(4)$

$C = 12.56$ inches

When asked to find the circumference of a circle, you will sometimes be given the radius of the circle, instead of the diameter.

EXAMPLE 2 Find the circumference of this circle.

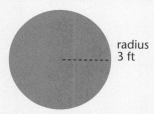

radius
3 ft

Step 1 To find the circumference of a circle, use the formula $C = \pi d$. In this circle, the diameter is not given.

Since the radius of any circle is one-half the length of the diameter, multiply the radius by 2 to find the diameter.

3 ft • 2 = 6 ft; the diameter is 6 feet.

Step 2 In the formula $C = \pi d$, substitute 3.14 for π and 6 for d. Then simplify and label your answer.

$C = \pi d$

$C = (3.14)(6)$

$C = 18.84$ feet

When asked to find the area of a circle, you will sometimes be given the diameter of the circle, instead of the radius.

EXAMPLE 3 Find the area of this circle.

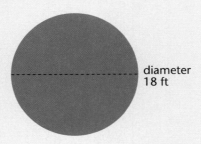

diameter
18 ft

Step 1 To find the area of a circle, use the formula $A = \pi r^2$. In this circle, the radius is not given.

Since the diameter of any circle is twice the length of the radius, divide the diameter by 2 to find the radius.

18 feet ÷ 2 = 9 feet; the radius is 9 feet.

Step 2 In the formula $A = \pi r^2$, substitute 3.14 for π and 9 for r. Then simplify and label your answer.

$$A = \pi r^2$$

$$A = (3.14)(9)^2$$

$$A = (3.14)(9)(9)$$

$$A = 254.34 \text{ ft}^2$$

Exercise A Find the circumference of a circle with the given radius or diameter. Use 3.14 for π.

1. radius = 3 in.

2. diameter = 3 ft

3. radius = 6 m

4. diameter = 5 cm

5. radius = 10 yd

Exercise B Find the area of a circle with the given radius or diameter. Use 3.14 for π.

6. radius = 4 m

7. diameter = 8 in.

8. diameter = 2 yd

9. radius = 7 cm

10. diameter = 12 m

Calculator Practice Many calculators have a π key. When a formula includes π, use the π key.

EXAMPLE 4 The radius of a circle is 15 mm. Find the area of the circle.

To find the area of a circle, use the formula $A = \pi r^2$.

On the calculator, press π × 15 x^2 = .

The display may read 706.8583471, depending on how many decimal places the calculator uses for its approximation of π.

Exercise C Use a calculator and the formula $A = \pi r^2$ to find the areas of circles with the following measures.

11. radius = 6.5 in.

12. radius = 150 ft

13. diameter = 2.4 m

14. radius = 67 mm

15. diameter = 1.15 mi

Estimation Activity

Estimate: Using π = 3, estimate the area of a circle with a diameter of 4 feet.

Solution: Use the formula for finding the area of a circle $A = \pi r^2$ where r = radius and 3 is used for π.
diameter = 4 feet → radius = 2 feet

Approximate area of circle = $(3)(2 \text{ ft})^2 = 12 \text{ ft}^2$

Sphere

A round solid figure in which all points on the surface are at an equal distance from the center

Cylinder

A solid figure with two equal circular bases that are parallel

In this lesson, you use pi to find the volume of a **sphere** and a **cylinder**.

A soup can is an example of a three-dimensional figure called a cylinder. To find the volume of a cylinder, use the formula $V = \pi r^2 h$.

EXAMPLE 1   Find the volume of this cylinder.

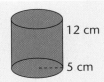
12 cm
5 cm

To find the volume of a cylinder, use the formula $V = \pi r^2 h$. Substitute 3.14 for π, 5 for r, and 12 for h. Then simplify and label your answer.

$V = \pi r^2 h$

$V = (3.14)(5)^2(12)$

$V = (3.14)(5)(5)(12)$

$V = 942 \text{ cm}^3$

A ball is an example of a three-dimensional figure known as a sphere. To find the volume of a sphere, use the formula $V = \frac{4}{3}\pi r^3$.

The formula $\frac{4\pi r^3}{3}$ can also be used to find the volume of a sphere.

EXAMPLE 2   Find the volume of this sphere.

2 ft

To find the volume of a sphere, use the formula $V = \frac{4}{3}\pi r^3$. Substitute 3.14 for π and 2 for the radius. Then simplify and label your answer.

$V = \frac{4}{3}\pi r^3$

$V = \frac{4}{3}(3.14)(2)^3$

$V = \frac{4}{3}(3.14)(2)(2)(2)$

$V = \frac{4}{3}(25.12)$

$V = \frac{4}{3} \cdot \frac{25.12}{1} = \frac{100.48}{3} = 33.493 \text{ ft}^3$

Writing About Mathematics

Would a cylindrical can 4 inches tall with a diameter of 6 inches have more volume than a cylindrical can 6 inches tall with a diameter of 4 inches? Explain your answer.

Exercise A Find the volume of a cylinder with the given height and radius or diameter. Use 3.14 for π.

1. diameter = 4 in.; height = 10 in.

2. radius = 20 cm; height = 50 cm

3. diameter = 16 mm; height = 10 mm

4. radius = 9 ft; height = 9 ft

Exercise B Find the volume of a sphere with the given radius or diameter. Use 3.14 for π.

5. radius = 5 cm

6. diameter = 24 in.

7. radius = 1 ft

8. diameter = 42 mm

PROBLEM SOLVING

Exercise C Solve each problem.

9. A globe is a model of Earth. Our classroom globe has a diameter of 12 inches. What is its volume?

10. Jamal is pouring rice from a rectangular box that is 6 by 4 by 1.5 inches into a canister that is a six-inch tall cylinder with a 3-inch diameter. Will the canister hold all of the rice?

Finding Room Measurements Many people use formulas that involve finding the area of a shape. For example, a family that is buying new carpeting uses an area formula to find the number of square yards of carpeting that is needed.

EXAMPLE 1 Find the number of square yards of carpet that must be purchased to cover the floor of a 12-foot by 14-foot rectangular room.

Step 1 Find the area of the floor. Since the floor is a rectangle, use $A = lw$.

$A = (12)(14) = 168$ square feet

Step 2 Find the number of square yards in 168 square feet. Since one square yard measures 1 yard by 1 yard or 3 feet by 3 feet, one square yard contains 3 feet • 3 feet or 9 square feet. So to find the number of square yards in 168 square feet, divide by 9.

$168 \div 9 = 18\frac{2}{3}$ square yards

The room will require $18\frac{2}{3}$ square yards of carpet.

Exercise Solve each problem.

1. The floor of a room measures 10 feet by 12 feet and is shaped like a rectangle. Find the number of square yards of carpet it would take to cover the floor.

2. A remodeling team wants to place new floor tiles in a kitchen. The floor of the kitchen measures 8 feet by 11 feet. How many 12-inch by 12-inch tiles should be purchased to cover the floor of the kitchen?

3. Suppose one gallon of paint covers 450 square feet. A room measures 16 feet long by 12 feet wide. All of the walls in the room are 8 feet high. How much paint will be required to paint all four walls in the room?

Chapter 9   R E V I E W

Write the letter of the correct answer.

1. Find the area of square *PQRS* with *s* = 1.5 m
   A 2 m²   **C** 2.5 m²
   B 2.25 m²   **D** 2.50 m²

2. Find the area of rectangle *ABCD* with *l* = 6 cm, *w* = 2 cm
   A 8 cm²   **C** 12 cm²
   B 6 cm²   **D** 24 cm²

3. Find the area of triangle *EFG* with *b* = 2 in. and *h* = 3 in.
   A 6 in.²   **C** 3 in.²
   B 7 in.²   **D** 4 in.²

Find the perimeter of each polygon shown.

4. A 15 m   **C** 6 m
   B 9 m   **D** 12 m

5. A 12 cm   **C** 13 cm
   B 9 cm   **D** 8 cm

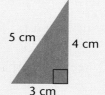

6. A 17 in.   **C** 26 in.
   B 32 in.   **D** 24 in.

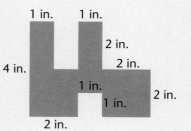

7. Find the circumference and the area of the circle.
   Use 3.14 for π.
   A 9.42 m; 4.71 m²
   B 9.42 m; 7.065 m²
   C 7.065 m; 9.42 m²
   D 4.71 m; 14.7894 m²

Find the area of each shape.

Example: 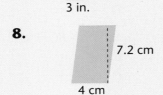 8 in.

3 in.

Solution: $A = bh = (3)(8) = 24$ in.^{2}

8.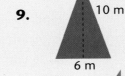
7.2 cm

4 cm

9.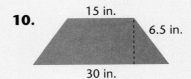
10 m

6 m

10.
15 in.

6.5 in.

30 in.

11.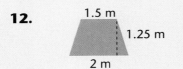
27 ft

18 ft

12.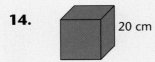
1.5 m

1.25 m

2 m

13.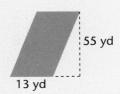
55 yd

13 yd

Find the volume of each shape.

Example: 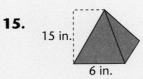 13 cm

Solution: $V = e^3$ $V = (13)^3 =$
$(13)(13)(13) = 2,197$ cm^3

14.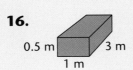
20 cm

15.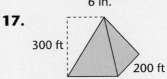
15 in.

6 in.

16.
0.5 m   3 m

1 m

17.
300 ft

200 ft

Use 3.14 for π to find area and circumference.

Example: Christina is tracing and coloring a circle with a radius of 10 cm on a poster she is making. What is the circle's circumference? What is its area?

Solution: $C = \pi d = (3.14)(20) = 62.8$ cm
$A = \pi r^2 = (3.14)(10)^2 = (3.14)(10)(10) = 314$ cm^2

18. The clock in the train station has a clock face with a 9-inch radius. What is the circumference and area of the clock face?

19. The company's logo is drawn inside a circle with a diameter of 12.2 cm. What is the circumference and area of the circle?

Use 3.14 for π to find the volume of each figure.

Example:  Solution: $V = \pi r^2 h = (3.14)(4)^2(16) = (3.14)(4)(4)(16) = 803.84$ in.^{3}

20. 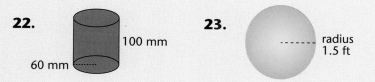 16 cm

3 cm

21. radius 7 in.

22. 100 mm

60 mm

23. radius 1.5 ft

24. The beach ball has a radius of 70 cm when it is fully inflated. What is its volume?

25. Cassie opens a can of soup for lunch. The can is a cylinder with a radius of 2.25 in. and a height of 6 in. What is its volume?

Test-Taking Tip

Drawing pictures or diagrams is one way to help you understand and solve problems.

Graphing

We think of Earth as a perfectly round globe, but it is not. Earth is wider at the equator and narrower near the poles. Flat maps do not show a true view of Earth, either. To map a sphere on flat paper or a computer screen is difficult. For centuries, people have worked at perfecting a way to measure and map Earth. Maps today are coordinate systems with latitude and longitude lines. The decimal degrees between lines represent distance. Mapmakers solve geometry equations to graph curves and angles onto flat surfaces.

In Chapter 10, you will use a coordinate system to graph linear equations.

Goals for Learning

- ◆ To graph solutions to equalities and inequalities on number lines
- ◆ To identify and graph ordered pairs of values
- ◆ To determine and graph points of a linear equation
- ◆ To identify the slope of a line
- ◆ To determine the values of slope, the *y*-intercept, and the *x*-intercept

Equality

The state of being equal; shown by the equal sign

Graphing

Showing on a number line the relationship of a set of numbers

Solution

The value of a variable that makes an open statement true

Recall that an equation is a mathematical sentence with an equal sign. Equations such as $4 + 5 = 9$ and $w = 12$ are examples of **equalities**. **Graphing** is a way to show the **solution** on a number line.

EXAMPLE 1   Suppose that $x = 3$ is the solution of an equality. Graph the solution on a number line.

Step 1   Draw a number line.

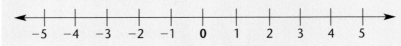

Step 2   A shaded circle is used to indicate an integer solution. Since the solution is $x = 3$, make a shaded circle on the number line at 3.

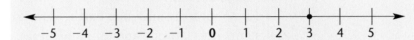

The solution to an equality will sometimes be a negative integer.

EXAMPLE 2   Suppose that $q = -4$ is the solution of an equality. Graph the solution on a number line.

Step 1   Draw a number line.

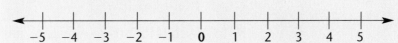

Step 2   A shaded circle is used to indicate an integer solution. Since the solution is $q = -4$, make a shaded circle on the number line at -4.

Exercise A Graph each solution on a number line.

1. $x = 8$ **4.** $p = 6$

2. $r = -2$ **5.** $n = -\dfrac{1}{2}$

3. $s = -6$

Exercise B Write a solution for each equality. Use x as the variable in each of the solutions.

6.

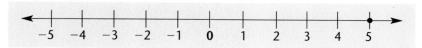

7.

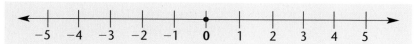

8.

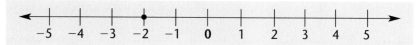

9.

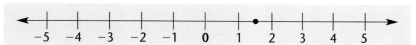

10.

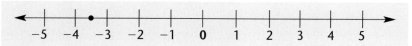

Inequality

Two quantities that are not the same; shown by the less than, greater than, and unequal to signs

An **inequality** is a mathematical sentence that contains a symbol such as > (greater than), < (less than), ≥ (greater than or equal to), ≤ (less than or equal to), and ≠ (unequal to). A number line can be used to graph the solution of an inequality.

EXAMPLE 1 Suppose that $n > 16$ is the solution of an inequality. Graph the solution on a number line.

Step 1 Draw a number line.

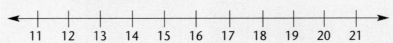

Step 2 Note that the inequality $n > 16$ means "n is greater than 16." The integer 16 is not a solution of the inequality.

Step 3 Graph the solution. To show all numbers greater than 16, but not including 16, make an open circle at 16. Draw a line extending to the right and place an arrow at the end of the line.

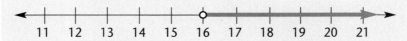

EXAMPLE 2 Suppose that $c < -5$ is the solution of an inequality. Graph the solution on a number line.

Step 1 Draw a number line.

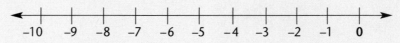

Recall that a shaded circle is used to show the solution to an equality. It can also be used to show an integer that is a solution to an inequality. An open circle is used to show an integer that is not a solution to an inequality.

Step 2 Note that the inequality $c < -5$ means "c is less than -5." The integer -5 is not a solution of the inequality.

Step 3 Graph the solution. To show all numbers less than -5, but not including -5, make an open circle at -5. Draw a line extending to the left and place an arrow at the end of the line.

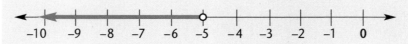

EXAMPLE 3 Suppose that $h \leq 10$ is the solution of an inequality. Graph the solution on a number line.

Step 1 Draw a number line.

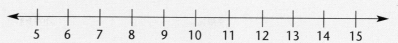

Step 2 Note that the inequality $h \leq 10$ means "h is less than or equal to 10." The integer 10 and all numbers less than 10 are solutions of the inequality.

Step 3 Graph the solution. To show all numbers that are less than or equal to 10, make a shaded circle at 10. Draw a line extending to the left and place an arrow at the end of the line.

EXAMPLE 4 Suppose that $a \geq -2$ is the solution of an inequality. Graph the solution on a number line.

Step 1 Draw a number line.

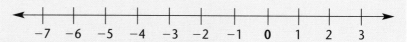

Step 2 Note that the inequality $a \geq -2$ means "a is greater than or equal to -2." The integer -2 and all numbers greater than -2 are solutions of the inequality.

Step 3 Graph the solution. To show all numbers that are greater than or equal to -2, make a shaded circle at -2. Draw a line extending to the right and place an arrow at the end of the line.

Exercise A Graph each solution on a number line.

1. $x < 8$ **4.** $r > -4$

2. $b < -1$ **5.** $m \geq -1$

3. $v > 12$ **6.** $d \leq 11$

Exercise B Write a solution for each inequality. Use x as the variable in each of the solutions.

7.

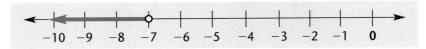

8.

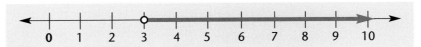

9.

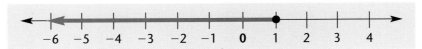

10.

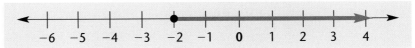

11.

12.

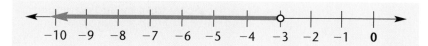

13.

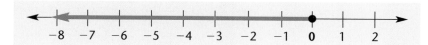

14.

15.

Algebra in Your Life

Graph That Goal!
People who write down their goals are more likely to achieve them. But how about graphing your goals? Set a goal for yourself to get an 85 or better on your pre-algebra tests. Then graph your goal on a number line. Draw a shaded circle at a giant 85 and a brightly colored arrow going right. Post your number line where you can see it when you study. Or carry it as a bookmark in your pre-algebra book. Imagine the results!

To graph an equality on a number line, you must first solve for the variable.

EXAMPLE 1   Solve $x - 3 = 6$ for x. Then graph the solution.

Step 1   Solve for x by adding 3 to each side of the equality.

$$x - 3 = 6$$
$$x - 3 + 3 = 6 + 3$$
$$x = 6 + 3$$
$$x = 9$$

Step 2   Graph the solution on a number line.

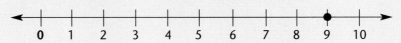

Step 3   To check your work, substitute 9 for x in the given equality.

$$x - 3 = 6$$
$$9 - 3 = 6$$
$$6 = 6 \quad \text{True}$$

EXAMPLE 2   Solve $x + 2 = -5$ for x. Then graph the solution.

Step 1   Solve for x by adding -2 to each side of the equality.

$$x + 2 = -5$$
$$x + 2 + (-2) = -5 + (-2)$$
$$x = -5 + (-2)$$
$$x = -7$$

Step 2   Graph the solution on a number line.

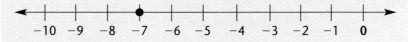

Step 3   To check your work, substitute -7 for x in the given equality.

$$x + 2 = -5$$
$$(-7) + 2 = -5$$
$$-5 = -5 \quad \text{True}$$

Exercise A Solve each equality for the variable. Then graph and check each solution.

1. $d + 4 = 7$

2. $x + 1 = 10$

3. $g + 12 = 7$

4. $t - 4 = -2$

5. $n - 6 = 0$

6. $-3 + w = -6$

PROBLEM SOLVING

Exercise B Write and solve an equality for each problem. Use x as the variable in the equality. Graph your solution on a number line.

7. Ariel has competed in 17 hurdle races this year. She has lost 8 of the races. How many has she won?

8. Kito has seen 13 movies he liked and 9 he disliked this year. How many movies has he seen this year?

9. Yesterday, the high temperature was 45°F. Today's high temperature is 15°F lower. What is today's high temperature?

10. The stock market was up 29 points today. If it gains 5 points tomorrow, how many points will it have gained in the two days?

To graph an inequality on a number line, use the same steps as you did for graphing an equality—first solve for the variable.

EXAMPLE 1   Solve $n - 3 \leq 1$ for n. Then graph the solution.

Step 1   Solve for n by adding 3 to each side of the inequality.

$$n - 3 \leq 1$$
$$n - 3 + 3 \leq 1 + 3$$
$$n \leq 1 + 3$$
$$n \leq 4$$

Step 2   Graph the solution on a number line.

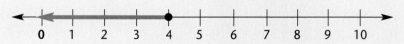

Step 3   To check your work, substitute 4 for n in the given inequality.

$$n - 3 \leq 1$$
$$4 - 3 \leq 1$$
$$1 \leq 1 \quad \text{True}$$

Substituting the value of the variable into the given equality or inequality is one way to check your work. Another way is to choose several points from the graph and substitute those points into the given equality or inequality.

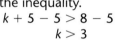

To solve $k + 5 > 8$ for k, subtract 5 from each side of the inequality.
$$k + 5 - 5 > 8 - 5$$
$$k > 3$$

EXAMPLE 2   Suppose this number line is a graph of the solution $k + 5 > 8$. Check the solution.

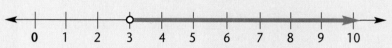

Substitute the points 2, 3, and 4 into the given inequality. Since the graph shows that 4 is a part of the solution, 4 is the only point that should make the given equation true.

$k + 5 > 8$	$k + 5 > 8$	$k + 5 > 8$
$(2) + 5 > 8$	$(3) + 5 > 8$	$(4) + 5 > 8$
$7 > 8$ False	$8 > 8$ False	$9 > 8$ True

Exercise A Solve each equality or inequality for the variable. Then graph and check each solution.

1. $d + 4 < 7$
2. $h - 7 > 0$
3. $1 + c < 4$
4. $s - 1 \geq -5$
5. $-9 + w \leq -7$
6. $p + 4 > 10$

7. $6 + r \leq -4$
8. $-1 + m < -1$
9. $z - 2 > -3$
10. $-5 + f \geq 5$
11. $-2 + v < -9$
12. $a + 11 < 6$

PROBLEM SOLVING

Exercise B Write and solve an inequality for each problem. Use x as the variable in the inequality. Graph your solution on a number line.

13. This month Bette used her cellular phone for 52 or more minutes. If she has to pay for any time over 35 minutes, how many minutes does she have to pay for?

14. One basketball player scores more than 18 points. The other players score 45 points together. How many points were scored in all?

15. For every ten people polled, three or fewer said they bought new cars this year. For every ten people, how many didn't buy new cars?

Vertical

Straight up and down

Horizontal

Left to right or parallel to the horizon

Coordinate system

A way of using number lines to locate points on a plane or in space

x-axis

The horizontal, or left-to-right, axis in a coordinate system

y-axis

The vertical, or up-and-down, axis in a coordinate system

Quadrant

One of four regions of a coordinate system bounded by the x-axis and y-axis

Origin

The point at which the x-axis and y-axis in the coordinate system intersect

Ordered pair

A set of two real numbers that locate a point in a plane

Have you ever used a mercury thermometer to see the temperature? A mercury thermometer is an example of a **vertical** number line. A vertical number line and a **horizontal** number line can be combined to form a coordinate system. A **coordinate system** is a way of using numbers to locate points on a plane or in space.

A coordinate system is shown here.

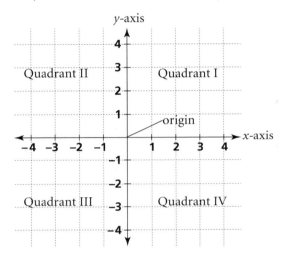

In a coordinate system, the **x-axis** and **y-axis** separate the system into four regions called **quadrants.** The intersection of the x-axis and y-axis is known as the **origin.**

Points in a coordinate system are given as **ordered pairs** of the form (*x, y*). To locate points in a coordinate system, write an ordered pair of the form (*x, y*) for each point.

In a coordinate system, ordered pairs are listed so that the *x* value is always given first and the *y* value second.

Whenever a point lies exactly on one axis, one value of the ordered pair describing the location of that point will be zero.

EXAMPLE 1 Locate Point *A*.

Step 1 Determine the *x* value of the ordered pair of the form (*x*, *y*) that will be used to describe the location of Point *A*. Begin at the origin and count the number of units the point is to the right or to the left of the *y*-axis. Since Point *A* is located 3 units to the right of the *y*-axis, the *x* value is +3.

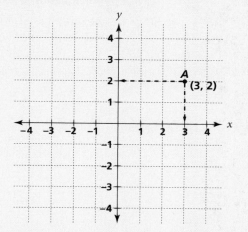

Step 2 Count the number of units the point is above or below the *x*-axis. Since Point *A* is located 2 units above the *x*-axis, the *y* value is +2.

Step 3 Write the ordered pair (3, 2) to describe the location of Point *A*.

The ordered pair (3, 2) describes the location of Point *A* with respect to the *x*- and *y*-axes.

In the coordinate system, the location of a point may sometimes be on an axis.

Technology Connection

Graphing Calculators

People used to have to draw their own graphs. Now calculators can draw graphs for you. Some graphing calculators have libraries of equations so that you just choose the one you need and presto—the calculator graphs the equation for you. Some calculators graph in three dimensions. You can plug some graphing calculators into a computer. Then you can see your graphs on a large monitor, print them out, and even share them over the Internet.

EXAMPLE 2 Locate each point.

Step 1 Locate Point *M*. The ordered pair (0, 3) describes the location of Point *M*.

Step 2 Locate Point *N*. The ordered pair (4, −1) describes the location of Point *N*.

Step 3 Locate Point *B*. The ordered pair (−4, 0) describes the location of Point *B*.

Step 4 Locate Point *T*. The ordered pair (−2, −3) describes the location of Point *T*.

Step 5 Locate Point *W*. The ordered pair (0, −4) describes the location of Point *W*.

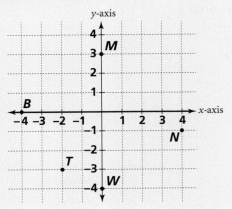

A point can be located in a specific quadrant by its *x*- and *y*-values.

In the coordinate system, Quadrant I is the upper-right quarter of the system, Quadrant II is the upper-left quarter of the system, Quadrant III is the lower-left quarter, and Quadrant IV is the lower-right quarter of the system.

EXAMPLE 3 Identify the quadrants in which Point *G*, Point *C*, Point *R*, and Point *P* are located.

Point *G* is located in Quadrant I.

Point *C* is located in Quadrant II.

Point *R* is located in Quadrant III.

Point *P* is located in Quadrant IV.

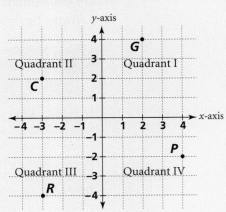

Exercise A Write an ordered pair to describe the location of each point.

1. Point *K*

2. Point *H*

3. Point *M*

4. Point *W*

5. Point *B*

6. Point *S*

7. Point *P*

8. Point *Q*

9. Point *D*

10. Point *L*

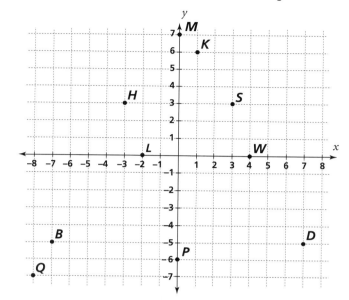

Exercise B Identify the quadrant in which each of these points is located.

11. Point *K*

12. Point *H*

13. Point *B*

14. Point *S*

15. Point *Q*

16. Point *D*

PROBLEM SOLVING

Exercise C Draw a coordinate system with *x* values from −10 to 10 and *y* values from −10 to 10. Suppose that the system stands for a grid of city blocks. Use it to answer the questions.

17. Kafi walks from $(0, 0)$ to $(2, 0)$. How many units does he walk?

18. Every morning, Mark jogs from $(0, 0)$ to $(0, -4)$ and back again. How many units does he jog?

19. Wendy left her home at $(3, 4)$, picked up Jessie at $(3, 5)$, and went to the library at $(5, 5)$. How far did Wendy go?

20. Part of the mail carrier's route takes her from $(-2, 6)$ to $(-2, -4)$ to $(6, -4)$ to $(6, 8)$. How many units is this part of her route?

In the coordinate system, the *x* value of an ordered pair (*x*, *y*) is a description of the horizontal distance a point is to the left or to the right of the *y*-axis, and the *y* value of an ordered pair is a description of the vertical distance a point is above or below the *x*-axis. This concept of horizontal and vertical distance is used when plotting points in the coordinate system.

EXAMPLE 1   Plot a point at (−4, 4).
Label the point Point *J*.

Step 1   Construct a coordinate system. Since the greatest value of the ordered pair (−4, 4) is 4, show at least four units on each axis. Label the *x*- and *y*-axes.

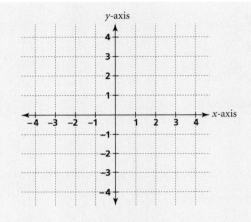

Step 2   To plot a point at (−4, 4), begin at the origin. Move 4 units to the left.

Step 3   Then move 4 units up.

Step 4   Make a shaded circle at (−4, 4).

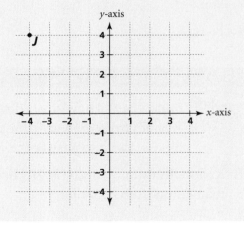

Each time you plot a point in the coordinate system, remember that the *x* value of the ordered pair describes the horizontal distance a point is to the left or to the right of the *y*-axis, and the *y* value of the ordered pair describes the vertical distance a point is above or below the *x*-axis.

EXAMPLE 2 Plot a point at $(2, -1)$. Label the point Point D.

Step 1 To plot a point at $(2, -1)$, begin at the origin. Move 2 units to the right.

Step 2 Then move 1 unit down.

Step 3 Make a shaded circle at $(2, -1)$.

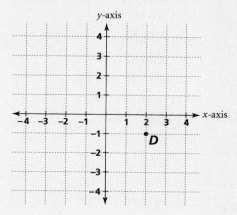

Exercise A On a sheet of graph paper, draw a coordinate system. Then use it to plot and label each point shown in problems 1–11.

1. Point $Z(-4, -2)$

2. Point $C(2, 3)$

3. Point $R(-5, 0)$

4. Point $N(6, 4)$

5. Point $Q(-3, 5)$

6. Point $B(-1, -6)$

7. Point $M(0, -1)$

8. Point $P(3, 0)$

9. Point $W(4, 1)$

10. Point $S(-2, 4)$

11. Point $V(0, 3)$

Exercise B The sign of each coordinate of an ordered pair is shown. In which quadrant is each point found?

12. $(+, +)$

13. $(-, -)$

14. $(+, -)$

15. $(-, +)$

Linear equation

An equation whose graph is a straight line

The equation $y = x + 2$ is an example of a **linear equation** because its graph is a straight line. The graph of any linear equation will intersect an infinite number of points in the coordinate system.

For example, the graph of the line $y = x + 2$ intersects $(-4, -2), (-2, 0), (1, 3)$, and many other points.

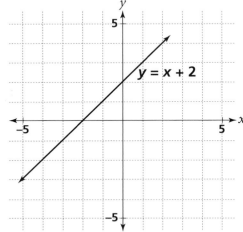

This table of values shows several points that are intersected by the line $y = x + 2$.

$y = x + 2$	
x	y
-4	-2
-2	0
1	3
2	4

In order to graph an equation of a line in the coordinate system, you must first find two or more points that the graph will intersect. To find two or more points, make a table of values.

EXAMPLE 1   Make a table of values for the line $y = x - 1$.

Step 1   Create a table that displays the equation of the line and space for at least three x and y values.

$y = x - 1$	
x	y

EXAMPLE 1   (continued)

Step 2   Choose a value for *x*. For example, choose *x* = −3. Write −3 in the table for *x*, then substitute *x* = −3 into the equation of the line *y* = *x* − 1 and solve for *y*.

y = x − 1	
x	y
−3	

$$y = x - 1$$
$$y = (-3) - 1$$
$$y = -4$$

y = x − 1	
x	y
−3	−4

The line passes through (−3, −4).

Step 3   Repeat Step 2. Choose a different value for *x*. For example, choose *x* = 0.

y = x − 1	
x	y
−3	
0	

$$y = x - 1$$
$$y = 0 - 1$$
$$y = -1$$

y = x − 1	
x	y
−3	−4
0	−1

The line passes through (0, −1).

Step 4   Repeat Step 2. Choose a different value for *x*. For example, choose *x* = 2.

y = x − 1	
x	y
−3	
0	
2	

$$y = x - 1$$
$$y = 2 - 1$$
$$y = 1$$

y = x − 1	
x	y
−3	−4
0	−1
2	1

The line passes through (2, 1).

A completed table of values shows that the graph of the line *y* = *x* − 1 passes through (−3, −4), (0, −1), and (2, 1). As long as you substitute a value for either *x* or *y*, you can solve for the other variable.

y = x − 1	
x	y
−3	−4
0	−1
2	1

Writing About
Mathematics

In several short
sentences, explain
why you can
substitute a value
for y or x in a
linear equation
and still graph the
same line.

EXAMPLE 2 Complete the table
of values for the
line $y = x + 4$.

y = x + 4	
x	y
−5	
	3
6	

Step 1 Substitute −5 for x and solve for y.

$y = x + 4$

$y = (-5) + 4$

$y = -1$

Step 2 Substitute 3 for y and solve for x.

$y = x + 4$

$3 = x + 4$

$3 + (-4) = x + 4 + (-4)$

$-1 = x$

Step 3 Substitute 6 for x and solve for y.

$y = x + 4$

$y = 6 + 4$

$y = 10$

Step 4 Complete the table
of values.

y = x + 4	
x	y
−5	−1
−1	3
6	10

Exercise A Complete each table of values.

1.

y = x + 1	
x	y
−1	
0	
1	

2.

y = x − 2	
x	y
−3	
	0
3	

3.

y = x + 3	
x	y
	−4
−1	
	−1

4.

y = 2x	
x	y
	−4
	0
	2

Exercise B Create a table of values for each equation of a line.

5.

y = x + 6	
x	y

6.

y = x − 5	
x	y

Calculator Practice

Use the [+/−] key on a calculator to help complete a table of values.

EXAMPLE 3 Complete the table of values for the line y = x − 3.

y = x − 3	
x	y
2	−1
0	−3
−2	

In the equation y = x − 3, substitute (−2) for x and use a calculator to find y.

y = (−2) − 3

Press 2 [+/−] [−] 3 [=].

The display reads −5.

Complete the table.

y = x − 3	
x	y
2	−1
0	−3
−2	−5

Exercise C Use a calculator to complete this table of values.

y = x − 12	
x	y
−53.2	**7.**
8.	−25
−89.9	**9.**
10.	−52.7

The graph of a straight line can be drawn using only two points. However, if you use only two points, you may find it difficult to tell whether an error has been made in graphing. For this reason, use three points whenever you graph linear equations.

EXAMPLE 1 Graph the linear equation $y = 3x - 1$.

Step 1 Create a table of values.

$y = 3x - 1$	
x	y

Step 2 Choose three different values for x.

$y = 3x - 1$	
x	y
-2	
0	
2	

Step 3 Solve for y.

$y = 3x - 1$	
x	y
-2	-7
0	-1
2	5

Step 4 Draw a coordinate system. Plot the points shown in the table of values. Draw a line to connect the points, make an arrow at each end of the line, and label the line $y = 3x - 1$.

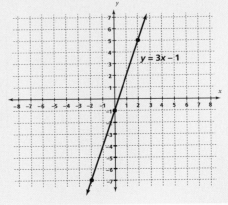

EXAMPLE 2 Graph the linear equation $y = -x + 1$.

Create and complete a table of values and then plot the points shown in the table and graph the line.

$y = -x + 1$	
x	y
-3	4
0	1
3	-2

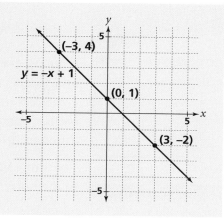

Exercise A Graph each linear equation.

1. $y = x + 5$

2. $y = x - 4$

3. $y = x$

4. $y = 2x + 2$

5. $y = -2x$

6. $y = -x + 2$

7. $y = 3x + 1$

8. $y = 2x - 3$

9. $y = -x - 1$

10. $y = 3x - 3$

TRY THIS On a grid, draw a straight line. Choose three points on the line. Give the ordered pairs for the points to a partner. Ask your partner to write a linear equation based on the ordered pairs given. For example, if your ordered pairs are (0, 2), (2, 4), and (3, 5), the equation would be $y = x + 2$.

Estimation Activity

Estimate: Estimate the population in 2010 based on the given graph.

Solution: The straight line increases by 10,000 every ten years. So in 2010 the population would be about 40,000.

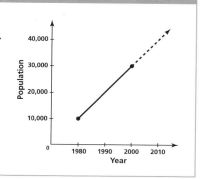

Slope

The measure of the steepness of a line

$$slope = \frac{rise}{run}$$

If you've ever pedaled a bicycle up a hill and coasted down the other side, you know that pedaling a bicycle up a hill requires a great deal more energy than coasting a bicycle down a hill. This happens because the slope of the hill in one direction is different from the slope of the hill in the other direction.

The **slope** of a line is the ratio of the vertical rise to the horizontal run and is written in the form $slope = \frac{rise}{run}$.

Recall that the fraction bar means _divide_. You can use the division symbol on the calculator to divide the rise by the run.

EXAMPLE 1   What is the slope of a street that is 800 feet long and rises 10 feet in that distance?

Step 1   Express the slope as the fraction $\frac{rise}{run}$.

Step 2 $\frac{rise}{run} = \frac{+10}{+800}$

Step 3   Simplify if possible. $\frac{+10}{+800} = \frac{1}{80}$

A slope of $\frac{1}{80}$ means for every 80 feet of horizontal distance, the street rises 1 foot.

The slope of a line may sometimes be a negative number.

EXAMPLE 2   What is the slope of a driveway that is 60 feet long and falls 2 feet in that distance?

Step 1   Express the slope as the fraction $\frac{rise}{run}$.

Step 2 $\frac{rise}{run} = \frac{-2}{+60}$

Step 3   Simplify if possible. $\frac{-2}{+60} = \frac{-1}{30}$

A slope of $\frac{-1}{30}$ means for every 30 feet of horizontal distance, the driveway falls 1 foot.

It is possible to decide whether the slope of a line is positive or negative simply by looking at the line.

A line has a _positive slope_ if it moves upward when viewed from left to right.

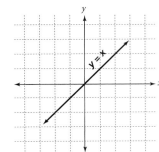

A line has a *negative slope* if it moves downward when viewed from left to right.

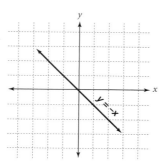

A line has *zero slope* if it is parallel to the *x*-axis.

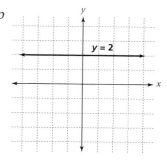

 **Calculator Practice**

You can use a calculator and the formula slope $= \frac{rise}{run}$ to determine slope of lines. Your answer will be given in decimal points.

EXAMPLE 3 Find the slope of a line that is 14.7 miles long and has a −9 mile change in elevation.
Press 9 $\boxed{+/-}$ $\boxed{÷}$ 14 $\boxed{.}$ 7 $\boxed{=}$.
The display reads −0.6122448980.

Exercise A In this chart, *Distance* is a horizontal measure and *Change in Elevation* is a vertical measure. Use a calculator to find slope.

	Distance	Change in Elevation		Distance	Change in Elevation
1.	16 in.	0.2 in.	**5.**	100 m	200 m
2.	1,200 mi	5 mi	**6.**	2.4 mm	−0.6 mm
3.	180 cm	−12 cm	**7.**	0.5 in.	6 in.
4.	10 yd	−50 yd			

Exercise B Describe the slope of each line. Write *positive slope, negative slope,* or *zero slope.*

8.

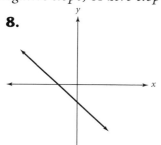

9.

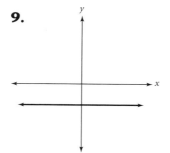

10.

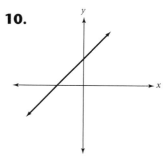

The ratio $\frac{\text{rise}}{\text{run}}$ is one way to determine the slope of a line. Another way is to use the formula $m = \frac{y_2 - y_1}{x_2 - x_1}$ where (x_1, y_1) and (x_2, y_2) are any two points on the line. In the formula, m represents slope. Use the formula whenever you are given two points through which a line passes.

EXAMPLE 1   A line passes through the points (0, 0) and (4, 2). Find the slope of the line.

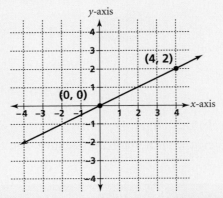

Step 1   Recall that points such as (0, 0) and (4, 2) are written in the form (x, y). Designate one of the points (x_1, y_1) and designate the other point (x_2, y_2).

$$
\begin{array}{cc}
(0, 0) & (4, 2) \\
\downarrow\ \downarrow & \downarrow\ \downarrow \\
(x_1, y_1) & (x_2, y_2)
\end{array}
$$

Step 2   Substitute the values for x_1, y_1, x_2, and y_2 into the formula.

$$m = \frac{y_2 - y_1}{x_2 - x_1} = \frac{2 - 0}{4 - 0}$$

Step 3   Simplify.

$$\frac{2 - 0}{4 - 0} = \frac{2}{4} = \frac{1}{2}$$

The slope of a line passing through the points (0, 0) and (4, 2) is $\frac{1}{2}$.

When you use two points and the formula $m = \frac{y_2 - y_1}{x_2 - x_1}$ to find the slope of a line, it does not matter which point you designate (x_1, y_1) and which point you designate (x_2, y_2).

EXAMPLE 2 Find the slope of a line that passes through the points $(-2, 3)$ and $(1, 0)$.

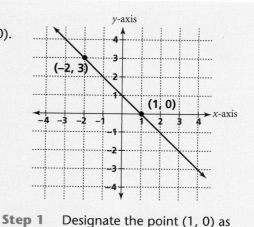

Step 1 Designate the point $(-2, 3)$ as (x_1, y_1) and designate the point $(1, 0)$ as (x_2, y_2).

$(-2, 3)$ $(1, 0)$
↓ ↓   ↓ ↓
(x_1, y_1) (x_2, y_2)

Step 2 Substitute the values for x_1, y_1, x_2, and y_2 into the formula.

$$m = \frac{y_2 - y_1}{x_2 - x_1} = \frac{0 - 3}{1 - (-2)}$$

Step 3 Simplify.

$$\frac{0 - 3}{1 - (-2)} = \frac{-3}{3} = -1$$

Step 1 Designate the point $(1, 0)$ as (x_1, y_1) and designate the point $(-2, 3)$ as (x_2, y_2).

$(1, 0)$ $(-2, 3)$
↓ ↓   ↓ ↓
(x_1, y_1) (x_2, y_2)

Step 2 Substitute the values for x_1, y_1, x_2, and y_2 into the formula.

$$m = \frac{y_2 - y_1}{x_2 - x_1} = \frac{3 - 0}{-2 (-1)}$$

Step 3 Simplify.

$$\frac{3 - 0}{-2 - 1} = \frac{3}{-3} = -1$$

The slope of a line passing through the points $(-2, 3)$ and $(1, 0)$ is -1.

Exercise A Find the slope of a line that passes through the given points.

1. $(5, 1)$ and $(0, 0)$

2. $(4, 4)$ and $(8, 8)$

3. $(-2, 10)$ and $(6, 1)$

4. $(1, -5)$ and $(2, -10)$

5. $(-8, 3)$ and $(3, 8)$

6. $(7, 5)$ and $(3, 15)$

7. $(-4, -6)$ and $(4, -6)$

8.

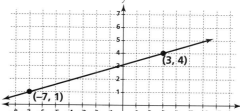

Calculator Practice

A calculator can be used to help find the slope of a line that passes through two points. Use the $+/-$ key to calculate negative integers.

EXAMPLE 3   Find the slope of a line that passes through the points $(-4, 6)$ and $(8, -1)$.

Step 1   Designate one of the points (x_1, y_1) and designate the other point (x_2, y_2).

$(-4, 6)$ $(8, -1)$
↓ ↓   ↓ ↓
(x_1, y_1) (x_2, y_2)

Step 2   Substitute the values for x_1, y_1, x_2, and y_2 into the formula.

$$m = \frac{y_2 - y_1}{x_2 - x_1} = \frac{-1 - 6}{8 - (-4)}$$

Step 3   Use a calculator to compute the numerator.

Press 1 $+/-$ $-$ 6 $=$.

The display reads -7.

Step 4   Use a calculator to compute the denominator.

Press 8 $-$ 4 $+/-$ $=$.

The display reads 12.

Step 5   Write the numerator over the denominator. Simplify if possible. The slope of a line passing through the points $(-4, 6)$ and $(8, -1)$ is $\frac{-7}{12}$.

Exercise B Find the slope of a line that passes through the given points. You may use a calculator.

9. $(-7, 3)$ and $(4, 5)$

10. $(2, -9)$ and $(1, -10)$

11. $(8, -1)$ and $(4, 8)$

12. $(2, 2)$ and $(-1, 1)$

13. $(-10, -5)$ and $(8, -7)$

Exercise C Answer each question.

14. Suppose the first half of a hiking trail has a slope of $\frac{-2}{25}$ and the last half of the trail has a slope of $\frac{1}{25}$. Which part of the trail is more difficult to hike? Explain.

15. Suppose the first half of a bicycle trail has a slope of $\frac{3}{20}$ and the last half of the trail has a slope of $\frac{5}{40}$. Which part of the trail is more difficult to bicycle? Explain.

TRY THIS Look at these shapes. Tell whether each line has a negative slope, a positive slope, or zero slope.

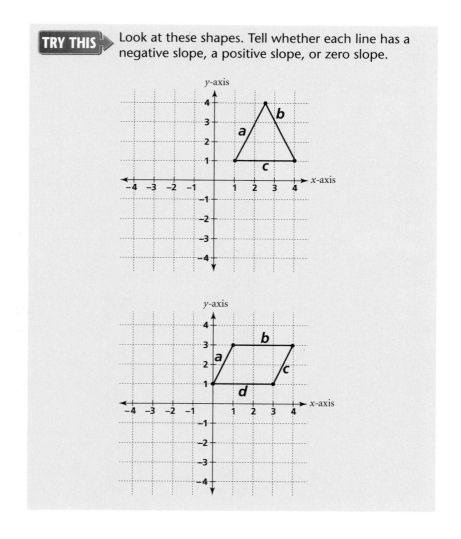

The graph of $y = 2x + 4$ is shown in this coordinate system.

x-intercept

The point at which a line crosses or intersects the x-axis

y-intercept

The point at which a line crosses or intersects the y-axis

Slope-intercept form

The slope-intercept form of a line in which m = *slope and* b = *y-intercept is* y = mx + b

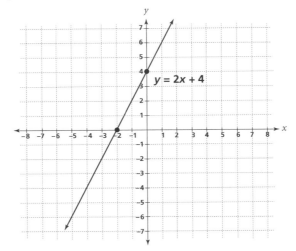

The line has three characteristics: it has slope, a point at which it crosses the x-axis, and a point at which it crosses the y-axis. The point at which a line crosses the x-axis is the **x-intercept** of the line. The point at which a line crosses the y-axis is the **y-intercept** of the line.

The graph of $y = 2x + 4$ can be used to determine that the x-intercept of the line is -2, the y-intercept is 4, and the slope is 2 (the line moves $+2$ units vertically for every $+1$ unit horizontally).

When a graph of a line is not given, it is still possible to determine the slope, x-intercept, and y-intercept of the line if the equation of the line is written in **slope-intercept form.** The slope-intercept form of a line is $y = mx + b$, where $m =$ slope and $b = y$-intercept.

EXAMPLE 1 Suppose the graph was not given and instead only the equation $y = 2x + 4$ was given. Find the slope, x-intercept, and y-intercept of the line $y = 2x + 4$.

Step 1 Determine the slope. Since $y = 2x + 4$ is written in slope-intercept form, the corresponding value for m is the slope of the line.

$$y = mx + b$$
$$\downarrow \qquad \text{The slope of the line is 2.}$$
$$y = 2x + 4$$

Step 2 Determine the y-intercept. Since $y = 2x + 4$ is written in slope-intercept form, the corresponding value for b is the y-intercept of the line.

$$y = mx + b$$
$$\downarrow \qquad \text{The } y\text{-intercept of the line is 4.}$$
$$y = 2x + 4$$

Step 3 To determine the x-intercept of a line written in slope-intercept form, substitute 0 for y in the equation of the line and solve for x.

$$y = 2x + 4$$
$$0 = 2x + 4$$
$$-4 = 2x$$
$$-2 = x \qquad \text{The } x\text{-intercept of the line is } -2.$$

To write the equation of a line in slope-intercept form, solve the equation for y.

EXAMPLE 2 Write the equation of the line $3y = 3x - 12$ in slope-intercept form.

Solve the equation for y.
$$3y = 3x - 12$$
$$\frac{3}{3}y = \frac{3}{3}x - \frac{12}{3}$$
$$y = x - 4$$

The slope-intercept form of $3y = 3x - 12$ is $y = x - 4$.

To find the slope, *x*-intercept, and *y*-intercept of a line, first write the equation of the line in slope-intercept form.

EXAMPLE 3 Find the slope, *x*-intercept, and *y*-intercept of the line $2y = -4x + 1$.

Step 1 Write the equation of the line in slope-intercept form by solving the equation for *y*.

$$2y = -4x + 1$$
$$\frac{2}{2}y = \frac{-4}{2}x + \frac{1}{2}$$
$$y = -2x + \frac{1}{2} \quad \text{slope-intercept form}$$

Step 2 Determine the slope. Since $y = -2x + \frac{1}{2}$ is written in slope-intercept form, the corresponding value for *m* is the slope of the line.

$$y = \quad mx + b$$
$$\qquad \downarrow \qquad \qquad \text{The slope of the line is } -2.$$
$$y = -2x + \frac{1}{2}$$

Step 3 Determine the *y*-intercept. Since $y = -2x + \frac{1}{2}$ is written in slope-intercept form, the corresponding value for *b* is the *y*-intercept of the line.

$$y = \quad mx + b$$
$$\qquad \qquad \downarrow \quad \text{The } y\text{-intercept of the line is } \frac{1}{2}.$$
$$y = -2x + \frac{1}{2}$$

Step 4 Determine the *x*-intercept. Substitute 0 for *y* in the equation of the line and solve for *x*.

$$y = -2x + \frac{1}{2}$$
$$0 = -2x + \frac{1}{2}$$
$$2x = \frac{1}{2}$$
$$x = \frac{1}{4} \qquad \text{The x-intercept of the line is } \frac{1}{4}.$$

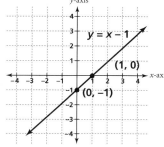

Writing About Mathematics

Describe a line that does not have a *x*-intercept. Describe a line that does not have a *y*-intercept.

Exercise A Identify the slope, *x*-intercept, and *y*-intercept of each line.

1.

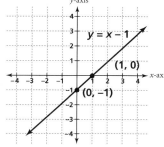

2.

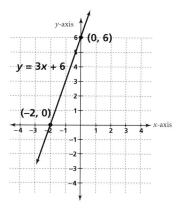

Exercise B Write each of these equations of a line in slope-intercept form.

3. $2y = 2x + 10$

4. $3y = 3x - 6$

5. $-4y = -8x + 4$

6. $-5y = -15x - 5$

7. $-2y = 2x + 2$

8. $-y = 2x + 2$

Exercise C Determine the slope, *x*-intercept, and *y*-intercept of each line.

9. $y = x - 3$

10. $y = 2x + 10$

11. $y = -2x - 4$

12. $y = -x + 1$

13. $-3y = -3x - 3$

14. $5y = 15x - 30$

15. $7y = 7x - 35$

16. $-6y = 18x - 18$

17. $-2y = 2x + 2$

18. $2y = 4x - 1$

19. $4y = 2x + 4$

20. $2y = -x + 3$

Graphing Commission Sales Some salespeople earn a salary plus commission. A commission is a percentage of sales. An equation can be written that shows the possible income of the salespeople, and a graph of that income can be drawn.

EXAMPLE 1   Trina earns $200 each week and also earns 10% of any merchandise she sells. Write and graph an equation that shows Trina's possible income each week.

Step 1   Write an equation in slope-intercept form.
Have s = amount of sales.

Trina's income =
10% of sales + $200 each week

$$i = 0.1s + \$200$$
$$\quad\uparrow\qquad\quad\uparrow$$
$$\text{slope}\quad y\text{-intercept}$$

Step 2   Graph the equation.

Exercise Use this information to complete each problem.

Ricardo earns a salary of $500 each week and earns a commission of 5% of any merchandise he sells.

1. Write an equation in slope-intercept form that describes Ricardo's potential income each month.

2. Graph the equation.

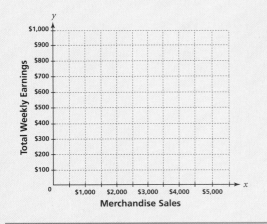

Chapter 10 R E V I E W

Write the letter of the correct answer.
Identify the solution shown by the number line.

1.

A $x \leq -13$	**C** $x = -13$
B $x = 13$	**D** $x \geq -13$

2.

A $x \geq -1$	**C** $x \geq 1$
B $x < 1$	**D** $x = -1$

---

3. Find the slope of a line that passes through points $(0, 0)$ and $(2, -2)$.

A 1	**C** -1
B 2	**D** -2

4. Find the slope of a line that passes through points $(3, -6)$ and $(6, 12)$.

A 3	**C** 2
B -6	**D** 6

5. How would the equation of the line $3y = 3x + 3$ be written in slope-intercept form?

A $y = 3x$	**C** $y = x + 3$
B $y = x + 1$	**D** $y = x - 1$

6. How would the equation of the line $5y = 15x - 5$ be written in slope-intercept form?

A $y = 75x - 25$	**C** $y = 3x - 5$
B $y = 5x - 1$	**D** $y = 3x - 1$

Chapter 10 R E V I E W - continued

Graph each solution on a number line.

Example: Graph the solution $x < -16$ on a number line.
Solution:

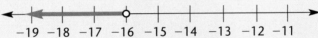

$$-19 \quad -18 \quad -17 \quad -16 \quad -15 \quad -14 \quad -13 \quad -12 \quad -11$$

7. $n = 9$ **9.** $m > -4$ **11.** $p \geq 5$

8. $x < 1$ **10.** $b \leq -3$ **12.** $y \leq 2$

Solve each equality or inequality for the variable. Then graph and check each solution.

Example: $h - 1 > 0$ for h Solution: $h - 1 > 0 = h > 1$

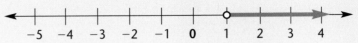

$$-5 \quad -4 \quad -3 \quad -2 \quad -1 \quad 0 \quad 1 \quad 2 \quad 3 \quad 4$$

13. $b - 2 \geq -3$ **15.** $5 + m < 6$

14. $z + 1 = 6$ **16.** $-8 + p \leq -4$

Use this coordinate system for problems 17–28.

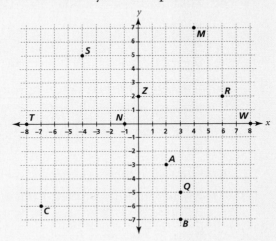

Identify the quadrant in which each of these points is located.

Example: Point M
Solution: Since Point M is located 4 units to the right of the y-axis and 7 units above the x-axis, the point is located in Quadrant I.

17. Point B **18.** Point C **19.** Point R **20.** Point S

Write an ordered pair to describe the location of each point.

Example: Point *A* Solution: (2, −3)

21. Point *R*   **23.** Point *B*   **25.** Point *S*   **27.** Point *C*

22. Point *T*   **24.** Point *N*   **26.** Point *Z*   **28.** Point *W*

On a sheet of graph paper, draw a coordinate system like the one on page 310. Then use it to plot and label the following points.

Example: Point *Q* (3, −5)   Solution: Locate the graph of Point *Q* on page 310.

29. Point *D* (−1, −2)   **31.** Point *V* (−7, 7)

30. Point *Y* (0, 5)   **32.** Point *G* (−6, 0)

Graph the equation of each line.

Example: $y = x - 3$ Solution: Complete a table of values and graph the points shown in the completed table.

$y = x - 3$	
x	**y**
−2	−5
0	−3
2	−1

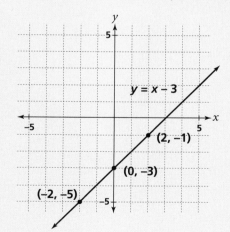

33. $y = x + 1$

34. $y = x - 2$

35. $y = -2x$

Test-Taking Tip

Make sure you have the same number of answers on your paper as there are items on the test.

11 Geometry

People have decorated buildings with polygons since ancient times. Polygons are used in all kinds of artwork. Mosaics like the one in the photo are pictures composed of hundreds of colored shapes—triangles, squares, trapezoids, and other polygons. A polygon is a plane figure made up of straight lines. The lines join together to form angles. Polygons are named for their number of sides, like a triangle. A square is a kind of quadrangle. The Pentagon in Washington, D.C., is a building named for its number of sides—five. If you see a red octagon by the road, watch out! It's probably a stop sign.

In Chapter 11, you will use geometry to learn about polygons.

Goals for Learning

◆ To measure and classify angles

◆ To name and classify triangles

◆ To find the measures of angles in triangles

◆ To identify quadrilaterals

◆ To determine the number of degrees in polygons

In geometry, you study the size, shape, and position of objects. One way to make that study easier is to concentrate on the outline of a figure, looking closely at the lines, angles, and **intersections** that make up the figure. Two of the most important geometric forms are **rays** and angles. Two rays form an angle, and their shared endpoint is called a **vertex.**

Intersection

A point at which two or more lines cross in a figure

Ray

Part of a line—a ray has one endpoint and extends indefinitely in one direction

Vertex

A common point to both sides of an angle

Protractor

A tool used to draw or measure angles

The symbol ∠ is used to show an angle. Any angle can be named in two ways. An angle is sometimes named by one letter or number.

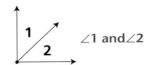 ∠1 and ∠2

 ∠a and ∠b

Recall that an angle is a figure made up of two sides, or rays, with a common endpoint.

The angle at the right can be named ∠ABC or ∠CBA. Each name has the letter B, the letter at the vertex, as the middle letter.

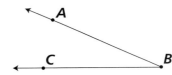

EXAMPLE 1 Name ∠a in two other ways.

Point P is the vertex of ∠a, so P must be the middle letter of the angle name. The angle has sides OP and PN. The angle can be named ∠OPN or ∠NPO.

A **protractor** is used to measure an angle in degrees. The basic unit of angle measure (m) is the degree (°).

EXAMPLE 2 What is the measure, m, of ∠XRT?

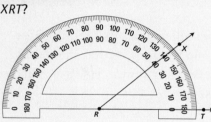

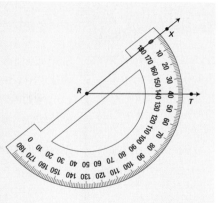

Step 1 Place the center point of the protractor at the vertex of the angle.

Step 2 Place the 0° line of the protractor along one side of the angle.

Step 3 Read the measure of the angle shown by the second side of the angle, m∠XRT = 40°

Exercise A Use the illustration to answer the following questions.

1. Give two other names for ∠1.

2. What is the vertex of ∠2?

3. What are two other names for ∠FPG?

4. What angle shares a side with both ∠2 and ∠3?

5. What rays form ∠2?

6. Name eight angles that have *CP* as a side.

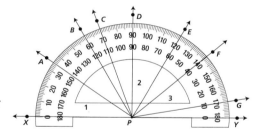

Exercise B Give the measure of each angle.

7. ∠DPY

8. ∠DPX

9. ∠FPY

10. ∠FPX

11. ∠XPA

12. ∠APY

Exercise C Find the following.

13. m∠CPY

14. m∠CPX

15. m∠EPY

Writing About Mathematics

Write directions telling how to find the measure of ∠2 in the illustration for the Exercises.

You can identify some angles by their position relative to other angles. Angles that share a common vertex and a common side are called **adjacent angles.**

∠BAC and ∠DAC are adjacent.

Adjacent angle

Two angles that have the same vertex and one side in common

Vertical angles

Pairs of opposite angles formed by intersecting lines—vertical angles have the same measure

Vertical angles are opposite pairs of angles formed by the intersection of two lines. Vertical angles have the same measure.

∠a and ∠b are vertical angles.

Acute

An angle less than 90 degrees

Obtuse

An angle with a measure between 90 and 180 degrees

You can classify an angle using its measure.

Measure (m) in Degrees		Name of Angle
0° < m < 90°		**acute**
m = 90°		right
90° < m < 180°		**obtuse**
m = 180°		straight

The symbol □ is sometimes used to show a right angle.

EXAMPLE 1   Name two angles adjacent to ∠APB. Tell what kind of angle each is.

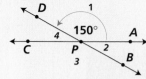

Step 1   To be adjacent, the angle must share the vertex, P. It must also share a common side. ∠APD and ∠BPC are each adjacent to ∠APB.

Step 2   m∠APD is greater than 90° but less than 180°, so m∠APD is an obtuse angle.

Step 3   ∠APD and ∠BPC form a pair of vertical angles, so m∠APD = m∠BPC. Therefore, ∠BPC must also be an obtuse angle.

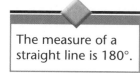

The measure of a straight line is 180°.

EXAMPLE 2 Give two names for the angle vertical to ∠2 in the Example on page 316. Tell what kind of angle it is.

Step 1 The angle opposite to ∠2 will be the vertical angle. ∠4 is opposite ∠2, so it is the vertical angle. ∠4 can also be named ∠CPD or ∠DPC.

Step 2 m∠4 is less than 90°, so ∠4 is an acute angle.

Exercise A Classify each angle. Write *acute*, *right*, *obtuse*, or *straight*.

1.

2.

3.

4.

78°

5.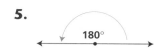

180°

Exercise B Use this illustration to answer the following questions.

6. Name any angles adjacent to ∠a.

7. Name any pairs of vertical angles.

8. What is m∠a? m∠b?

9. What is m∠c? m∠d? Explain.

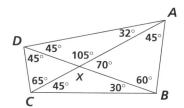

a, 140°

d   *b*

c

Exercise C Identify these angles. Write *vertical* or *adjacent*, *acute*, *right*, *obtuse*, or *straight*. An angle may have more than one description.

A
32° 45°
D 45° 105°
45° 70°
65° X
45° 30° 60°
C B

10. ∠AXB and ∠DXC

11. ∠DXC and ∠AXD

12. ∠BXC and ∠AXD

Exercise D Tell whether the following statements are *true* or *false*.

13. A pair of vertical angles can also be acute angles.

14. The sum of the measures of two obtuse angles is always greater than 180°.

15. The sum of the measures of a right angle and a straight angle is 270°.

Complementary angles

Two angles whose sum of their measures is 90 degrees

Supplementary angles

Two angles whose sum of their measures is 180 degrees

Some pairs of angles are related by their measures. If the sum of the measures of two angles is 90°, the angles are **complementary angles.** Angles do not have to be adjacent to be complementary.

Examples of Complementary Angles

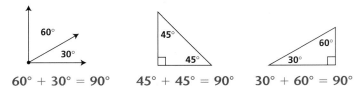

$60° + 30° = 90°$ $45° + 45° = 90°$ $30° + 60° = 90°$

EXAMPLE 1 Angles *a* and *b* are complementary. m∠*b* = 37°. What is the m∠*a*?

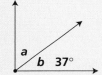

Step 1 The sum of the measures of complementary angles is 90°. Write an equation for the sum of the measures of ∠*a* and ∠*b*.

$$m\angle a + 37° = 90°$$

Step 2 Solve the equation for m∠*a*.

$$m\angle a + 37° = 90°$$
$$m\angle a = 90° - 37°$$
$$m\angle a = 53°$$

Step 3 Check. $53° + 37° = 90°$

If the sum of the measures of two angles is 180°, the angles are **supplementary angles.** Angles do not have to be adjacent to be supplementary.

Examples of Supplementary Angles

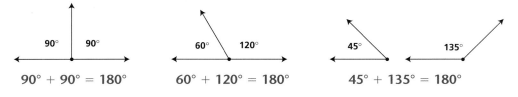

$90° + 90° = 180°$ $60° + 120° = 180°$ $45° + 135° = 180°$

EXAMPLE 2 | Angles *a* and *b* are supplementary angles. m∠*b* is two times greater than m∠*a*. What is the measure of each angle?

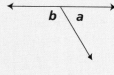

Step 1 The sum of the measures of supplementary angles is 180°. Write an equation for the sum of the measures of ∠*a* and ∠*b*. Let m∠*b* = 2m∠*a*.

$$m∠a + 2m∠a = 180°$$

Step 2 Solve the equation for m∠*a*.

$$m∠a + 2m∠a = 180°$$
$$3m∠a = 180°$$
$$m∠a = 180° ÷ 3$$
$$m∠a = 60°$$

Since m∠*b* = 2m∠*a*, m∠*b* = 2(60°) = 120°.

Step 3 Check. 60° + 120° = 180°

The measure of ∠*a* = 30°. What is m∠*b*? m∠*c*? m∠*d*?

EXAMPLE 3

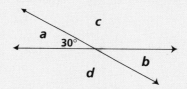

Step 1 Find the measure of ∠*c*. Note that ∠*a* and ∠*c* are adjacent and supplementary angles. The sum of the measures of supplementary angles is 180°.

$$m∠a + m∠c = 180°$$
$$30º + m∠c = 180°$$
$$m∠c = 180° − 30°$$
$$m∠c = 150°$$

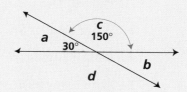

Writing About Mathematics

Tell how you could use the fact that vertical angles are equal to find the measures of the angles in the figure shown in the example to the right.

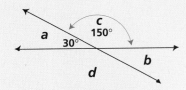

EXAMPLE 3 *(continued)*

Step 2 Find the measure of $\angle d$. Note that $\angle a$ and $\angle d$ are adjacent and supplementary angles.

$$m\angle a + m\angle d = 180°$$
$$30° + m\angle d = 180°$$
$$m\angle d = 180° - 30°$$
$$m\angle d = 150°$$

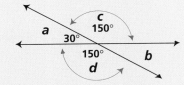

Step 3 Find the measure of $\angle b$. Note that $\angle b$ and $\angle d$ are adjacent and supplementary angles.

$$m\angle b + m\angle d = 180°$$
$$m\angle b + 150° = 180°$$
$$m\angle b = 180° - 150°$$
$$m\angle b = 30°$$

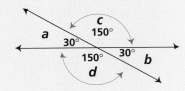

Exercise A Use the figure at the right.

1. Which angles are complementary?

2. Which angles are supplementary?

3. Which angles are adjacent but neither complementary nor supplementary?

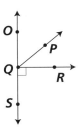

Show that the supplement of a right angle is always a right angle.

Exercise B Find the measure of the complement of ∠X.

4. m∠X = 45°

5. m∠X = 20°

6. m∠X = 30°

7. m∠X = 55°

8. m∠X = 75°

9. m∠X = 80°

Exercise C Find the measure of the supplement of ∠Y.

10. m∠Y = 20°

11. m∠Y = 105°

12. m∠Y = 90°

13. m∠Y = 150°

14. m∠Y = 135°

15. m∠Y = 120°

Exercise D Answer each question.

16. The measure of one supplementary angle is 120°. What is the measure of the other angle?

17. The measure of one complementary angle is 22°. What is the measure of the other angle?

18. The measure of one supplementary angle is 100°. What is the measure of the other angle?

19. The measure of one supplementary angle is 3 times greater than the measure of the other angle. What is the measure of each angle?

20. The measure of one complementary angle is 3 times greater than the measure of the other angle. What is the measure of each angle?

Estimation Activity

Estimate: Estimate the measure of the angle at the right.

Solution: Think of a circle and a 90° angle over the given angle. The length of the arc between the sides of the angle is about $\frac{1}{2}$ of the 90° arc. So the angle is about $\frac{1}{2}$ of 90° or about 45°.

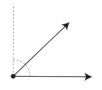

Buildings, signs, staircases, and kites all depend on one geometric figure, the triangle. A triangle is a closed geometric figure with three sides and three angles. There are many different relationships among the sides and angles of triangles. If you try this experiment with several different triangles, you will find the results will be the same.

The symbol △ is used to denote a triangle.

EXAMPLE 1 Discover the relationship among the measures of the three angles of a triangle.

Step 1 Draw a triangle similar to △ABC. Be sure to label each angle.

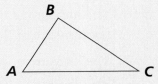

Step 2 Using scissors, cut off each angle of the triangle.

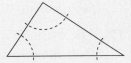

Step 3 Place the angles adjacent to each other along a straight line.

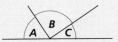

The angles form a straight angle.

$$m\angle A + m\angle B + m\angle C = 180°$$

The sum of the measures of the angles in a triangle is 180°.

You can use this information to find the missing measure of an angle in a triangle.

EXAMPLE 2 One angle in a triangle measures 45°. Another angle measures 30°. What is the measure of the third angle?

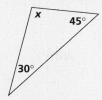

Step 1 Write an equation for the sum of the measures of the angles.

$$x + 45° + 30° = 180°$$

Step 2 Solve the equation for x.

$$x + 45° + 30° = 180°$$
$$x = 180° - (+45°) - (+30°)$$
$$x = 180° - 75°$$
$$x = 105°$$

Step 3 Check. $105° + 45° + 30° = 180°$

There are many other relationships that exist in triangles. In $\triangle ABC$, for example, angles A, B, and C are **interior angles.** Extending one side of the triangle at any vertex forms an **exterior angle.**

In $\triangle ABC$, $\angle DCB$ is an exterior angle.

Note that $\angle DCB$ and $\angle ACB$ are supplementary angles.

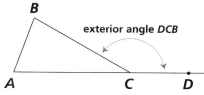

exterior angle *DCB*

Any exterior angle of a triangle is supplementary to the adjacent interior angle.

Technology Connection

Making Tracking and Navigation Easy

A global positioning system (GPS) works on a geometric principle called *triangulation*. GPS uses satellites to calculate a location. GPS shows a location by the intersection of distances from the location and three (and sometimes four) satellites. GPS was built by the U.S. government, but now GPS is available to everyone. Many cities use GPS to get their police and ambulances to people who call 911. Some people who fish even use GPS so they can return to their best fishing spots.

EXAMPLE 3 Find the measure of exterior angle 1.

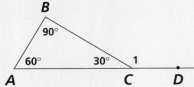

Step 1 Angle 1 and ∠BCA are supplementary. Write an equation using this information.

$$m\angle 1 + 30° = 180°$$

Step 2 Solve the equation for $m\angle 1$.

$$m\angle 1 + 30° = 180°$$
$$m\angle 1 = 180° - 30°$$
$$m\angle 1 = 150°$$

Step 3 Check. $150° + 30° = 180°$

Note that $m\angle B + m\angle A = 90° + 60° = 150°$. So for this triangle, the measure of the exterior angle at one vertex is equal to the sum of the measures of the two nonadjacent interior angles. In fact, this is true for any triangle.

> The measure of the exterior angle is equal to the sum of the measures of the two nonadjacent interior angles.

EXAMPLE 4 Given $\triangle RST$, find $m\angle x$.

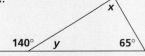

Step 1 The measure of the exterior angle is 140°. Angle x is one of the two nonadjacent angles. The measure of the other nonadjacent angle is 65°. Write an equation using this information.

$$140° = x + 65°$$

Step 2 Solve the equation for x.

$$140° = x + 65°$$
$$140° - 65° = x$$
$$75° = x$$

Step 3 Check. $65° + 75° = 140°$

Exercise A Find m∠x.

1.
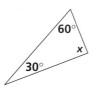
60°
x
30°

2.

x
45° 90°

3.
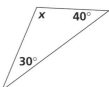
x 40°
30°

4.
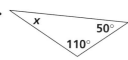
x
50°
110°

5.

75°
35° x

Exercise B Find ∠y.

6.
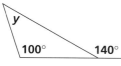
y
100° 140°

7.

y
90° 60°

8.
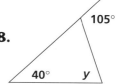
105°
40° y

9.
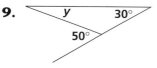
y 30°
50°

10.
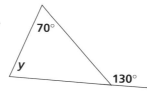
70°
y
130°

Exercise C Find ∠z. You may need more than one step.

11.
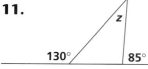
z
130° 85°

12.
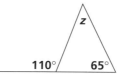
z
110° 65°

13.
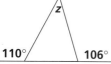
z
110° 106°

14.
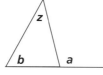
z
b a

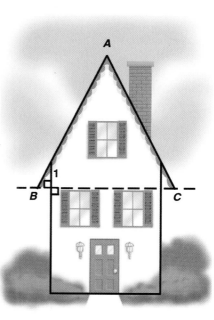

PROBLEM SOLVING

Exercise D Solve the problem.

15. The pitch (m∠ABC) of the roof is
38°. What is the m∠1, the angle the
roof makes with the outside wall of
the house?

You've already learned to name and identify triangles using the lengths of the sides of the triangle. Short lines, called **ticks,** may be used to mark the sides of a triangle or other geometric figure. One tick represents one length, two ticks represent another, and three ticks represent a third length. For example, a triangle that has a single tick marking each side has three sides of equal length.

Tick

A short line used to mark the side of a triangle

Acute triangle

A triangle with three acute angles

Obtuse triangle

A triangle with one obtuse angle

Equiangular triangle

A triangle with three equal angles, each measuring 60°

Scalene Triangle

Isosceles Triangle

Equilateral Triangle

Recall that each side of a scalene triangle is a different length, two sides of an isosceles triangle have the same length, and all sides of an equilateral triangle have the same length.

Triangles can also be classified by their angles. In addition to right triangles, which you've already studied, there are **acute, obtuse,** and **equiangular** triangles.

Arcs are used like ticks to show angles. If a triangle has two angles marked with a single arc, those two angles are of equal measure.

Acute Triangle

Obtuse Triangle

Equiangular Triangle

Right Triangle

Each angle of an acute triangle measures less than 90°.
One angle of an obtuse triangle measures more than 90°.
Each angle of an equiangular triangle measures 60°.
You can use the characteristics of triangles to name or classify triangles.

Writing About Mathematics

Do you think a triangle can be both right and obtuse? Write an explanation of why or why not.

EXAMPLE 1 What name or names best describe this triangle?

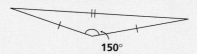

150°

Step 1 Look at the angles of the triangle. Because one angle measures more than 90°, it is an obtuse triangle.

Step 2 Look at the sides of the triangle. Two of the sides are the same length. Therefore, the triangle is an isosceles triangle.

Step 3 Name the triangle. The triangle is an obtuse, isosceles triangle.

Exercise A Name each triangle.

1.

2.

3.

4.
75°
45° 70°

5.

6.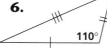
110°

7.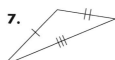

8.
140°

9.

10.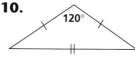
120°

Algebra in Your Life

Triangles in Nature
A triangle is a very pleasing geometric form. Perhaps that's because triangles are so often seen in nature. Think about it. The profile of your nose, for example, is shaped like a triangle. A flock of geese flies in a triangle. In photos, pine trees look like triangles. And of course, mountains look like triangles against the sky. Next time you go for a walk, try finding triangles in nature. You'll be surprised at how many you'll find once you start looking.

Congruent

Figures that have the same size and shape

Geometric figures, such as triangles, that have exactly the same size and shape are **congruent.** The symbol for congruent is ≅. $\triangle ABC \cong \triangle DEF$ is read "triangle ABC is congruent to triangle DEF."

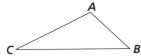
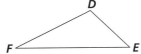

There are three sets of conditions that determine whether two triangles are congruent.

Side-Angle-Side (SAS)

If two sides and the included angle of two triangles are equal, then the triangles are congruent.

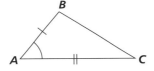
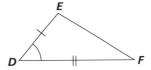

Side-Side-Side (SSS)

If the corresponding sides of two triangles are equal, then the triangles are congruent.

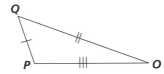
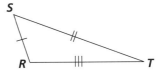

Angle-Side-Angle (ASA)

If two angles and the included side of two triangles are equal, then the triangles are congruent.

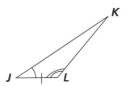
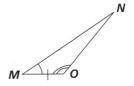

EXAMPLE 1 Determine if △ABC is congruent to △DEF. m∠A = m∠D, side *AB* = side *DE* and side *AC* = side *DF*. If the triangles are congruent, tell which condition they satisfy.

Step 1 Make a sketch and label the conditions.

Step 2 Note that two sides and the included angles of the triangles are equal.

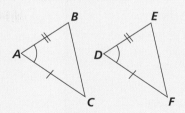

△ABC ≅ △DEF.

They satisfy the SAS condition.

EXAMPLE 2 Determine if triangles *HJK* and *DFG* are congruent. m∠H = m∠D, side *JK* = side *FG*, and side *HJ* = side *DF*. If the triangles are congruent, name the condition they satisfy.

Step 1 Make a sketch and label the conditions.

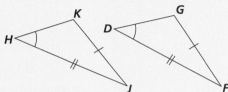

Step 2 The triangles have two sides and an angle that are equal. However, the angle that is equal is not the angle included between the two equal sides. Therefore, the triangles are not congruent.

Exercise A Name the condition that makes these pairs of triangles congruent.

1.   **2.** 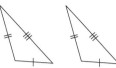   **3.**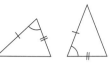

Exercise B Tell whether each pair of triangles is congruent. Tell why or why not.

4. 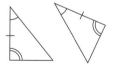   **5.**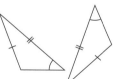

Similar

Figures that have the same shape but not the same size

Corresponding angles

Interior or exterior angles of figures in the same position as those of figures with the same shape

Sometimes, geometric figures such as triangles can have exactly the same shape but be different sizes. Figures that have the same shape but not the same size are **similar.** The symbol for similar is ~. $\triangle ABC \sim \triangle DEF$ is read "triangle ABC is similar to triangle DEF."

Similar triangles have equal **corresponding angles** but not equal corresponding sides. These triangles are similar because their corresponding angles are equal.

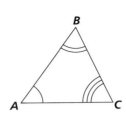

Corresponding angles are marked like this. If the corresponding angles of two triangles are equal, then the triangles are similar.

EXAMPLE 1 $\triangle ABC \sim \triangle DEF$, $m\angle A = 60°$, $m\angle C = 50°$. Find $m\angle E$.

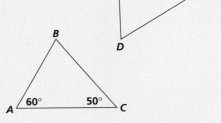

Step 1   Since the triangles are similar, their corresponding angles are equal, and $m\angle E = m\angle B$.

Step 2   Find $m\angle B$.

$$m\angle A + m\angle B + m\angle C = 180°$$
$$60° + m\angle B + 50° = 180°$$
$$m\angle B = 180° - 60° - 50°$$
$$m\angle B = 70°$$
$$m\angle E = 70° \text{ (from Step 1)}$$

Similar triangles have other characteristics in common. In similar triangles, the lengths of the corresponding sides form equal ratios. You may remember from an earlier chapter that a ratio can be expressed as a fraction. For example,

if $\triangle ABC \sim \triangle DEF$, then $\frac{AB}{DE} = \frac{BC}{EF} = \frac{AC}{DF}$.

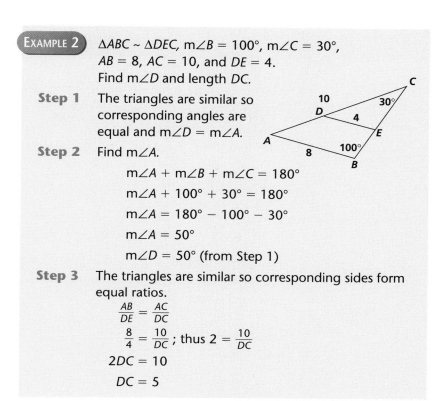

EXAMPLE 2 $\triangle ABC \sim \triangle DEC$, m$\angle B = 100°$, m$\angle C = 30°$,
$AB = 8$, $AC = 10$, and $DE = 4$.
Find m$\angle D$ and length DC.

Step 1 The triangles are similar so
corresponding angles are
equal and m$\angle D$ = m$\angle A$.

Step 2 Find m$\angle A$.

$$m\angle A + m\angle B + m\angle C = 180°$$
$$m\angle A + 100° + 30° = 180°$$
$$m\angle A = 180° - 100° - 30°$$
$$m\angle A = 50°$$
$$m\angle D = 50° \text{ (from Step 1)}$$

Step 3 The triangles are similar so corresponding sides form
equal ratios.

$$\frac{AB}{DE} = \frac{AC}{DC}$$
$$\frac{8}{4} = \frac{10}{DC} \text{ ; thus } 2 = \frac{10}{DC}$$
$$2DC = 10$$
$$DC = 5$$

Exercise A Tell whether the triangles in each pair are similar.
Answer *yes, no,* or *not enough information.*

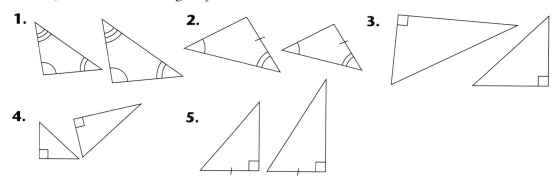

1.   **2.**   **3.**

4.   **5.**

Exercise B Answer *true* or *false.*

6. All isosceles triangles are similar.

7. All equilateral triangles are similar.

8. All right isosceles triangles are similar.

9. All congruent triangles are similar.

10. All similar triangles are congruent.

You've studied triangles—polygons made up of three intersecting lines. There are other types of polygons, and some of these polygons are made of sets of parallel lines. The symbol for parallel is ||. $m\|n$ is read "m is parallel to n."

m and n are intersecting lines   **m and n are parallel lines**

Polygons with four sides and four angles are called quadrilaterals. Quadrilaterals can be classified by whether or not they are made up of parallel lines.

Quadrilateral
• four sides

Parallelogram
• two pairs of parallel sides
• opposite sides are the same length
• opposite angles are equal

Rectangle
• parallelogram
• all angles 90°

Square
• rectangle
• all sides same length

Rhombus
• parallelogram
• all sides same length

Trapezoid
• quadrilateral
• one pair of parallel sides

| EXAMPLE 1 | Identify this quadrilateral. $AB \parallel DC$, $\angle A$ and $\angle D$ are right angles. |

Step 1 The figure has only two right angles so it cannot be a square or a rectangle.

Step 2 *ABCD* has one set of parallel sides. Therefore, *ABCD* is a trapezoid.

Exercise A Identify each polygon. Write *quadrilateral, parallelogram, rectangle, square, rhombus,* or *trapezoid.*

1.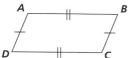

2.

3.

Exercise B Tell whether each statement is *true* or *false.*

4. All squares are rectangles.

5. A square is a rhombus with right angles.

6. A rhombus has only two parallel sides, four equal sides, and equal opposite angles.

7. A trapezoid is a parallelogram with two pairs of parallel sides.

8. A rectangle with four equal sides is a square.

PROBLEM SOLVING

Exercise C Solve each problem.

9. Anna Marie wants to make a log-cabin quilt. What kinds of quadrilaterals will she need to use to duplicate this quilt pattern?

10. Armand plans to make several birdhouses. He is using this completed house as a model. What kind of quadrilaterals will he use for the base, sides, front, back, and roof of the house?

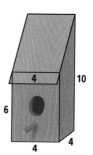

Diagonal

A line segment connecting two vertices that are not next to each other

A line connecting the opposite vertices of a quadrilateral is called a **diagonal.** A diagonal can be used to divide quadrilaterals into two triangles. For example, BD is a diagonal of square $ABCD$. If you fold the square along the diagonal, the two triangles would match exactly. That is, $\triangle BAD \cong \triangle DCB$.

EXAMPLE 1 | $ABCD$ is a rectangle, with DB the diagonal. Determine if $\triangle BAD \cong \triangle DCB$.

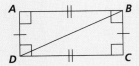

Step 1 Because $ABCD$ is a rectangle, $\angle A = \angle C$, $AD = CB$, and $AB = DC$.

Step 2 Because triangles BAD and DCB meet the Side-Angle-Side condition, $\triangle BAD \cong \triangle DCB$.

There are more relationships you can discover about the diagonals of quadrilaterals. For instance, the sum of the angle measures in any quadrilateral is 360°. You can show this using the diagonal of a quadrilateral. Two triangles make up every quadrilateral, and the sum of the angle measures in each triangle is 180°.

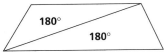

EXAMPLE 2 | In trapezoid $ABCD$, m$\angle A = 90°$, m$\angle B = 50°$, $\angle A$ and $\angle D$ are supplementary angles. What is the m$\angle C$? m$\angle D$?

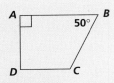

Step 1 $\angle A$ and $\angle D$ are supplementary angles so

$$m\angle A + m\angle D = 180°$$
$$90° + m\angle D = 180°$$
$$m\angle D = 90°$$

EXAMPLE 2 (continued)

Step 2 The sum of the angles in a quadrilateral is 360°.

$$m\angle A + m\angle B + m\angle C + m\angle D = 360°$$
$$90° + 50° + m\angle C + 90° = 360°$$
$$m\angle C = 360° - 90° - 50° - 90°$$
$$m\angle C = 130°$$

EXAMPLE 3 The lengths of the sides of a rectangle are shown in the illustration. What is the length of the diagonal DB?

Step 1 Because $ABCD$ is a rectangle, $\angle A$ is a right angle and $\triangle DAB$ is a right triangle with legs AD and AB.

Step 2 From the Pythagorean theorem,

$$a^2 + b^2 = c^2$$
$$3^2 + 4^2 = c^2$$
$$9 + 16 = c^2$$
$$25 = c^2$$
$$\sqrt{25} = \sqrt{c^2}$$
$$5 = c$$

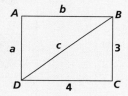

Exercise A Answer the questions about rectangle $ABCD$.
Remember, $\triangle ABD$ and $\triangle CDB$ are congruent.

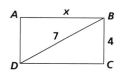

1. What is $m\angle A$?

3. What is $m\angle B$?

2. What is x?

4. What is the length of AC?

Calculator Practice You can use a calculator to find the squares and square roots of numbers.

EXAMPLE 4 Use a calculator to find the value of 17^2.

Press 17 $\boxed{x^2}$.   The displays reads 289.

Find the value of $\sqrt{63}$.

Press 63 $\boxed{\sqrt{}}$.   The display reads 7.937.

Exercise B Use a scientific calculator to find these values.
Round to the nearest hundredth.

5. 6.9^2

7. $\sqrt{124}$

9. $\sqrt{42}$

6. $\sqrt{7.3}$

8. 7.4^2

10. $\sqrt{53}$

You've seen that the sum of the measures of the angles in a triangle is 180°. And you've seen that the sum of the measures of the angles in a quadrilateral is 360°. It is possible to predict the total number of degrees in any polygon. In each of these polygons, all the possible diagonals from one vertex have been drawn.

Polygon	Number of Sides	Number of Triangles	Sum of the Angle Measures
	3	1	180°
	4	2	$2 \cdot 180° = 360°$
	5	3	$3 \cdot 180° = 540°$
	6	4	$4 \cdot 180° = 720°$
	7	5	$5 \cdot 180° = 900°$
	8	6	$6 \cdot 180° = 1,080°$
n-gon	n	$n - 2$	$(n - 2)180°$

EXAMPLE 1   Find the sum of the angle measures of a dodecagon, a polygon with 12 sides.

For a dodecagon, $n = 12$ and $n - 2 = 10$.

$(10)180° = 1,800°$. The sum of the angle measures in a dodecagon is 1,800°.

In a regular polygon, all the angles are of equal measure.

Writing About Mathematics

Explain why the measure of each angle of a regular *n*-gon is
$[(n - 2)180] \div n$.

EXAMPLE 2 Find the measure of each angle of a regular pentagon, a five-sided polygon.

Step 1 First find the sum of all the angles in a pentagon.

$$(5 - 2)180° = (3)180° = 540°$$

Step 2 The measure of one angle equals the sum of the measures of all angles divided by the number of angles.

$$540° \div 5 = 108°$$

EXAMPLE 3 What is the measure of each exterior angle, $\angle e$ of a regular pentagon, a five-sided polygon?

The interior and exterior angles are supplementary.

$$m\angle i + m\angle e = 180°$$
$$108° + m\angle e = 180°$$
$$m\angle e = 180° - 108°$$
$$m\angle e = 72°$$

Exercise A Copy the chart and fill in the missing information. The first two answers are given.

Regular Polygon, Number of Sides	Sum of Interior Angles Measures	Measure of Each Interior Angle	Measure of Each Exterior Angle
3 (triangle)	180°	60°	120°
4 (quadrilateral)	360°	90°	90°
5 (pentagon)	540°	**6.**	**10.**
1. 6 (hexagon)	720°	**7.**	60°
8 (octagon)	**4.**	135°	**11.**
2. 10 (decagon)	1,440°	144°	**12.**
12 (dodecagon)	**5.**	**8.**	**13.**
20	3,240°	**9.**	**14.**
3.	17,640°	176.4°	**15.**

Drawing Polygon Tessellations A tessellation is an arrangement of shapes that completely covers a surface. There are no gaps in a tessellation and none of the shapes overlap.

You can see tessellations on wallpaper and tiled floors and walls. Many classroom ceilings are covered with square or rectangular tessellations.

You can test to see if a polygon can form a tessellation.

EXAMPLE 1 Find out if triangles can tessellate—cover a surface without overlapping or leaving gaps.

Step 1 Mark a point *P* on a sheet of paper.

Step 2 Trace several triangles around point *P*. Each triangle should have a vertex at *P*.

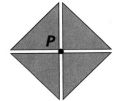

The resulting arrangement of triangles has no gaps and no overlaps. Therefore, triangles can tessellate.

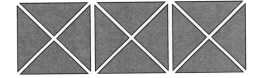

Exercise Draw tessellations.

1. Draw a tessellation using squares.

2. Draw a tessellation using rectangles.

3. Draw a tessellation using squares and equilateral triangles.

Chapter 11 R E V I E W

Write the letter of the correct answer.

1. Find x in the triangle.

    A 90°

    B 100°

    C 110°

    D 290°

2. Find x in the triangle.

    A 20°

    B 60°

    C 70°

    D 50°

3. Is this pair of triangles congruent?
If yes, why?

    A yes, SSS

    B no

    C yes, ASA

    D yes, SAS

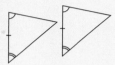

4. Name this polygon.

    A rhombus

    B pentagon

    C trapezoid

    D square

5. Name this quadrilateral.

    A rhombus

    B square

    C trapezoid

    D rectangle

6. *ABCD* is a rectangle. What the value of x to the tenths place?

    A 12.2

    B 149

    C 14.9

    D 122

Use this illustration for problems 7 to 17.

Example: m∠BXC
Solution: C at 90°, B at 35°
90° − 35° = 55° = m∠BXC

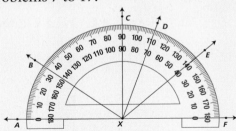

7. m∠AXB

8. m∠AXD

9. m∠FXD

10. m∠FXE

11. m∠AXE

12. Name two right angles.

13. Name three obtuse angles.

14. Angle AXB and angle ■ are supplementary.

15. Angle AXD and angle ■ are supplementary.

16. Angle AXB and angle ■ are complementary.

17. Angle CXD and angle ■ are complementary.

Use the intersecting lines for problems 18 to 22. Write *vertical, adjacent, complementary, equal,* or *supplementary.* More than one name may apply.

Example: ∠2 and ∠3   Solution: adjacent and supplementary

18. ∠1 and ∠2 are ____ angles.

19. ∠1 and ∠3 are ____ angles.

20. ∠1 and ∠4 are ____ angles.

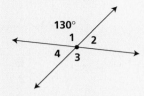

Find the measure of each angle.

Example: m∠4   Solution: 180° − 130° = 50° = m∠4

21. m∠3

22. m∠2

Find x in the triangles.

Example:
Solution: $180° = 55° + 90° + x$ $180° = 145° + x$ $x = 35°$

23.

24.

25.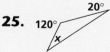

26.

27.

28.

Tell whether these triangles are similar or not. Explain your answer.

Example: Solution: Yes, corresponding angles are equal.

29.

30.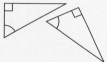

Test-Taking Tip

When taking a mathematics test, complete the answers that you know before tackling more difficult problems.

Data, Statistics, and Probability

What are the chances of winning a chess game? Chess has nothing to do with chance or probability. All the pieces are visible, and the moves are seen by both players. Winning has to do with skill and strategy. However, you can predict the odds of one chess player beating another player. People collect statistics on how different players play and how often they win. This helps them to make predictions. People collect and analyze data about all kinds of things. Data about the weather, baseball teams, population, and television programs all are of interest to us. Your teacher collects data on your homework, records your attendance, and calculates the range of all your test scores.

In Chapter 12, you will solve problems involving data, statistics, and probability.

Goals for Learning

◆ To construct graphs and interpret information illustrated by them

◆ To record and understand data in a frequency table

◆ To find measures of central tendency and range

◆ To construct and understand box-and-whiskers plots

◆ To solve problems involving probability and the fundamental principle of counting

Statistics

Numerical facts about people, places, or things

Data

Information given in numbers

Bar graph

A way of comparing information using rectangular bars

Interval

Set of all numbers between two stated numbers

Statistics are numerical facts about people or things. Facts, information, and statistics are examples of **data.** Data can be organized and displayed in different ways.

A **bar graph** is a way to organize and display data using rectangular bars. A bar graph has the following parts:

- a title

- a horizontal axis with labels

- a vertical axis with labels

- data

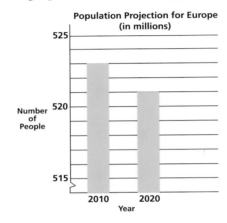

Whenever you see a bar graph with a break in the vertical axis, you know that it does not begin at zero.

In this bar graph, the title tells you that the graph is describing the projected population of Europe, in millions of people. The horizontal axis shows that the graph is describing the years 2010 and 2020. The vertical axis shows the number of people.

The **interval** of this vertical axis is 5 numbers from one labeled number to the next. For example, the interval between 520 and 525 of the vertical axis is 520, 521, 522, 523, and 524. Since the title of the graph tells you the data is stated in millions, the vertical axis represents 516 million, or 516,000,000, people; 517,000,000 people; 518,000,000 people; and so on.

The graph shows that for the year 2010, the projected population of Europe is 523,000,000 people, and for the year 2020, the projected population is 521,000,000 people.

Sometimes an axis of a graph, such as the vertical axis of the graph above, does not begin at zero. Whenever an axis of a graph does not begin at zero, it must be shown as a broken, or jagged, line.

Exercise A Answer the questions about this bar graph.

1. What data is displayed by the graph?

2. What is the interval of the vertical axis?

3. Why is the vertical axis broken and not a straight line?

4. Are all of the counties in the state of Wyoming shown on the graph? Tell how you know.

5. Of the counties shown on the graph, which county covers the greatest number of square miles?

6. Of the counties shown on the graph, which county covers the least number of square miles?

7. Order the counties shown in the graph by area from least to greatest.

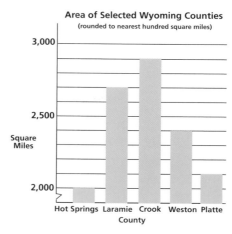

Area of Selected Wyoming Counties
(rounded to nearest hundred square miles)

8. Suppose that two counties were added to the graph and the bar for each county reads 2,500 square miles. Is it likely that both counties have exactly the same area? Explain.

9. Is it possible for the bars of a bar graph to be horizontal instead of vertical? Explain.

Exercise B Draw a bar graph that organizes and displays the data shown in this table.

10.

Number of Minutes of Tutoring This Week	
Monday	35
Tuesday	50
Wednesday	45
Thursday	75

TRY THIS Find a set of data in a newspaper, a magazine, an almanac, or on the Internet. Display the data in a bar graph.

Another way in which data can be shown is a **circle graph.** A circle graph represents data using parts of a circle.

Circle graph

A way to present information using the parts of a circle

A circle graph is also known as a pie chart.

EXAMPLE 1   This circle graph shows how 30 students responded when asked if they listen to music more than two times each week. How many students responded yes? How many students responded no?

To find the number of students who responded yes, find 60% of 30.

60% of 30 = 0.60 • 30 = 18; 18 students responded yes.

To find the number of students who responded no, find 40% of 30.

40% of 30 = 0.40 • 30 = 12; 12 students responded no.

Music Listeners

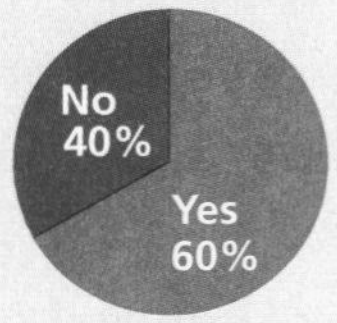

No 40%

Yes 60%

30 students surveyed

You can use data to make a circle graph.

EXAMPLE 2   Make a circle graph that organizes and displays the data in this table.

Have you ever studied 90 minutes without stopping?	
16 students surveyed	
Yes	12 students
No	4 students

Step 1   Draw a circle.

Step 2   Find the fractional part for the total number of votes for each response.

$$\text{Yes: } \frac{12}{16} \text{ votes or } \frac{3}{4}$$

$$\text{No: } \frac{4}{16} \text{ votes or } \frac{1}{4}$$

Step 3   Multiply each fractional part by 360°—the number of degrees in a circle.

$$\frac{3}{4} \cdot 360° = 270° \qquad \frac{1}{4} \cdot 360° = 90°$$

Writing About Mathematics

Write a news report about an election. Answer these questions: What was the election for? Who won? When was it? Where? Make a circle graph to illustrate the election results.

EXAMPLE 2 *(continued)*

Step 4 Use a protractor to divide the circle into two parts. The central angle of one part should measure 270° to represent $\frac{3}{4}$ and the central angle of the other part should measure 90° to represent $\frac{1}{4}$. Label each part and write a title for your graph.

Have You Ever Studied 90 Minutes Without Stopping?

No 4 Students

Yes 12 Students

Exercise A Answer the questions about the circle graph shown.

1. What data does the circle graph organize and display?

2. What percent of students responded *yes*?

3. What percent of students responded *no*?

4. How many students were surveyed altogether?

5. How many students responded *yes*?

6. How many students responded *no*?

7. How many degrees of the circle are represented by *yes* votes?

8. How many degrees of the circle are represented by *no* votes?

Do You Usually Sleep More Than 8 Hours Each Night?

No 20%

Yes 80%

40 students surveyed

9. Suppose the circle graph represented twice the number of students—80 instead of 40. Would the circle contain twice the number of degrees—720° instead of 360°? Explain.

Exercise B Draw a circle graph that organizes and displays the data shown in this table.

10.

Class Election	
Candidate A	9 votes
Candidate B	5 votes
Candidate C	10 votes

Another way data can be shown is a **frequency table.** A frequency table is a way of **tallying** data in intervals. This frequency table describes the ages of 20 people selected at random.

Frequency

The number of times an event, value, or characteristic occurs

Frequency table

A chart showing the number of times something happened

Tally

A mark of each count

For the tally part of a frequency table, check marks (✓) are sometimes used instead of other kinds of marks.

Ages of 20 People Selected at Random

Frequency Table		
Interval	Tally	Frequency
0–9	|||	3
10–19			1
20–29	|||	3
30–39	||||	4
40–49		0
50–59			1
60–69	||	2
70–79	~~||||~~	5
80–89			1
90–99		0
100–109		0

The column titled *Interval* shows the interval of the frequency table. The interval of this frequency table is ten years: 0–9, 10–19, 20–29, and so on. Other frequency tables may have other intervals—it depends on the table and the data that is described by the table.

The column titled *Tally* contains a tally mark for each time an age in any interval was recorded. Tallies are often arranged in groups of five. Look at the tally marks for the interval 70–79: the fifth tally mark is drawn in a different direction. Grouping tallies in groups of five helps anyone who reads the frequency table interpret the data more quickly.

The column titled *Frequency* shows the exact number of tallies in each interval. In any frequency table, the sum of the numbers in the Frequency column must be the same as the sum of the tallies in the Tally column. Since this frequency table shows the ages of 20 people, the sum of both the Tally column and the Frequency column must be 20.

Frequency tables help you interpret data by showing how data is grouped, or clustered. In the frequency table on page 348, the interval 40–49 seems to break the data into halves—about one-half of the data is below the interval and about one-half of the data is above. Also, the interval 70–79 contains the greatest number of tallies, and the intervals 40–49, 90–99, and 100–109 contain the least number of tallies.

Exercise A Use this frequency table for problems 1–4.

Quiz Scores

Frequency Table		
Interval	Tally	Frequency
50–59		0
60–69	I I	2
70–79	I I I I	4
80–89	⊬⊬⊬ ⊬⊬⊬ I I	12
90–99	⊬⊬⊬ I	6

1. How many students took the quiz? Tell how you know.

2. What was the highest quiz score? Explain.

3. What was the lowest quiz score? Explain.

4. Suppose that any student who scores 80 or more on the quiz earns an A. How many students earned an A?

Exercise B

5. Survey your classmates and ask each of them to estimate the number of minutes they studied last week. Organize the data you collect and display it in a frequency table.

Technology Connection

Virtual Data Collection and Analysis
Computer software can take the place of paper and pen when it comes to collecting and analyzing data. Some of the professionals who use these "virtual" data collectors are medical researchers, microbiologists, economists, political scientists, and geographers. Look on the Internet, and you can find a dozen products to help these professionals do their work faster and more accurately. Some word processing programs even let you make bar charts and circle graphs.

Mean

The sum of the values in a set of data divided by the number of pieces of data in the set

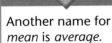

Another name for *mean* is *average*.

The **mean** of a set of data is the sum of the values in the set divided by the number of data in the set.

EXAMPLE 1 Find the mean of the set of data
{12, 29, 7, 33, 20, 15, 2, 24}.

Step 1 Use addition to find the sum of the values in the set.

```
  12
  29
   7
  33
  20
  15
   2
+ 24
 142
```

Step 2 Count the number of pieces of data.
{12, 29, 7, 33, 20, 15, 2, 24} = 8 pieces of data

Step 3 Divide the sum of the values by the number of pieces of data.
142 ÷ 8 = 17.75
The mean of {12, 29, 7, 33, 20, 15, 2, 24} is 17.75.

Exercise A Find the mean of each set of data.

1. daily newspaper prices each day for a week: $0.35, $0.35, $0.35, $0.35, $0.35, $0.35, $1.75

2. minutes of long-distance phone calls on bill: 7, 5, 22, 4, 9, 14, 8, 19, 1, 15

3. points scored by high school football team this season: 7, 17, 10, 21, 13, 31, 0, 14

4. height in feet of the 5 tallest buildings in town: 455, 210, 623, 280, 514

5. height of students in inches: 48, 52, 60, 57, 49, 53, 60, 51, 62, 49

Calculator Practice

A calculator can be used to find the mean of a set of data.

EXAMPLE 2 Find the mean of this set of data:
{106.25, 181.049, 127.4}

Step 1 Use a calculator to find the sum of the values in the set of data.
Press $106 \cdot 25 + 181 \cdot 049 + 127 \cdot 4 =$.
The display reads *414.699*.

Step 2 Divide the sum by the number of values in the set of data.
Press $\div 3 =$.
The display reads *138.233*.
The mean of {106.25, 181.049, 127.4} is 138.233.

Exercise B Use a calculator to find the mean of each set of data.

6. {18.2, 34, 28.004, 5.080}

7. {1,099; 1,405; 1,834; 1,970; 1,582}

8. {13,721; 42,858; 39,121}

9. {5.075, 3.2, 6.104, 8.4, 6.0605}

10. {84, 48, 10, 28, 74, 37, 5, 44, 39, 4}

11. {14.5, 6.2, 33.1, 25.6, 6}

12. {121, 218, 483, 912, 219, 555}

13. {22, 25, 21, 31, 42, 27, 29, 21}

PROBLEM SOLVING

Exercise C Find the mean of the set of data in each problem.

14. The ages of five Presidents at their first inauguration were 61, 52, 69, 64, and 46. What is the mean of their ages at the time of inauguration?

15. The number of times each of the first 16 Presidents vetoed a bill passed by Congress is shown. {2, 0, 0, 7, 1, 0, 12, 1, 0, 10, 3, 0, 0, 9, 7, 7} What is the mean of the number of bills vetoed by the first 16 Presidents?

Lesson 5 | **Median**

Median

The middle value in an ordered set of data

Note that one-half of the values of a set of data are above the median and one-half are below the median.

The **median** of a set of data is the middle value when the set is ordered from greatest to least or least to greatest.

EXAMPLE 1 Find the median of this set of data:
{163, 179, 140, 196, 158}

Step 1 Order the values in the set from greatest to least or least to greatest.

140   158   163   179   196

Step 2 Cross off the greatest and least values in the set.

~~140~~   158   163   179   ~~196~~

Continue crossing off greatest and least pairs until one value remains in the middle of the set.

~~140~~   ~~158~~   163   ~~179~~   ~~196~~

The median of {163, 179, 140, 196, 158} is 163.

The set of data {163, 179, 140, 196, 158} has an *odd* number of values. Any set of data that has an odd number of values will always have a piece of data as its median. However, a set of data may have an even number of values. To find the median of such a set, arrange the values in order from greatest to least or least to greatest, and cross off greatest and least pairs until two values remain in the middle of the set. The median is the mean, or average, of these two pieces of data.

Writing About Mathematics

Cathryn believes it is possible for a set of data to have the same mean and median. Mario does not believe it is possible. Who is correct? Tell why.

EXAMPLE 2 Find the median of this set of data:
{75, 71, 85, 67, 63, 88}

Step 1 Order the values in the set from greatest to least or least to greatest.

88   85   75   71   67   63

Step 2 Cross off the greatest and least values in the set.

~~88~~   85   75   71   67   ~~63~~

Continue crossing off greatest and least pairs until two values remain in the middle of the set.

~~88~~   ~~85~~   75   71   ~~67~~   ~~63~~

EXAMPLE 2 *(continued)*

Step 3 Find the mean of the two values in the middle of the set. Add the values, then divide by 2 because there are 2 values in the set.

$$75 + 71 = 146 \qquad 146 \div 2 = 73$$

The median of {75, 71, 85, 67, 63, 88} is 73.

Exercise A Use the data in the following table to answer each question.

Attendance		
	7 P.M.	9:30 P.M.
Movie 1	106	91
Movie 2	85	98
Movie 3	172	180
Movie 4	141	119
Movie 5	52	95

1. Find the median of the data for the movies shown at 7 P.M.

2. Find the median of the data for the movies shown at 9:30 P.M.

3. Find the median of the data for both times together.

PROBLEM SOLVING

Exercise B Find the median for each set of data given.

4. Six U.S. cities that have high annual average amounts of snow are Juneau, Alaska, with 101.3 inches; Portland, Maine, with 70.6 inches; Sault Sainte Marie, Michigan, with 115.5 inches; Duluth, Minnesota, with 78.2 inches; Buffalo, New York, with 91.0 inches; and Burlington, Vermont, with 77.5 inches. What is the median amount of annual snowfall?

5. The heights of several active volcanoes in Africa are 13,354 feet; 1,650 feet; 5,981 feet; 8,000 feet; 3,011 feet; 10,028 feet; 11,400 feet; and 9,469 feet. What is the median height?

Estimation Activity

Estimate: Determine the median from an odd set of ordered data:

30, 9, 7, 39, 4, 31, 21, 18, 9

Solution: Order the values, then strike out the left and right most numbers. Repeat.

4, 7, 9, 9, (18) 21, 30, 31, 39

18 is not an estimate but the actual, correct median. The process, however, is easy and mechanical.

Mode

The value or values that occur most often in a set of data

Measures of central tendency

The mean, median, and mode of a set of data

The **mode** of a set of data is the value or values that occur most often. The mean, the median, and the mode of a set of data are **measures of central tendency.**

To compute the mode of a set of data, count the number of times each value appears. The value or values that appear most often are the mode.

EXAMPLE 1   Find the mode or modes of the set of data
$$\{1\tfrac{1}{2}, 2\tfrac{1}{8}, 1\tfrac{1}{4}, 3\tfrac{3}{4}, 1\tfrac{1}{2}, 2\tfrac{5}{8}\}.$$

Step 1   Order the data from least to greatest or greatest to least value.
$$1\tfrac{1}{4} \quad 1\tfrac{1}{2} \quad 1\tfrac{1}{2} \quad 2\tfrac{1}{8} \quad 2\tfrac{5}{8} \quad 3\tfrac{3}{4}$$

Step 2   Find the value or values that occur most often.

The value $1\tfrac{1}{2}$ occurs two times. All other values occur only once. Since $1\tfrac{1}{2}$ occurs more often than any other value, $1\tfrac{1}{2}$ is the mode of
$$\{1\tfrac{1}{2}, 2\tfrac{1}{8}, 1\tfrac{1}{4}, 3\tfrac{3}{4}, 1\tfrac{1}{2}, 2\tfrac{5}{8}\}.$$

If two or more values appear the same number of times, the set of data has two or more modes.

EXAMPLE 2   Find the mode or modes of the set of data
$$\{70, 75, 71, 72, 82, 94, 71, 98, 85, 94\}.$$

Step 1   Order the data from least to greatest or greatest to least value.

98   94   94   85   82   75   72   71   71   70

Step 2   Find the value or values that occur most often. The values 94 and 71 occur twice each. All other values occur once. The set of data has two modes: 71 and 94.

If each value in a set of data occurs the same number of times, the set of data has no mode.

EXAMPLE 3 Find the mode of the set of data
{$32.40, $100.00, $67.95, $8.50, $599.99}.

Step 1 Order the data from least to greatest or greatest to least value.

$8.50 $32.40 $67.95 $100.00 $599.99

Step 2 Find the value or values that occur most often. Since each value in the set of data occurs the same number of times (1), the set of data has no mode.

Exercise A Look at each set of data. Identify the number of modes each set has.

1. Magnitudes of Largest Earthquakes	
Kuril Islands	8.0
Jordan	7.2
Sumatra Island, Indonesia	7.0
Mexico	7.2
Papua New Guinea	7.8
Chile	7.8
Myanmar	7.2
Kermadec Islands, New Zealand	7.1

2. Road Mileage from Chicago	
Atlanta	674 miles
Boston	963 miles
Dallas	917 miles
Denver	996 miles
Detroit	266 miles
Los Angeles	2,054 miles
New York	802 miles
San Francisco	2,142 miles
Washington, DC	671 miles

3. Record-High Temperatures in Selected States	
Alaska	100°F
Arizona	128°F
Florida	109°F
Hawaii	100°F
Kansas	121°F
Maryland	109°F
Nevada	125°F
Oregon	119°F

Exercise B Determine the mode or modes for each set of data.

4. Number of stories in tallest buildings in Toronto, Ontario:
    49, 36, 31, 30, 32, 28, 29, 27, 29, 28.

5. Number of stories in tallest buildings in Memphis, Tennessee: 37, 31, 32, 31.

6. Number of stories in tallest buildings in Newark, New Jersey:
    36, 37, 26, 24, 26, 26, 31, 38.

7. Number of stories in tallest buildings in Fort Worth, Texas: 38, 40, 40, 33, 35, 30.

8. Number of stories in tallest buildings in Montreal, Quebec: 34, 30, 30, 30.

9. Number of stories in tallest buildings in San Diego, California:
    34, 34, 39, 30, 41, 23, 27, 27, 27, 24, 25.

10. Number of stories in tallest buildings in Phoenix, Arizona:
    40, 31, 20, 20, 26, 28, 26.

Range

The difference between the greatest and least values in a set of data

The mean, median, and mode of a set of data are measures of central tendency. The **range** of a set of data is the difference between the greatest and least values. To compute the range, subtract the least value from the greatest value.

EXAMPLE 1   Find the range of the set of data
{181, 370, 199, 267}.

Step 1   Identify the greatest and least values in the set of data.

370   →   greatest value

181   →   least value

Step 2   Subtract the least value from the greatest value.

370   →   greatest value

− 181   →   least value

189

The range of {181, 370, 199, 267} is 189.

Often, you will be given only the least and greatest values of a set of data. Then you do not have to locate these values in the set. You just subtract the least value from the greatest value to determine the range.

EXAMPLE 2   Find the range of the areas of the 50 states in the United States.

Rhode Island, the smallest state, has an area of 1,045 square miles. Alaska, the largest state, has an area of 570,374 square miles.

570,374   →   greatest value

− 1,045   →   least value

569,329

The range of the areas of the 50 states is 569,329 square miles.

Exercise A Solve each problem.

1. On three math quizzes, Jeremy scored 82, 88, and 99 points. What is the range of his quiz scores?

2. At 20,320 feet, Mount McKinley is the tallest of the 78 highest mountain peaks in North America. At 14,072 feet, Mount Augusta is the shortest of the 78 peaks. What is the range of the tallest and shortest peaks?

3. The average daily circulation for specific newspapers follows. Find the range in the papers' circulation.

Austin Tribune	113,031
Long Island Post	684,366
Oakland News	105,624
Orlando Times	1,763,140
Toronto Post	793,660

4. Jenessa bought seven items at the store. Their prices were $3.98, $0.49, $12.99, $6.18, $1.35, $4.32, $0.85. What is the range of the prices?

5. Lake Ontario, the smallest Great Lake, has an area of 34,850 square miles. Lake Superior, the largest Great Lake, has an area of 81,000 square miles. What is the range of the areas of the Great Lakes?

6. The Olympic gold medal winners in the men's downhill skiing event completed the course in these times: 1 min 45.50 sec, 1 min 45.59 sec, 1 min 59.63 sec, 1 min 50.37 sec, and 1 min 45.75 sec. What is the range of times?

7. The Olympic gold medal winners in the women's 10-kilometer race had these finishing times: 30 min 31.54 sec, 31 min 44.2 sec, 30 min 08.3 sec, 25 min 53.7 sec, and 27 min 30.1 sec. What is the range of times?

8. A general in the military with 26 years of service receives $9,845.40 a month. A general with 2 years of service receives $7,397.10 a month. What is the range of pay?

9. Ten years ago, Americans spent $3,761.2 billion for personal expenses. Five years ago, Americans spent $4,924.9 billion. What is the range in expenses?

10. The more than 600 stone statues on Easter Island have heights from 3.4 meters to 12 meters. What is the range in the statues' heights?

Box-and-whiskers plot

A way to show the spread of data in a set of numbers

Lower extreme

The least value of a set of data

Upper extreme

The greatest value of a set of data

Lower quartile

The median of scores below the median

Upper quartile

The median of scores above the median

A **box-and-whiskers plot** is a visual way to describe the concentration and the spread of data in a set. A box-and-whiskers plot contains a box and two whiskers, and looks like this:

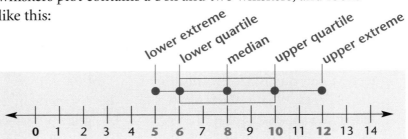

In this example, 5 is the **lower extreme,** 8 is the median, 12 is the **upper extreme,** 6 is the **lower quartile,** and 10 is the **upper quartile.**

EXAMPLE 1 Suppose you were asked to construct a box-and-whiskers plot for the data set below. The data represent the number of years different students have gone to school together.

{12, 5, 8, 16, 15, 9, 19}

Step 1 Arrange the data in order from least to greatest.

5 8 9 12 15 16 19

Step 2 Identify the greatest and least values of the data. These values are called the upper and lower extremes.

5 8 9 12 15 16 19
↑   ↑
lower extreme   upper extreme

Step 3 Find the median of the data.

5 8 9 12 15 16 19
↑
median

Step 4 Find the median of all of the scores below the median. This median is called the lower quartile. Then find the median of all of the scores above the median. This median is called the upper quartile.

5 8 9 12 15 16 19
  ↑   ↑
lower quartile   upper quartile

EXAMPLE 1 (continued)

Step 5 Draw a number line that can display all of the data in the set.

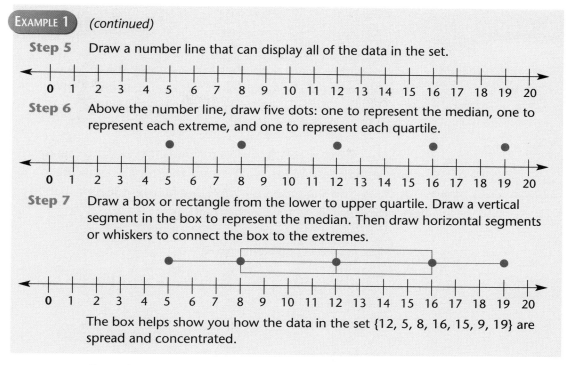

Step 6 Above the number line, draw five dots: one to represent the median, one to represent each extreme, and one to represent each quartile.

Step 7 Draw a box or rectangle from the lower to upper quartile. Draw a vertical segment in the box to represent the median. Then draw horizontal segments or whiskers to connect the box to the extremes.

The box helps show you how the data in the set {12, 5, 8, 16, 15, 9, 19} are spread and concentrated.

Exercise A Use the data set {12, 8, 17, 10, 2, 13, 9, 20, 11, 4, 14}.

1. Arrange the data in order from least to greatest.

2. Identify the greatest value of the data. Label your answer *upper extreme*.

3. Identify the least value of the data. Label your answer *lower extreme*.

4. Find the median of the data. Label your answer *median*.

5. Find the median of all of the scores above the median. Label your answer *upper quartile*.

6. Find the median of all of the scores below the median. Label your answer *lower quartile*.

7. Draw a number line that can display all of the data in the set.

8. Above the number line, draw five dots: one to represent the median, one to represent each extreme, and one to represent each quartile.

9. Draw a box or rectangle from the lower to upper quartile. Draw a vertical segment in the box to represent the median. Then draw horizontal segments or whiskers to connect the box to the extremes.

Exercise B Answer the question.

10. Suppose a set of data was displayed in a box-and-whiskers plot. How could you use the plot to compute the range of the data?

Probability

The chance or likelihood of an event occurring

Outcome

A result of a probability experiment

Perhaps you've heard a weather forecaster say something like "Tomorrow there is a 40% chance of precipitation." A 40% chance of precipitation is an example of **probability**—the chance or likelihood that something will occur.

Probability experiments always include an event and one or more **outcomes.** A word that means the same as *outcome* is *result.* To find the probability *(P)* that an event in a probability experiment will occur, use the fraction

$$P = \frac{\text{number of favorable outcomes}}{\text{number of possible outcomes}}$$

EXAMPLE 1 Suppose a coin is tossed once. What is the probability that the coin will land with the tails side facing up?

Step 1 Use the probability fraction.

$$P = \frac{\text{number of favorable outcomes}}{\text{number of possible outcomes}}$$

Step 2 Find the denominator. Since there are two possible outcomes when the coin is tossed—the coin will either land heads up or tails up—the denominator is two.

$$P = \frac{\text{number of favorable outcomes}}{2}$$

Step 3 Find the numerator. Since one outcome is favorable—the coin landing tails up—the numerator is one.

$$P = \frac{1}{2}$$

The probability of tossing a coin and having it land tails up is $\frac{1}{2}$.

If you choose to express the probability as a percent, the probability would be 50%, because

$\frac{1}{2} = 0.5 = 50\%$.

Algebra in Your Life

Predicting the Weather
Temperature, wind, and air pressure all determine the kind of weather we'll see the next day. Radar, computers, and the forecasters' experience go into forecasting tomorrow's weather. But the weather forecast isn't always accurate. Forecasting the weather uses probability, so it is not always accurate.

EXAMPLE 2 The faces of the number cube at the right are labeled 1, 2, 3, 4, 5, and 6. Suppose the cube is rolled once. What is the probability of rolling an odd number?

Step 1 Use the probability fraction.

$$P = \frac{\text{number of favorable outcomes}}{\text{number of possible outcomes}}$$

Step 2 Find the denominator. Since there are six possible outcomes when the cube is rolled—1, 2, 3, 4, 5, and 6—the denominator is six.

$$P = \frac{\text{number of favorable outcomes}}{6}$$

Step 3 Find the numerator. Since three outcomes are favorable—1, 3, and 5—the numerator is three.

$$P = \frac{3}{6}$$

Step 4 Simplify if possible.

$$P = \frac{3}{6} = \frac{1}{2}$$

The probability (P) of rolling a 1–6 number cube and rolling an odd number is $\frac{1}{2}$ or 50%.

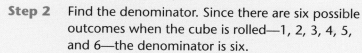

Exercise A Answer each question.

1. What is the probability of tossing a coin and getting an outcome of heads? Express your answer as a fraction in simplest form and as a percent.

2. What is the probability of rolling a 1–6 number cube and getting an outcome of an even number? Express your answer as a fraction in simplest form.

3. An example of a prime number is the number 3. A prime number has exactly two factors—the number itself and 1. (The factors of 3 are 3 and 1.) What is the probability of tossing a 1–6 number cube and getting an outcome of a prime number?

Exercise B In a probability experiment, a painted cube is rolled once. One side of the cube is painted green, two sides are painted blue, and three sides are painted orange. Express the probability of each outcome as a fraction in simplest form.

4. P (orange)

5. P (blue)

TRY THIS Integers can be described by the set {..., −3, −2, −1, 0, 1, 2, 3, ...}. The probability of any outcome can never be less than what integer? The probability of any outcome can never be greater than what integer?

Fundamental principle of counting

A general rule that states if one task can be completed a different ways, and a second task can be completed b different ways, the first task followed by the second task can be completed a • b or ab different ways

There are infinite numbers of arrangements in the world. One example of an arrangement is found in a dictionary. The words in a dictionary are arranged, or ordered, from *A* to *Z*. Another example of an arrangement is found in a library. Books in a library are arranged in a certain order.

Arrangement problems can be solved different ways.

EXAMPLE 1 Suppose a classroom contains three desks, all in a row. Three students—Angela, Barry, and Caitlin— enter the classroom. How many different ways can Angela, Barry, and Caitlin sit at the desks?

One way to solve the problem is to draw a diagram.

Step 1 Show all of the possible arrangements with Angela sitting at the first desk.

Angela	Barry	Caitlin
Angela	Caitlin	Barry

Step 2 Show all of the possible arrangements with Barry sitting at the first desk.

Barry	Caitlin	Angela
Barry	Angela	Caitlin

Step 3 Show all of the possible arrangements with Caitlin sitting at the first desk.

Caitlin	Angela	Barry
Caitlin	Barry	Angela

Angela, Barry, and Caitlin can sit at three desks six different ways. There are two ways with Angela first, two ways with Barry first, and two ways with Caitlin first.

The fundamental principle of counting is also called the *basic counting principle.*

Another way to solve the problem is to use the **fundamental principle of counting.** The fundamental principle of counting is a general rule that states if one task can be completed *a* different ways, and a second task can be completed *b* different ways, the first task followed by the second task can be completed *a* • *b* or *ab* different ways.

EXAMPLE 2 Again consider the original problem: suppose a classroom contains three desks in a row. Three students—Angela, Barry, and Caitlin—enter the classroom. How many different ways can Angela, Barry, and Caitlin sit at the desks?

Use the fundamental principle of counting.

Any of the 3 students can sit at the first desk.

Once a student is sitting at the first desk, either of the remaining 2 students can sit at the second desk.

Once a student is sitting at the first desk and a student is sitting at the second desk, only 1 student remains, and that student must sit at the last desk.

Three students can arrange themselves 3 • 2 • 1 or 6 different ways.

These examples show you that the problem can be solved by drawing a diagram or by using the fundamental principle of counting. If used correctly, either method will produce the correct answer. However, you may find that as arrangement problems becoming lengthier, using the fundamental principle of counting requires much less time than drawing a diagram.

Exercise A Use the fundamental principle of counting to answer these questions.

1. Choose any two digits. How many different ways can those digits be arranged?

2. Choose any three letters of the alphabet. How many different ways can those letters be arranged?

3. Suppose you had to complete four chores, and you could complete the chores in any order. In how many different ways could you complete the chores?

Exercise B Use a calculator to find each product.

4. 100 • 99 • 98

5. 15 • 14 • 13 • 12 • 11 • 10

Making a Budget A budget is a plan. Many individuals and families budget their income and their expenses each month.

> **EXAMPLE 1** Each month, the Smith family budgets 15% of their income for food. If the family earns $2,800 each month, how much money is budgeted for food?
>
> To find 15% of $2,800, change 15% to a decimal and multiply.
>
> $$0.15 \cdot \$2,800 = \$420$$
>
> Each month, the Smith family budgets $420 for food.

Exercise Use the circle graph.

1. Find the amount of money budgeted for each portion of the graph.

2. Which expenses consume $\frac{1}{2}$ of the monthly income?

3. Suppose you earned $200 each month. How would you budget your earnings?

Monthly Budget—Monthly Income $3,000

Mortgage/Rent 28%
Car Payment 8%
Clothing 3%
Utilities 7%
Taxes 7%
Food 18%
Recreation 6%
Insurance 5%
Savings 4%
Miscellaneous Expenses 14%

Chapter 12 REVIEW

Write the letter of the correct answer.
Use the table to answer questions 1 through 4.

1. What is the range of the data?

7	2	6
4	1	0
5	7	8
3	9	5

   A 8   **C** 12

   B 9   **D** 4

2. What is the mean of the data?

   A 9   **C** 5

   B 7.45   **D** 4.75

3. What is the median of the data?

   A 7   **C** 4.75

   B 9   **D** 5

4. What is the mode (or modes) of the data?

   A 5 and 7   **C** 7 and 2

   B 3   **D** 9

Use the box and whiskers plot to answer questions 5 through 7.

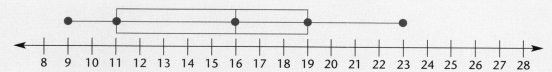

5. Which value represents the median?

   A 16   **C** 9

   B 23   **D** 15.25

6. Which values represent the extremes?

   A 11 and 19   **C** 9 and 23

   B 11 and 23   **D** 9 and 11

7. Which values represent the quartiles?

   A 9 and 23   **C** 16 and 23

   B 11 and 19   **D** 9 and 19

Create a bar graph that organizes and displays the data shown in the table below.

Example: Draw a bar graph that organizes and displays the data shown in this table.

Class Attendance Last Week	
Monday	18 students
Tuesday	20 students
Wednesday	19 students
Thursday	15 students
Friday	17 students

Solution:

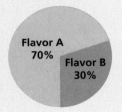

8.

How Do I Spend My Time?	
Sleeping	9 hours
Eating	1 hour
Working/Doing Chores	1 hour
Recreation/Exercise	3 hours
Studying	2 hours
School	8 hours

Create a circle graph that organizes and displays the data shown in the table below.

Example: How many degrees of the circle graph are represented by Flavor A?

Solution: 0.70 • 360° = 252°

Which Flavor?

Flavor A 70%

Flavor B 30%

9.

Taste Test—Which Flavors Is Your Favorite?	
Flavor A	12 votes
Flavor B	3 votes
Flavor C	5 votes

Use the following frequency table.

Example: How many packages weighing less than 10 pounds were shipped?
Solution: 15

Shipping Weights of Packages

Weight in Pounds	Tally	Frequency
> 0 but < 10	卌 卌 卌	15
> 10 but < 20	卌 IIII	9
> 20 but < 30	卌 卌 I	11
> 30 but < 40	III	3
> 40 but < 50	I	1

10. How many packages were shipped?

11. What was the weight of the heaviest package? Explain.

12. What was the weight of the lightest package? Explain.

Find the probability. Express your answer as a fraction in simplest form and as a percent rounded to the nearest whole number.

Example: Suppose a coin is tossed once. What is the probability that the coin will land heads up?

Solution: $P = \frac{\text{number of favorable outcomes}}{\text{number of possible outcomes}} = \frac{1}{2} = 0.50 = 50\%$

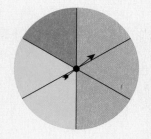

13. Suppose the spinner is spun once. Find the probability of the spinner landing on orange.

14. Suppose the spinner is spun once. Find the probability of the spinner landing on red.

Use the fundamental principle of counting to solve the problem.

Example: How many different ways can three people stand in a straight line?

Solution: Three people can stand in a straight line 3 • 2 • 1 or 6 different ways.

15. Evelyn has a first name, 2 middle names, and a last name. In how many different ways could Evelyn arrange the initials of her name?

Test-Taking Tip

It is a good idea to double-check the location of numbers or other data that you identify in a table or chart.

Chapter 1   Supplementary Problems

Find each sum.

1. 3,289 + 6,573

2. 324,905 + 8,713

3. 984 + 321

4. 5,075 + 837

5. 64,829 + 92,081

6. 573 + 43,807

Find each difference.

7. 12,306 − 8,729

8. 5,537 − 723

9. 625 − 98

10. 329,610 − 32,106

11. 485,287 − 251,876

12. 3,082 − 93

Find each product.

13. 589 × 251

14. 41 × 57

15. 67 × 32

16. 24 × 9

17. 630 × 8

18. 49 × 34

Find each quotient. Remember to write any remainder as part of the quotient.

19. 5,544 ÷ 66

20. 576 ÷ 24

21. 166 ÷ 40

22. 23,137 ÷ 32

23. 10,908 ÷ 8

24. 756 ÷ 36

Estimate each answer.

25. 82,573 + 15,987

26. 614 × 321

27. 5,920 + 5,231

28. 192,309 − 47,367

29. 73,582 ÷ 67

30. 25,308 ÷ 39

Tell whether each statement is *true, false,* or *open.*

31. $24 - n = 15$ **33.** $826n = 24{,}078$ **35.** $64 \div 8 = n$

32. $11 \times 11 = 111$ **34.** $12 + 3 = 36$ **36.** $634 \times 7 = 4{,}438$

Classify each expression as *numerical* or *algebraic.* Then name the operation(s) and identify any variables.

37. $816 \div 15$ **40.** $w \div 33$

38. $15x$ **41.** $4 + 3 \times 9$

39. $3y - 14$ **42.** $5a + 6$

Evaluate each expression.

43. $16 + n$ when $n = 14$. **45.** $49 - z$ when $z = 13$.

44. $125 \div c$ when $c = 5$. **46.** $16 - 3n$ when $n = 3$.

Write *true* or *false.*

47. $3m = 42$ when $m = 15$. **49.** $y \div 42 = 6$ when $y = 252$.

48. $24 - e = 9$ when $e = 15$. **50.** $31 + n = 49$ when $n = 80$.

Identify place or value.

1. the place of 6 in the decimal 135.0861

2. the value of 3 in the decimal 8,346.05

3. the place of 4 in 267.0914

4. the value of 9 in 89.43

Add or subtract.

5. $0.978 + 6.84$

6. $4.7301 - 2.73$

7. $8 - 0.318$

8. $\$80 - \$29.98$

9. $35.45 + 1.035$

10. $6.4 + 5.31 + 0.675$

Multiply. Round to the nearest thousandth when necessary.

11. 200×8.183

12. 0.497×3.25

13. $\$16.88 \times 3.75$

14. 84.51×6.2

15. 4.135×6.512

16. 6.57×10^3

Divide. If necessary, round to the nearest thousandth.

17. $32.6 \div 100$

18. $651 \div 9.3$

19. $32.9 \div 0.4$

20. $94.58 \div 3.6$

21. $57.81 \div 10^2$

22. $64.4 \div 10^3$

Write each decimal as a fraction. Simplify your answer.

23. 0.750

25. 0.375

24. 0.500

26. 0.120

Write each fraction as a decimal. Round to the nearest hundredth if necessary.

27. $\frac{3}{11}$

29. $\frac{27}{100}$

28. $\frac{15}{16}$

30. $\frac{7}{9}$

Find the interest earned. Use the formula $I = prt$.

31. What is the interest earned on $32,000 at $6\frac{1}{2}$% for 5 years?

32. What is the interest earned on $2,500 at 5.3% for 4 years?

Evaluate each expression. Round to the nearest hundredth if necessary.

33. $y + 3.14$ when $y = 12.84$

34. $2l + 2w$ when $l = 4.6$ and $w = 6.25$

35. $4.5c - 6.9b$ when $c = 4.6$ and $b = 2.4$

36. $x \div 3.2$ when $x = 45.73$

Write *true* or *false*.

37. Is $4.2s = 25.2$ a *true* or *false* statement when $s = 6$?

38. Is $403.2 \div s = 4.2$ a *true* or *false* statement when $s = 9.6$?

39. Is $21.7 + s = 38.1$ a *true* or *false* statement when $s = 16.4$?

40. Is $s + 0.375 = 0.380$ a *true* or *false* statement when $s = 5$?

Evaluate each statement. Write *true* or *false.*

1. 6|32

2. 7|84

3. 10|3,560

4. 3|265

5. 4|76

6. 2|843

7. 8|448

8. 9|4,509

Is each number divisible by 2? by 3? by 4? by 5? by 6? by 8? by 9? by 10?

9. 84

10. 430

11. 3,120

12. 32,022

Decide whether each number is *prime* or *composite.*

13. 123

14. 196

15. 101

16. 187

Find the greatest common divisor.

17. (21, 28)

18. (6, 16)

19. (3y, 42)

20. (8, 64a)

Use the distributive property to find the product of each expression.

21. 5(6 + 4)

22. 7(3 + 4)

23. 6(b + 9)

24. 21(5 + 3x)

25. 4(c + 15 + 5a)

26. 17(8 + d + 6p)

Find the greatest common divisor.

27. 12c + 24

28. 15 + 25y

29. 9xc + 18x

30. 6j + 18k

31. 12z + 20h

32. 13y + 21t

Factor each expression.

33. $3y + 21$

34. $25x + 35$

35. $10c + 5$

36. $6u + 4$

37. $24s + 28m$

38. $12q + 18n$

39. $7z + 14b$

40. $6j + 15k$

Find the LCM.

41. LCM $(5, 30)$

42. LCM $(16, 24)$

43. LCM $(9, 30)$

44. LCM $(15, 50)$

45. LCM $(64, 16)$

46. LCM $(12, 20)$

Use a calculator and find the value of each expression.

47. $6 \cdot 8^3$

48. $3^3 \cdot 4^6$

49. $8 \cdot 13 \cdot 23^3$

50. $5^2 \cdot 3^4 \cdot 2^5$

Write in scientific notation.

51. 35,210,000,000

52. 4,500,000

53. 0.0000375

54. 0.000000089

55. 49.7

Express each improper fraction as a mixed number and express each mixed number as an improper fraction.

1. $2\frac{2}{3}$

2. $\frac{11}{3}$

3. $\frac{32}{5}$

4. $1\frac{7}{8}$

5. $\frac{15}{7}$

6. $6\frac{5}{9}$

7. $3\frac{3}{4}$

8. $\frac{21}{4}$

Write two equivalent fractions for each fraction.

9. $\frac{7}{8}$

10. $\frac{3}{5}$

11. $\frac{1}{8}$

12. $\frac{5}{14}$

13. $\frac{9}{15}$

14. $\frac{11}{12}$

15. $\frac{1}{50}$

16. $\frac{1}{10}$

Express each fraction in simplest form.

17. $\frac{10}{25}$

18. $\frac{4}{30}$

19. $\frac{6}{42}$

20. $\frac{15}{45}$

21. $\frac{3}{27}$

22. $\frac{18}{24}$

23. $\frac{8}{18}$

24. $\frac{21}{30}$

Order from least to greatest.

25. $\dfrac{1}{2}$ $\dfrac{1}{5}$ $\dfrac{3}{10}$

26. $\dfrac{5}{12}$ $\dfrac{2}{3}$ $\dfrac{1}{4}$

27. $\dfrac{2}{9}$ $\dfrac{5}{6}$ $\dfrac{5}{18}$

28. $\dfrac{19}{21}$ $\dfrac{3}{7}$ $\dfrac{2}{3}$

Add, subtract, multiply, or divide. Simplify your answer if possible.

29. $\dfrac{3}{10} + \dfrac{4}{5}$

30. $\dfrac{2}{3} - \dfrac{1}{2}$

31. $4\dfrac{1}{2} \cdot 3\dfrac{3}{4}y$

32. $1\dfrac{3}{24} - \dfrac{11}{12}$

33. $\dfrac{5}{6} \div \dfrac{7}{8}$

34. $3\dfrac{3}{16} + 5\dfrac{3}{4}$

35. $\dfrac{4}{7} \cdot \dfrac{4}{7}$

36. $2\dfrac{5}{8} - 1\dfrac{3}{24}$

37. $9\dfrac{1}{3}g + 6\dfrac{2}{5}g$

38. $2\dfrac{6}{7} \cdot 2\dfrac{4}{5}$

39. $4\dfrac{7}{8} \div \dfrac{5}{8}$

40. $5\dfrac{1}{2} - 3\dfrac{3}{16}$

41. $\dfrac{4}{7} \div \dfrac{1}{2}$

42. $3\dfrac{1}{8} + 2\dfrac{15}{16}$

43. $3\dfrac{3}{5} \div 2\dfrac{1}{4}$

44. $1\dfrac{7}{12} \div 1\dfrac{1}{3}$

45. $6\dfrac{5}{12}m \cdot 1\dfrac{1}{3}$

46. $5\dfrac{1}{3}n + 5\dfrac{5}{6}n$

47. $2\dfrac{1}{4} \cdot 6\dfrac{2}{3}$

48. $3\dfrac{6}{7} \div 4\dfrac{1}{2}$

49. $1\dfrac{8}{9} \cdot 3\dfrac{3}{5}$

50. $4\dfrac{1}{4} - 2\dfrac{15}{16}$

Simplify each expression by following the order of operations.

1. $6 + 3 \cdot 8$

2. $12 \div 3 \cdot (3 + 4)$

3. $28 - 20 \div 5$

4. $12(10 - 9) + 3 \cdot 5$

5. $6 \cdot 7 \div 3 + 4$

6. $(5 + 7) \div 4 + 3 \cdot 2$

7. $11 + 3(10 - 7)$

8. $5 + 4 - 3 \cdot 6 \div 2$

Evaluate each expression from $n = 6$.

9. $n + 6$

10. $n - 3$

11. $50 - 3n$

12. $8n + 5$

13. $\frac{n}{11} + 21$

14. $\frac{n}{3} - 2$

15. $6n - 30$

16. $1 + \frac{1}{n}$

17. $\frac{2n}{3} + \frac{3}{2n}$

18. $5n - 3n$

Tell whether each equation is *true* or *false* when the given number is substituted for x.

19. $5(7) - x = 30$ when $x = 5$

20. $x + 4(x) = 40$ when $x = 10$

21. $26 + x = 20$ when $x = 6$

22. $30 - 3x = 9$ when $x = 7$

23. $15 + 4x = 23$ when $x = 2$

24. $3x \cdot 4 = 16$ when $x = 4$

25. $6 + 8x = 62$ when $x = 7$

Solve for x. Write your answer in simplest form.

26. $x + 18 = 23$

27. $32 - x = 18$

28. $\frac{2}{3}x + \frac{2}{3} = 5\frac{2}{3}$

29. $\frac{6}{7} + 3x = 12\frac{6}{7}$

30. $3\frac{3}{4} - x = 2\frac{1}{8}$

31. $\frac{1}{2}x - \frac{1}{2} = 5$

32. $\frac{7}{8} + \frac{3}{8}x = 6\frac{7}{8}$

Simplify each complex fraction.

33. $\dfrac{\frac{2}{3}}{\frac{1}{3}}$

35. $\dfrac{\frac{3}{4}}{2}$

37. $\dfrac{\frac{1}{4}}{\frac{1}{16}}$

39. $\dfrac{10}{\frac{2}{3}}$

34. $\dfrac{\frac{4}{5}}{\frac{4}{7}}$

36. $\dfrac{6}{\frac{7}{8}}$

38. $\dfrac{\frac{2}{3}}{6}$

40. $\dfrac{\frac{15}{16}}{4}$

Simplify. Write your answers in simplest form.

41. $\dfrac{2}{7b} + \dfrac{1}{7b}$

45. $\dfrac{13}{16a} - \dfrac{1}{2a}$

42. $\dfrac{19}{20x} - \dfrac{1}{4x}$

46. $\dfrac{7}{8j} + \dfrac{3}{8j} + \dfrac{5}{8j}$

43. $\dfrac{7}{24g} + \dfrac{3}{8g}$

47. $\dfrac{8}{9y} - \dfrac{1}{9y} + \dfrac{2}{9y}$

44. $\dfrac{9}{10t} - \dfrac{3}{4t}$

48. $\dfrac{3}{4c} - \dfrac{2}{3c} + \dfrac{1}{6c}$

Multiply. Write your answer in simplest form.

49. $\dfrac{3}{5} \cdot \dfrac{5}{6z}$

53. $\dfrac{2}{7h} \cdot \dfrac{21}{24}$

50. $\dfrac{3}{8e} \cdot \dfrac{8}{15}$

54. $\dfrac{3}{5m} \cdot \dfrac{8}{9}$

51. $\dfrac{24}{25} \cdot \dfrac{5p}{8}$

55. $\dfrac{5}{12} \cdot \dfrac{7}{15f}$

52. $\dfrac{15}{16k} \cdot \dfrac{8}{9}$

Express each ratio as a fraction in simplest form.

1. 50 to 2

2. 18:24

3. $\frac{60}{22}$

4. 52:12

5. 8 to 64

6. $\frac{6}{42}$

7. 108:9

8. $\frac{15}{35}$

Is each proportion a true proportion? Write *yes* or *no*.

9. $\frac{3}{4} = \frac{15}{20}$

10. $\frac{5}{9} = \frac{30}{72}$

11. $\frac{15}{35} = \frac{3}{5}$

12. $\frac{5}{16} = \frac{30}{96}$

Solve for the variable in each proportion.

13. $\frac{v}{8} = \frac{9}{24}$

14. $\frac{5}{6} = \frac{35}{n}$

15. $\frac{1}{x} = \frac{16}{48}$

16. $\frac{c}{7} = \frac{42}{49}$

17. $\frac{6}{8} = \frac{3}{n}$

18. $\frac{10}{d} = \frac{50}{30}$

19. $\frac{28}{16} = \frac{s}{4}$

20. $\frac{9}{t} = \frac{72}{80}$

Express each decimal as a percent.

21. 0.53

22. 0.1

23. 0.91

24. 0.42

25. 0.16

26. 0.7

27. 0.84

28. 0.32

29. 0.27

30. 0.66

Express each fraction as a percent.

31. $\frac{3}{10}$ **34.** $\frac{15}{16}$ **37.** $\frac{6}{25}$ **40.** $\frac{67}{100}$

32. $\frac{4}{5}$ **35.** $\frac{3}{4}$ **38.** $\frac{13}{20}$

33. $\frac{3}{8}$ **36.** $\frac{7}{10}$ **39.** $\frac{39}{50}$

Write each percent as a decimal.

41. 25%   **44.** 8%   **47.** 9%   **50.** 79%

42. 32%   **45.** 55%   **48.** 43%

43. 16%   **46.** 81%   **49.** 63%

Solve each problem.

51. Jenny bought a calculator that originally cost $80 for $52. What was her percent of savings on the calculator purchase?

52. Eric is buying two round-trip boat tickets to Alaska for $3,150. The tax on the tickets is 12%. How much is the total cost of the tickets with tax?

53. Amy deposits $2,300 in a certificate of deposit that pays 8.5% interest compounded annually. How much money will she have in the account after 4 years? Remember, the compound interest formula is $A = P(1 + i)^n$.

54. Steve works part-time at the local video store. On Thursday, he rented out 200 videos. On Friday, he rented out 354 videos. What was the percent of increase in the number of videos he rented out on Friday?

55. Jose works as a reporter for a large newspaper. Last year he worked 240 days out of 250 work days. What percent of the year did he work?

Chapter 7   Supplementary Problems

Find the absolute value or distance from zero.

1. $|6|$

3. $|25|$

5. $|-93|$

2. $|-40|$

4. $|-3|$

Name the opposite of each integer.

6. 15

8. -9

10. -32

7. 21

9. 5

Compare each pair. Use $<$, $>$, or $=$.

11. 6 ■ -6

13. 5 ■ -10

15. -3 ■ $|5|$

12. -2 ■ 0

14. 15 ■ $|-15|$

Find each sum.

16. $8 + 5$

21. $-8 + (-6)$

17. $3 + 7$

22. $-9 + 5$

18. $7 + (-3)$

23. $-3 + (-1)$

19. $-5 + (-4)$

24. $2 + (-7)$

20. $-3 + 3$

25. $-4 + (-4)$

Find each difference.

26. $-4 - (-10)$ **29.** $15 - (-5)$ **32.** $-5 - (-6)$ **35.** $9 - (+4)$

27. $6 - (+3)$ **30.** $-8 - (-6)$ **33.** $-4 - (-8)$

28. $-7 - (-6)$ **31.** $2 - (-3)$ **34.** $-9 - (-7)$

Find each product or quotient.

36. $(4)(6)$ **41.** $(6)(9)$ **46.** $42 \div 7$ **51.** $72 \div 9$

37. $(6)(-3)$ **42.** $(2)(-12)$ **47.** $10 \div (-5)$ **52.** $64 \div (-8)$

38. $(-5)(4)$ **43.** $(-7)(-5)$ **48.** $-48 \div 12$ **53.** $-24 \div -4$

39. $(-7)(-7)$ **44.** $(-4)(8)$ **49.** $-7 \div -7$ **54.** $50 \div (-5)$

40. $(-12)(-4)$ **45.** $(-5)(9)$ **50.** $-150 \div (-50)$ **55.** $-32 \div (-8)$

Solve each problem.

56. Anita can scuba dive 15 feet in a minute. At what depth will she be in 6 minutes?

57. What is the difference between the top of a building, which is 453 feet above ground, and the basement, which is 24 feet below ground?

58. The temperature Wednesday was $-10°F$. Thursday's temperature was $2°F$. How much did the temperature increase?

59. For the first three holes in golf, John scored one point over par $(+1)$, three points under par (-3), and one point under par (-1). What was his score for the first three holes?

60. The top long jump in Phil's gym class was 107 inches. Phil jumped 98 inches. How far was he from the top long jump?

Rewrite each of the following using exponents.

1. $5 \cdot 5 \cdot 5 \cdot 5 \cdot 5$

2. $8 \cdot 8 \cdot 8$

3. $3 \cdot 3 \cdot 3 \cdot 3 \cdot 3$

4. $(-6) \cdot (-6)$

5. $(-8) \cdot (-8) \cdot (-8)$

6. $(-t) \cdot (-t) \cdot (-t) \cdot (-t)$

7. $y \cdot y$

8. $c \cdot c \cdot c \cdot c$

9. $e \cdot e$

10. $(-n) \cdot (-n) \cdot (-n)$

Find the value of each expression.

11. 2^5

12. 8^3

13. 35^2

14. $(-6)^3$

15. 3^4

Simplify each expression.

16. $6^2 \cdot 6^5$

17. $8^7 \div 8^3$

18. $12^5 \cdot 12^2$

19. $3^9 \div 3^4$

20. $7^4 \div 7^2$

Write an expression for the area of each square. Then find the area.

21. 3

22.  2

23.  x

24. 5

25. y

Write an expression for the volume of each cube. Then find the volume.

26. 5

28. 7

30. 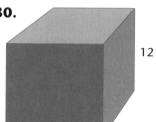 12

27.  9

29. m

Estimate the square root of each number.

31. $\sqrt{10}$

33. $\sqrt{37}$

35. $\sqrt{47}$

32. $\sqrt{56}$

34. $\sqrt{93}$

Find the approximate length of a side of each square. Round to the nearest tenth.

36. Area = 49

38. Area = 67

40. Area = 2,000

37. Area = 351

39. Area = 100

Use the Pythagorean theorem to find x.

41. x 6 8

44. 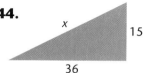 x 15 36

42. 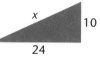 x 10 24

45. 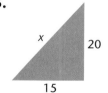 x 20 15

43. x 9 12

Find each perimeter.

1.

5.3 cm

8.1 cm

2.

5 ft

4 ft

8 ft

3.

14 yd

4.

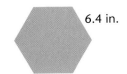

6.4 in.

5.

36 mm

6.

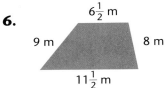

$6\frac{1}{2}$ m

9 m   8 m

$11\frac{1}{2}$ m

The measures of various squares and rectangles are given below. Find the area of each.

7. Square *NLIP* with *s* = 25 mm

8. Rectangle *JHGF* with *l* = 8.5 in.; *w* = 3 in.

9. Rectangle *CDEF* with *l* = 9 cm; *w* = 12 cm

10. Square *ACEG* with *s* = 7.3 ft

Find the area of each shape.

11.

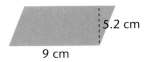

5.2 cm

9 cm

12.

15 m

11 m

13.

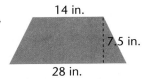

14 in.

7.5 in.

28 in.

14.

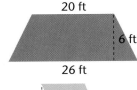

20 ft

6 ft

26 ft

15.

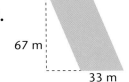

67 m

33 m

16.

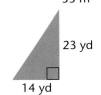

23 yd

14 yd

Find the volume of each shape.

17.

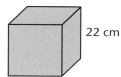

22 cm

18.

8.4 in.

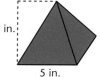

5 in.

19.

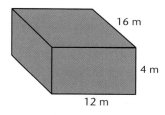

16 m

4 m

12 m

20.

30 ft

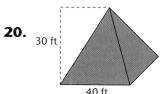

40 ft

21. Zari mailed a package to her mom that is a cube with sides 23 inches long. What is the volume of the package?

22. Melissa is shipping a model boat in a box that is a rectangular prism. Its length is 43 inches, its width is 18 inches, and its height is 15 inches. What is the volume of the box?

Use 3.14 for π to find the area and circumference.

23. On the outside of city hall in Cookport is a clock face with a 24- inch radius. What is the circumference and area of the clock face?

24. A school's logo of a tiger is painted inside a circle on the front door of the building. It has a diameter of 30 cm. What is the circumference and area of the circle?

Use 3.14 for π to find the volume of each figure. Round to the nearest hundredth.

25.

25 m

14 m

26.

radius 2.5 ft

27.

30 mm

9 mm

28.

radius 6 in.

29. Find the volume of a basketball with a radius of 22 cm.

30. As part of the Thanksgiving dinner, Marshall opens a can of cranberries from a cylinder can that is 8 inches high and has a radius of 3 inches. What is the volume of the can?

Graph each solution on a number line.

1. $c = 4$ **4.** $y < -1$ **7.** $p \le -4$

2. $d > -3$ **5.** $g \ge 6$ **8.** $t \ge -5$

3. $x \le 7$ **6.** $a > 0$ **9.** $s = -2$

Identify the solution shown by each number line.

10.

11.

Solve each equality or inequality for the variable. Then graph and check each solution.

12. $c - 3 \le 5$ **14.** $4 + j > 3$ **16.** $t + 16 < 24$

13. $m + 8 = 10$ **15.** $-6 + e \ge -3$

Use this coordinate system for problems 17–28.

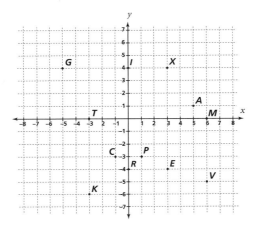

Identify the quadrant for each point.

17. Point C **18.** Point A **19.** Point E **20.** Point G

Write an ordered pair to describe the location of each point.

21. Point I **24.** Point P **27.** Point V

22. Point K **25.** Point R **28.** Point X

23. Point M **26.** Point T

On a sheet of graph paper, draw a coordinate system as shown on page 386. Then use it to plot and label the following points.

29. Point $B\,(6, -3)$ **31.** Point $F\,(0, -3)$ **33.** Point $J\,(-4, 4)$

30. Point $D\,(-1, -5)$ **32.** Point $H\,(2, 3)$ **34.** Point $L\,(-5, 0)$

Graph the equation of each line.

35. $y = x + 2$ **36.** $y = x - 1$ **37.** $y = -3x$

Find the slope of a line that passes through the given points.

38. $(6, 13)$ and $(4, 9)$ **40.** $(-1, -5)$ and $(0, -4)$

39. $(2, 10)$ and $(7, 25)$ **41.** $(0, 1)$ and $(-2, 3)$

Write each of these equations of a line in slope-intercept form.

42. $3y = 6x + 3$ **44.** $-y = -3x - 5$

43. $4y = 16x - 12$ **45.** $-2y = 2x + 4$

Use a protractor to give the measure of each angle.

1. angle *BAC*

2. angle *CAD*

3. angle *CAE*

4. angle *GAF*

5. angle *DAF*

6. angle *GAE*

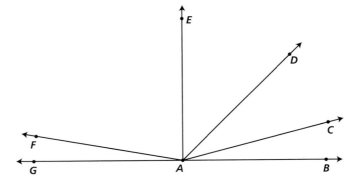

Use this illustration to answer the following questions.

7. Name any angles adjacent to angle 1.

8. Name all pairs of vertical angles.

9. What is the measure of angle 3?

10. What is the measure of angle 4?

11. Angles 3 and 4 form what type of angle?

12. Angle 2 is what type of angle?

13. Angle 3 is what type of angle?

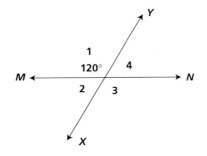

Find the measure of the complement and supplement of angle *J*.

14. measure angle *J* = 25° **16.** measure angle *J* = 75° **18.** measure angle *J* = 89°

15. measure angle *J* = 80° **17.** measure angle *J* = 38°

Find the measure of angle *x*.

19.

20.

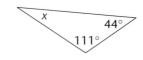

Find the measure of angle *x*.

21.

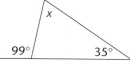

22.

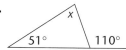

Name each triangle.

23.

24.

25.

Name the condition that makes each pair of triangles congruent.

26.

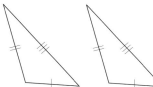

27.

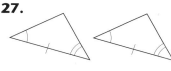

28.

Tell whether the triangles in each pair are similar.
Answer *yes, no,* or *not enough information.*

29.

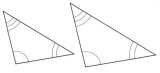

30.

31.

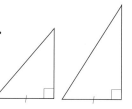

Tell whether each statement is *true* or *false.*

32. All polygons with four sides are called quadrilaterals.

33. All squares have two pairs of parallel sides and are rectangles.

34. A trapezoid is a parallelogram with one pair of parallel sides.

35. A rhombus is a square in the shape of a diamond.

Chapter 12   Supplementary Problems

Create a bar graph that organizes and displays the data shown in the table below.

1.

Type of Music Students Prefer the Most	
Rock	83
Country	25
Heavy Metal	62
Rap	27
Jazz	42
Folk	18
Top 40	73

Create a circle graph that organizes and displays the data shown in the table below.

2.

Sales by Student Council	
tablets	47
t-shirts	16
notebooks	37

Use the following frequency table.

Food Drive Results

Frequency Table		
Type	Tally	Frequency
Canned Vegetables	卌 IIII	9
Canned Meats	卌 III	8
Boxed Cereal	卌 卌 III	13
Powdered Milk	IIII	4
Boxed Dried Fruit	II	2

3. How many items were brought in for the food drive?

4. How many items were canned?

5. Explain why the total number of boxed items may be 15, 16, 17, 18, or 19.

Use the table. Find the measures of central tendency and range.

6. Find the range of the data.

7. Find the mean of the data.

8. Find the median of the data.

9. Find the mode or modes of the data.

Data		
3	0	5
1	0	2
5	5	8

Use the box-and-whiskers plot shown.

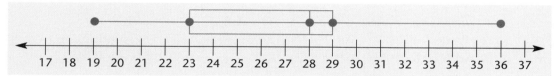

10. Which value represents the median?

11. Which values represent the extremes?

12. Which values represent the quartiles?

Find the probability. Express your answer as a fraction in simplest form and as a percent rounded to the nearest whole number.

13. Suppose the spinner is spun once. Find the probability of the spinner landing on a number less than 4.

14. Suppose the spinner is spun once. Find the probability of the spinner landing on a prime number.

Use the fundamental principle of counting to solve the problem.

15. Eric, Amanda, Alyssa, and Jenny ran in a 100-meter dash. In how many different ways can they place first, second, third, and fourth?

Selected Answers and Solutions

CHAPTER 1

Lesson 1, pages 4–5

1. 32; To add 23 + 9, add the ones first; 3 + 9 = 12. Regroup 12 ones as 1 ten and 2 ones. Write 2 in the ones column. Write 1 in the tens column. Add the tens; 1 + 2 = 3; 23 + 9 = 32 **3.** 63 **5.** 71 **7.** 63 **9.** 993 **11.** 2,803 **13.** 160x **15.** 76a **16.** 377; To add 41 + 329 + 7 vertically, add the ones first; 1 + 9 + 7 = 17. Regroup 17 ones as 1 ten and 7 ones. Write 7 in the ones column and 1 in the tens column. Add the tens; 1 + 4 + 2 = 7. Write 7 in the tens column and add the hundreds; write 3 in the hundreds column. **17.** 1,092 **19.** 574 **21.** 2,114 **23.** 268a **25.** 224; Enter 135 and press $+$. Enter 89 and press $=$. The display reads 224. **27.** 1,096 **29.** 1,545 **31.** $140; To solve, you add $85 + $55. Add the ones first; 5 + 5 = 10. Regroup 10 ones as 1 ten and 0 ones. Write 0 in the ones column. Write 1 in the tens column. Add the tens; 1 + 8 + 5 = 14 **33.** 875 miles **35)** $381

Lesson 2, pages 7–9

1. 6; To subtract 74 − 68, you cannot subtract 8 from 4. Rename 7 tens 4 ones as 6 tens 14 ones and then subtract; 14 − 8 = 6; 6 − 6 = 0 **3.** 49 **5.** 29 **7.** 29a **9.** 18x **10.** 1,021; To subtract 1,400 − 379 in vertical form, first rename 4 hundreds as 3 hundreds 9 tens and 10 ones. Then subtract the ones; 10 − 9 = 1. Subtract the tens; 9 − 7 = 2. Subtract the

hundreds; 3 − 3 = 0. Subtract the thousands; 1 − 0 = 1 **11.** 4,252 **13.** 24,689 **15.** 148,878y **17.** 116,189a **19.** 46; Enter 135 and press $-$. Enter 89 and press $=$. The display reads 46. **21.** 696 **23.** 13,081 **25.** 5,543 **27.** 162 bushels; To solve, subtract 223 from 385. Subtract the ones first; 5 − 3 = 2. Then subtract the tens; 8 − 2 = 6. Subtract the hundreds; 3 − 2 = 1 **29.** 2,195 books

Try This

Answers will vary. Use subtraction to find the answer. (Price of item) − (Amount on coupon) = Price paid

Lesson 3, page 11

1. 1,400; Round each addend to its greatest place value. Round 643 down to 600. Round 821 down to 800. Add 600 + 800. **3.** 21,300 **5.** 179,080 **6.** 500; Round each number to its greatest place value. Round 875 up to 900. Round 397 up to 400. Subtract 400 from 900. **7.** 1,500 **9.** 60,000 **11.** 100; 101; Round 28 up to 30. Round 73 down to 70. Add 30 + 70 = 100 for estimated answer; 28 + 73 = 101 **13.** 1,500; 1,468 **15.** 1,400; 1,408 **17.** 13,000; 13,294 **19.** 30,000; 29,853

Lesson 4, page 13

1. 24; 4 times 6 is the same as 4 + 4 + 4 + 4 + 4 + 4. **3.** 2,484 **5.** 32 **7.** 8,091 **9.** 6,048 **11.** 56 **13.** 45 **15.** 3,608 **17.** 54a **19.** 576x **21.** 108,072; To multiply 237 times 456 vertically, multiply the ones first; 237 times 6 = 1,422. Then multiply the tens; 237 times 50 = 11,850. Then multiply the hundreds; 237 times 400 = 94,800. Add the products; 1,422 + 11,850 + 94,800 **23.** 65,709 **24.** 104 offices; Multiply 26 times 4. First multiply the ones; 6 times 4 = 24. Then multiply the tens; 20 times 4 = 80. Add the products; 24 + 80 = 104 **25.** 1,500 sheets

Lesson 5, pages 15–17

1. 9; 45 ÷ 5 = 9. To check, multiply the quotient by the divisor; 9 times 5 = 45 **3.** 9 **5.** 8 **7.** 8c **9.** 8a **11.** 82 r2; Divide 412 by 5. First see that 5 does not go into 4, but 5 goes into 41 eight times. Multiply 5 by 8. Subtract 40 from 41. Bring down the 2. Next, 5 goes into 12 two times. Multiply 5 by 2. Subtract 10 from 12. The remainder is 2. **13.** 173 r1 **15.** 84 r1 **17.** 61 r1 **19.** 137 r5 **21.** 581 r2; Divide 4,650 by 8. First see that 8 does not go into 4, but 8 goes into 46 five times. Multiply 8 by 5. Subtract 40 from 46. Bring down the 5. Next, 8 goes into 65 eight times. Multiply 8 by 8. Subtract 64 from 65. Bring down 0. Eight goes into 10 one time. Multiply 8 by 1. Subtract 8 from 10. The remainder is 2. **23.** 588 r8 **25.** 967 r35 **27.** 26; Enter 910 and press ÷ . Enter 35 and press = . The display reads 26. **29.** 45 **31.** 37 **33.** 439,331 **35.** 13,261 **37.** 16 cartons; To find how many cartons, divide 320 (the total number of packages) by 20 (the number of packages in each carton). **39.** 24 rows

Try This
Multiplication. Sample example:
24 ÷ 6 = 4, 4 • 6 = 24

Lesson 6, page 19

1. 5,400; Round 92 down to 90. Round 64 down to 60. Multiply 90 by 60. **3.** 3,500 **5.** 360,000 **7.** 900 **9.** 40,000 **11.** 60; Find compatible numbers for the dividend and divisor. 37 becomes 36, because 36 ÷ 6 is a basic fact. An estimated quotient is 60. **13.** 100 **15.** 400 **17.** 80 **19.** 1,000 **21.** 2,100,000 and 2,228,036; Round 3,412 down to 3,000 and round 653 up to 700. Multiply 3,000 by 700 for an estimated answer. **23.** 4,000 and 3,184 **25.** 200 and 213 r2

Try This
Answers will vary.

Lesson 7, page 21

1. true; To check addition, use subtraction; 9 − 4 = 5 **3.** true **5.** false **7.** false **9.** true **11.** true; To check addition, use subtraction; 12 − 5 = 7. This statement is not open because it does not contain a letter used as a placeholder. **13.** open **15.** false **17.** open **19.** true **21.** Thirty-four divided by some number; The ÷ symbol means division, and n is the placeholder for an unknown number. **23.** Sixteen minus some number **25.** Some number divided by eight

Lesson 8, page 23

1. x; x is the letter used as a placeholder for a number **3.** a **5.** t **7.** h **9.** n **11.** addition; The + symbol means addition **13.** division **15.** multiplication, addition **17.** multiplication, addition **19.** subtraction **21.** numerical, addition; This expression does not contain any variables, so it is a numerical expression; the + symbol means addition

23. algebraic, division, *y* **25.** algebraic, multiplication, addition, *y* **27.** algebraic, multiplication, addition, *m* **29.** algebraic, multiplication, *n*

Lesson 9, pages 24–25
1. *n* + 5; An algebraic expression contains at least one variable and an operation; *n* is the variable (some number), and the operation is addition (+). **3.** 15 ÷ *n* **5.** 2*n* + 5 **7.** 10 − *n* **9.** *n* ÷ 9 **11.** 29; Substitute the number 14 for *m* and then perform the operation (addition); 14 + 15 **13.** 84 **15.** 13 **17.** 7 **19.** 5 **21.** false; Substitute 3 for *n* and then perform the operation; 5 + 3 does not equal 12 **23.** true **24.** true; Substitute 7 for *x*. Enter 35 and press ÷ . Enter 7 and press = . The display reads 5; 35 ÷ 7 = 5 **25.** false **27.** true **29.** false

Chapter 1 Application, page 26
1. 108 sq ft **3.** 168 sq ft

Chapter 1 Review, pages 27–29
1. C **3.** A **5.** C **7.** 37,104 **9.** 933 **11.** 38,788 **13.** 101,368 **15.** 90,387 **17.** 128 **19.** 34 r10 **21.** 5 r8 **23.** 120,000 **25.** 50,000 **27.** open **29.** false **31.** algebraic, multiplication, addition, *m* **33.** algebraic, division, *g* **35.** algebraic, multiplication, *x* **37.** false **39.** true

CHAPTER 2

Lesson 1, page 33
1. tenths; 1 is in the tenths place **3.** thousandths **5.** hundreds **7.** tens **9.** ones **10.** 0.3; 3 is in the tenths place, so its value is 3 times 0.1 **11.** 0.0009 **13.** 80 **15.** 2 **17.** 1,000 **19.** 3,000 **21.** 0.007 **23.** 0.0009 **25.** 0.001; 1 is in the thousandths place, so its value is 1 times 0.001 **27.** 0.0003 **29.** 0.006

Try This
Answers will vary.

Lesson 2, page 35
1. 5.403 > 5.03; First add one zero to 5.03 so that each decimal has the same number of places to the right of the decimal point. Next, compare the decimals; .403 is greater than .030. **3.** 91.8 < 91.8135 **5.** 2.04 < 2.044 **7.** 403.079 > 403.07 **9.** 30.19 < 300.19 **11.** 2.6; 2.63; 2.635; When rounding 2.6345 to the tenth and hundredth places, there are no changes, since 3 and 4 (digits to the right of the place you are rounding to) are less than 5. When rounding to the thousandth place, one was added to the thousandth place, since 5 was to the right. **13.** 0.9; 0.90; 0.902 **15.** 6.5; 6.46; 6.463 **17.** 2.8; 2.80; 2.800 **19.** 14.0; 14.04; 14.037 **21.** 5.7; 5.65; 5.654 **23.** 20.0; 19.99; 19.987 **25.** 523.7; 523.67; 523.675

Try This
Answers will vary. Sample example: number found 4.179 rounded to 4.18

Lesson 3, page 37

1. 10.11; Include zeros and then line up the decimal points. Add 3.20 + 0.91 + 6.00. **3.** 1.53 **5.** 31.3 **7.** 125.4 **9.** 22.92 **11.** 17.108 **13.** 2.671; Press 1 $\boxed{\cdot}$ 5 $\boxed{+}$ $\boxed{\cdot}$ 21 $\boxed{+}$ $\boxed{\cdot}$ 35 $\boxed{+}$ $\boxed{\cdot}$ 611 $\boxed{=}$. The display reads 2.671. **15.** 5.95679 **17.** 933.9648 **19.** $17.54 **21.** $129.56 **22.** 19.75 miles; Include zeros, line up the decimal points, and then add; 5.00 + 6.05 + 8.70 **23.** $4.05 **25.** exactly $0.017 more or about $0.02 more

Lesson 4, page 39

1. 236; Since the number of zeros in 10^2 is two, move the decimal point in 2.36 two places to the right. **3.** 2,700 **5.** 1,441 **7.** 771,000 **9.** 73,000 **11.** 84.104 **13.** 7,690 **15.** 4,044 **17.** 1,011,200 **19.** 890.7 **21.** true; Since the number of zeros in 10^1 is one, the decimal point in 3.3 is moved one place to the right. **23.** false **25.** open **27.** true **29.** open

Lesson 5, page 41

1. 21.24; First multiply the numbers as if they were whole numbers. Then count the number of decimal places in both original factors (two) and move the decimal point that many places in the product. The product 2124 becomes 21.24. **3.** 39.1 **5.** 20.59 **7.** 6.648 **9.** 0.2862 **11.** 85.618 **13.** 31.4 in.; Use the formula $C = \pi d$. Use 3.14 for π. 10 times 3.14 = 31.4. **15.** 157 in. **16.** 0.36864; Press 3 $\boxed{\cdot}$ 2 $\boxed{\times}$ 6 $\boxed{\cdot}$ 4 $\boxed{\times}$ $\boxed{\cdot}$ 018 $\boxed{=}$. The display reads 0.36864. **17.** 0.16074 **19.** 15.2724 **21.** 0.00006 **22.** $559.13; Multiply 355 by 1575. The product is 559125. Since there were three decimal places in the original factors, and

you round to the nearest cent, the answer is $559.13. **23.** $2.07 **25.** 159.25 miles

Lesson 6, page 43

1. 0.66; There is one zero in 10. To divide by 10, move the decimal point one place to the left; 6.6 ÷ 10 = 0.66 **3.** 0.093 **5.** 0.0203 **7.** 0.0115 **9.** 0.244 **11.** 0.2432 **13.** 0.736 **15.** 0.0000005 **17.** 0.000003 **19.** 30.005 **21.** true; Since there is one zero in 10, to divide 6.5 by 10, move the decimal point one place to the left. This is not an open statement because it does not contain a variable. **23.** true **25.** true **27.** false **29.** true

Lesson 7, page 45

1. 1.30; Since the divisor is a whole number, first write a decimal point in the quotient. Then divide 5.21 by 4. **3.** 14.42 **5.** 4.72 **7.** 1,578.57 **9.** 267.50 **11.** 0.598; Press 16 $\boxed{\cdot}$ 5 $\boxed{÷}$ 27 $\boxed{\cdot}$ 58 $\boxed{=}$. The display reads 0.598. **13.** 0.129 **15.** 2.245 **17.** $1.06; To solve, divide $8.45 by 8. Since the divisor is a whole number, first write a decimal point in the quotient and then divide. **19.** $14.50

Lesson 8, page 47

1. $\frac{7}{25}$; The place value of the last digit in 0.28 is the hundredths place, so the denominator is 100. Use the numeral in the decimal for the numerator; $\frac{28}{100}$. Then simplify the fraction. **3.** $\frac{27}{50}$ **5.** $\frac{1}{250}$ **7.** $\frac{29}{100}$ **9.** $\frac{3}{400}$ **11.** $5\frac{1}{20}$ **13.** $\frac{11}{10,000}$ **15.** $\frac{9}{200}$ **17.** 0.3; Since the denominator of $\frac{3}{10}$ is a power of ten, you can identify the place value as tenths. Write the decimal using the numeral in the numerator; 0.3. **19.** 0.25 **21.** 0.6 **23.** 0.124 **25.** 0.3 **27.** 6.5 **29.** 0.504 **31.** 0.5625 **33.** $9.36; First change the mixed number $3\frac{1}{2}$ to the decimal 3.5. Then divide $32.75 by 3.5. **35.** $81

Lesson 9, page 49

1. $0.\overline{3}$; 1 divided by 3 is 0.33333 or $0.\overline{3}$. **3.** $0.8\overline{3}$ **5.** $0.\overline{6}$ **7.** $0.\overline{81}$ **9.** $0.\overline{8}$ **10.** 17°C; First, substitute 62° Fahrenheit into the formula; $C = \frac{5}{9}(62 - 32)$. Then simplify; $C = \frac{5}{9}(30)$; $C = \frac{150}{9}$; $C = 16.\overline{6}$. To write $16.\overline{6}$ as a whole number, round up to 17°C. **11.** 12°C **13.** 31°C **15.** 35°C **17.** 4°C **19.** 26°C

Try This
77°F; $F = \frac{9}{5}(25) + 32 = 45 + 32 = 77°F$

Lesson 10, page 51

1. 0.05; Locate the decimal point, move it two places to the left, and drop the % sign. **3.** 0.045 **5.** 0.006 **7.** 0.008 **9.** $165; Before using the formula $I = prt$, change 5.5% to the decimal 0.055; $I = (3,000)(0.055)(1) = $165. **11.** $287.50 **12.** $220; Before using the formula $I = prt$, change 5.5% to the decimal 0.055; $I = (2,000)(0.055)(2) = $220. **13.** $38 **15.** $219.38 per year; $18.28 per month

Lesson 11, page 53

1. 5.155; Substitute 3.085 for m. Perform the arithmetic operation; $3.085 + 2.07 = 5.155$ **3.** 8.164 **5.** 21.176 **7.** 55.386 **9.** 5.2195121 **11.** false; Substitute 3.5 for s. Perform the arithmetic operation; 4 times 3.5 does not equal 18. **13.** false **15.** false **17.** true **19.** false

Chapter 2 Application, page 54

1. 83.277 liters **3.** 50 m (49.99); 25 m (24.99)

Chapter 2 Review, pages 55–57

1. B **3.** A **5.** B **7.** D **9.** ten-thousandths **11.** tenths **13.** 2.254 **15.** 11.716 **17.** 63.085 **19.** 8,720 **21.** 114.167 **23.** 0.637 **25.** $\frac{1}{4}$ **27.** $\frac{7}{8}$ **29.** 0.88 **31.** $4,080 **33.** 5.74 **35.** 27.83

CHAPTER 3

Lesson 1, page 63

1. true; 12 is divisible by 2 because its last digit is 2. **3.** true **5.** false **7.** false **9.** true **11.** true **13.** 90 is divisible by 2, 3, 5, 6, 9, and 10; 90 is divisible by 2, 5, and 10 because its last digit is 0; it is divisible by 3 and 9 because the sum of its digits are divisible by 3 and by 9; it is divisible by 6 because it is divisible by 2 and by 3. **15.** by 2, 3, 4, 5, 6, 8, 9, and 10 **17.** by 3 and 9 **19.** Answers will vary. Sample answer: 12,000,960

Try This, page 64

30 years old, or any multiple of 30 years

Lesson 2, page 65

1. numbers circled in the text, plus 53, 59, 61, 67, 71, 73, 79, 83, 89, 97; These numbers were left on the grid after crossing out multiples of 2, 3, 5, and 7. **2.** composite; 108 has factors other than 1 and 108. **3.** prime **5.** composite **7.** composite **9.** composite **11.** prime **13.** No; for two numbers greater than 3 to be consecutive, one number must be an even number, and every even number is a composite number because it is a multiple of 2. **15.** Answers will vary. Sample answer: The factors of 169 are 1, 13, and 169

Lesson 3, page 67

1. 10; List all the factors of each term; 10: 1, 2, 5, 10; 50: 1, 2, 5, 10, 25, 50. They share 1, 2, 5, and 10 as factors. 10 is the greatest common factor. **3.** 3 **5.** 4 **7.** 4 **9.** 6 **11.** 2 **13.** 7 **15.** $5h$ **17.** $9d$ **19.** $13v$

Try This

Answers will vary.

Lesson 4, pages 70–71

1. 24; $3(2 + 6) = (3 \cdot 2) + (3 \cdot 6) = 6 + 18 = 24$ **3.** $2a + 10$ **5.** $20m + 20$ **7.** $4n + 12p + 8$ **9.** $2v + 26 + 4x$ **11.** 2; List all the factors of each term; $2x$: 1, 2, x; 10: 1, 2, 5, 10. The GCD is 2. **13.** 4 **15.** 1 **17.** $2d + 9$; List all the factors of each term; $2d$: 1, 2, d; 9: 1, 3, 9. The GCD is 1. When the GCD of any group of numbers or terms is 1, the expression cannot be factored. **19.** $3(3j + 1)$ **21.** $3(5w + 2y)$ **23.** $23b + 4n$ **25.** $2(11x + y)$ **27.** 22 CDs; Jarrod and Nadine have $6 + 5$ CDs. Double that number is $2(6 + 5)$; $(2 \cdot 6) + (2 \cdot 5) = 12 + 10 = 22$ **29.** $6(3 + 4)$

Lesson 5, pages 74–75

1. 24; First write the prime factorization of 8 and 12. Identify the greatest power of each prime factor. The greatest power of the prime factor 2 is 2^3. The greatest power of the prime factor 3 is 3. Find the product of the greatest power of each prime factor; $2^3 \cdot 3 = 24$; LCM = 24. **3.** 39 **5.** 176 **7.** 288 **9.** 1,344 **11.** 90 **13.** 250; multiply $5 \cdot 5 \cdot 5 \cdot 2$ **15.** 108 **17.** 229,957 **18.** One day; if today

represents Kayla's sixth day off and today represents Tia's fourth day off, both Kayla and Tia will be off again tomorrow **19.** 5.6 min or 5 min 36 sec

Lesson 6, page 77

1. 6.2×10^4; Make 62,000 a number between 1 and 10 by moving the decimal point to the left; 6.2. The decimal point was moved four places to the left or 10^4. The scientific notation is 6.2×10^4. **3.** 3.06×10^8 **5.** 1.2×10^4 **7.** 6.221×10^6 **9.** 3.34×10^4 **11.** 1.194×10^{11} **13.** 5.0×10^{-3}; Make 0.005 a number between 1 and 10 by moving the decimal point to the right; 5. The decimal point was moved three places to the right. Moving the decimal point to the right makes the exponent negative; 10^{-3}. The scientific notation is 5.0×10^{-3}. **15.** 4.402×10^{-1} **17.** 6.66×10^{-4} **19.** 4.0×10^{-10} **21.** true; To check if $2.4 \times 10^4 = 24,000$, move the decimal point four places (10^4) to the right; 2.4 becomes 24,000. **23.** false **25.** true

Try This

3.688×10^8

Chapter 3 Application, page 78

1. $3 + 5$ **3.** $7 + 13$ **5.** $13 + 19$ **7.** $17 + 23$ **9.** $29 + 29$

Chapter 3 Review, pages 79–81

1. C **3.** A **5.** A **7.** D **9.** true **11.** false **13.** 624 is divisible by 2, 3, 4, 6, 8 **15.** 90,200 is divisible by 2, 4, 5, 8, 10 **17.** composite **19.** composite **21.** 34 **23.** $3b + 30 + 15x$ **25.** 7 **27.** 1 **29.** $4(2j + 1)$ **31.** $6(3w + k)$ **33.** $3(3f + 8m)$ **35.** 120 **37.** 300

39. 1,728 **41.** 13,824 **43.** 8.9×10^9
45. 4.28×10^{-2}

CHAPTER 4

Lesson 1, page 85

1. $\frac{3}{8}$; Three out of eight shapes are shaded. **3.** $\frac{1}{5}$ **4.** $\frac{0}{2}, \frac{1}{2}$; The number line is divided into two parts between 0 and 1. In a proper fraction, the numerator is less than the denominator; $\frac{2}{2}$ is not a proper fraction. **5.** $\frac{0}{4}, \frac{1}{4}, \frac{2}{4}, \frac{3}{4}$ **6.** Sample answer: $\frac{2}{8}, \frac{3}{8}, \frac{4}{8}, \frac{5}{8}, \frac{6}{8}$ **7.** Check your drawing. $\frac{7}{10}$ of your set should be shaded. ●●●●●●●○○○

9. $\frac{5}{6}$ of the total distance; Jamal walked 5 of the 6 blocks, or $\frac{5}{6}$ of the total distance.

Lesson 2, pages 88–89

1. $\frac{4}{4}, \frac{5}{4}, \frac{6}{4}, \frac{7}{4}, \frac{8}{4}$; In any improper fraction, the numerator is greater than or equal to the denominator. **3.** proper; The numerator (3) is smaller than the denominator (8). **5.** proper **7.** proper **9.** improper **11.** 1; Divide the numerator by the denominator; $2 \div 2 = 1$. **13.** $2\frac{3}{4}$ **15.** $2\frac{9}{10}$ **17.** $1\frac{7}{12}$ **19.** $3\frac{7}{8}$ **21.** $\frac{13}{3}$; First multiply the whole number by the denominator of the fraction; $4 \cdot 3 = 12$. Add the numerator to this number; $1 + 12 = 13$. Write this sum as the numerator in the improper fraction, and write the denominator of the mixed fraction as the denominator of the improper fraction; $\frac{13}{3}$ **23.** $\frac{25}{2}$ **25.** $\frac{75}{8}$ **27.** $\frac{133}{16}$ **29.** $\frac{2,001}{20}$

31. $3\frac{4}{9}$; Begin with the improper fraction $\frac{31}{9}$. Divide the numerator by the denominator and list the remainder as a fraction of the divisor; $31 \div 9 = 3$ r4; $3\frac{4}{9}$; Eric has only 3 complete sets. **33.** $4\frac{5}{6}$, or 5 sheets **35.** $5\frac{2}{3}$ ounces

Lesson 3, pages 91–93

Sample answers shown for **1–13.**

1. $\frac{2}{6}$ and $\frac{3}{9}$ **3.** $\frac{14}{16}$ and $\frac{21}{24}$ **5.** $\frac{6}{20}$ and $\frac{9}{30}$ **7.** $\frac{6}{16}$ and $\frac{9}{24}$ **9.** $\frac{18}{20}$ and $\frac{27}{30}$ **11.** $\frac{1}{2}$ and $\frac{5}{10}$ **13.** $\frac{4}{10}$ and $\frac{2}{5}$ **15.** yes; Press 1 $\boxed{\div}$ 5 $\boxed{=}$. The display reads 0.2. Press 10 $\boxed{\div}$ 50 $\boxed{=}$. The display reads 0.2. **17.** no **19.** no

Try This
Answers will vary.

Lesson 4, page 95

1. 8; The factors of 8 are 1, 2, 4, 8. The factors of 16 are 1, 2, 4, 8, 16. Shared factors are 1, 2, 4, 8. The greatest common factor is the GCD; 8. **3.** 6 **5.** 2 **7.** $\frac{5}{8}$; GCD (10, 16) = 2. Divide the numerator and denominator of $\frac{10}{16}$ by 2; $\frac{10 \div 2}{16 \div 2} = \frac{5}{8}$. **9.** $\frac{1}{3}$ **11.** $\frac{3}{5}$ **13.** $\frac{5}{6}$ **15.** $\frac{4}{5}$ **17.** $\frac{11}{12}$ **19.** $\frac{7}{8}$ **21.** $\frac{5}{12}$ **23.** Yes. Sample explanation: In each class, $\frac{3}{8}$ of the students are male. If the same number of students are enrolled in each class, each class will have the same number of males ($\frac{3}{8}$) and females ($\frac{5}{8}$). **25.** The enrollment in each class is 8, or a multiple of 8, because the fractions are in eighths.

Lesson 5, pages 98–99

1. $\frac{3}{8}$; On the number line, the fraction farther to the right is greater. **3.** $>$; When comparing fractions with like denominators, the fraction with the greater numerator is the greater in value. **5.** $>$ **7.** $<$ **9.** $>$ **11.** $<$ **13.** $>$ **15.** $\frac{3}{4}, \frac{2}{3}, \frac{1}{2}$; Write equivalent fractions using the LCM of the denominators (12) as the denominator. $\frac{1}{2} = \frac{6}{12}, \frac{2}{3} = \frac{8}{12}, \frac{3}{4} = \frac{9}{12}$. Then compare the fractions with like denominators. **17.** $\frac{11}{12}, \frac{7}{8}, \frac{5}{6}$ **19.** $\frac{1}{2}, \frac{5}{8}, \frac{3}{4}$; Write equivalent fractions using the LCM of the denominators (8) as the denominator and then compare the fractions with like denominators. **21.** $\frac{1}{2}, \frac{4}{7}, \frac{9}{14}$ **23.** Terrence; Write equivalent fractions for $\frac{5}{6}$ and $\frac{7}{8}$ using the LCM (24) as the denominator and then compare the fractions with like denominators. **25.** James

Try This

Answers will vary. Sample: Change each fraction to a decimal by dividing the numerator of each fraction by its denominator. Align the decimal points, then compare and order the decimals.

Lesson 6, pages 102–103

1. $\frac{1}{2}$; Subtract the numerators of the fractions; $\frac{3-1}{4} = \frac{2}{4}$. Keep the same denominator; $\frac{2}{4}$. Simplify; $\frac{2}{4} = \frac{1}{2}$. **3.** $\frac{2}{5}$ **5.** $6\frac{1}{6}$ **7.** $16\frac{1}{2}$ **8.** $\frac{3x}{4}$; Subtract the numerators of the fractions; $\frac{7x-x}{8} = \frac{6x}{8}$. Keep the same denominator; $\frac{6x}{8}$. Simplify;

$\frac{6x}{8} = \frac{3x}{4}$. **9.** $\frac{2x}{3}$ **11.** $\frac{x-1}{y}$ **13.** $\frac{y-3}{x}$ **15.** x **16.** 1; Subtract the numerators of the fractions first; $\frac{4-1}{5} = \frac{3}{5}$. Keep the same denominator; $\frac{3}{5}$. Add $\frac{3}{5} + \frac{2}{5} = \frac{5}{5} = 1$. **17.** 1 **19.** $1\frac{1}{2}$ **21.** $\frac{7}{12}$ **23.** $\frac{3x}{8}$ **25.** $\frac{x}{2}$

Lesson 7, pages 106–107

1. $1\frac{1}{12}$; Write equivalent fractions using the LCM of the denominators (12) as the denominator. Add; $\frac{4}{12} + \frac{9}{12} = \frac{13}{12}$. Simplify; $\frac{13}{12} = 1\frac{1}{12}$. **3.** $\frac{13}{20}$ **5.** $\frac{2}{15}$ **7.** $\frac{79}{80}$ **9.** $1\frac{1}{63}$ **11.** $\frac{1}{3}x$; Write equivalent fractions. Subtract; $\frac{5}{6}x - \frac{3}{6}x = \frac{2}{6}x = \frac{1}{3}x$. **13.** $\frac{23x}{24}$ **15.** $\frac{x}{40}$ **16.** $1\frac{1}{4}$; Write equivalent fractions. Subtract the numerators of the fractions; subtract the whole numbers; $2\frac{3}{4} - 1\frac{2}{4} = 1\frac{1}{4}$. **17.** $11\frac{1}{8}$ **19.** $1\frac{27}{40}$ **21.** $23\frac{7}{24}$ **23.** $46\frac{43}{60}$ **25.** $5\frac{29}{80}x$

Lesson 8, page 109

1. $1\frac{1}{2}$; You cannot subtract $\frac{3}{4}$ from $\frac{1}{4}$. You must rename before subtracting; $3\frac{1}{4} = 2\frac{5}{4}$. Subtract; $2\frac{5}{4} - 1\frac{3}{4} = 1\frac{2}{4} = 1\frac{1}{2}$. **3.** $5\frac{3}{5}$ **5.** $2\frac{2}{3}$ **7.** $\frac{2}{3}$ **9.** $13\frac{15}{16}$ **11.** $9\frac{17}{40}$ **13.** $\frac{29}{30}$ **15.** $21\frac{59}{84}$ **16.** $9\frac{1}{4}$ hours; Rename $5\frac{1}{2}$ to $5\frac{2}{4}$. Add $3\frac{3}{4} + 5\frac{2}{4} = 8\frac{5}{4} = 9\frac{1}{4}$. **17.** $178\frac{5}{16}$ pounds **19.** $34\frac{11}{12}$ miles

Lesson 9, page 111

1. $\frac{1}{12}$; Multiply the numerators; $\frac{1}{4} \cdot \frac{1}{3} = \frac{1 \cdot 1}{3} = \frac{1}{3}$. Multiply the denominators; $\frac{1}{4} \cdot \frac{1}{3} = \frac{1}{4 \cdot 3} = \frac{1}{12}$. **3.** $\frac{2}{15}$ **5.** $\frac{5}{48}$ **7.** $\frac{1}{64}$ **9.** $\frac{1}{16y}$

11. $2\frac{1}{4}$; Change mixed numbers to improper fractions; $1\frac{1}{2} \cdot 1\frac{1}{2} = \frac{3}{2} \cdot \frac{3}{2}$. Multiply the numerators; $\frac{3 \cdot 3}{} = \frac{9}{}$. Multiply the denominators; $\frac{9}{2 \cdot 2} = \frac{9}{4} = 2\frac{1}{4}$. **13.** $3\frac{8}{9}$ **15.** $7\frac{5}{9}$ **17.** $1\frac{41}{50}$ **19.** $3\frac{3}{8}x$

21. not correct; Press 1 $\div$ 4 $\times$ 7 $\div$ 8 $=$. The display reads 0.21875. **23.** correct

25. correct

Lesson 10, pages 114–115

1. $1\frac{1}{5}$; Find the reciprocal of the divisor (the second fraction). The reciprocal of $\frac{5}{8}$ $= \frac{8}{5}$. Multiply the dividend by this reciprocal; $\frac{3}{4} \cdot \frac{8}{5} = \frac{24}{20} = 1\frac{1}{5}$. **3.** $\frac{3}{8}$ **5.** $1\frac{2}{3}$

7. $\frac{2m}{3}$ **9.** $2\frac{1}{12}$; Express each mixed number as an improper fraction; $2\frac{1}{2} \div 1\frac{1}{5}$ $= \frac{5}{2} \div \frac{6}{5}$. Find the reciprocal of the divisor; $\frac{6}{5} = \frac{5}{6}$. Multiply the dividend by this reciprocal; $\frac{5}{2} \cdot \frac{5}{6} = \frac{25}{12} = 2\frac{1}{12}$. **11.** $\frac{8}{25}$

13. $\frac{6}{7}$ **15.** $1\frac{5}{13}h$ **17.** $\frac{9}{14}k$ **18.** $\frac{3}{8}$ of the court; To solve, divide $13\frac{1}{2}$ by $\frac{36}{1}$. Express the mixed number as an improper fraction; $13\frac{1}{2} = \frac{27}{2}$. Multiply the dividend by the reciprocal of the divisor; $\frac{27}{2} \cdot \frac{1}{36} = \frac{27}{72} = \frac{3}{8}$. **19.** $43\frac{3}{4}$ pieces

Try This

$1\frac{1}{4}$

Chapter 4 Application, page 116

1. $4\frac{1}{12}$ cups **3.** $1\frac{3}{4}$ cups

Chapter 4 Review, pages 117–119

1. B **3.** C **5.** C **7.** D **9.** $3\frac{1}{3}$ **11.** $\frac{12}{5}$

13. $\frac{10}{3}$ Sample answers shown for **15–19.**
15. $\frac{2}{8}$ and $\frac{3}{12}$ **17.** $\frac{14}{20}$ and $\frac{21}{30}$
19. $\frac{10}{24}$ and $\frac{15}{36}$ **21.** $\frac{2}{3}$ **23.** $\frac{1}{4}$ **25.** $\frac{7}{15}$
27. $\frac{2}{3}, \frac{5}{6}, \frac{11}{12}$ **29.** $\frac{13}{24}, \frac{9}{16}, \frac{5}{8}$ **31.** $\frac{9}{16}$ **33.** $\frac{8}{9}$
35. $17\frac{1}{12}$ **37.** $13\frac{17}{24}$ **39.** $2\frac{13}{24}$ **41.** $5\frac{29}{32}$
43. $13\frac{5}{12}h$ **45.** $\frac{a}{6}$

CHAPTER 5

Lesson 1, pages 124–125

1. 22; Follow the order of operations and divide first; $8 \div 4 = 2$. Then subtract; $24 - 2 = 22$. **3.** 12 **5.** 35 **7.** 27 **9.** 17
11. 106 **13.** 80 **15.** 11 **16.** 3; Press 10 $-$ 2 $\times$ 4 $+$ 1 $=$. The display reads 3.
17. 19 **19.** 26

Try This

Answers will vary. Sample answer: $2 + 3(4) = 20$. Error: First multiply and then add. $2 + 3(4) = 14$.

Lesson 2, page 129

1. $8\frac{1}{3}$; Substitute 9 for a in the expression. $9 - \frac{2}{3} = \frac{9}{1} - \frac{2}{3} = \frac{27}{3} - \frac{2}{3} = \frac{25}{3} = 8\frac{1}{3}$
3. 14 **5.** 1 **7.** 35 **9.** $1\frac{1}{2}$ **11.** 36; Substitute 12 for x in the expression. $12 + 2(12) = 12 + 24 = 36$. **13.** $1\frac{1}{8}$ **15.** $1\frac{7}{12}$ **17.** 24
18. Kareem is 14; his sister is 15; $x + (x + 1) = 2x + 1 = 29$; $2x = 28$; $x = 14$; $x + 1 = 15$. **19.** Sherry is 22; Sara is 24

Lesson 3, page 131

1. false; Substitute 2 for x in the equation $4x - 3 = 13$; $4(2) - 3 = 8 - 3 = 5$, not 13. **3.** true **5.** false **6.** 2; Substitute numbers for x in the equation until the sides are equal to each other; $17 - 3(2) = 17 - 6 = 11$ **7.** 4 **9.** 0 **11.** 1 **13.** 3 **15.** 7

Lesson 4, page 133

1. $\frac{2}{3}$; Subtracting $\frac{2}{3}$ from the expression would isolate x. **3.** 4 **5.** 14; Isolate the variable by subtracting 3 from each side of the equation; $a + 3 - 3 = 17 - 3$. Perform each operation; $a = 14$. **7.** 17 **9.** $\frac{2}{5}$ **11.** $\frac{1}{2}$ **13.** $\frac{1}{4}$ **15.** $\frac{3}{8}$

Lesson 5, page 135

1. 36; Isolate the variable by adding 14 to each side of the equation; $x - 14 + 14 = 22 + 14$. Perform each operation; $x = 36$. **3.** 65 **5.** $\frac{4}{5}$ **7.** $1\frac{1}{4}$ **9.** 141 million miles; Isolate the variable by adding 48 to each side of the equation; $x - 48 + 48 = 93 + 48$. Perform each operation; $x = 141$.

Try This

19, 3, 14, 20

Lesson 6, pages 138–139

1. $\frac{3}{4}$; Rewrite the complex fraction horizontally; $\frac{1}{2} \div \frac{2}{3}$. Multiply the dividend by the reciprocal of the divisor; $\frac{1}{2} \cdot \frac{3}{2} = \frac{3}{4}$. **3.** 9 **5.** $3\frac{3}{4}$ **7.** 10 **9.** $4\frac{1}{6}$ **11.** $\frac{2}{3}$ **13.** $28\frac{4}{5}$ **15.** $\frac{7}{128}$ **17.** $28\frac{4}{7}$ **19.** not correct; Press 1 $\boxed{a^{b/c}}$ 4 $\div$ 1 $\boxed{a^{b/c}}$ 8 $\boxed{=}$. The display reads 2. **21.** correct **23.** not correct **25.** not correct

Lesson 7, page 141

1. $\frac{3}{4a}$; To simplify $\frac{1}{8a} + \frac{5}{8a}$ only add the numerators; $\frac{1}{8a} + \frac{5}{8a} = \frac{6}{8a} = \frac{3}{4a}$. **3.** $\frac{6}{5c}$ **5.** $\frac{5y}{4}$ or $1\frac{1}{4}y$ **7.** $\frac{7}{9t}$ **9.** $\frac{1}{2b}$ **11.** $\frac{6}{5n}$; Add the numerators; $\frac{7}{10n} + \frac{5}{10n} = \frac{12}{10n} = \frac{6}{5n}$. **13.** $\frac{5d}{4}$ or $1\frac{1}{4}d$ **15.** $\frac{17}{12b}$

Lesson 8, page 143

1. $\frac{1}{2a}$; To simplify $\frac{5}{8a} - \frac{1}{8a}$ only subtract the numerators; $\frac{5}{8a} - \frac{1}{8a} = \frac{4}{8a} = \frac{1}{2a}$. **3.** $\frac{2}{5c}$ **5.** $\frac{y}{2}$ **7.** $\frac{5}{9t}$ **9.** $\frac{1}{4b}$ **11.** $\frac{1}{5n}$; To simplify $\frac{7}{10n} - \frac{1}{2n}$ convert the fractions to equivalent fractions with like denominators; $\frac{7}{10n} - \frac{5}{10n} = \frac{2}{10n} = \frac{1}{5n}$. **13.** $\frac{7}{12d}$ **15.** $\frac{5}{12b}$ **17.** $\frac{13q}{18}$ **18.** $\frac{1}{4}$ dollar more; To solve $\frac{1}{2} - \frac{1}{4}$ convert the fractions to equivalent fractions with like denominators; $\frac{2}{4} - \frac{1}{4} = \frac{1}{4}$. **19.** $\frac{2}{3}$ left

Lesson 9, page 145

1. $\frac{1}{6}$; Multiply the numerators and the denominators; $\frac{1}{4} \cdot \frac{2}{3} = \frac{2}{12} = \frac{1}{6}$. **3.** $\frac{27}{110}$ **5.** $\frac{16}{135}$ **7.** $\frac{8}{135}$ **9.** $\frac{32}{63a}$ **11.** $\frac{5}{12}$ **13.** $\frac{2}{3y}$ **15.** $\frac{75p}{112}$ **16.** 21 years old; $\frac{3}{5} \cdot \frac{35}{1} = \frac{105}{5} = 21$. **17.** $\frac{4}{9}$ of the cereal **19.** $\frac{15}{32}$ of the casserole

Chapter 5 Application, page 146

1. $5\frac{1}{2}$ feet **3.** 2,500 meters

Chapter 5 Review, pages 147–149

1. B **3.** D **5.** D **7.** C **9.** false **11.** true **13.** true **15.** false **17.** 6 **19.** 11 **21.** 6 **23.** $\frac{2}{3}$ **25.** 8 **27.** 2 **29.** $12\frac{4}{5}$ **31.** $\frac{1}{2c}$ **33.** $\frac{21}{16r}$ **35.** $\frac{19}{30z}$ **37.** $\frac{17}{12w}$ **39.** $\frac{1}{9x}$ **41.** $\frac{9}{88w}$ **43.** $\frac{14p}{45}$ **45.** $\frac{5}{18a}$

Lesson 1, page 153

1. $\frac{4}{3}$; 4:3 3. 7 to 2; 7:2 5. 5 to 11; 5:11

7. $\frac{1}{2}$; Divide 9 and 18 by 9, the GCD.

9. $\frac{17}{2}$ 11. $\frac{32}{9}$ 13. $\frac{1}{6}$ 15. $\frac{4}{7}$; There are 14 students and 6 are boys, so $14 - 6$, or 8, are girls. In simplest form, $\frac{8}{14} = \frac{4}{7}$. 17. 4 boys 19. Even, because there are $3 + 1$ coins, or some multiple of 4 coins, in the collection.

Lesson 2, page 155

1. no; The cross products are 90 and 100. In a true proportion, the cross products are equal. 3. No 5. Yes

7. 3; Multiply the cross products, $(2)(12) = (n)(8)$, and divide each side of the equation by 8. 9. 16 11. 7 13. 12 15. 6

Lesson 3, page 157

1. 160 hits; Write and solve the proportion $\frac{1 \text{ hit}}{3 \text{ at bats}} = \frac{n \text{ hits}}{480 \text{ at bats}}$. 3. 420 frames 5. 2 perfect scores 7. 54 players

9. 105 children

Lesson 4, pages 160–161

1. $\frac{53}{100}$; The grid contains 100 squares; of those squares, 53 are shaded. 3. $\frac{83}{100}$

4. 7%; Seven out of 100 squares are shaded. The ratio 7:100 can be written as the fraction $\frac{7}{100}$. A percent is the numerator of a fraction whose denominator is 100. 5. 47% 7. 91%

8. 22%; Denominator is 100, write numerator with %. 9. 95% 11. 53%

13. 33% 15. 9%

Try This

$\frac{4,000}{10,000} = \frac{4}{10} = \frac{2}{5}$ is shaded;

$\frac{6,000}{10,000} = \frac{3}{5}$ is not shaded; $\frac{2}{5} + \frac{3}{5} = 1$

Lesson 5, pages 164–165

1. 75%; To express a decimal as a percent, move the decimal point two places to the right, and add a percent symbol. 3. 18%

5. 78% 7. 88% 9. 10% 10. 50%; To express a fraction as a percent, first use division to change the fraction to a decimal. Then move the decimal point two places to the right and add a percent symbol. 11. 25% 13. 40% 15. 70%

17. 76% 19. 0.11; To express a percent as a decimal, move the decimal point two places to the left and leave off the percent symbol. 21. 0.68 23. 0.17 25. 0.05

27. 0.83 28. Yes. Possible answer: For example, a test score can increase by more than 100% when compared to a previous test score. 29. 20% 31. 350% 33. 10%

35. Sample answer: Marc should choose an increase of $\frac{1}{5}$ because $\frac{1}{5} = 0.2 = 20\%$.

Lesson 6, page 167

1. 1.44; Change the percent to a decimal, then multiply 0.12 by 12. 3. 480 5. 936

7. 134 9. 655.5

Lesson 7, page 169

1. 250%; $(n)(4) = 10$; $4n = 10$; $n = \frac{10}{4} = 2.5 = 250\%$ 3. 37.5% or $37\frac{1}{2}\%$ 5. 5%

6. 13.5; Press 75 $\boxed{\times}$ 18 $\boxed{\%}$. The display reads 13.5. 7. 0.15 9. 392

Lesson 8, page 171

1. $3.50; Subtract $4.00 from $7.50
3. Increase; 15.625%; Find the amount of increase ($1,850 − $1,600 = $250) and then solve the equation $250 = $(x)($1,600)$. **5.** 8%

Lesson 9, page 173

1. $551.25; $A = P(1 + i)^n$; $A = 500(1 + .05)^2$; $A = 551.25$ **3.** $3,589.07
5. $10,049.50

Try This
7 years

Chapter 6 Application, page 174
1. $18.36 **3.** 6%

Chapter 6 Review, pages 175–177
1. D **3.** A **5.** C **7.** A **9.** 12% **11.** 55%
13. 50% **15.** 10% **17.** 25% **19.** 16%
21. 58% **23.** 0.21 **25.** 0.19 **27.** 0.11
29. 0.79 **31.** 50% **33.** $1,837.56
35. 57.1%

CHAPTER 7

Lesson 1, pages 182–183
1. 3; 3 is 3 units from zero. **3.** 10 **5.** 12
7. 73 **9.** −4; The opposite of a positive integer is a negative integer. **11.** 73 **13.** −8
15. −1 **17.** A, B, C; These letters represent real numbers to the right of zero. **19.** E
21. +3; The team moves forward 3 yards.
23. −40 **25.** −13 **27.** −10 **29.** +2,500

Lesson 2, page 185
1. >; On a number line, 5 is farther to the right than 2. **3.** > **5.** > **7.** = **9.** >
11. = **13.** > **15.** > **17.** > **19.** =

Lesson 3, page 187
1. <; On a number line, 2 is farther to the left than 5. **3.** = **5.** = **7.** = **9.** <
11. < **13.** < **15.** < **17.** < **19.** <
21. Yes, the integers follow one another in order and none are missing. **23.** −5 is farther left, so −5 < −3

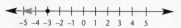

25. No, you need to know whether the integer is 8 units to the left or to the right of zero.

Lesson 4, page 189
1. even; Digit in the ones place is even.
3. even **5.** odd **6.** 876, even; Digit in the ones place is even. **7.** 171, odd **9.** 1,376, even **11.** 4,692, even **13.** 98, even
15. 330, even **16.** 864, even; Digit in the ones place is even. **17.** 1,404, even
19. 946, even **21.** •, 20; even • odd = even
23. +, 9 or −, 3 **25.** •, 27

Try This
even ÷ even = even or odd (64 ÷ 8 = 8, 44 ÷ 4 = 11)
even ÷ odd = even (24 ÷ 3 = 8)
odd ÷ odd = odd (35 ÷ 5 = 7)

Lesson 5, page 191
1. 11; Adding a positive to a positive gives a result farther to the right on a number line. **3.** 5 **5.** 0 **7.** 3 **9.** −5 **11.** −8 **13.** 5
15. 2 **16.** 1,630; 652 $\boxed{+}$ 978 $\boxed{=}$. The display reads 1,630 **17.** −202 **19.** 727

Lesson 6, page 193
1. −9; Adding a negative to a negative gives a result farther to the left on a number line. **3.** −11 **5.** 8 **7.** −602; 359 $\boxed{+/-}$ $\boxed{+}$ 243 $\boxed{+/-}$ $\boxed{=}$. The display reads

−602 **9.** −1,071 **11.** 870 **13.** 27,000 ft;
25,000 ft + 2,000 ft **15.** 1,017 ft

Lesson 7, pages 196–197

1. 4 + (−5) = −1; Adding a negative to
a positive gives a result farther to the left
on the number line. **3.** −6 + 5 = −1
5. 7 + (−5) = 2 **7.** −2 + (−4) = −6
9. 7 + 4 = 11 **11.** −4; Subtracting 7 is
the same as adding −7. **13.** 0 **15.** 7
17. −8 **19.** 12 **21.** 30,340 feet; 29,028 ft
+ 1,312 ft **23.** 221°F **25.** 75 minutes

Lesson 8, page 199

1. 20; (+5) • (+4) = (+20) **3.** −24 **5.** 99
7. −20 **9.** −70 **11.** −21 **13.** 49 **15.** −15
17. −104 **19.** −27 **21.** positive; (Positive)
• (Positive) = (Positive) **23.** negative
25. positive **27.** negative **29.** positive

Lesson 9, page 201

1. positive; (Negative) • (Negative) =
(Positive) **3.** negative **5.** positive
7. negative **9.** positive **11.** 15 points
under par; −5 • 3 = −15 **13.** −$36
15. −$30.00

Lesson 10, page 203

1. 2; Like signs give positive quotients.
3. −6 **5.** 3 **7.** −5 **9.** −2 **11.** 3 **13.** −1
15. −3 **17.** −8 **19.** −3 **21.** positive; Like
signs give positive quotients. **23.** positive
25. positive **27.** negative **29.** 240 seats;
1,440 ÷ 6 = 240

Try This
−20, −5

Chapter 7 Application, page 204

1. Mariana Trench **3.** 7,608 feet deeper

Chapter 7 Review, pages 205–207

1. B **3.** D **5.** A **7.** C **9.** 14 **11.** 71

13. 4 **15.** −43 **17.** 4 > 0 **19.** −2 < |−5|
21. 10 **23.** 0 **25.** −3 **27.** −18 **29.** −2
31. −3 **33.** −7 **35.** −42 **37.** 96 **39.** −40
41. −4 **43.** 4 **45.** −7 **47.** 39,730 feet
49. −7

CHAPTER 8

Lesson 1, page 211

1. 2; In 4^2; 4 is the base, 2 is the exponent.
3. 3 **5.** 3 **7.** 5 **9.** 1 **11.** 2^3; 2 to the third
power. **13.** 4^3 **15.** 5^4 **17.** x^4 **19.** m^6
21. 1,024; Press 2 $\boxed{y^x}$ 10 $\boxed{=}$. The display
reads 1024. **23.** 4,096 **25.** 0.25

Lesson 2, page 213

1. 4^4; To multiply numbers with the same
base, add their exponents. **3.** 2^7 **5.** 4^8 **7.** a^8
9. x^7 **11.** 2^{2n} **13.** true; $2^3 • 2^5 = 2^{3+5} = 2^8$
15. false, the two terms in this expression
do not have the same base. **17.** false, 3^{3+1}
= 3^4 **19.** true **21.** false, $n^{6+2} = n^8$
23. true **25.** true

Try This
x^{n+m}, a^{x+y}

Lesson 3, page 215

1. 7; To divide numbers with the same
base, subtract their exponents. Any
number to the first power is the number
itself. **3.** 2 **5.** 9^2 **7.** h^3 **9.** k^3 **11.** y
13. false, $2^{8-2} = 2^6$ **15.** false, $9^{3-1} = 9^2$
17. false, $3^{3-1} = 3^2$ **19.** false, $x^{12-3} = x^9$
21. false, $(−s)^{6-2} = (−s)^4$ **23.** false,
$x^{15-3} = x^{12}$ **25.** true

Try This
$19^{x-w}, 1$

Lesson 4, page 217

1. 2^2; Area = $s^2 = 2 • 2 = 2^2$ **3.** y^2 **5.** p^2
6. 49 sq cm; Area = $s^2 = 7 • 7 = 49$

7. 81 sq cm **9.** 16 sq cm **11.** $s^2 = 12^2 = 144$ sq ft **13.** $s^2 = 7^2 = 49$ sq ft **15.** $s^2 = 800^2 = 640,000$ sq m

Lesson 5, pages 218–219
1. 27 cu in.; $3 \cdot 3 \cdot 3 = 27$ **3.** 125 cu in.
4. 4^3; Volume $= s^3 = 4 \cdot 4 \cdot 4 = 4^3$ **5.** 2^3
7. y^3 **9.** 512 cu cm; Press 8 $\boxed{y^x}$ 3 $\boxed{=}$. The display reads 512. **11.** 8 cu cm
13. 5,832 cu cm **14.** 1 cu ft; Volume $= s^3 = 1 \cdot 1 \cdot 1 = 1$ **15.** 27 cu ft

Lesson 6, pages 222–223
1. 1, 2; 1.73; Press 3 $\boxed{\sqrt{}}$. The display reads 1.732050808; Round to the nearest hundredth. **3.** 2, 3; 2.45 **5.** 2, 3; 2.83
7. 3, 4; 3.61 **9.** 9, 10; 9.95 **11.** 10, 11; 10.25 **13.** 14, 15; 14.70 **15.** 20, 21; 20.66
16. 4; Side of square $= \sqrt{16}$ **17.** 3.2
19. 2.8

Lesson 7, page 225
Answers will vary. **1.** 3.2; 10 is between 9 and 16, so the $\sqrt{10}$ is between 3 and 4.
3. 5.5 **5.** 7.1 **7.** 8.1 **9.** 9.2

Try This
$\sqrt{81} = 9$, rational
$\sqrt{91} \approx 9.5$, irrational
$\sqrt{111} \approx 10.5$, irrational
$\sqrt{121} = 11$, rational

Lesson 8, pages 228–229
1. 25; $x = \sqrt{7^2 + 24^2}$; $x = \sqrt{625}$; $x = 25$
3. 29 **5.** 24 **6.** 4.4; $x^2 = 10^2 - 9^2$; $x = \sqrt{100 - 81}$; $x = \sqrt{19}$; $x = 4.4$ **7.** 40.3
9. 5.9

Try This
Be sure to draw a triangle with a 90° angle. Check your classmate's calculations.

Lesson 9, page 231
1. 5, no, no, yes; $c = \sqrt{3^2 + 4^2}$; $c = \sqrt{25}$; $c = 5$; This triangle does not have three or two sides of equal length. It is scalene because it has no equal sides. **3.** no, yes, no **5.** 6, yes, no, yes

Chapter 8 Application, page 232
1. 29.7 miles **3.** 11.2 meters

Chapter 8 Review, pages 233–235
1. B **3.** B **5.** D **7.** A **9.** m^2 **11.** 6^2, 36
13. 6^3, 216 **15.** s^3 **17.** 5^3, 125
19. between 8 and 9 **21.** between 9 and 10
23. 8.7 **25.** 31.6 **27.** 11.4 **29.** 11.3

CHAPTER 9

Lesson 1, pages 240–241
1. 12 ft; $P = 3$ ft $+ 4$ ft $+ 5$ ft **3.** 7.125 cm
4. $14\frac{3}{4}$ in.; $P = 3\frac{1}{8}$ in. $+ 3\frac{1}{8}$ in. $+ 8\frac{1}{2}$ in.
5. 4.66 m **7.** 611.75 ft **8.** 86.2 m; Subtract the two given sides (each 42.5 m) from the perimeter. Divide the difference (172.4) by 2. **9.** 31.67 mm or $31\frac{2}{3}$ mm

Try This
$P = s + s + s + s$, $P = 4s$

Lesson 2, pages 244–245
1. 18 cm; $P = 6$ cm $+ 6$ cm $+ 6$ cm
3. 111 in. **5.** 117 yd **7.** 10 sides; Divide 82.5 by 8.25 to find the number of sides.
9. Yes. Sample explanation: Find the perimeters of the square and rectangle. A 20 by 10 rectangle has the same perimeter (60 in.) as a 15 by 15 square.

Try This

Sample answer: $P = nm$ where $n =$ the number of sides of a regular polygon and $m =$ the measure of one side.

Lesson 3, pages 248–249

1. $8\frac{5}{6}$; $P = 2 + 3 + 1\frac{1}{2} + 2\frac{1}{3}$ **3.** 94.5 cm
5. 11.71 m **6.** 1, 10; Since the measure of the side opposite the missing side is 2, the measure of the missing side is $2 - 1$ or 1.
$P = 2 + 3 + 1 + 1 + 1 + 2 = 10$ **7.** $1\frac{1}{4}$, 9
9. 16.5 in., 109.5 in.

Lesson 4, pages 251–253

1. 84 cm^2; Use the formula $A = lw$; $A = 12 \cdot 7$. **3.** 102 mm^2 **5.** $3\frac{3}{4}$ yd^2 **7.** 81 mm^2;
Use the formula $A = s^2$; $A = 9^2$ or $9 \cdot 9$.
9. 19.36 m^2 **11.** $6\frac{1}{4}$ ft^2 **13.** 400 m^2; Press
20 $\boxed{x^2}$ The display reads 400. **15.** 56.25 ft^2
17. 1.2544 mi^2 **19.** 144 m^2; Use the formula $A = s^2$; $A = 12^2 = 12 \cdot 12$

Lesson 5, page 255

1. 80 in.^{2}; Use the formula $A = \frac{1}{2}bh = \frac{1}{2}(10)(16)$ **3.** 261 ft^2 **5.** 21 **6.** 4 in.; Use the formula $A = \frac{1}{2}bh$; $36 = \frac{1}{2}(18)h$; $\frac{36}{1} \cdot \frac{2}{18}$
$= \frac{h(18)}{2} \cdot \frac{2}{18} = \frac{72}{18} = 4 = h$ **7.** 4 ft **9.** 10 ft;
Use the formula $A = \frac{1}{2}bh$; $60 = \frac{1}{2}(12)h$;
$\frac{60}{1} \cdot \frac{2}{12} = \frac{b(12)}{2} \cdot \frac{2}{12} = \frac{120}{12} = 10 = h$

Lesson 6, page 257

1. 160 mm^2; Use the formula $A = bh$; $A = 8 \cdot 20$ **3.** 30 ft^2 **5.** 47,200 mm^2 **7.** 3.5 ft;
Use the formula $A = bh$; $7 = b(2)$; $7 \cdot \frac{1}{2}$
$= b(\frac{2}{1}) \cdot \frac{1}{2}$; $3\frac{1}{2} = b$ **9.** 2 in.

Lesson 7, page 259

1. 70 units^2; $(2 \cdot 3) + (8 \cdot 8) = 6 + 64$

3. 442.5 units^2 **5.** 632 units^2

Lesson 8, pages 262–263

1. 125 cm^3; Use the formula $V = e^3$;
$5 \cdot 5 \cdot 5$ **3.** 30 m^3 **4.** 27,000 mm^3; Press
30 $\boxed{y^x}$ 3 $\boxed{=}$ The display reads 27000
5. 262.144 in.^{3} **7.** 1,906,624 in.^{3} **9.** 60 in.^{3};
$(4 \cdot 4 \cdot 4) - (1 \cdot 1 \cdot 4) = 64 - 4 = 60$

Lesson 9, pages 266–267

1. 18.84 in.; Since radius $= 3$, then diameter $= 6$. Now use the formula $C = \pi d$; $C = 3.14 \cdot 6$ **3.** 37.68 m **5.** 62.8 yd
6. 50.24 m^2; Use the formula $A = \pi r^2$;
$A = 3.14 \cdot 4^2 = 3.14 \cdot 16$ **7.** 50.24 in.^{2}
9. 153.86 cm^2 **11.** 132.7322896 in.^{2};
Press $\boxed{\pi}$ $\boxed{\times}$ 6.5 $\boxed{x^2}$ $\boxed{=}$. The display reads 132.7322896. **13.** 4.523893421 m^2
15. 1.038689071 mi^2

Lesson 10, page 269

1. 125.6 in.^{3}; Use the formula $V = \pi r^2 h$;
$V = (3.14)(2)^2(10)$; $(3.14)(2)(2)(10)$
3. 2,009.6 mm^3 **5.** 523.$\overline{3}$ cm^3; Use the
formula $V = \frac{4}{3}\pi r^3$; $V = \frac{4}{3}(3.14)(5)^3$;
$\frac{4}{3}(392.5)$; $\frac{4}{3} \cdot \frac{392.5}{1} = \frac{1,570}{3} = 523.\overline{3}$
7. 4.18$\overline{6}$ ft^3 **9.** 904.32 in.^{3}; Use the
formula $V = \frac{4}{3}\pi r^3$; $V = \frac{4}{3}(3.14)(6)^3$;
$\frac{4}{3}(678.24) = \frac{4}{3} \cdot \frac{678.24}{1} = \frac{2,712.96}{3} = 904.32$

Chapter 9 Application, page 270

1. $13\frac{1}{3}$ square yards **3.** 1 gallon

Chapter 9 Review, pages 271–273

1. B **3.** C **5.** A **7.** B **9.** 30 m^2 **11.** 243 ft^2
13. 715 yd^2 **15.** 180 in.^{3} **17.** 4,000,000 ft^3
19. $C = 38.308$ cm $A = 116.8394$ cm^2
21. 1,436.02$\overline{6}$ in.^{3} **23.** 14.13 ft^3
25. 95.3775 in.^{3}

CHAPTER 10

Lesson 1, page 277

1. Shaded circle indicates the solution.

3.

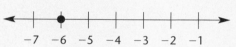

5.

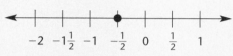

6. $x = 5$; A shaded circle indicates an integer solution. **7.** $x = 0$ **9.** $x = 1\frac{1}{2}$

Lesson 2, pages 280–281

1.

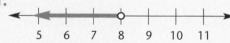

The open circle on 8 and the heavy line to the left show that all numbers less than 8 are solutions to the inequality.

3.

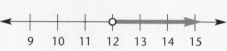

5.

7. $x < -7$; The open circle on -7 and heavy line to the left show that all numbers less than -7 are solutions to the inequality. **9.** $x \le 1$ **11.** $x \ge 5$ **13.** $x \le 0$ **15.** $x \le -4$

Lesson 3, page 283

1. $d = 3$; $3 + 4 = 7$

3. $g = -5$

5. $n = 6$

7. $x + 8 = 17$ or $17 - x = 8$; The shaded circle at 9 shows that it is the solution. $9 + 8 = 17$ or $17 - 9 = 8$; $x = 9$

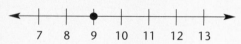

9. $45 - x = 15$ or $15 + x = 45$; $x = 30$

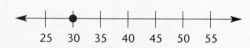

Lesson 4, page 285

1. $d < 3$; All numbers less than 3 solve the inequality.

3. $c < 3$

5. $w \le 2$

7. $r \leq -10$

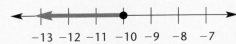

9. $z > -1$

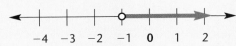

11. $v < -7$

13. $x + 35 \geq 52$; $x \geq 17$; 17 and all numbers greater than 17 solve the inequality.

15. $10 - x \leq 3$; $7 \leq x$

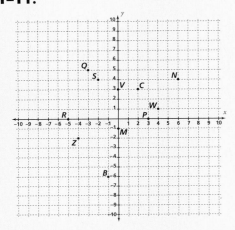

Lesson 5, page 289

1. $(1, 6)$; Point K is 1 unit to the right of the y-axis and 6 units above the x-axis.
3. $(0, 7)$ **5.** $(-7, -5)$ **7.** $(0, -6)$
9. $(7, -5)$ **11.** Quadrant I; Point K is in the upper right quarter of the system.
13. Quadrant III **15.** Quadrant III
17. 2 units; Plot points $(0, 0)$ and $(2, 0)$. The distance between these points is 2 units. **19.** 3 units

Lesson 6, page 291
1–11.

12. Quadrant I; Since the first coordinate of the ordered pair is positive, the point lies to the right of the y-axis, and since the second coordinate of the ordered pair is positive, the point lies above the x-axis.
13. Quadrant III **15.** Quadrant II

Lesson 7, pages 294–295
1. $y = x + 1$; $x = -1, 0, 1$; $y = 0, 1, 2$; Substitute the values for x and y; $0 = -1 + 1$; $1 = 0 + 1$; $2 = 1 + 1$ **3.** $y = x + 3$; $x = -7, -1, -4$; $y = -4, 2, -1$
5. Answers will vary. Sample answer shown. $y = x + 6$; $x = -1, 0, 1$; $y = 5, 6, 7$
7. -65.2; Substitute -53.2 for x in the equation and find y; $-53.2 \boxed{-} 12 \boxed{=}$. The display reads -65.2. **9.** -101.9

Lesson 8, page 297

Sample answers shown.

1. $y = x + 5$; $x = -2, 0, 2$; $y = 3, 5, 7$

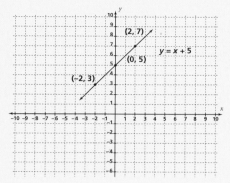

3.

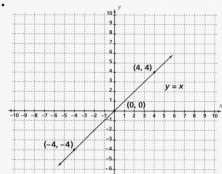

5.

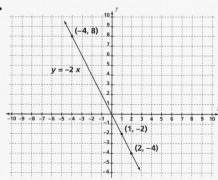

7.

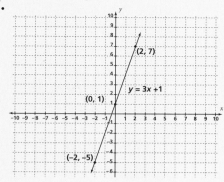

9.

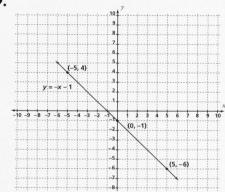

Try This

Check your partner's work to be sure the equation was written correctly.

Lesson 9, page 299

1. 0.0125; Use the formula slope $= \dfrac{\text{rise}}{\text{run}}$. Press .2 $\boxed{\div}$ 16 $\boxed{=}$. The display reads 0.0125 **3.** -0.066666667 **5.** 2 **7.** 12

8. negative slope; The line moves downward when viewed from left to right.

9. zero slope

Lesson 10, pages 301–303

1. $\dfrac{1}{5}$; Simplify $\dfrac{0 - 1}{0 - 5} = \dfrac{-1}{-5} = \dfrac{1}{5}$. **3.** $\dfrac{-9}{8}$

5. $\dfrac{5}{11}$ **7.** 0 **9.** $\dfrac{2}{11}$; $m = \dfrac{y_2 - y_1}{x_2 - x_1} = \dfrac{5 - 3}{4 - (-7)}$

$= \dfrac{2}{11}$ **11.** $\dfrac{-9}{4}$ **13.** $\dfrac{-1}{9}$ **14.** Sample answer: The last half of the trail is more difficult because it has a positive, or uphill, slope. The first half of the trail has a negative slope. It is downhill. **15.** Sample answer: The first half of the trail is more difficult. Since an equivalent fraction for $\frac{3}{20}$ is $\frac{6}{40}$, the slope of the first half of the trail ($\frac{6}{40}$) is greater than the slope of the second half of the trail ($\frac{5}{40}$).

Try This
Triangle: a has a positive slope, b has a negative slope, and c has zero slope. Parallelogram: a and c have positive slopes and b and d have zero slopes.

Lesson 11, page 307
1. slope $= m = 1$; y-intercept $= -1$; x-intercept $= 1$; The slope of the line is 1 because the line moves 1 unit vertically for every 1 unit horizontally. The y-intercept is -1 because the line crosses the y-axis at -1. The x-intercept is 1 because the line crosses the x-axis at $+1$. **3.** $y = x + 5$; Divide each side of the equation by 2. **5.** $y = 2x - 1$ **7.** $y = -x - 1$ **9.** $m = 1$; y-intercept $= -3$; x-intercept $= 3$; In the equation $y = x - 3$, the slope and y-intercept are the corresponding values for m and b in the equation $y = mx + b$. To find the x-intercept, substitute 0 for y in the equation $y = x - 3$ and solve for x. **11.** $m = -2$; y-intercept $= -4$; x-intercept $= -2$ **13.** $m = 1$; y-intercept $= 1$; x-intercept $= -1$ **15.** $m = 1$; y-intercept $= -5$; x-intercept $= 5$ **17.** $m = -1$; y-intercept $= -1$; x-intercept $= -1$ **19.** $m = \frac{1}{2}$; y-intercept $= 1$; x-intercept $= -2$

Chapter 10 Application, page 308
1. Sample answers: y-intercept $= \$500$; $i = 0.05s + \$500$ where $i =$ income and $s =$ sales **2.** Sample graph shown.

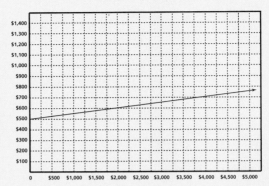

Chapter 10 Review, pages 309–311
1. C **3.** C **5.** B
7.

9.

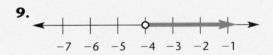

11.

13. $b \geq -1$

15. $m < 1$

17. Quadrant IV **19.** Quadrant I
21. (6, 2) **23.** (3, −7) **25.** (−4, 5)
27. (−7, −6)
29–32.

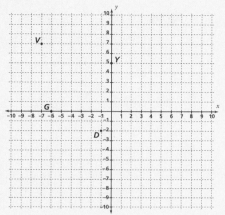

33. Sample answer: $y = x + 1$; $x = -2, 3,$ -1; $y = -1, 4, 0$ **35.** Sample answer: $y = -2x$; $x = -3, -2, -1$; $y = 6, 4, 2$

CHAPTER 11

Lesson 1, page 315
1. ∠XPA, ∠APX; Each name has letter P, the vertex, as the middle letter. **3.** ∠3, ∠GPF **5.** $\overrightarrow{PD}$ and $\overrightarrow{PE}$ **7.** 90°; The 0° line of the protractor is on side PY of the angle, and side PD is on 90°. **9.** 40° **11.** 35° **13.** 110°; The 0° line of the protractor is on side PY of the angle, and side PC is on 110°. **15.** 60°

Lesson 2, page 317
1. right; The symbol inside the angle shows a right angle. **3.** obtuse **5.** straight **6.** d, b; These angles share a vertex and a common side with ∠a. **7.** a, c; b, d **9.** 140°, 40°; Vertical angles have the same measure, so m∠a = m∠c and m∠b = m∠d. **10.** vertical, acute; These are opposite pairs of angles formed by the

intersection of two lines, and they are less than 90°. **11.** adjacent, one acute and one obtuse **13.** true; Vertical angles are opposite pairs of angles formed by the intersection of two lines. Their angles can be acute or obtuse. **15.** true

Lesson 3, pages 320–321
1. ∠OQP and ∠PQR; The sum of the measures of these angles equals 90°.
3. ∠PQR and ∠RQS **4.** 45°; The sum of the measures of complementary angles equals 90°; 90° − 45° = 45° **5.** 70° **7.** 35° **9.** 10° **10.** 160°; The sum of the measures of supplementary angles equals 180°; 180° − 20° = 160° **11.** 75° **13.** 30° **15.** 60° **16.** 60°; The sum of the measures of supplementary angles equals 180°; 180° − 120° = 60° **17.** 68° **19.** 45°, 135°

Try This
The sum of the measures of supplementary angles equals 180°; of right angles, 90°. 180° = 90° + x; x = 90°

Lesson 4, page 325
1. 90°; The sum of the measures of the angles in a triangle is 180°; 30° + 60° + x = 180°; x = 90° **3.** 110° **5.** 70° **6.** 40°; The supplement to the exterior angle (140°) is 40°. The sum of the measures of the angles in a triangle is 180°; 100° + 40° + y = 180°; y = 40° **7.** 30° **9.** 20° **11.** 35°; The supplement to the exterior angle (130°) is 50°; the supplement to the other exterior angle (85°) is 95°; 50° + 95° + z = 180°; z = 35° **13.** 36° **15.** 128°; m∠ABC + m(right angle) = m∠1; 38° + 90° = m∠1, m∠1 = 128°

Lesson 5, page 327

1. right isosceles; This triangle has a right angle and two sides of equal length.
3. equilateral and equiangular
5. isosceles **7.** scalene **9.** equiangular

Lesson 6, page 329

1. ASA; Two angles and the included side are equal. **3.** SAS **4.** yes, ASA **5.** no, angle is not included angle

Lesson 7, page 331

1. yes; These triangles are the same shape but not the same size. **3.** not enough information **5.** not enough information **6.** false; Isosceles triangles can have many different shapes. For all of them to be similar, they would all need the same shape. **7.** true **9.** true

Lesson 8, page 333

1. parallelogram; This polygon has two pairs of parallel sides, opposite sides of the same length, and opposite angles that are equal. **3.** trapezoid **4.** true; Rectangles are parallelograms with all angles 90°. This also describes squares. **5.** true **7.** false **9.** square, rectangle, parallelogram

Lesson 9, page 335

1. 90°; All angles in a rectangle are right angles. **3.** 90°; All angles in a rectangle are right angles. **5.** 47.61; Press 6.9 x^2. The display reads 47.61. **7.** 11.14 **9.** 6.48

Lesson 10, page 337

1. 6; A polygon whose interior angles equal 720° is a hexagon. **3.** 100 **5.** 1,800° **7.** 120° **9.** 162° **11.** 45° **13.** 30° **15.** 3.6°

Chapter 11 Application, page 338

1. Answers will vary. Sample tessellation:

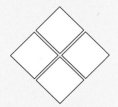

3. Answers will vary. Sample tessellation:

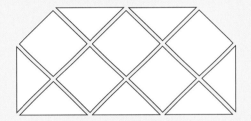

Chapter 11 Review, pages 339–341

1. C **3.** C **5.** C **7.** 35° **9.** 70° **11.** 140° **13.** *BXE, AXE, AXD, FXB* **15.** *DXF* **17.** *DXF* **19.** vertical and equal **21.** 130° **23.** 60° **25.** 40° **27.** 110° **29.** yes, corresponding angles are equal

Lesson 1, page 345

1. The graph displays the area, rounded to the nearest one hundred square miles, of selected Wyoming counties; the title of a graph describes the data it displays. **3.** The axis does not begin at zero. **5.** Crook County **7.** Hot Springs; Platte; Weston; Laramie; Crook **9.** Yes. Sample explanation: A horizontal bar graph is a vertical bar graph rotated 90° clockwise. **10.** Sample bar graph:

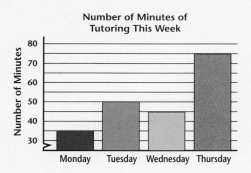

Try This

Answers will vary. Be sure to label the vertical axis and horizontal axis. Give your graph a title that describes the data shown.

Lesson 2, page 347

1. The graph describes how 40 students responded when asked if they usually sleep more than 8 hours each night; the title of a graph describes the data it displays. **3.** 20% **5.** 32 students **7.** 288° **9.** No; A circle cannot measure more than or less than 360°. **10.** Draw a circle. Find the fractional part for the total number of votes for each candidate. Candidate A: $\frac{9}{24}$ or $\frac{3}{8}$ Candidate B: $\frac{5}{24}$ votes

Candidate C: $\frac{10}{24}$ votes or $\frac{5}{12}$ Multiply each fractional part by 360°—the number of degrees in a circle. $\frac{9}{24}$ or $\frac{3}{8} \cdot 360° = 135°$ $\frac{5}{24} \cdot 360° = 75°$ $\frac{10}{24}$ or $\frac{5}{12} \cdot 360° = 150°$ Use a protractor to divide the circle into two parts. Measure and mark a 135° angle; label this part *Candidate A*. Then measure and mark a 75° angle, label this part *Candidate B*. The remaining part of the circle should measure 150°; label it *Candidate C*.

Sample circle graph:

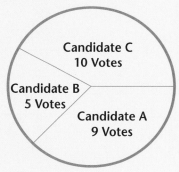

Lesson 3, page 349

1. 24 students; there are 24 tallies, and the sum of the numbers displayed in the frequency column is 24. **3.** The lowest quiz score was one number from 60–69. The interval in which the lowest quiz scored occurred is 60–69, but the exact score of the lowest quiz cannot be determined from the frequency table. **5.** Answers will vary. Make a frequency table with three columns labeled *Interval, Tally,* and *Frequency.* Determine the intervals for the minutes studied and list them. Survey your classmates and make a tally mark for each interval reported. Grouping tallies in groups of five will help anyone reading the frequency table interpret the data more quickly. Record the exact number of tallies for each interval in the *Frequency* column. The sum of the numbers in the *Frequency* column must be the same as the sum of the tallies in the *Tally* column. Write a title for your frequency table. Sample frequency table:

Frequency Table		
Interval	Tally	Frequency
0–20	IIII	4
21–40	IIII	4
41–60	IIII	4
61–80	I	1
81–100	I	1

Lesson 4, pages 350–351

1. $0.55; Use addition to find the sum of the values in the set. $0.35 + $0.35 + $0.35 + $0.35 + $0.35 + $0.35 + $1.75 = $3.85 Count the pieces of data in {$0.35, $0.35, $0.35, $0.35, $0.35, $0.35, $1.75} = 7 pieces of data. Divide the sum of the values by the number of pieces of data. $3.85 ÷ 7 = $0.55 **3.** 14.125 points **5.** 54.1 inches **6.** 21.321; Press 18.2 $+$ $+$ 34 $+$ 28.004 $+$ 5.080 $=$. The display reads 85.284. Divide the sum by the number of values in the set of data. Press $÷$ 4 $=$. The display reads 21.321. **7.** 1,578 **9.** 5.7679 **11.** 17.08 **13.** 27.25 **14.** 58.4 years old; Use addition to find the sum of the values in the set. 61 + 52 + 69 + 64 + 46 = 292 Count the pieces of data in {61, 52, 69, 64, 46} = 5 pieces of data. Divide the sum of the values by the number of pieces of data. 292 ÷ 5 = 58.4 **15.** 3.6875 bills

Lesson 5, page 353

1. 106; Order the values in the set from the greatest to the least or the least to the greatest. 52, 85, 106, 141, 172. Cross off the greatest and least pairs (172, 52; 141, 85) until one value (106) remains in the middle of the set. **3.** 102 **4.** 84.6 in.; Order the values in the set from the greatest to the least or the least to the greatest. 70.6, 77.5, 78.2, 91.0, 101.3, 115.5 Cross off the greatest and least pairs (115.5, 70.6; 101.3, 77.5) until two values (78.2, 91.0) remain in the middle of the set. Add the values, then divide by two because there are two values in the set. 78.2 + 91.0 = 169.2 ÷ 2 = 84.6 **5.** 8,734.5 ft

Lesson 6, page 355

1. 1; Order the data from least to greatest or greatest to least value. 7.0, 7.1, 7.2, 7.2, 7.2, 7.8, 7.8, 8.0. Find the value that occurs most often. 7.2 occurs three times. No other value occurs that often. **3.** 2 modes **4.** 28, 29; Order the data from least to greatest or greatest to least value. 27, 28, 28, 29, 29, 30, 31, 32, 36, 49. Find the values that occur most often. 28 and 29 each occur twice. No other values occur that often. **5.** 31 **7.** 40 **9.** 27

Lesson 7, page 357

1. 17 points; Identify the greatest and least values in the set of data {82, 88, 99}. 99 is the greatest value; 82 is the least value. Subtract the least value from the greatest value. 99 − 82 = 17 **3.** 1,657,516 papers **5.** 46,150 square miles **7.** 5 minutes and 50.5 seconds **9.** $1,163.7 billion

Lesson 8, page 359

1. {2, 4, 8, 9, 10, 11, 12, 13, 14, 17, 20}
3. 2, lower extreme **5.** 14, upper quartile
7.

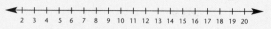

9.

10. Sample answer: Subtract the lower extreme from the upper extreme.

Lesson 9, page 361

1. $\frac{1}{2}$ or 50%; Since there are two possibilities when the coin is tossed—the coin will either land heads up or tails up—the denominator is two. Since one outcome is favorable—the coin landing heads up—the numerator is one. The probability of tossing a coin and having it land heads up is $\frac{1}{2}$ or 50%. **3.** $\frac{3}{6}$ or $\frac{1}{2}$ or 50% **4.** Since there are six possible outcomes when the cube is rolled, the denominator is six. Since there are three orange sides, the numerator is 3. The probability of the cube landing on orange is $\frac{1}{2}$. **5.** $\frac{1}{3}$

Try This

The probability can never be less than 0 and can never be greater than 1.

Lesson 10, page 363

1. 2 ways; If, for example, the digits were 5 and 8, the digits could be arranged as 58 or 85. No other arrangements are possible for two digits. **3.** 24 ways **4.** 970,200; Press 100 ☒ 99 ☒ 98 ☐. The display reads 970200. **5.** 3,603,600

Chapter 12 Application, page 364

1. food: $540 car payment: $240 savings: $120 mortgage: $840 misc. expenses: $420 recreation: $180 utilities: $210 clothing: $90 insurance: $150 taxes: $210
3. Answers will vary. Sample answer: savings 15% ($30) recreation 20% ($40) clothing 20% ($40) food 20% ($40) music lessons 15% ($30) guitar rental 10% ($20) All percentages must add to a total of 100%. All amounts must add to a total of $200.

Chapter 12 Review, pages 365–367

1. B **3.** D **5.** A **7.** B
9. Flavor A; $\frac{12}{20} = 60\%$
　　Flavor B; $\frac{3}{20} = 15\%$
　　Flavor C; $\frac{5}{20} = 25\%$

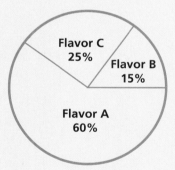

11. The package that weighed the most weighed more than 40 pounds but less than 50 pounds. Its exact weight is not known. **13.** $\frac{1}{2}$; 50% **15.** 24 ways

Supplementary Problems

CHAPTER 1

Pages 368–369

1. 9,862 **2.** 333,618 **3.** 1,305 **4.** 5,912
5. 156,910 **6.** 44,380 **7.** 3,577 **8.** 4,814
9. 527 **10.** 297,504 **11.** 233,411 **12.** 2,989
13. 147,839 **14.** 2,337 **15.** 2,144 **16.** 216
17. 5,040 **18.** 1,666 **19.** 84 **20.** 24
21. 4 r6 **22.** 723 r1 **23.** 1,363 r4 **24.** 21
25. 100,000 **26.** 180,000 **27.** 11,000
28. 150,000 **29.** 1,000 **30.** 750 **31.** open
32. false **33.** open **34.** false **35.** open
36. true **37.** numerical; division
38. algebraic; multiplication, x
39. algebraic; multiplication, subtraction, y
40. algebraic; division, w
41. numerical; addition, multiplication
42. algebraic; multiplication, addition, a
43. 30 **44.** 25 **45.** 36 **46.** 7 **47.** false
48. true **49.** true **50.** false

CHAPTER 2

Pages 370–371

1. thousandths place **2.** $3 \times 100 = 300$
3. ten-thousandths place **4.** $9 \times 1 = 9$
5. 7.818 **6.** 2.0001 **7.** 7.682 **8.** $50.02
9. 36.485 **10.** 12.385 **11.** 1,636.6
12. 1.615 **13.** $63.30 **14.** 523.962
15. 26.927 **16.** 6,570 **17.** 0.326 **18.** 70
19. 82.25 **20.** 26.272 **21.** 0.578 **22.** 0.064
23. $\frac{3}{4}$ **24.** $\frac{1}{2}$ **25.** $\frac{3}{8}$ **26.** $\frac{3}{25}$ **27.** 0.27
28. 0.94 **29.** 0.27 **30.** 0.78 **31.** $10,400
32. $530 **33.** 15.98 **34.** 21.7 **35.** 4.14
36. 14.29 **37.** true **38.** false **39.** true
40. false

CHAPTER 3

Pages 372–373

1. false **2.** $7 \cdot 12 = 84$ true **3.** $10 \cdot 356 = 3,560$ true **4.** false **5.** $4 \cdot 19 = 76$ true
6. false **7.** $8 \cdot 56 = 448$ true **8.** $9 \cdot 501 = 4,509$ true **9.** 84 is divisible by 2, 3, 4, 6.
10. 430 is divisible by 2, 5, 10. **11.** 3,120 is divisible by 2, 3, 4, 5, 6, 8, 10.
12. 32,022 is divisible by 2, 3, 6, 9.
13. composite **14.** composite **15.** prime
16. prime **17.** 7 **18.** 2 **19.** 3 **20.** 8
21. 50 **22.** 49 **23.** $6b + 54$ **24.** $105 + 63x$
25. $4c + 60 + 20a$ **26.** $136 + 17d + 102p$
27. 12 **28.** 5 **29.** $9x$ **30.** 6 **31.** 4 **32.** 1
33. $3(y + 7)$ **34.** $5(5x + 7)$ **35.** $5(2c + 1)$
36. $2(3u + 2)$ **37.** $4(6s + 7m)$
38. $6(2q + 3n)$ **39.** $7(z + 2b)$
40. $3(2j + 5k)$ **41.** 30 **42.** 48 **43.** 90
44. 150 **45.** 64 **46.** 60 **47.** 3,072
48. 110,592 **49.** 1,265,368 **50.** 64,800
51. $3.521 \cdot 10^{10}$ **52.** $4.5 \cdot 10^{6}$
53. $3.75 \cdot 10^{-5}$ **54.** $8.9 \cdot 10^{-8}$ **55.** $4.97 \cdot 10$

CHAPTER 4

Pages 374–375

1. $\frac{8}{3}$ **2.** $3\frac{2}{3}$ **3.** $6\frac{2}{5}$ **4.** $\frac{15}{8}$ **5.** $2\frac{1}{7}$ **6.** $\frac{59}{9}$
7. $\frac{15}{4}$ **8.** $5\frac{1}{4}$ **9.** possible answers: $\frac{14}{16}$ $\frac{21}{24}$
10. possible answers: $\frac{6}{10}$ $\frac{9}{15}$ **11.** possible answers: $\frac{2}{16}$ $\frac{3}{24}$ **12.** possible answers: $\frac{10}{28}$ $\frac{15}{42}$ **13.** possible answers: $\frac{18}{30}$ $\frac{27}{45}$

14. possible answers: $\frac{22}{24}$ $\frac{33}{36}$ **15.** possible answers: $\frac{2}{100}$ $\frac{3}{150}$ **16.** possible answers: $\frac{2}{20}$ $\frac{3}{30}$ **17.** $\frac{2}{5}$ **18.** $\frac{2}{15}$ **19.** $\frac{1}{7}$ **20.** $\frac{1}{3}$ **21.** $\frac{1}{9}$ **22.** $\frac{3}{4}$ **23.** $\frac{4}{9}$ **24.** $\frac{7}{10}$ **25.** $\frac{1}{5}$ $\frac{3}{10}$ $\frac{1}{2}$ **26.** $\frac{1}{4}$ $\frac{5}{12}$ $\frac{2}{3}$ **27.** $\frac{2}{9}$ $\frac{5}{18}$ $\frac{5}{6}$ **28.** $\frac{3}{7}$ $\frac{2}{3}$ $\frac{19}{21}$ **29.** $1\frac{1}{10}$ **30.** $\frac{1}{6}$ **31.** $16\frac{7}{8}y$ **32.** $\frac{5}{24}$ **33.** $\frac{20}{21}$ **34.** $8\frac{15}{16}$ **35.** $\frac{16}{49}$ **36.** $1\frac{1}{2}$ **37.** $15\frac{11}{15}g$ **38.** 8 **39.** $7\frac{4}{5}$ **40.** $2\frac{5}{16}$ **41.** $1\frac{1}{7}$ **42.** $6\frac{1}{16}$ **43.** $1\frac{3}{5}$ **44.** $1\frac{3}{16}$ **45.** $8\frac{5}{9}m$ **46.** $11\frac{1}{6}n$ **47.** 15 **48.** $\frac{6}{7}$ **49.** $6\frac{4}{5}$ **50.** $1\frac{5}{16}$

CHAPTER 5

Pages 376–377

1. 30 **2.** 28 **3.** 24 **4.** 27 **5.** 18 **6.** 9 **7.** 20 **8.** 0 **9.** 12 **10.** 3 **11.** 32 **12.** 53 **13.** $21\frac{6}{11}$ **14.** 0 **15.** 6 **16.** $1\frac{1}{6}$ **17.** $4\frac{1}{4}$ **18.** 12 **19.** true **20.** false **21.** false **22.** true **23.** true **24.** false **25.** true **26.** 5 **27.** 14 **28.** $7\frac{1}{2}$ **29.** 4 **30.** $1\frac{5}{8}$ **31.** 11 **32.** 16 **33.** 2 **34.** $1\frac{2}{5}$ **35.** $\frac{3}{8}$ **36.** $6\frac{6}{7}$ **37.** 4 **38.** $\frac{1}{9}$ **39.** 15 **40.** $\frac{15}{64}$ **41.** $\frac{3}{7b}$ **42.** $\frac{7}{10x}$ **43.** $\frac{2}{3g}$ **44.** $\frac{3}{20t}$ **45.** $\frac{5}{16a}$ **46.** $1\frac{7}{8j}$ **47.** y **48.** $\frac{1}{4c}$ **49.** $\frac{1}{2z}$ **50.** $\frac{1}{5e}$ **51.** $\frac{3p}{5}$ **52.** $\frac{5}{6k}$ **53.** $\frac{1}{4h}$ **54.** $\frac{8}{15m}$ **55.** $\frac{7}{36f}$

CHAPTER 6

Pages 378–379

1. $\frac{25}{1}$ **2.** $\frac{3}{4}$ **3.** $\frac{30}{11}$ **4.** $\frac{13}{3}$ **5.** $\frac{1}{8}$ **6.** $\frac{1}{7}$ **7.** $\frac{12}{1}$ **8.** $\frac{3}{7}$ **9.** yes **10.** no **11.** no **12.** yes **13.** 3 **14.** 42 **15.** 3 **16.** 6 **17.** 4 **18.** 6 **19.** 7 **20.** 10 **21.** 53% **22.** 10% **23.** 91% **24.** 42% **25.** 16% **26.** 70% **27.** 84% **28.** 32% **29.** 27% **30.** 66% **31.** 30% **32.** 80% **33.** 37.5% **34.** 93.75% **35.** 75% **36.** 70% **37.** 24% **38.** 65% **39.** 78% **40.** 67% **41.** 0.25 **42.** 0.32 **43.** 0.16 **44.** 0.08 **45.** 0.55 **46.** 0.81 **47.** 0.09 **48.** 0.43 **49.** 0.63 **50.** 0.79 **51.** 35% **52.** $3,528 **53.** $3,187.48 **54.** 77% **55.** 96%

CHAPTER 7

Pages 380–381

1. 6 **2.** 40 **3.** 25 **4.** 3 **5.** 93 **6.** −15 **7.** −21 **8.** 9 **9.** −5 **10.** 32 **11.** > **12.** < **13.** > **14.** = **15.** < **16.** 13 **17.** 10 **18.** 4 **19.** −9 **20.** 0 **21.** −14 **22.** −4 **23.** −4 **24.** −5 **25.** −8 **26.** 6 **27.** 3 **28.** −1 **29.** 20 **30.** −2 **31.** 5 **32.** 1 **33.** 4 **34.** −2 **35.** 5 **36.** 24 **37.** −18 **38.** −20 **39.** 49 **40.** 48 **41.** 54 **42.** −24 **43.** 35 **44.** −32 **45.** −45 **46.** 6 **47.** −2 **48.** −4 **49.** 1 **50.** 3 **51.** 8 **52.** −8 **53.** 6 **54.** −10 **55.** 4 **56.** −90 feet **57.** 477 feet **58.** 12°F **59.** −3 or three points under par **60.** 9 inches

CHAPTER 8

Pages 382–383

1. 5^5 **2.** 8^3 **3.** 3^5 **4.** $(-6)^2$ **5.** $(-8)^3$
6. $(-t)^4$ **7.** y^2 **8.** c^4 **9.** e^2 **10.** $(-n)^3$
11. 32 **12.** 512 **13.** 1,225 **14.** -216
15. 81 **16.** 6^7 **17.** 8^4 **18.** 12^7 **19.** 3^5
20. 7^2 **21.** $3 \cdot 3 = 3^2 = 9$ **22.** $2 \cdot 2 = 2^2$
$= 4$ **23.** $x \cdot x = x^2$ **24.** $5 \cdot 5 = 5^2 = 25$
25. $y \cdot y = y^2$ **26.** $5 \cdot 5 \cdot 5 = 5^3 = 125$
27. $9 \cdot 9 \cdot 9 = 9^3 = 729$ **28.** $7 \cdot 7 \cdot 7 = 7^3$
$= 343$ **29.** $m \cdot m \cdot m = m^3$ **30.** $12 \cdot 12 \cdot$
$12 = 12^3 = 1,728$ **31.** $\sqrt{10}$ is between 3
and 4 **32.** $\sqrt{56}$ is between 7 and 8
33. $\sqrt{37}$ is between 6 and 7 **34.** $\sqrt{93}$ is
between 9 and 10 **35.** $\sqrt{47}$ is between 6
and 7 **36.** $s = 7$ **37.** $s = 18.7$ **38.** $s = 8.2$
39. $s = 10$ **40.** $s = 44.7$ **41.** 10 **42.** 26
43. 15 **44.** 39 **45.** 25

CHAPTER 9

Pages 384–385

1. 26.8 cm **2.** 17 ft **3.** 56 yd **4.** 38.4 in.
5. 144 mm **6.** 35 m **7.** 625 mm^2
8. 25.5 in.^{2} **9.** 108 cm^2 **10.** 53.29 ft^2
11. 46.8 cm^2 **12.** 82.5 m^2 **13.** 157.5 in.^{2}
14. 138 ft^2 **15.** 2,211 m^2 **16.** 161 yd^2
17. 10,648 cm^3 **18.** 70 in.^{3} **19.** 768 m^3
20. 16,000 ft^3 **21.** 12,167 in.^{3}
22. 11,610 in.^{3} **23.** 150.72 in.; 1,808.64 in.^{2}
24. 94.2 cm; 706.5 cm^2 **25.** 15,386 m^3
26. 65.42 ft^3 **27.** 7,630.2 mm^3
28. 904.32 in.^{3} **29.** 44,579.63 cm^3
30. 226.08 in.^{3}

CHAPTER 10

Pages 386–387

1.

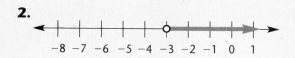

2.

3.

4.

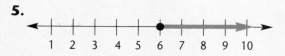

5.

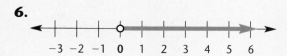

6.

7.

8.

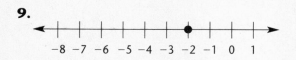

9.

10. $x \le 15$ **11.** $x > -6$
12. $c \le 8$

13. $m = 2$

14. $j > -1$

15. $e \ge 3$

16. $t < 8$

17. Quadrant III **18.** Quadrant I
19. Quadrant IV **20.** Quadrant II
21. $(0, 4)$ **22.** $(-3, -6)$ **23.** $(6, 0)$
24. $(1, -3)$ **25.** $(0, -4)$ **26.** $(-3, 0)$
27. $(6, -5)$ **28.** $(3, 4)$
29–34.

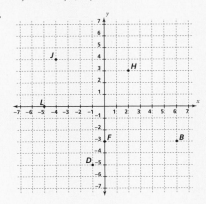

35. $y = x + 2$

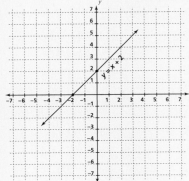

36. $y = x - 1$

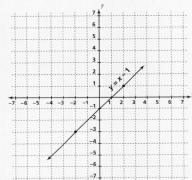

37. $y = -3x$

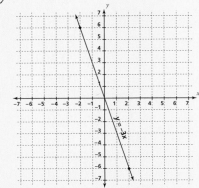

38. 2 **39.** 3 **40.** 1 **41.** -1 **42.** $y = 2x + 1$
43. $y = 4x - 3$ **44.** $y = 3x + 5$
45. $y = -x - 2$

CHAPTER 11

Pages 388–389

1. 15° **2.** 30° **3.** 75° **4.** 10° **5.** 125° **6.** 90°
7. angles 2 and 4 **8.** angles 1 and 3; angles 2 and 4 **9.** 120° **10.** 60° **11.** straight
12. acute **13.** obtuse **14.** 65°; 155°
15. 10°; 100° **16.** 15°; 105° **17.** 52°; 142°
18. 1°; 91° **19.** 89° **20.** 25° **21.** 64°
22. 59° **23.** isosceles triangle **24.** scalene triangle **25.** acute triangle or scalene triangle **26.** SSS **27.** ASA **28.** SAS
29. yes **30.** no **31.** not enough information **32.** true **33.** true **34.** false
35. false

CHAPTER 12

Pages 390–391

1.

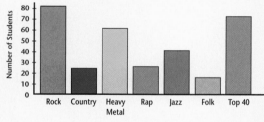

Type of Music Students Prefer the Most

2.

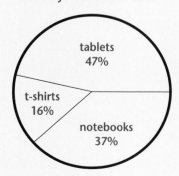

Sales by Student Council

3. 36 items **4.** 17 items **5.** We cannot tell from this frequency table if the powdered milk was canned, bagged, or boxed. **6.** 8
7. 3.2 **8.** 3 **9.** 5 **10.** 28 **11.** 19 and 36
12. 23 and 29 **13.** $\frac{3}{8} = 0.375 = 38\%$
14. $\frac{1}{2} = 0.50 = 50\%$ **15.** 24 ways

Review of Basic Skills

Review of Basic Skills 1, page 427
1. ones **2.** tens **3.** hundreds
4. hundreds **5.** tens **6.** ones
7. thousands **8.** hundreds **9.** tens
10. ones **11.** hundreds **12.** thousands
13. ones **14.** ten-thousands **15.** ten-thousands **16.** hundred-thousands
17. thousands **18.** millions
19. hundred-thousands **20.** hundred-millions

Review of Basic Skills 2, page 428
1. 10 **2.** 20 **3.** 190 **4.** 360 **5.** 1,890
6. 2,390 **7.** 4,020 **8.** 55,490 **9.** 63,560
10. 250,960 **11.** 100 **12.** 100 **13.** 300
14. 600 **15.** 800 **16.** 8,700 **17.** 13,400
18. 64,800 **19.** 267,500 **20.** 416,300
21. 1,000 **22.** 1,000 **23.** 5,000 **24.** 9,000
25. 10,000 **26.** 21,000 **27.** 46,000
28. 148,000 **29.** 250,000 **30.** 864,000

Review of Basic Skills 3, page 429
1. 6 **2.** 9 **3.** 8 **4.** 15 **5.** 19 **6.** 27 **7.** 113
8. 510 **9.** 1,017 **10.** 36 **11.** 118 **12.** 112
13. 377 **14.** 43,888 **15.** 110,682
16. 104,248 **17.** 256,818 **18.** 1,050
19. 2,107 **20.** 6,628

Review of Basic Skills 4, page 430
1. 4 **2.** 5 **3.** 10 **4.** 11 **5.** 32 **6.** 37
7. 141 **8.** 160 **9.** 404 **10.** 506 **11.** 309
12. 411 **13.** 736 **14.** 950 **15.** 40,736
16. 49,654 **17.** 1,692 **18.** 4,052 **19.** 873
20. 80,033 **21.** 59,960 **22.** 17,785
23. 493,000 **24.** 490,000 **25.** 400,000

Review of Basic Skills 5, page 431
1. 2, 4, 6, 8, 10, 12, 14, 16, 18, 20
2. 3, 6, 9, 12, 15, 18, 21, 24, 27, 30
3. 4, 8, 12, 16, 20, 24, 28, 32, 36, 40
4. 5, 10, 15, 20, 25, 30, 35, 40, 45, 50
5. 6, 12, 18, 24, 30, 36, 42, 48, 54, 60
6. 7, 14, 21, 28, 35, 42, 49, 56, 63, 70
7. 8, 16, 24, 32, 40, 48, 56, 64, 72, 80
8. 9, 18, 27, 36, 45, 54, 63, 72, 81, 90
9. 10, 20, 30, 40, 50, 60, 70, 80, 90, 100
10. 138 **11.** 182 **12.** 315 **13.** 252
14. 576 **15.** 162 **16.** 1,610 **17.** 987
18. 1,443 **19.** 3,312 **20.** 2,997 **21.** 3,087
22. 2,163 **23.** 6,768 **24.** 21,298
25. 48,020

Review of Basic Skills 6, page 432
1. 30 **2.** 500 **3.** 7,000 **4.** 60 **5.** 1,000
6. 1,400 **7.** 12,000 **8.** 270 **9.** 2,700
10. 27,000 **11.** 430 **12.** 4,300
13. 43,000 **14.** 2,670 **15.** 26,700
16. 267,000 **17.** 3,490 **18.** 34,900
19. 349,000 **20.** 3,490,000 **21.** 830
22. 8,300 **23.** 83,000 **24.** 5,860
25. 58,600 **26.** 586,000 **27.** 41,840
28. 418,400 **29.** 4,184,000
30. 41,840,000

Review of Basic Skills 7, page 433
1. 8 **2.** 7 **3.** 2 **4.** 4 **5.** 10 **6.** 6 **7.** 7 **8.** 7
9. 6 **10.** 9 **11.** 9 **12.** 9 **13.** 9 **14.** 7
15. 6 **16.** 23 **17.** 53 **18.** 123 **19.** 121
20. 207 **21.** 47 **22.** 17 **23.** 15 **24.** 50
25. 57

Review of Basic Skills 8, page 434

1. $27\frac{3}{14}$ **2.** $15\frac{1}{39}$ **3.** $45\frac{18}{21} = 45\frac{6}{7}$ **4.** $9\frac{7}{71}$
5. $24\frac{7}{20}$ **6.** 591.52 **7.** 423.10 **8.** 2,838.33
9. 7,467.47 **10.** 17,082.15

Review of Basic Skills 9, page 435

1. 170 **2.** 304 **3.** 120 **4.** 460 **5.** 360
6. 502 **7.** 610 **8.** 6,011 **9.** 21,100
10. 4,300

Review of Basic Skills 10, page 436

1. 9 **2.** 16 **3.** 25 **4.** 36 **5.** 49 **6.** 64
7. 81 **8.** 100 **9.** 32 **10.** 625 **11.** 16
12. 27 **13.** 125 **14.** 1,000 **15.** 64
16. 900 **17.** 8,000 **18.** 121
19. 1,000,000 **20.** 1,000,000 **21.** 2^3
22. 2^4 **23.** 3^3 **24.** 9^2 **25.** 7^5 **26.** 10^5
27. 81^2 **28.** 92^3 **29.** 46^4 **30.** 10^6 **31.** 4^3
32. 4^4 **33.** 6^3 **34.** 6^5 **35.** 90^5 **36.** 43^3
37. 5^8 **38.** 36^4 **39.** 94^4 **40.** 100^5

Review of Basic Skills 11, page 437

1. 7 **2.** 6 **3.** 12 **4.** 8 **5.** 23 **6.** 1 **7.** 8
8. 8 **9.** 5 **10.** 35 **11.** 43 **12.** 15 **13.** 25
14. 159 **15.** 22 **16.** 23 **17.** 45 **18.** 0
19. 10 **20.** 3

Review of Basic Skills 12, page 438

1. 47.4 **2.** 64.2 **3.** 53.2 **4.** 70.7 **5.** 62.7
6. 50.7 **7.** 61.7 **8.** 53.7 **9.** 68.6 **10.** 51.6
11. 103.5 **12.** 54.7 **13.** 95.3 **14.** 42.7
15. 41.2

Review of Basic Skills 13, page 439

1. < **2.** > **3.** < **4.** < **5.** < **6.** > **7.** <
8. < **9.** < **10.** > **11.** < **12.** < **13.** >
14. < **15.** < **16.** > **17.** < **18.** <
19. > **20.** <

Review of Basic Skills 14, page 440

1. $\frac{15}{30}$ **2.** $\frac{10}{24}$ **3.** $\frac{9}{21}$ **4.** $\frac{12}{18}$ **5.** $\frac{21}{36}$ **6.** $\frac{27}{39}$
7. $\frac{20}{35}$ **8.** $\frac{15}{40}$ **9.** $\frac{30}{35}$ **10.** $\frac{90}{100}$ **11.** $\frac{9}{33}$ **12.** $\frac{18}{39}$
13. $\frac{25}{60}$ **14.** $\frac{18}{45}$ **15.** $\frac{36}{64}$ **16.** $\frac{15}{65}$ **17.** $\frac{15}{51}$
18. $\frac{12}{38}$ **19.** $\frac{30}{550}$ **20.** $\frac{14}{630}$

Review of Basic Skills 15, page 441

1. $\frac{1}{2}$ **2.** $\frac{1}{23}$ **3.** $\frac{5}{11}$ **4.** $\frac{1}{5}$ **5.** $\frac{1}{3}$ **6.** $\frac{28}{29}$ **7.** $\frac{7}{9}$
8. $\frac{1}{9}$ **9.** $\frac{1}{7}$ **10.** $\frac{3}{4}$ **11.** $\frac{1}{5}$ **12.** $\frac{1}{4}$ **13.** $\frac{1}{2}$
14. $\frac{2}{11}$ **15.** $\frac{1}{2}$ **16.** $\frac{1}{4}$ **17.** $\frac{1}{3}$ **18.** $\frac{5}{22}$
19. $\frac{5}{26}$ **20.** $\frac{1}{2}$

Review of Basic Skills 16, page 442

1. $3\frac{3}{5}$ **2.** 6 **3.** $3\frac{1}{6}$ **4.** $4\frac{2}{3}$ **5.** $5\frac{3}{4}$ **6.** 6 **7.** $7\frac{3}{5}$
8. 6 **9.** $5\frac{1}{11}$ **10.** $3\frac{4}{5}$ **11.** $1\frac{5}{8}$ **12.** $6\frac{7}{8}$
13. $4\frac{2}{3}$ **14.** 8 **15.** 30 **16.** $7\frac{3}{4}$ **17.** $8\frac{1}{3}$
18. $8\frac{2}{7}$ **19.** $5\frac{1}{5}$ **20.** $12\frac{1}{3}$

Review of Basic Skills 17, page 443

1. $\frac{17}{5}$ **2.** $\frac{32}{5}$ **3.** $\frac{31}{6}$ **4.** $\frac{86}{12}$ **5.** $\frac{13}{6}$ **6.** $\frac{19}{2}$
7. $\frac{37}{9}$ **8.** $\frac{90}{11}$ **9.** $\frac{17}{3}$ **10.** $\frac{25}{3}$ **11.** $\frac{88}{13}$ **12.** $\frac{50}{3}$
13. $\frac{59}{8}$ **14.** $\frac{47}{3}$ **15.** $\frac{191}{14}$ **16.** $\frac{29}{3}$ **17.** $\frac{61}{10}$
18. $\frac{62}{3}$ **19.** $\frac{341}{21}$ **20.** $\frac{89}{8}$

Review of Basic Skills 18, page 444

1. $\frac{1}{3}$ **2.** $\frac{1}{2}$ **3.** $\frac{21}{52}$ **4.** $\frac{2}{15}$ **5.** $\frac{3}{7}$ **6.** $\frac{6}{55}$ **7.** $\frac{4}{63}$
8. $\frac{5}{44}$ **9.** $\frac{1}{27}$ **10.** $\frac{5}{24}$ **11.** $\frac{1}{22}$ **12.** $\frac{8}{45}$
13. $\frac{1}{14}$ **14.** $\frac{13}{112}$ **15.** $\frac{1}{6}$ **16.** $\frac{5}{104}$ **17.** $\frac{1}{8}$
18. $\frac{5}{9}$ **19.** $\frac{1}{2}$ **20.** $\frac{1}{8}$

Review of Basic Skills 19, page 445

1. $\frac{5}{6}$ **2.** $\frac{3}{5}$ **3.** $\frac{8}{21}$ **4.** $\frac{8}{35}$ **5.** $2\frac{2}{5}$ **6.** $1\frac{2}{15}$

7. $1\frac{39}{56}$ **8.** $1\frac{1}{4}$ **9.** 3 **10.** $3\frac{3}{25}$ **11.** $6\frac{1}{14}$

12. $11\frac{11}{35}$ **13.** $6\frac{1}{5}$ **14.** $2\frac{4}{9}$ **15.** $2\frac{41}{56}$

16. $17\frac{7}{8}$ **17.** $4\frac{1}{5}$ **18.** $5\frac{5}{8}$ **19.** 8 **20.** $5\frac{7}{8}$

Review of Basic Skills 20, page 446

1. $1\frac{2}{5}$ **2.** $2\frac{1}{2}$ **3.** $2\frac{2}{7}$ **4.** $4\frac{4}{5}$ **5.** $\frac{12}{35}$ **6.** $\frac{3}{4}$

7. $\frac{24}{25}$ **8.** $1\frac{1}{9}$ **9.** $2\frac{1}{12}$ **10.** 5 **11.** $1\frac{3}{5}$ **12.** $\frac{1}{2}$

13. $\frac{9}{10}$ **14.** $1\frac{1}{3}$ **15.** $\frac{2}{3}$ **16.** $1\frac{2}{3}$ **17.** $1\frac{7}{48}$

18. $\frac{35}{48}$ **19.** $\frac{7}{10}$ **20.** 2 **21.** $1\frac{7}{9}$ **22.** $\frac{7}{8}$

23. $2\frac{1}{6}$ **24.** $1\frac{1}{3}$ **25.** 1

Review of Basic Skills 21, page 447

1. 3 **2.** $7\frac{1}{3}$ **3.** $2\frac{2}{5}$ **4.** $3\frac{1}{4}$ **5.** $\frac{1}{10}$ **6.** $\frac{26}{45}$

7. $2\frac{1}{10}$ **8.** 10 **9.** 7 **10.** $4\frac{1}{2}$ **11.** 2 **12.** $3\frac{1}{2}$

13. 8 **14.** 6 **15.** 7 **16.** $8\frac{1}{3}$ **17.** $4\frac{1}{7}$

18. $7\frac{1}{9}$ **19.** $13\frac{1}{2}$ **20.** $15\frac{4}{5}$ **21.** $\frac{2}{3}$ **22.** $2\frac{1}{6}$

23. $1\frac{4}{5}$ **24.** $5\frac{2}{3}$ **25.** $2\frac{8}{11}$ **26.** $5\frac{2}{3}$ **27.** $1\frac{16}{19}$

28. $2\frac{16}{21}$ **29.** $1\frac{1}{4}$ **30.** $2\frac{22}{27}$

Review of Basic Skills 22, page 448

1. 3 **2.** $5\frac{1}{2}$ **3.** 8 **4.** 13 **5.** $7\frac{2}{3}$ **6.** $8\frac{1}{4}$ **7.** 10

8. $8\frac{1}{2}$ **9.** $8\frac{5}{16}$ **10.** $3\frac{1}{2}$ **11.** $11\frac{1}{2}$ **12.** $4\frac{13}{16}$

13. $6\frac{3}{16}$ **14.** $9\frac{4}{5}$ **15.** $7\frac{15}{16}$ **16.** $9'$ **17.** $4'$

18. $17'$ **19.** $7'$ **20.** $12'$

Review of Basic Skills 23, page 449

1. $\frac{3}{4}$ **2.** $\frac{8}{15}$ **3.** $1\frac{1}{4}$ **4.** $\frac{7}{10}$ **5.** $\frac{11}{12}$ **6.** $\frac{17}{30}$

7. $\frac{19}{30}$ **8.** $\frac{3}{4}$ **9.** $\frac{13}{14}$ **10.** $\frac{2}{3}$ **11.** $3\frac{5}{6}$ **12.** $7\frac{5}{6}$

13. $5\frac{1}{4}$ **14.** $5\frac{11}{12}$ **15.** $6\frac{7}{10}$ **16.** $5\frac{5}{12}$

17. $4\frac{5}{6}$ **18.** $10\frac{14}{15}$ **19.** $12\frac{11}{24}$ **20.** $12\frac{1}{32}$

Review of Basic Skills 24, page 450

1. $\frac{1}{4}$ **2.** $\frac{3}{7}$ **3.** $3\frac{1}{4}$ **4.** $4\frac{1}{4}$ **5.** $1\frac{2}{5}$ **6.** $2\frac{1}{2}$

7. $1\frac{1}{6}$ **8.** $2\frac{1}{4}$ **9.** $3\frac{1}{5}$ **10.** $3\frac{1}{2}$ **11.** $2\frac{1}{8}$ **12.** $\frac{1}{4}$

13. $1\frac{1}{8}$ **14.** $2\frac{1}{4}$ **15.** $3\frac{2}{5}$ **16.** 1 **17.** $2\frac{1}{17}$

18. $5\frac{11}{39}$ **19.** $2\frac{1}{5}$ **20.** $2\frac{1}{2}$

Review of Basic Skills 25, page 451

1. $\frac{1}{8}$ **2.** $\frac{1}{4}$ **3.** $1\frac{1}{8}$ **4.** $2\frac{1}{4}$ **5.** $4\frac{7}{20}$ **6.** $1\frac{1}{6}$

7. $3\frac{1}{8}$ **8.** $4\frac{1}{8}$ **9.** $3\frac{27}{100}$ **10.** $1\frac{31}{100}$ **11.** $7\frac{5}{8}$

12. $2\frac{1}{2}$ **13.** $4\frac{4}{9}$ **14.** $2\frac{1}{10}$ **15.** 7

Review of Basic Skills 26, page 452

1. $3\frac{3}{4}$ **2.** $3\frac{1}{4}$ **3.** $7\frac{1}{2}$ **4.** $2\frac{2}{3}$ **5.** $1\frac{1}{3}$ **6.** $2\frac{2}{5}$

7. $2\frac{3}{4}$ **8.** $2\frac{4}{7}$ **9.** $4\frac{7}{10}$ **10.** $4\frac{7}{9}$ **11.** $3\frac{1}{2}$

12. $3\frac{2}{3}$ **13.** $4\frac{3}{5}$ **14.** $1\frac{5}{6}$ **15.** $1\frac{7}{8}$ **16.** $4\frac{3}{4}$

17. $2\frac{5}{6}$ **18.** $6\frac{5}{6}$ **19.** $4\frac{1}{2}$ **20.** $4\frac{3}{5}$

Review of Basic Skills 27, page 453

1. tenths **2.** thousandths

3. ten-thousandths **4.** thousandths

5. hundred-thousandths **6.** millionths

7. thousandths **8.** hundreds

9. hundredths **10.** hundred-thousandths

11. > **12.** < **13.** < **14.** < **15.** >

16. < **17.** > **18.** < **19.** > **20.** <

Review of Basic Skills 28, page 454

1. 2.1, 2.06, 2.063 **2.** 0.1, 0.09, 0.089

3. 1.0, 1.04, 1.035 **4.** 0.2, 0.15, 0.155

5. 32.7, 32.70, 32.704 **6.** 7.6, 7.63, 7.630

7. 19.8, 19.81, 19.809 **8.** 34.0, 34.00,

34.004 **9.** 2.1, 2.06, 2.061 **10.** 139.4,

139.42, 139.418

Review of Basic Skills 29, page 455

1. $18.03 **2.** $13.73 **3.** $18.20 **4.** $13.42
5. $18.64 **6.** $15.78 **7.** $33.09 **8.** $26.26
9. $26.25 **10.** $29.93 **11.** 15.32
12. 20.13 **13.** 12.11 **14.** 31.383
15. 64.403 **16.** 18.099 **17.** 11.617
18. 24.098 **19.** 86.0991 **20.** 28.8514

Review of Basic Skills 30, page 456

1. $16.33 **2.** $3.11 **3.** $11.35 **4.** $10.00
5. $2.11 **6.** $27.18 **7.** $8.26 **8.** $8.28
9. $13.37 **10.** $5.19 **11.** 5.09 **12.** 0.66
13. 1.09 **14.** 5.29 **15.** 5.79 **16.** 74.51
17. 21.81 **18.** 35.13 **19.** 36.73 **20.** 80.63

Review of Basic Skills 31, page 457

1. 2.8 **2.** 12 **3.** 18.9 **4.** 14.7 **5.** 33.5
6. 3.12 **7.** 15.86 **8.** 15.99 **9.** 8.04
10. 58.48 **11.** 3.159 **12.** 17.748
13. 7.408 **14.** 26.568 **15.** 14.094
16. 11.993 **17.** 36.036 **18.** 8.838
19. 27.434 **20.** 55.188

Review of Basic Skills 32, page 458

1. $2.9 \cdot 10^3$ **2.** $3.6 \cdot 10^3$ **3.** $8.75 \cdot 10^3$
4. $6.32 \cdot 10^3$ **5.** $3.5 \cdot 10^4$ **6.** $4.6 \cdot 10^4$
7. $7.11 \cdot 10^4$ **8.** $4.0 \cdot 10^5$ **9.** $4.0 \cdot 10^6$
10. $1.7 \cdot 10^9$ **11.** $3.8 \cdot 10^{-4}$ **12.** $3.9 \cdot 10^{-1}$
13. $4.1 \cdot 10^{-1}$ **14.** $7.2 \cdot 10^{-2}$ **15.** $7.2 \cdot 10^{-3}$
16. $8.1 \cdot 10^{-3}$ **17.** $7.4 \cdot 10^{-4}$ **18.** $1.2 \cdot 10^{-5}$
19. $1.23 \cdot 10^{-3}$ **20.** $2.46 \cdot 10^{-4}$

Review of Basic Skills 33, page 459

1. 2.35 **2.** 0.26 **3.** 0.25 **4.** 3.17 **5.** 6.5
6. 3.1 **7.** 7.1 **8.** 0.21 **9.** 7.1 **10.** 2.1
11. 3.1 **12.** 3.3 **13.** 20.5 **14.** 9.09
15. 6.1 **16.** 1.202 **17.** 6.1 **18.** 0.51
19. 1.02 **20.** 0.5

Review of Basic Skills 34, page 460

1. 7.2 **2.** 12.3 **3.** 11 **4.** 14.9 **5.** 55.7
6. 37.4 **7.** 96.7 **8.** 427 **9.** 0.002
10. 210.5 **11.** 210.5 **12.** 6,460 **13.** 810
14. 81 **15.** 8.1 **16.** 707 **17.** 33 **18.** 6,620
19. 532 **20.** 0.98

Review of Basic Skills 35, page 461

1. $\frac{14}{100}$ $\frac{7}{50}$ **2.** $\frac{15}{100}$ $\frac{3}{20}$ **3.** $\frac{75}{100}$ $\frac{3}{4}$
4. $\frac{36}{100}$ $\frac{9}{25}$ **5.** $\frac{79}{100}$ **6.** $\frac{15}{100}$ $\frac{3}{20}$ **7.** $\frac{159}{1,000}$
8. $\frac{375}{1,000}$ $\frac{3}{8}$ **9.** $\frac{875}{1,000}$ $\frac{7}{8}$ **10.** $\frac{999}{1,000}$
11. $\frac{42}{100}$ $\frac{21}{50}$ **12.** $\frac{65}{100}$ $\frac{13}{20}$ **13.** $\frac{60}{100}$ $\frac{3}{5}$
14. $\frac{45}{100}$ $\frac{9}{20}$ **15.** $\frac{50}{100}$ $\frac{1}{2}$ **16.** $\frac{168}{1,000}$ $\frac{21}{125}$
17. $\frac{22}{100}$ $\frac{11}{50}$ **18.** $\frac{98}{100}$ $\frac{49}{50}$ **19.** $\frac{568}{1,000}$ $\frac{71}{125}$
20. $\frac{72}{100}$ $\frac{18}{25}$

Review of Basic Skills 36, page 462

1. 0.1 **2.** 0.2 **3.** 0.5 **4.** 0.12 **5.** 0.18
6. 0.35 **7.** 0.36 **8.** 0.006 **9.** 0.024
10. 0.118 **11.** 0.4285714 **12.** 0.7142857
13. 0.6666666 **14.** 0.2222222
15. 0.3846153 **16.** 0.117647
17. 0.1578947 **18.** 0.2173913
19. 0.2068965 **20.** 0.1612903

Review of Basic Skills 1

Place Value of Whole Numbers

Recall that 1,234 means 1 thousand + 2 hundreds + 3 tens + 4 ones.
So the place value of 1 is thousands, 2 is hundreds, 3 is tens, and 4 is ones.

> **EXAMPLE 1** Write the place value of the underlined digit.
>
> 4,301   thousands
> 4,301   hundreds
> 4,301   tens
> 4,301   ones

Exercise Write the place value of the underlined digit.

1. 356   **3.** 356   **5.** 981   **7.** 3,401   **9.** 3,401

2. 356   **4.** 981   **6.** 981   **8.** 3,401   **10.** 3,401

You may use this place value chart for larger numbers.

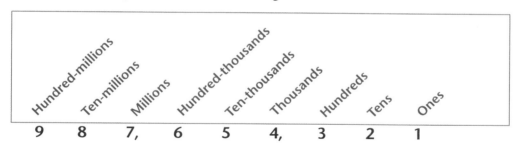

11. 3,485   **16.** 999,999

12. 6,379   **17.** 4,676,000

13. 21,397   **18.** 9,462,391

14. 86,477   **19.** 56,926,400

15. 191,945   **20.** 879,940,604

Rounding Whole Numbers

EXAMPLE 1	Round to the nearest:	Ten	Hundred	Thousand
Step 1	Find the place to be rounded.	1,582	1,582	1,582
Step 2	If the digit to the right is 5 or larger, add 1 to the place to be rounded.	1,582 ↑	1,582 ↑	1,582 ↑
Step 3	Change all digits to the right of the rounded place to 0s.	1,580	1,600	2,000

Exercise Round to the nearest ten.

1. 9

2. 16

3. 191

4. 356

5. 1,888

6. 2,394

7. 4,017

8. 55,487

9. 63,561

10. 250,960

Round to the nearest hundred.

11. 89

12. 51

13. 284

14. 561

15. 840

16. 8,696

17. 13,401

18. 64,789

19. 267,476

20. 416,313

Round to the nearest thousand.

21. 787

22. 806

23. 5,350

24. 8,634

25. 9,500

26. 21,435

27. 46,187

28. 147,831

29. 250,011

30. 864,217

Review of Basic Skills 3

Adding Whole Numbers

EXAMPLE 1   Try these in your head.

$7 + 3 = \blacksquare$ **Answer** 10 $7 + 13 + 0 = \blacksquare$ **Answer** 20

$3 + 5 + 19 = \blacksquare$ **Answer** 27

EXAMPLE 2 $2 + 451 + 26 = \blacksquare$ **EXAMPLE 3**   Find the perimeter.

Solution
$$
\begin{array}{r}
26 \\
451 \\
+ \;\; 2 \\
\hline
479
\end{array}
$$
26, 451, +2 → Addends   479 Sum

Solution
$$
\begin{array}{r}
30 \\
40 \\
+ \;\; 50 \\
\hline
120
\end{array}
$$

30, 50, 40

Exercise Do these in your head. Just write your answers.

1. $2 + 4$

2. $2 + 4 + 3$

3. $2 + 5 + 1 + 0$

4. $2 + 0 + 3 + 10$

5. $3 + 7 + 5 + 4$

6. $6 + 7 + 4 + 10$

7. $2 + 5 + 6 + 100$

8. $500 + 2 + 7 + 1$

9. $3 + 5 + 9 + 1,000$

Write in vertical form, then add.

10. $9 + 27$

11. $3 + 29 + 86$

12. $7 + 14 + 91$

13. $2 + 69 + 5 + 301$

14. $26,487 + 17,401$

15. $37,091 + 73,591$

16. $100,847 + 3,401$

17. $217,401 + 39,417$

Find the perimeters.

18.

19.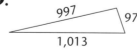

20.

Review of Basic Skills 4

Subtracting Whole Numbers

EXAMPLE 1   Try these in your head.

$7 - 3 = \blacksquare$ **Answer 4** $13 - 3 + 0 = \blacksquare$ **Answer 10**

$28 - 10 = \blacksquare$ **Answer 18**

EXAMPLE 2   Subtract 26 from 235.

Solution	235	Minuend
	$- \ \ 26$	Subtrahend
	209	Difference

Check.	26
	$+ \ 209$
	235

EXAMPLE 3 $208 - 35$

Solution	208
	$- \ \ 35$
	173

Check.	173
	$+ \ \ 35$
	208

Exercise Do these in your head. Just write the answers.

1. $9 - 5$ **3.** $14 - 4$ **5.** $42 - 10$ **7.** $143 - 2$ **9.** $409 - 5$

2. $8 - 3$ **4.** $19 - 8$ **6.** $57 - 20$ **8.** $167 - 7$ **10.** $536 - 30$

Write in vertical form, then subtract.

11. subtract 26 from 335

12. subtract 39 from 450

13. subtract 48 from 784

14. subtract 341 from 1,291

15. subtract 481 from 41,217

16. subtract 346 from 50,000

Write in vertical form, then subtract.

17. $2,113 - 421$ **20.** $81,573 - 1,540$ **23.** $493,146 - 146$

18. $8,101 - 4,049$ **21.** $72,451 - 12,491$ **24.** $493,146 - 3,146$

19. $6,714 - 5,841$ **22.** $63,456 - 45,671$ **25.** $493,146 - 93,146$

Multiplying Whole Numbers

Multiplication is repeated addition.

6 • 3 means 6 threes. $\underbrace{3 + 3 + 3 + 3 + 3 + 3}_{18}$

6 • 3 = 18

You may want to practice your times tables before doing these problems.

EXAMPLE 1   23 • 6 = ■
Solution

$$\begin{array}{r} 23 \\ \times\ 6 \\ \hline 138 \end{array}$$

23 Factors
138 Product

EXAMPLE 2   46 • 35 = ■
Solution

$$\begin{array}{r} 46 \\ \times\ 35 \\ \hline 230 \\ +\ 1\ 38 \\ \hline 1,610 \end{array}$$

46 Factors
1,610 Product

Exercise Do these in your head. Just write your answers.

1. 1 • 2, 2 • 2, 3 • 2, 4 • 2, 5 • 2, 6 • 2, 7 • 2, 8 • 2, 9 • 2, 10 • 2

2. 1 • 3, 2 • 3, 3 • 3, 4 • 3, 5 • 3, 6 • 3, 7 • 3, 8 • 3, 9 • 3, 10 • 3

3. 1 • 4, 2 • 4, 3 • 4, 4 • 4, 5 • 4, 6 • 4, 7 • 4, 8 • 4, 9 • 4, 10 • 4

4. 1 • 5, 2 • 5, 3 • 5, 4 • 5, 5 • 5, 6 • 5, 7 • 5, 8 • 5, 9 • 5, 10 • 5

5. 1 • 6, 2 • 6, 3 • 6, 4 • 6, 5 • 6, 6 • 6, 7 • 6, 8 • 6, 9 • 6, 10 • 6

6. 1 • 7, 2 • 7, 3 • 7, 4 • 7, 5 • 7, 6 • 7, 7 • 7, 8 • 7, 9 • 7, 10 • 7

7. 1 • 8, 2 • 8, 3 • 8, 4 • 8, 5 • 8, 6 • 8, 7 • 8, 8 • 8, 9 • 8, 10 • 8

8. 1 • 9, 2 • 9, 3 • 9, 4 • 9, 5 • 9, 6 • 9, 7 • 9, 8 • 9, 9 • 9, 10 • 9

9. 1 • 10, 2 • 10, 3 • 10, 4 • 10, 5 • 10, 6 • 10, 7 • 10, 8 • 10, 9 • 10, 10 • 10

Multiply.

10. 23 • 6

11. 26 • 7

12. 35 • 9

13. 63 • 4

14. 72 • 8

15. 54 • 3

16. 46 • 35

17. 47 • 21

18. 37 • 39

19. 46 • 72

20. 81 • 37

21. 49 • 63

22. 309 • 7

23. 423 • 16

24. 926 • 23

25. 196 • 245

Multiplying Whole Numbers by Powers of 10

EXAMPLE 1 $267 \cdot 10 = $ ■

Solution
$$\begin{array}{r} 267 \\ \times\ \underline{10} \leftarrow \text{One zero} \\ 2{,}670 \leftarrow \text{One zero} \end{array}$$

EXAMPLE 2 $342 \cdot 100 = $ ■

Solution
$$\begin{array}{r} 342 \\ \times\ \underline{100} \leftarrow \text{Two zeros} \\ 34{,}200 \leftarrow \text{Two zeros} \end{array}$$

Exercise Do these in your head. Just write the answers.

1. $3 \cdot 10$
2. $5 \cdot 100$
3. $7 \cdot 1{,}000$
4. $3 \cdot 20$

5. $5 \cdot 200$
6. $7 \cdot 200$
7. $6 \cdot 2{,}000$
8. $9 \cdot 30$

9. $9 \cdot 300$
10. $9 \cdot 3{,}000$

Multiply.

11. $43 \cdot 10$
12. $43 \cdot 100$
13. $43 \cdot 1{,}000$
14. $267 \cdot 10$
15. $267 \cdot 100$
16. $267 \cdot 1{,}000$
17. $349 \cdot 10$

18. $349 \cdot 100$
19. $349 \cdot 1{,}000$
20. $349 \cdot 10{,}000$
21. $83 \cdot 10$
22. $83 \cdot 100$
23. $83 \cdot 1{,}000$
24. $586 \cdot 10$

25. $586 \cdot 100$
26. $586 \cdot 1{,}000$
27. $4{,}184 \cdot 10$
28. $4{,}184 \cdot 100$
29. $4{,}184 \cdot 1{,}000$
30. $4{,}184 \cdot 10{,}000$

Review of Basic Skills 7

Division of Whole Numbers

Division is repeated subtraction:

$21 \div 3 = 7$ because $21 - 3 = 18, 18 - 3 = 15, 15 - 3 = 12, 12 - 3 = 9,$

$9 - 3 = 6, 6 - 3 = 3, 3 - 3 = 0$ There are 7 threes in 21.

You may want to practice basic division facts through $\div 9$ before doing these problems.

Division of Whole Numbers with Zero Remainders

EXAMPLE 1 $576 \div 12 = n$

Solution

$$\begin{array}{r} 48 \\ 12\overline{)576} \\ -48 \\ \hline 96 \\ -96 \\ \hline 0 = \text{Remainder} \end{array}$$

Check.

$$\begin{array}{r} 48 \\ \times\ 12 \\ \hline 96 \\ +\ 48 \\ \hline 576 \end{array}$$

Exercise Do these in your head. Just write the answers.

1. $24 \div 3$
2. $14 \div 2$
3. $14 \div 7$
4. $12 \div 3$
5. $30 \div 3$

6. $24 \div 4$
7. $35 \div 5$
8. $49 \div 7$
9. $48 \div 8$
10. $18 \div 2$

11. $45 \div 5$
12. $63 \div 7$
13. $81 \div 9$
14. $56 \div 8$
15. $54 \div 9$

Divide.

16. $138 \div 6$
17. $371 \div 7$
18. $369 \div 3$
19. $484 \div 4$

20. $621 \div 3$
21. $564 \div 12$
22. $323 \div 19$
23. $540 \div 36$

24. $4,100 \div 82$
25. $1,539 \div 27$

Review of Basic Skills 8

Division of Whole Numbers with Fractional Remainders

EXAMPLE 1 $3,191 \div 25 = \blacksquare$

Solution

$$127\tfrac{16}{25}$$
$$25\overline{)3,191}$$
$$-25$$
$$\overline{69}$$
$$-50$$
$$\overline{191}$$
$$-175$$
$$\overline{16}$$

Write the remainder over the divisor.

Check.

$$127$$
$$\times\ 25$$
$$\overline{635}$$
$$+\ 254$$
$$\overline{3,175}$$
$$+\ \ 16 \quad \text{Remainder}$$
$$\overline{3,191}$$

Exercise Divide. Write remainders as fractions.
(These cannot be done with a calculator.)

1. $381 \div 14$

2. $586 \div 39$

3. $963 \div 21$

4. $646 \div 71$

5. $487 \div 20$

Estimate the quotients to the nearest thousand first, then use a calculator.
Copy the calculator answer to the nearest hundreth.

6. $19,520 \div 33$

7. $30,040 \div 71$

8. $51,090 \div 18$

9. $126,947 \div 17$

10. $341,643 \div 20$

Review of Basic Skills 9

Division of Whole Numbers with Zeros in the Quotient

EXAMPLE 1 $2,380 \div 14 = \blacksquare$

Solution
```
      170
14 ) 2,380
   - 14
      98
    - 98
      00
```

Check.
```
    170
  × 14
    680
+ 1 70
  2,380
```

EXAMPLE 2 $4,864 \div 16 = \blacksquare$

Solution
```
      304
16 ) 4,864
   - 48
      064
    -  64
        0
```

Check.
```
    304
  ×  16
  1,824
+ 3 04
  4,864
```

Exercise Divide. Do not use a calculator.

1. $2,380 \div 14$
2. $4,864 \div 16$
3. $2,040 \div 17$
4. $5,980 \div 13$
5. $16,200 \div 45$
6. $31,626 \div 63$
7. $19,520 \div 32$
8. $138,253 \div 23$
9. $738,500 \div 35$
10. $103,200 \div 24$

Numbers with Exponents

2^4 means $2 \cdot 2 \cdot 2 \cdot 2$.
So $2^4 = 2 \cdot 2 \cdot 2 \cdot 2 = 16$.

2^4

Base   Exponent

2 is the base, 4 is the exponent.

EXAMPLE 1   Find the value of 3^4.
Solution $3^4 = 3 \cdot 3 \cdot 3 \cdot 3$
$3^4 = 81$

EXAMPLE 2   Write with an exponent $2 \cdot 2 \cdot 2$.
Solution $2 \cdot 2 \cdot 2 = 2^3$

Exercise Find the value of each.

1. 3^2
2. 4^2
3. 5^2
4. 6^2
5. 7^2
6. 8^2
7. 9^2

8. 10^2
9. 2^5
10. 25^2
11. 2^4
12. 3^3
13. 5^3
14. 10^3

15. 4^3
16. 30^2
17. 20^3
18. 11^2
19. $1,000^2$
20. 10^6

Write with an exponent.

21. $2 \cdot 2 \cdot 2$
22. $2 \cdot 2 \cdot 2 \cdot 2$
23. $3 \cdot 3 \cdot 3$
24. $9 \cdot 9$
25. $7 \cdot 7 \cdot 7 \cdot 7 \cdot 7$
26. $10 \cdot 10 \cdot 10 \cdot 10 \cdot 10$
27. $81 \cdot 81$

28. $92 \cdot 92 \cdot 92$
29. $46 \cdot 46 \cdot 46 \cdot 46$
30. $10 \cdot 10 \cdot 10 \cdot 10 \cdot 10 \cdot 10$
31. $4 \cdot 4 \cdot 4$
32. $4 \cdot 4 \cdot 4 \cdot 4$
33. $6 \cdot 6 \cdot 6$
34. $6 \cdot 6 \cdot 6 \cdot 6 \cdot 6$

35. $90 \cdot 90 \cdot 90 \cdot 90 \cdot 90$
36. $43 \cdot 43 \cdot 43$
37. $5 \cdot 5 \cdot 5 \cdot 5 \cdot 5 \cdot 5 \cdot 5 \cdot 5$
38. $36 \cdot 36 \cdot 36 \cdot 36$
39. $94 \cdot 94 \cdot 94 \cdot 94$
40. $100 \cdot 100 \cdot 100 \cdot 100 \cdot 100$

Using the Order of Operations

> **Rule**
> 1. Evaluate exponents first.
> 2. Multiply and divide from left to right in order.
> 3. Add and subtract from left to right in order.

EXAMPLE 1

$$2 \quad + \quad 3 \cdot 4 \quad - \quad 8 \div 4 \quad = \quad \blacksquare$$

Solution
$$2 \quad + \quad 3 \cdot 4 \quad - \quad 8 \div 4 \quad =$$
$$\qquad\qquad \downarrow \qquad\qquad \downarrow$$
$$2 \quad + \quad 12 \quad - \quad 2 \quad = \quad 12$$

EXAMPLE 2

$$2^3 \quad + \quad 3 \cdot 4 \div 2 \quad - \quad 48 \div 4^2 \quad = \quad \blacksquare$$

Solution
$$8 \quad + \quad 3 \cdot 4 \div 2 \quad - \quad 48 \div 16 \quad =$$
$$\qquad\qquad \downarrow \qquad\qquad\qquad \downarrow$$
$$\qquad\qquad 12 \div 2 \qquad\qquad 3 \qquad =$$
$$\qquad\qquad \downarrow \qquad\qquad\qquad \downarrow$$
$$8 \quad + \quad 6 \quad - \quad 3 \quad = \quad 11$$

Exercise Use the rules for the order of operations. Find the answers.

1. $3 + 8 \cdot 2 \div 4$

2. $5 + 9 \cdot 4 \div 12 - 2$

3. $8 - 8 \div 4 + 3 \cdot 2$

4. $13 - 16 \cdot 3 \div 12 - 1$

5. $9 + 6 \cdot 3 - 8 \cdot 2 \div 4$

6. $1 + 16 \cdot 3 \div 12 - 4$

7. $14 + 32 \div 16 - 4 \cdot 2$

8. $32 \div 16 + 9 \div 3 \cdot 2$

9. $5 - 16 \div 4 + 1 + 3$

10. $35 - 25 \cdot 4 \div 20 + 5$

11. $2^3 + 8 \cdot 2^2 + 3$

12. $8 - 6^2 \div 12 + 2 \cdot 5$

13. $15 + 8^2 \div 4 - 6$

14. $25 + 11^2 + 8 \cdot 2 - 3$

15. $39 \div 13 + 12^2 \div 6 - 5$

16. $52 + 12 \div 2^2 - 82 \div 2 + 3^2$

17. $35 + 2^5 \div 2^4 \cdot 3^2 - 2^3$

18. $18 \div 3^2 + 6 \cdot 8 \div 4^2 - 5$

19. $4 \cdot 3 \cdot 5 \div 10 + 8 \cdot 2^3 \div 2^4$

20. $9 - 16 \cdot 3 \div 12 + 8 \div 2^2 - 2^2$

Review of Basic Skills 12

Finding an Average (Mean)

The word *mean* is sometimes used for *average*.

> **Rule**
>
> **1.** Add the numbers whose average or mean you want.
>
> **2.** Divide the sum by the number of addends. The quotient is the average or mean.

EXAMPLE 1   Find the average of 98, 88, 80, and 60.

Solution Add the numbers.

$$
\begin{array}{r}
98 \\
88 \\
80 \\
+\ 60 \\
\hline
326
\end{array}
\left.\vphantom{\begin{array}{r}98\\88\\80\\60\end{array}}\right\}\text{4 addends}
$$

Then divide.

$$
\begin{array}{r}
81.5 \\
4\,)\overline{326.0} \\
-32 \\
\hline
06 \\
-\ 4 \\
\hline
20 \\
-20 \\
\hline
0
\end{array}
$$

Answer The average is 81.5.

Exercise Find the average for each set of numbers. Round to the nearest tenth.

1. 25, 63, 48, 52, 49

2. 98, 53, 42, 56, 72

3. 39, 40, 39, 62, 53, 86

4. 95, 83, 39, 42, 88, 77

5. 88, 62, 42, 53, 96, 35

6. 53, 60, 72, 43, 35, 39, 53

7. 91, 62, 39, 50, 42, 88, 60

8. 36, 19, 41, 63, 72, 64, 81

9. 39, 41, 62, 73, 96, 81, 92, 65

10. 40, 49, 51, 73, 29, 86, 29, 56

11. 100, 103, 96, 105, 105, 97, 102, 120

12. 36, 42, 85, 92, 30, 33, 88, 29, 62, 50

13. 109, 156, 95, 108, 90, 83, 45, 80, 90, 98, 93, 96

14. 40, 42, 43, 40, 41, 42, 43, 48, 44, 42, 45, 42

15. 40, 38, 37, 35, 42, 43, 36, 49, 48, 53, 42, 39, 34

Review of Basic Skills 13

Comparing Fractions

Comparing fractions with *like* denominators—

> **Rule**
> Compare numerators: the larger the numerator, the larger the fraction.

EXAMPLE 1 Compare $\frac{5}{8}$ and $\frac{7}{8}$.

Solution The denominators are alike.
$5 < 7$, therefore $\frac{5}{8} < \frac{7}{8}$.

Comparing fractions with *unlike* denominators—

> **Rule**
> Change each fraction to a decimal. You may use a calculator. Compare decimals.

EXAMPLE 2 Compare $\frac{5}{8}$ and $\frac{3}{4}$.

Solution $\frac{5}{8}$ is

$$
\begin{array}{r}
0.625 \\
8\,)\overline{5.0} \\
-4\,8 \\
\hline
20 \\
-16 \\
\hline
40 \\
-40 \\
\hline
0
\end{array}
$$

$\frac{3}{4}$ is

$$
\begin{array}{r}
0.75 \\
4\,)\overline{3.0} \\
-2\,8 \\
\hline
20 \\
-20 \\
\hline
0
\end{array}
$$

$0.625 < 0.75$, therefore $\frac{5}{8} < \frac{3}{4}$.

Exercise Compare the fractions. Write $<$ or $>$.

1. $\frac{1}{8}$ $\frac{3}{8}$ 6. $\frac{5}{3}$ $\frac{2}{3}$ 11. $\frac{3}{4}$ $\frac{7}{8}$ 16. $\frac{3}{10}$ $\frac{3}{11}$

2. $\frac{6}{7}$ $\frac{5}{7}$ 7. $\frac{8}{5}$ $\frac{9}{5}$ 12. $\frac{3}{5}$ $\frac{3}{4}$ 17. $\frac{9}{13}$ $\frac{11}{12}$

3. $\frac{3}{8}$ $\frac{5}{8}$ 8. $\frac{1}{3}$ $\frac{2}{3}$ 13. $\frac{6}{7}$ $\frac{5}{8}$ 18. $\frac{6}{11}$ $\frac{7}{9}$

4. $\frac{7}{3}$ $\frac{11}{3}$ 9. $\frac{4}{7}$ $\frac{5}{7}$ 14. $\frac{3}{8}$ $\frac{5}{9}$ 19. $\frac{7}{13}$ $\frac{8}{15}$

5. $\frac{5}{4}$ $\frac{7}{4}$ 10. $\frac{11}{13}$ $\frac{9}{13}$ 15. $\frac{6}{10}$ $\frac{7}{11}$ 20. $\frac{9}{13}$ $\frac{6}{7}$

Changing Fractions to Higher Terms

EXAMPLE 1   Write $\frac{5}{6}$ as a fraction with 30 as the new denominator.

Step 1 $\frac{5}{6} = \frac{\blacksquare}{30}$

Step 2   Divide 30 by 6. $6\overline{)30}^{\;5}$

Step 3   Multiply $\frac{5}{6}$ by $\frac{5}{5}$. $\frac{5 \cdot 5}{6 \cdot 5} = \frac{25}{30}$

Exercise Write each fraction with a new denominator.

1. $\frac{3}{6} = \frac{\blacksquare}{30}$

2. $\frac{5}{12} = \frac{\blacksquare}{24}$

3. $\frac{3}{7} = \frac{\blacksquare}{21}$

4. $\frac{6}{9} = \frac{\blacksquare}{18}$

5. $\frac{7}{12} = \frac{\blacksquare}{36}$

6. $\frac{9}{13} = \frac{\blacksquare}{39}$

7. $\frac{4}{7} = \frac{\blacksquare}{35}$

8. $\frac{3}{8} = \frac{\blacksquare}{40}$

9. $\frac{6}{7} = \frac{\blacksquare}{35}$

10. $\frac{9}{10} = \frac{\blacksquare}{100}$

11. $\frac{3}{11} = \frac{\blacksquare}{33}$

12. $\frac{6}{13} = \frac{\blacksquare}{39}$

13. $\frac{5}{12} = \frac{\blacksquare}{60}$

14. $\frac{6}{15} = \frac{\blacksquare}{45}$

15. $\frac{9}{16} = \frac{\blacksquare}{64}$

16. $\frac{3}{13} = \frac{\blacksquare}{65}$

17. $\frac{5}{17} = \frac{\blacksquare}{51}$

18. $\frac{6}{19} = \frac{\blacksquare}{38}$

19. $\frac{6}{110} = \frac{\blacksquare}{550}$

20. $\frac{7}{315} = \frac{\blacksquare}{630}$

Renaming Fractions in Simplest Terms

Simplest terms means using the *smallest* numbers in both the numerator and the denominator of a fraction.

EXAMPLE 1 Rename $\frac{75}{100}$ in simplest terms.

Solution $\frac{75 \div 25}{100 \div 25} = \frac{3}{4}$

Choose a number that divides both the numerator and the denominator. If you do not use the largest common divisor, you may have to divide more than once.

EXAMPLE 2 Rename $\frac{24}{30}$ in simplest terms.

Solution $\frac{24 \div 3}{30 \div 3} = \frac{8}{10}$

The division process may occur more than once if the divisor is not large enough in the first step.

$$\frac{8 \div 2}{10 \div 2} = \frac{4}{5}$$

Answer $\frac{24}{30} = \frac{4}{5}$

Exercise Rename these fractions in simplest terms.

1. $\frac{24}{48}$

2. $\frac{10}{230}$

3. $\frac{45}{99}$

4. $\frac{5}{25}$

5. $\frac{13}{39}$

6. $\frac{56}{58}$

7. $\frac{63}{81}$

8. $\frac{6}{54}$

9. $\frac{16}{112}$

10. $\frac{39}{52}$

11. $\frac{12}{60}$

12. $\frac{16}{64}$

13. $\frac{18}{36}$

14. $\frac{22}{121}$

15. $\frac{53}{106}$

16. $\frac{18}{72}$

17. $\frac{5}{15}$

18. $\frac{55}{242}$

19. $\frac{10}{52}$

20. $\frac{48}{96}$

Renaming Improper Fractions as Mixed Numbers

EXAMPLE 1 Rename $\frac{13}{5}$ as a mixed number.

Solution Divide numerator by denominator.
Write the remainder as a fraction.

$$5 \overline{)13} \quad \begin{array}{c} 2 \\ \end{array}$$
$$\underline{-10}$$
$$3 \quad \text{Remainder}$$

Answer $2\frac{3}{5}$ Write the remainder over the divisor.

Mixed Numbers in Lowest Terms

Write mixed numbers in lowest terms.
This means to write the fraction part of a mixed number in lowest terms.

EXAMPLE 2 Write $3\frac{5}{15}$ in lowest terms.

Solution Rename $\frac{5}{15}$ in lowest terms.

$\frac{5 \div 5}{15 \div 5} = \frac{1}{3}$, so $3\frac{5}{15} = 3\frac{1}{3}$

Exercise Rename as mixed numbers in lowest terms or whole numbers.

1. $\frac{18}{5}$ 6. $\frac{12}{2}$ 11. $\frac{52}{32}$ 16. $\frac{62}{8}$

2. $\frac{18}{3}$ 7. $\frac{38}{5}$ 12. $\frac{55}{8}$ 17. $\frac{50}{6}$

3. $\frac{19}{6}$ 8. $\frac{66}{11}$ 13. $\frac{28}{6}$ 18. $\frac{58}{7}$

4. $\frac{14}{3}$ 9. $\frac{56}{11}$ 14. $\frac{32}{4}$ 19. $\frac{52}{10}$

5. $\frac{23}{4}$ 10. $\frac{19}{5}$ 15. $\frac{90}{3}$ 20. $\frac{37}{3}$

Renaming Mixed Numbers as Improper Fractions

EXAMPLE 1 Write $2\frac{3}{4}$ as an improper fraction.

Step 1 Multiply the whole number by the denominator.

$$2 \cdot 4 = 8$$

Step 2 Add the numerator to the product from Step 1.

$$3 + 8 = 11$$

Step 3 Write the sum over the old denominator.

$$\frac{11}{4}$$

Answer $2\frac{3}{4} = \frac{11}{4}$

Exercise Rename these mixed numbers as improper fractions.

1. $3\frac{2}{5}$

2. $6\frac{2}{5}$

3. $5\frac{1}{6}$

4. $7\frac{2}{12}$

5. $2\frac{1}{6}$

6. $9\frac{1}{2}$

7. $4\frac{1}{9}$

8. $8\frac{2}{11}$

9. $5\frac{2}{3}$

10. $8\frac{1}{3}$

11. $6\frac{10}{13}$

12. $16\frac{2}{3}$

13. $7\frac{3}{8}$

14. $15\frac{2}{3}$

15. $13\frac{9}{14}$

16. $9\frac{2}{3}$

17. $5\frac{11}{10}$

18. $20\frac{2}{3}$

19. $16\frac{5}{21}$

20. $11\frac{1}{8}$

Multiplying Fractions

To multiply fractions, follow this simple rule.

Rule

To multiply two fractions, multiply numerator times numerator and denominator times denominator.

EXAMPLE 1 $\frac{5}{6} \cdot \frac{3}{4} = \blacksquare$

Solution $\frac{5 \cdot 3}{6 \cdot 4} = \frac{15}{24}$

$\frac{15}{24} = \frac{5}{8}$

Answer $\frac{5}{8}$

EXAMPLE 2 $7 \cdot \frac{4}{5} = \blacksquare$

Solution $\frac{7 \cdot 4}{1 \cdot 5} = \frac{28}{5}$

$\frac{28}{5} = 5\frac{3}{5}$

Answer $5\frac{3}{5}$

Exercise Multiply. Write your answers in lowest terms.

1. $\frac{1}{2} \cdot \frac{2}{3}$

2. $\frac{3}{5} \cdot \frac{5}{6}$

3. $\frac{7}{8} \cdot \frac{6}{13}$

4. $\frac{2}{9} \cdot \frac{3}{5}$

5. $\frac{6}{7} \cdot \frac{1}{2}$

6. $\frac{3}{11} \cdot \frac{2}{5}$

7. $\frac{2}{7} \cdot \frac{2}{9}$

8. $\frac{5}{11} \cdot \frac{1}{4}$

9. $\frac{1}{6} \cdot \frac{2}{9}$

10. $\frac{5}{6} \cdot \frac{1}{4}$

11. $\frac{3}{11} \cdot \frac{2}{12}$

12. $\frac{4}{5} \cdot \frac{2}{9}$

13. $\frac{4}{7} \cdot \frac{1}{8}$

14. $\frac{3}{16} \cdot \frac{13}{21}$

15. $\frac{5}{21} \cdot \frac{7}{10}$

16. $\frac{5}{24} \cdot \frac{3}{13}$

17. $\frac{6}{28} \cdot \frac{7}{12}$

18. $\frac{2}{3} \cdot \frac{5}{6}$

19. $\frac{12}{21} \cdot \frac{7}{8}$

20. $\frac{13}{32} \cdot \frac{8}{26}$

Multiplying Mixed Numbers

To multiply mixed numbers
    1. Change them to improper fractions.
    2. Multiply the fractions.
    3. Reduce to lowest terms.

EXAMPLE 1 $3\frac{2}{3} \bullet 1\frac{1}{2} = \blacksquare$

    Solution $3\frac{2}{3} \bullet 1\frac{1}{2} = \frac{11}{1\cancel{3}} \bullet \frac{\cancel{3}^{1}}{2} = \frac{11}{2} = 5\frac{1}{2}$

    Answer $3\frac{2}{3} \bullet 1\frac{1}{2} = 5\frac{1}{2}$

Exercise Multiply. Write your answers in lowest terms.

1. $2\frac{1}{2} \bullet \frac{1}{3}$

2. $\frac{1}{2} \bullet 1\frac{1}{5}$

3. $\frac{2}{7} \bullet 1\frac{1}{3}$

4. $\frac{1}{5} \bullet 1\frac{1}{7}$

5. $3\frac{1}{5} \bullet \frac{3}{4}$

6. $5\frac{2}{3} \bullet \frac{1}{5}$

7. $\frac{5}{7} \bullet 2\frac{3}{8}$

8. $1\frac{1}{2} \bullet \frac{15}{18}$

9. $4\frac{5}{7} \bullet \frac{7}{11}$

10. $2\frac{3}{5} \bullet 1\frac{1}{5}$

11. $2\frac{3}{7} \bullet 2\frac{1}{2}$

12. $5\frac{1}{7} \bullet 2\frac{1}{5}$

13. $5\frac{1}{6} \bullet 1\frac{1}{5}$

14. $1\frac{5}{6} \bullet 1\frac{1}{3}$

15. $1\frac{2}{7} \bullet 2\frac{1}{8}$

16. $6\frac{1}{2} \bullet 2\frac{3}{4}$

17. $2\frac{2}{5} \bullet 1\frac{3}{4}$

18. $4\frac{1}{2} \bullet 1\frac{1}{4}$

19. $3\frac{3}{7} \bullet 2\frac{1}{3}$

20. $5\frac{2}{9} \bullet 1\frac{1}{8}$

Dividing Fractions

Rule

To divide one fraction by another fraction, invert the divisor and multiply.

EXAMPLE 1 $\frac{4}{7} \div \frac{1}{2} = \blacksquare$

$\frac{4}{7} \div \frac{1}{2} = \blacksquare$ ← Invert the divisor. Then multiply.

$\frac{4}{7} \bullet \frac{2}{1} = \frac{8}{7}$

$\frac{8}{7} = 1\frac{1}{7}$

Answer $1\frac{1}{7}$

Exercise Divide. Write your answers in lowest terms.

1. $\frac{2}{5} \div \frac{2}{7}$

2. $\frac{5}{6} \div \frac{1}{3}$

3. $\frac{2}{7} \div \frac{1}{8}$

4. $\frac{4}{5} \div \frac{1}{6}$

5. $\frac{2}{7} \div \frac{5}{6}$

6. $\frac{3}{8} \div \frac{1}{2}$

7. $\frac{4}{5} \div \frac{5}{6}$

8. $\frac{8}{9} \div \frac{4}{5}$

9. $\frac{5}{6} \div \frac{2}{5}$

10. $\frac{5}{11} \div \frac{2}{22}$

11. $\frac{8}{11} \div \frac{5}{11}$

12. $\frac{5}{12} \div \frac{5}{6}$

13. $\frac{3}{8} \div \frac{5}{12}$

14. $\frac{2}{11} \div \frac{3}{22}$

15. $\frac{8}{13} \div \frac{24}{26}$

16. $\frac{3}{9} \div \frac{1}{5}$

17. $\frac{11}{12} \div \frac{24}{30}$

18. $\frac{5}{7} \div \frac{48}{49}$

19. $\frac{1}{2} \div \frac{5}{7}$

20. $\frac{5}{7} \div \frac{5}{14}$

21. $\frac{8}{9} \div \frac{3}{6}$

22. $\frac{3}{4} \div \frac{6}{7}$

23. $\frac{13}{14} \div \frac{3}{7}$

24. $\frac{8}{15} \div \frac{2}{5}$

25. $\frac{1}{2} \div \frac{1}{2}$

Dividing Mixed Numbers

Rule

Rename the mixed numbers as improper fractions. Invert the divisor and multiply.

EXAMPLE 1 $2\frac{3}{4} \div 3\frac{1}{3} = \blacksquare$

Solution $2\frac{3}{4} \div 3\frac{1}{3} = \blacksquare$

$\frac{11}{4} \div \frac{10}{3} = \blacksquare$ ← Rename as improper fractions.

$\frac{11}{4} \cdot \frac{3}{10} = \blacksquare$ ← Invert the divisor and multiply.

$\frac{11 \cdot 3}{4 \cdot 10} = \frac{33}{40}$

Answer $\frac{33}{40}$

Exercise Divide. Write your answer in lowest terms.

1. $1\frac{1}{2} \div \frac{1}{2}$

2. $3\frac{2}{3} \div \frac{1}{2}$

3. $1\frac{1}{5} \div \frac{1}{2}$

4. $2\frac{1}{6} \div \frac{2}{3}$

5. $\frac{3}{12} \div 2\frac{1}{2}$

6. $\frac{13}{15} \div 1\frac{1}{2}$

7. $1\frac{2}{5} \div \frac{2}{3}$

8. $1\frac{3}{7} \div \frac{1}{7}$

9. $3\frac{1}{2} \div \frac{1}{2}$

10. $1\frac{1}{2} \div \frac{1}{3}$

11. $1\frac{5}{7} \div \frac{6}{7}$

12. $2\frac{1}{3} \div \frac{2}{3}$

13. $3\frac{1}{5} \div \frac{2}{5}$

14. $4\frac{1}{2} \div \frac{3}{4}$

15. $2\frac{5}{8} \div \frac{3}{8}$

16. $6\frac{1}{4} \div \frac{3}{4}$

17. $3\frac{5}{8} \div \frac{7}{8}$

18. $5\frac{1}{3} \div \frac{3}{4}$

19. $6\frac{3}{4} \div \frac{1}{2}$

20. $7\frac{9}{10} \div \frac{1}{2}$

21. $1\frac{1}{2} \div 2\frac{1}{4}$

22. $3\frac{1}{4} \div 1\frac{1}{2}$

23. $2\frac{1}{4} \div 1\frac{1}{4}$

24. $6\frac{3}{8} \div 1\frac{1}{8}$

25. $7\frac{1}{2} \div 2\frac{3}{4}$

26. $8\frac{1}{2} \div 1\frac{1}{2}$

27. $4\frac{3}{8} \div 2\frac{3}{8}$

28. $7\frac{1}{4} \div 2\frac{5}{8}$

29. $6\frac{3}{7} \div 5\frac{1}{7}$

30. $9\frac{1}{2} \div 3\frac{3}{8}$

Adding Mixed Numbers with Like Denominators

EXAMPLE 1 $3\frac{1}{8} + 2\frac{3}{8}$ **Solution**

$$3\frac{1}{8}$$
$$+ 2\frac{3}{8}$$
$$\overline{5\frac{4}{8}}$$

Answer $5\frac{1}{2}$

Step 1 Write in vertical form.
Step 2 Add numerators. $1 + 3 = 4$
Step 3 Add whole numbers. $3 + 2 = 5$
Step 4 Reduce fraction.

EXAMPLE 2 Add the sides to get the perimeter of the rectangle. Measurements are in feet.

Solution $1\frac{1}{4} + 1\frac{1}{4} + 2\frac{3}{4} + 2\frac{3}{4}$ Add the four sides.

Step 1 Add numerators.

$1 + 1 + 3 + 3 = 8$ $\frac{8}{4}$

Step 2 Add whole numbers.

$1 + 1 + 2 + 2 = 6$

Step 3 Simplify. $\frac{8}{4} = 2$ $6 + 2 = 8$ Answer 8'

$1\frac{1}{4}'$

$2\frac{3}{4}'$

Exercise Add the mixed numbers.

1. $1\frac{1}{2} + 1\frac{1}{2}$

2. $3\frac{1}{4} + 2\frac{1}{4}$

3. $6\frac{3}{4} + 1\frac{1}{4}$

4. $5\frac{1}{2} + 7\frac{1}{2}$

5. $3\frac{1}{3} + 4\frac{1}{3}$

6. $7\frac{1}{8} + 1\frac{1}{8}$

7. $3\frac{1}{4} + 6\frac{3}{4}$

8. $7\frac{3}{8} + 1\frac{1}{8}$

9. $5\frac{1}{16} + 3\frac{4}{16}$

10. $1\frac{1}{8} + 2\frac{3}{8}$

11. $5\frac{1}{16} + 6\frac{7}{16}$

12. $3\frac{5}{16} + 1\frac{8}{16}$

13. $4\frac{17}{32} + 1\frac{21}{32}$

14. $8\frac{9}{15} + 1\frac{3}{15}$

15. $6\frac{19}{32} + 1\frac{11}{32}$

Find the perimeter of the rectangles.

16. $1\frac{3}{4}'$

$2\frac{3}{4}'$

17. $\frac{1}{2}'$

$1\frac{1}{2}'$

18. 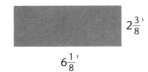 $2\frac{3}{8}'$

$6\frac{1}{8}'$

19. 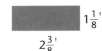 $1\frac{1}{8}'$

$2\frac{3}{8}'$

20.  $1\frac{3}{4}'$

$4\frac{1}{4}'$

Adding Fractions with Unlike Denominators

To add fractions with *unlike* denominators, you must first rewrite the fractions so that they have *like* denominators. Then you can add.

EXAMPLE 1 $\frac{2}{3} + \frac{1}{5} = \blacksquare$ $3 \cdot 5 = 15$ is a common denominator

Solution $\frac{2}{3} = \frac{2 \cdot 5}{3 \cdot 5} = \frac{10}{15}$

$+ \frac{1}{5} = \frac{1 \cdot 3}{5 \cdot 3} = \frac{3}{15}$

Add $\frac{13}{15}$ **Answer** $\frac{13}{15}$

Adding Mixed Numbers with Unlike Denominators

EXAMPLE 2 $1\frac{1}{2} + 2\frac{1}{3} = \blacksquare$

Solution $1\frac{1}{2}$ $\frac{1}{2} = \frac{1 \cdot 3}{2 \cdot 3} = \frac{3}{6}$ $1\frac{3}{6}$ Rewrite with common denominators.

$+ 2\frac{1}{3}$ $\frac{1}{3} = \frac{1 \cdot 2}{3 \cdot 2} = \frac{2}{6}$ $+ 2\frac{2}{6}$ Add.

$3\frac{5}{6}$ Simplify if needed.

Answer $3\frac{5}{6}$

Exercise Add the fractions. Watch for unlike denominators.

1. $\frac{1}{2} + \frac{1}{4}$

2. $\frac{1}{3} + \frac{1}{5}$

3. $\frac{3}{4} + \frac{1}{2}$

4. $\frac{3}{5} + \frac{1}{10}$

5. $\frac{7}{12} + \frac{1}{3}$

6. $\frac{1}{10} + \frac{7}{15}$

7. $\frac{3}{10} + \frac{1}{3}$

8. $\frac{7}{12} + \frac{1}{6}$

9. $\frac{3}{7} + \frac{1}{2}$

10. $\frac{3}{8} + \frac{7}{24}$

11. $1\frac{1}{2} + 2\frac{1}{3}$

12. $6\frac{1}{2} + 1\frac{1}{3}$

13. $3\frac{3}{4} + 1\frac{1}{2}$

14. $3\frac{1}{4} + 2\frac{2}{3}$

15. $5\frac{2}{5} + 1\frac{3}{10}$

16. $3\frac{7}{12} + 1\frac{5}{6}$

17. $1\frac{1}{12} + 3\frac{3}{4}$

18. $4\frac{2}{5} + 6\frac{8}{15}$

19. $5\frac{1}{2} + 6\frac{23}{24}$

20. $5\frac{17}{32} + 6\frac{1}{2}$

Review of Basic Skills 24

Subtracting Mixed Numbers with Like Denominators

EXAMPLE 1

$14\frac{5}{11}$

$-\ 6\frac{2}{11}$

$\overline{\quad 8\frac{3}{11}}$

Step 1 Subtract numerators 2 from 5.　　$5 - 2 = 3$

Step 2 Keep the denominator.

Step 3 Subtract the whole numbers.　　$14 - 6 = 8$

Answer　$8\frac{3}{11}$

Exercise Subtract and write in lowest terms.

1. $\frac{3}{8} - \frac{1}{8}$

2. $\frac{5}{7} - \frac{2}{7}$

3. $4\frac{3}{8} - 1\frac{1}{8}$

4. $5\frac{7}{8} - 1\frac{5}{8}$

5. $3\frac{7}{10} - 2\frac{3}{10}$

6. $5\frac{3}{4} - 3\frac{1}{4}$

7. $6\frac{7}{12} - 5\frac{5}{12}$

8. $7\frac{15}{32} - 5\frac{7}{32}$

9. $9\frac{41}{100} - 6\frac{21}{100}$

10. $5\frac{99}{100} - 2\frac{49}{100}$

11. $6\frac{5}{16} - 4\frac{3}{16}$

12. $\frac{3}{4} - \frac{2}{4}$

13. $2\frac{5}{8} - 1\frac{4}{8}$

14. $5\frac{3}{4} - 3\frac{2}{4}$

15. $6\frac{3}{5} - 3\frac{1}{5}$

16. $2\frac{1}{2} - 1\frac{1}{2}$

17. $3\frac{2}{17} - 1\frac{1}{17}$

18. $10\frac{18}{39} - 5\frac{7}{39}$

19. $3\frac{3}{10} - 1\frac{1}{10}$

20. $4\frac{3}{4} - 2\frac{1}{4}$

Subtracting with Unlike Denominators

EXAMPLE 1   Rewrite fractions with a like denominator.

$$8\frac{2}{3} \qquad \frac{2}{3} = \frac{2 \cdot 2}{3 \cdot 2} = \frac{4}{6} \qquad 8\frac{4}{6}$$

$$-\,5\frac{1}{2} \qquad \frac{1}{2} = \frac{1 \cdot 3}{2 \cdot 3} = \frac{3}{6} \qquad -\,5\frac{3}{6}$$

$$\overline{} \qquad\qquad\qquad\qquad\qquad \overline{3\frac{1}{6}}$$

Subtract numerators and whole numbers.

Answer $3\frac{1}{6}$

Exercise   Subtract and write in lowest terms.

1. $\frac{5}{8} - \frac{1}{2}$

2. $\frac{3}{4} - \frac{1}{2}$

3. $2\frac{5}{8} - 1\frac{1}{2}$

4. $5\frac{3}{4} - 3\frac{1}{2}$

5. $6\frac{3}{5} - 2\frac{1}{4}$

6. $2\frac{1}{2} - 1\frac{1}{3}$

7. $4\frac{3}{8} - 1\frac{1}{4}$

8. $6\frac{7}{8} - 2\frac{3}{4}$

9. $9\frac{3}{10} - 6\frac{3}{100}$

10. $7\frac{51}{100} - 6\frac{1}{5}$

11. $7\frac{3}{4} - \frac{1}{8}$

12. $2\frac{6}{11} - \frac{1}{22}$

13. $5\frac{7}{9} - 1\frac{1}{3}$

14. $3\frac{1}{5} - 1\frac{1}{10}$

15. $8\frac{1}{19} - 1\frac{2}{38}$

Subtracting with Renaming

EXAMPLE 1

$$12$$
$$- 3\frac{1}{4}$$

You need to rename 12 to $11\frac{4}{4}$ first.

Then you can subtract the fractions and the whole numbers.

$$
\begin{array}{l}
12 \\
- 3\frac{1}{4}
\end{array}
= 11 + 1 =
\begin{array}{l}
11\frac{4}{4} \\
- 3\frac{1}{4} \\
\hline
8\frac{3}{4}
\end{array}
\quad \textbf{Answer} \quad 8\frac{3}{4}
$$

EXAMPLE 2

$$5\frac{1}{4}$$
$$- 1\frac{3}{4}$$

You need to rename $5\frac{1}{4}$ to $4\frac{5}{4}$ first.

Then you can subtract the fractions and the whole numbers.

$$
\begin{array}{l}
5\frac{1}{4} = 4 + 1 + \frac{1}{4} = 4 + \frac{4}{4} + \frac{1}{4} = \\
- 1\frac{3}{4}
\end{array}
\qquad
\begin{array}{l}
4\frac{5}{4} \\
- 1\frac{3}{4} \\
\hline
3\frac{2}{4}
\end{array}
\quad \text{Simplify.}
$$

$$\textbf{Answer} \quad 3\frac{1}{2}$$

Exercise Subtract and write in lowest terms.

1. $5 - 1\frac{1}{4}$

2. $6 - 2\frac{3}{4}$

3. $9 - 1\frac{1}{2}$

4. $6 - 3\frac{1}{3}$

5. $7 - 5\frac{2}{3}$

6. $4 - 1\frac{3}{5}$

7. $8 - 5\frac{1}{4}$

8. $9 - 6\frac{3}{7}$

9. $10 - 5\frac{3}{10}$

10. $15 - 10\frac{2}{9}$

11. $5\frac{1}{4} - 1\frac{3}{4}$

12. $6\frac{1}{3} - 2\frac{2}{3}$

13. $6\frac{3}{10} - 1\frac{7}{10}$

14. $4\frac{5}{12} - 2\frac{7}{12}$

15. $8\frac{5}{8} - 6\frac{3}{4}$

16. $7\frac{1}{2} - 2\frac{3}{4}$

17. $5\frac{1}{3} - 2\frac{1}{2}$

18. $9\frac{1}{2} - 2\frac{2}{3}$

19. $10\frac{1}{5} - 5\frac{7}{10}$

20. $11\frac{1}{2} - 6\frac{9}{10}$

Identifying Place Value with Decimals

EXAMPLE 1 Write the place value of the underlined digits.

1. 23.0<u>6</u>71   Hundredths

2. 105.106<u>2</u>   Ten-Thousandths

EXAMPLE 2 Compare 2.38 and 2.4.
Use the symbol < or >.
    < is "less than." > is "more than."

Insert zeros to give each decimal the same number of places.

1. 2.38 and 2.4

2. 2.38 and 2.40 (after inserting zero)

Since 38 is less than 40, then 2.38 < 2.40.

Ten-Thousands	Thousands	Hundreds	Tens	Ones	.	Tenths	Hundredths	Thousandths	Ten-Thousandths
			2	3	.	0	6	7	1
	1	0	5	.		1	0	6	2

Exercise Write the place name for each underlined digit.

1. 35.<u>06</u>

2. 0.52<u>6</u>03

3. 5.681<u>1</u>

4. 1.06<u>11</u>

5. 0.5811<u>1</u>

6. 0.40101<u>5</u>

7. 0.00<u>2</u>731

8. <u>2</u>76.03

9. 2.0<u>8</u>35

10. 0.2850<u>1</u>

Write < or >.

11. 2.38 ■ 2.37

12. 6.19 ■ 6.91

13. 3.7 ■ 3.71

14. 6.8 ■ 6.81

15. 9.73 ■ 9.3

16. 4.03 ■ 4.3

17. 6.76 ■ 6.7

18. 4.801 ■ 4.81

19. 6.73 ■ 6.703

20. 8.701 ■ 8.71

Review of Basic Skills 28

Rounding Decimals

EXAMPLE 1　Round 2.7017 to the nearest thousandth.

　　Solution　2.7017　Number (7) to the right of the thousandths place
　　　　　　　is 5 or more, so add 1 to the thousandths place
　　　　　　　and drop all digits to the right.

　　Answer　2.7017 ≈ 2.702 (≈ means "approximately equal to.")

EXAMPLE 2　Round 8.1649 to the nearest hundredth.

　　Solution　8.1649　Number (4) to the right of the hundredth place is
　　　　　　　less than 5, so drop all digits to the right of 6.

　　Answer　8.1649 ≈ 8.16

Exercise　Round each decimal to the places named.

	Tenths	Hundredths	Thousandths
1. 2.063	_____	_____	_____
2. 0.0891	_____	_____	_____
3. 1.0354	_____	_____	_____
4. 0.15454	_____	_____	_____
5. 32.70391	_____	_____	_____
6. 7.63	_____	_____	_____
7. 19.808964	_____	_____	_____
8. 34.00354	_____	_____	_____
9. 2.061155	_____	_____	_____
10. 139.4181891	_____	_____	_____

Review of Basic Skills 29

Adding Decimals

> **Rule**
> Remember to line up all decimal points, then add.

EXAMPLE 1 $13.11 + $2 + $1.91

Solution
```
    $13.11
    $ 2.00   ← Insert zeros
  + $ 1.91
    $17.02
```

EXAMPLE 2   23 + .62 + 1.9

Solution
```
    23.00   ← Insert zeros
      .62
  +  1.90   ← Insert zero
    25.52
```

Exercise Write in vertical form, then add.

1. $13.10 + $3 + $1.93

2. $5.10 + $1 + $7.63

3. $6.03 + $7.17 + $5

4. $3.41 + $4.01 + $6

5. $3 + $14.63 + $1.01

6. $4.63 + $5 + $6.15

7. $9 + $18 + $6.09

8. $16.09 + $7.17 + $3

9. $10 + $0.05 + $16.20

10. $14 + $6.37 + $9.56

11. 4.3 + 6.02 + 5

12. 6.37 + 4 + 9.76

13. 5 + 3.01 + 4.1

14. 6.37 + 6 + 19.013

15. 41 + 16.1 + 7.303

16. 6.1 + 7.23 + 4.769

17. 4 + 3.01 + 4.607

18. 16.1 + 3.23 + 4.768

19. 19.02 + 4 + 63.0791

20. 16.778 + 3 + 9.0734

Subtracting Decimals

Rule

Remember to line up the decimal points first, then subtract.

EXAMPLE 1 $29.48 − $5.15   Write in vertical form.
         Solution $29.48   Line up decimals.
                  − $ 5.15   Subtract.
                  $24.33

EXAMPLE 2 $12 − $3.74   Write in vertical form.
         Solution $12.00 ←   Insert zeros.
                  − $3.74   Subtract.
                  $8.26

EXAMPLE 3   6.5 − 1.41   Write in vertical form.
         Solution   6.50 ←   Insert zero.
                  − 1.41   Subtract.
                  5.09

Exercise Write in vertical form, then subtract.

1. $21.48 − $5.15

2. $13.41 − $10.30

3. $16.71 − $5.36

4. $14.70 − $4.70

5. $18.41 − $16.30

6. $41.86 − $14.68

7. $12.00 − $3.74

8. $15.00 − $6.72

9. $19.00 − $5.63

10. $15.00 − $9.81

11. 6.5 − 1.41

12. 3.6 − 2.94

13. 6.7 − 5.61

14. 8.96 − 3.67

15. 10.46 − 4.67

16. 91.14 − 16.63

17. 41.62 − 19.81

18. 98.14 − 63.01

19. 43.1 − 6.37

20. 84.73 − 4.1

Multiplying Decimals

By adding the decimal places in the factors, you know exactly how many decimal places are in the product.

EXAMPLE 1 $1.3 \cdot 2 = \blacksquare$

Solution	1.3	one place
	$\times\ \ 2$	no decimal
Answer	2.6	one place $1 + 0 = 1$

EXAMPLE 2 $1.3 \cdot 2.43 = \blacksquare$

Solution	1.3	one place
	$\times\ \ 2.43$	two places
	39	
	52	
	$+\ 2\ 6$	
Answer	3.159	three places $1 + 2 = 3$

Exercise Write in vertical form, then multiply.

1. $1.4 \cdot 2$

2. $2.4 \cdot 5$

3. $6.3 \cdot 3$

4. $4.9 \cdot 3$

5. $6.7 \cdot 5$

6. $1.3 \cdot 2.4$

7. $6.1 \cdot 2.6$

8. $3.9 \cdot 4.1$

9. $6.7 \cdot 1.2$

10. $8.6 \cdot 6.8$

11. $1.3 \cdot 2.43$

12. $6.8 \cdot 2.61$

13. $4.63 \cdot 1.6$

14. $9.84 \cdot 2.7$

15. $4.86 \cdot 2.9$

16. $6.7 \cdot 1.79$

17. $7.8 \cdot 4.62$

18. $4.91 \cdot 1.8$

19. $9.46 \cdot 2.9$

20. $6.3 \cdot 8.76$

Scientific Notation

Scientific notation expresses any number as a product of a number 1 or greater but less than 10 and a power of ten.

EXAMPLE 1   Express 2,800 in scientific notation.

         Solution $2,800 = 2.8 \bullet 10^3$ Move the decimal point 3 places to the left.

         Answer $2.8 \bullet 10^3$

EXAMPLE 2   Express 0.00039 in scientific notation.

         Solution $0.00039 = 3.9 \bullet 10^{-4}$ Move the decimal point 4 places to the right.

         Use the negative sign ($^{-4}$) when the decimal is moved to the right.

         Answer $3.9 \bullet 10^{-4}$

Exercise   Write these numbers in scientific notation.

1. 2,900
2. 3,600
3. 8,750
4. 6,320
5. 35,000
6. 46,000
7. 71,100
8. 400,000
9. 4,000,000
10. 1,700,000,000

11. 0.00038
12. 0.39
13. 0.41
14. 0.072
15. 0.0072
16. 0.0081
17. 0.00074
18. 0.000012
19. 0.00123
20. 0.000246

Dividing Decimals by Whole Numbers

EXAMPLE 1 $0.168 \div 14 = \blacksquare$

Solution
```
        .012
14 ) .168
    − 14
      28
    − 28
       0
```
Place the decimal point in the quotient directly above the one in the dividend.

EXAMPLE 2 $68.6 \div 28 = \blacksquare$

Solution
```
        2.45
28 ) 68.60
   − 56
     12 6
   − 11 2
      1 40
    − 1 40
        0
```
Add a zero to complete the division.

Exercise Divide each decimal by the whole number.

1. $4.7 \div 2$

2. $0.78 \div 3$

3. $1.25 \div 5$

4. $6.34 \div 2$

5. $19.5 \div 3$

6. $21.7 \div 7$

7. $35.5 \div 5$

8. $1.68 \div 8$

9. $42.6 \div 6$

10. $18.9 \div 9$

11. $12.4 \div 4$

12. $23.1 \div 7$

13. $184.5 \div 9$

14. $36.36 \div 4$

15. $42.7 \div 7$

16. $8.414 \div 7$

17. $36.6 \div 6$

18. $25.5 \div 50$

19. $25.5 \div 25$

20. $12.5 \div 25$

Review of Basic Skills 34

Dividing Decimals by Decimals

EXAMPLE 1 $8.04 \div 0.6 = \blacksquare$

Solution

$$
\begin{array}{r}
13.4 \\
6\,)\overline{80.4} \\
-6 \\
\hline
20 \\
-18 \\
\hline
2\,4 \\
-2\,4 \\
\hline
0
\end{array}
$$

Step 1 Make the divisor a whole number. Multiply both divisor and dividend by ten.

$8.04 \bullet 10 \div 0.6 \bullet 10 = 80.4 \div 6$

Step 2 Divide. Place the decimal point straight up into the quotient.

Answer   13.4

Exercise Divide each decimal. Watch where you put the decimal point.

1. $1.44 \div 0.2$

2. $3.69 \div 0.3$

3. $5.50 \div 0.5$

4. $13.41 \div 0.9$

5. $16.71 \div 0.3$

6. $14.96 \div 0.4$

7. $1.934 \div 0.02$

8. $21.35 \div 0.05$

9. $0.0014 \div 0.7$

10. $6.315 \div 0.03$

11. $42.10 \div 0.2$

12. $32.30 \div 0.005$

13. $56.7 \div 0.07$

14. $5.67 \div 0.07$

15. $5.67 \div 0.7$

16. $636.3 \div 0.9$

17. $13.2 \div 0.4$

18. $132.4 \div 0.02$

19. $159.6 \div 0.3$

20. $7.938 \div 8.1$

Rewriting Decimals as Fractions

EXAMPLE 1   Rewrite 0.13 as a fraction.

Solution   0.1 3 means 13 hundredths.
              ↑ ↑
            tenths   hundredths
            so 0.13 = $\frac{13}{100}$ Answer $\frac{13}{100}$

Exercise Write these decimals as fractions. Then write the fractions in lowest terms.

1. 0.14

2. 0.15

3. 0.75

4. 0.36

5. 0.79

6. 0.150

7. 0.159

8. 0.375

9. 0.875

10. 0.999

11. 0.42

12. 0.65

13. 0.60

14. 0.45

15. 0.50

16. 0.168

17. 0.22

18. 0.98

19. 0.568

20. 0.72

Review of Basic Skills 36

Renaming Fractions as Decimals

Write decimals with denominators 10, 100, 1,000, and 10,000 or use a calculator to divide numerator by denominator.

EXAMPLE 1 Rewrite $\frac{2}{5}$ as a decimal.

Solution $\frac{2}{5} = \frac{2 \cdot 2}{5 \cdot 2} = \frac{4}{10}$ Rewrite with a denominator of 10.

$\frac{4}{10} = 0.4$ **Answer** 0.4

EXAMPLE 2 Rewrite $\frac{2}{7}$ as a decimal.

Solution Since 7 cannot be made into 10 or a multiple of 10, use your calculator.

$2 \div 7 = 0.2857142$ **Answer** 0.2857142

Exercise Write as decimals.

1. $\frac{1}{10}$

2. $\frac{1}{5}$

3. $\frac{1}{2}$

4. $\frac{3}{25}$

5. $\frac{9}{50}$

6. $\frac{7}{20}$

7. $\frac{9}{25}$

8. $\frac{3}{500}$

9. $\frac{6}{250}$

10. $\frac{59}{500}$

Use a calculator. Copy the display.

11. $\frac{3}{7}$

12. $\frac{5}{7}$

13. $\frac{2}{3}$

14. $\frac{2}{9}$

15. $\frac{5}{13}$

16. $\frac{2}{17}$

17. $\frac{3}{19}$

18. $\frac{5}{23}$

19. $\frac{6}{29}$

20. $\frac{5}{31}$

Calculator Practice

Although the symbols may differ depending on the calculator, most scientific calculators have keys that are useful in algebra. For example,

$\sqrt{}$ or $\sqrt{x}$ for square root; $1/x$ for reciprocals;

y^x, x^2, or $\wedge$ for powering;

π for pi; and $x!$ for factorial;

$\pm$, $+/-$ or $-$ for changing the sign (positive or negative) of a number.

It is easy to use your calculator to help you do arithmetic. Check the display after you key in each number to make sure you have entered the number correctly.

To add:
Press 46 $+$ 31 $=$.
The display will read 77.
46 + 31 = 77

To subtract:
Press 84 $-$ 32 $=$.
The display will read 52.
84 − 32 = 52

To multiply:
Press 12 $\times$ 6 $=$.
The display will read 72.
12 · 6 = 72

To divide:
Press 42 $\div$ 7 $=$.
The display will read 6.
42 ÷ 7 = 6

Use the $($ and $)$ for expressions to be evaluated separately within another expression. For example, to find 8 · (4 − 2), press 8 $\times$ $($ 4 $-$ 2 $)$ $=$.
The display will read 16.
8 · (4 − 2) = 16

Use the $\sqrt{}$ on your calculator to find the square root of a number. For example, to find the square root of 81, press 81 $\sqrt{}$.
The display will read 9.

To find the squared value of a number, use x^2. For example, to find 12 squared, press 12 x^2. The display will read 144.

To raise a number to a specified power, use the y^x. For example, to find 5 to the third power, press 5 y^x 3 $=$.
The display will read 125.

Calculator Practice

To find the decimal value of the reciprocal of the number, use $\boxed{1/x}$. For example, to find the reciprocal of 8, press 8 $\boxed{1/x}$. The display will read 0.125. The decimal for the reciprocal of 8 is 0.125.

To make a calculation including a fraction, use $\boxed{a^{b/c}}$. For example, to find the answer to $3 - \frac{3}{4}$, press 3 $\boxed{-}$ 3 $\boxed{a^{b/c}}$ 4 $\boxed{=}$. The display will read $2\frac{1}{4}$.

$$3 - \frac{3}{4} = 2\frac{1}{4}$$

A scientific calculator contains an exponential shift key $\boxed{EE}$ or $\boxed{EXP}$. Use this key to enter numbers that are written in scientific notation.

- To multiply $3.64 \cdot 10^6$, press 3.64 $\boxed{EE}$ 6 $\boxed{=}$. The display will read 3640000. The answer is 3,640,000.

- To divide $3.64 \cdot 10^6$ by $1.4 \cdot 10^{-5}$, press 3.64 $\boxed{EE}$ 6 $\boxed{\div}$ 1.4 $\boxed{EE}$ $\boxed{+/-}$ 5 $\boxed{=}$. The display will read $2.6\ 11$, so the answer is $2.6 \cdot 10^{11}$, or 260,000,000,000.

To find the sine, cosine, or tangent of angles, use $\boxed{SIN}$, $\boxed{COS}$, or $\boxed{TAN}$. For example, to find the cosine of a 30° angle, press 30 $\boxed{COS}$. The display will read 0.866025404.

Sometimes you want to use the same number, or constant, in a series of calculations. You can store the number in memory. For example, suppose you want to find the answers to $18 \cdot 4$, $18 \cdot 12$, and $18 \cdot 31$.

- Press 18 $\boxed{STO}$ 1. The number 18 is stored in memory 1.

- Press $\boxed{RCL}$ 1 $\boxed{\times}$ 4 $\boxed{=}$. The display will read 72.

- Press $\boxed{RCL}$ 1 $\boxed{\times}$ 12 $\boxed{=}$. The display will read 216.

- Press $\boxed{RCL}$ 1 $\boxed{\times}$ 31 $\boxed{=}$. The display will read 558.

On some calculators, the key used to store a number in memory is $\boxed{M+}$ instead of $\boxed{STO}$. The key used to display the stored number is $\boxed{MR}$ instead of $\boxed{RCL}$. On some calculators, you press $\boxed{ON/AC}$ to clear the memory. On other calculators, you must press $\boxed{MC}$ to clear the memory. Read the instructions for your calculator to find out how to store and recall numbers.

Decimal, Percent, and Fraction Conversion

Renaming Decimals as Percents

Example   Rename 0.75 as a percent.

Solution   0.75

0.75 = 75%

Step 1   Move the decimal point two places to the right.

Step 2   Then insert a percent symbol.

Example   Rename 0.5 as a percent.

Solution   0.5 = .50

0.5 = 50%

Renaming Percents as Decimals

Example   Rename 80% as a decimal.

Solution   80% = 80.%

80% = 0.80

= 0.8 ⟵ You can always drop zeros at the end of a decimal.

Step 1   Move the decimal point two places to the left.

Step 2   Then drop the percent symbol.

Renaming Fractions as Decimals

Example   Rename $\frac{7}{20}$ as a decimal.

Solution   **Method 1**

$$\frac{7}{20} = \frac{7 \times 5}{20 \times 5} = \frac{35}{100}$$

$$= 0.35$$

Choose a multiplier that makes the denominator a power of 10 (10, 100, 1,000, . . .)

Method 2

$$\frac{7}{20} = 20 \overline{)7.00} \quad .35$$

$$\begin{array}{r} -6\,0 \\ \hline 1\,00 \\ -1\,00 \end{array}$$

Divide the numerator by the denominator.

Decimal, Percent, and Fraction Conversion

Renaming Decimals as Fractions

Example   Rename 0.025 as a fraction.

Solution   First, read the decimal: "25 thousandths."

Then write the fraction and simplify.

$$0.025 = \frac{25}{1,000} = \frac{25 \div 25}{1,000 \div 25} = \frac{1}{40}$$

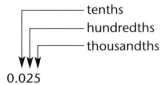

Renaming Fractions as Percents

Example   Rename $\frac{9}{25}$ as a percent.

Solution   **Method 1**

Write as an equivalent fraction with denominator 100.

$$\frac{9}{25} = \frac{9 \times 4}{25 \times 4} = \frac{36}{100} = 36\%$$

Percent means per 100.
So, 36 hundredths is 36%.

Method 2

$$\frac{9}{25} = 0.36 = 36\%$$

Step 1   Divide the numerator by the denominator.

Step 2   Rewrite the decimal as a percent.

Renaming Percents as Fractions

Example   Rename 2% as a fraction.

Solution $2\% = \frac{2}{100}$ ◀——   *Percent* means *per 100.*

$\quad\quad\quad = \frac{1}{50}$ ◀——   Simplify.

Measurement Conversion Factors

Metric Measures

Length
1,000 meters (m) = 1 kilometer (km)
100 centimeters (cm) = 1 m
10 decimeters (dm) = 1 m
1,000 millimeters (mm) = 1 m
10 cm = 1 decimeter (dm)
10 mm = 1 cm

Area
100 square millimeters (mm^2) = 1 square centimeter (cm^2)
10,000 cm^2 = 1 square meter (m^2)
10,000 m^2 = 1 hectare (ha)

Volume
1,000 cubic meters (m^3) = 1 cubic centimeter (cm^3)
100 cm^3 = 1 cubic decimeter (dm^3)
1,000,000 cm^3 = 1 cubic meter (m^3)

Capacity
1,000 milliliters (mL) = 1 liter (L)
1,000 L = 1 kiloliter (kL)

Mass
1,000 kilograms (kg) = 1 metric ton (t)
1,000 grams (g) = 1 kg
1,000 milligrams (mg) = 1 g

Temperature Degrees Celsius (°C)
0°C = freezing point of water
37°C = normal body temperature
100°C = boiling point of water

Time
60 seconds (sec) = 1 minute (min)
60 min = 1 hour (hr)
24 hr = 1 day

Customary Measures

Length
12 inches (in.) = 1 foot (ft)
3 ft = 1 yard (yd)
36 in. = 1 yd
5,280 ft = 1 mile (mi)
1,760 yd = 1 mi
6,076 feet = 1 nautical mile

Area
144 square inches (sq in.) = 1 square foot (sq ft)
9 sq ft = 1 square yard (sq yd)
43,560 sq ft = 1 acre (A)

Volume
1,728 cubic inches (cu in.) = 1 cubic foot (cu ft)
27 cu ft = 1 cubic yard (cu yard)

Capacity
8 fluid ounces (fl oz) = 1 cup (c)
2 c = 1 pint (pt)
2 pt = 1 quart (qt)
4 qt = 1 gallon (gal)

Weight
16 ounces (oz) = 1 pound (lb)
2,000 lb = 1 ton (T)

Temperature Degrees Fahrenheit (°F)
32°F = freezing point of water
98.6°F = normal body temperature
212°F = boiling point of water

Measurement Conversion Factors

To change	To	Multiply by	To change	To	Multiply by
centimeters	inches	0.3937	meters	feet	3.2808
centimeters	feet	0.03281	meters	miles	0.0006214
cubic feet	cubic meters	0.0283	meters	yards	1.0936
cubic meters	cubic feet	35.3145	metric tons	tons (long)	0.9842
cubic meters	cubic yards	1.3079	metric tons	tons (short)	1.1023
cubic yards	cubic meters	0.7646	miles	kilometers	1.6093
feet	meters	0.3048	miles	feet	5,280
feet	miles (nautical)	0.0001645	miles (statute)	miles (nautical)	0.8684
feet	miles (statute)	0.0001894	miles/hour	feet/minute	88
feet/second	miles/hour	0.6818	millimeters	inches	0.0394
gallons (U.S.)	liters	3.7853	ounces avdp	grams	28.3495
grams	ounces avdp	0.0353	ounces	pounds	0.0625
grams	pounds	0.002205	pecks	liters	8.8096
hours	days	0.04167	pints (dry)	liters	0.5506
inches	millimeters	25.4000	pints (liquid)	liters	0.4732
inches	centimeters	2.5400	pounds avdp	kilograms	0.4536
kilograms	pounds avdp	2.2046	pounds	ounces	16
kilometers	miles	0.6214	quarts (dry)	liters	1.1012
liters	gallons (U.S.)	0.2642	quarts (liquid)	liters	0.9463
liters	pecks	0.1135	square feet	square meters	0.0929
liters	pints (dry)	1.8162	square meters	square feet	10.7639
liters	pints (liquid)	2.1134	square meters	square yards	1.1960
liters	quarts (dry)	0.9081	square yards	square meters	0.8361
liters	quarts (liquid)	1.0567	yards	meters	0.9144

Addition Table

+	0	1	2	3	4	5	6	7	8	9	10
0	0	1	2	3	4	5	6	7	8	9	10
1	1	2	3	4	5	6	7	8	9	10	11
2	2	3	4	5	6	7	8	9	10	11	12
3	3	4	5	6	7	8	9	10	11	12	13
4	4	5	6	7	8	9	10	11	12	13	14
5	5	6	7	8	9	10	11	12	13	14	15
6	6	7	8	9	10	11	12	13	14	15	16
7	7	8	9	10	11	12	13	14	15	16	17
8	8	9	10	11	12	13	14	15	16	17	18
9	9	10	11	12	13	14	15	16	17	18	19
10	10	11	12	13	14	15	16	17	18	19	20

Subtraction Table

−	0	1	2	3	4	5	6	7	8	9	10
0	0	−1	−2	−3	−4	−5	−6	−7	−8	−9	−10
1	1	0	−1	−2	−3	−4	−5	−6	−7	−8	−9
2	2	1	0	−1	−2	−3	−4	−5	−6	−7	−8
3	3	2	1	0	−1	−2	−3	−4	−5	−6	−7
4	4	3	2	1	0	−1	−2	−3	−4	−5	−6
5	5	4	3	2	1	0	−1	−2	−3	−4	−5
6	6	5	4	3	2	1	0	−1	−2	−3	−4
7	7	6	5	4	3	2	1	0	−1	−2	−3
8	8	7	6	5	4	3	2	1	0	−1	−2
9	9	8	7	6	5	4	3	2	1	0	−1
10	10	9	8	7	6	5	4	3	2	1	0

Note: To use this table, look at the numbers in the far left vertical column. Select a number from the vertical column. Then subtract from that number by selecting a number in the top horizontal row. The difference is listed where the column and row meet. For example, subtract 4 in the top horizontal row from 1 in the vertical column. The answer is −3, which is the number located where the column and row meet. You must subtract the numbers in the horizontal row from the numbers in the vertical column for this chart to work.

Multiplication Table

×	2	3	4	5	6	7	8	9	10	11	12
2	4	6	8	10	12	14	16	18	20	22	24
3	6	9	12	15	18	21	24	27	30	33	36
4	8	12	16	20	24	28	32	36	40	44	48
5	10	15	20	25	30	35	40	45	50	55	60
6	12	18	24	30	36	42	48	54	60	66	72
7	14	21	28	35	42	49	56	63	70	77	84
8	16	24	32	40	48	56	64	72	80	88	96
9	18	27	36	45	54	63	72	81	90	99	108
10	20	30	40	50	60	70	80	90	100	110	120
11	22	33	44	55	66	77	88	99	110	121	132
12	24	36	48	60	72	84	96	108	120	132	144

Division Table

÷1	÷2	÷3	÷4	÷5
0 ÷ 1 = 0	0 ÷ 2 = 0	0 ÷ 3 = 0	0 ÷ 4 = 0	0 ÷ 5 = 0
1 ÷ 1 = 1	2 ÷ 2 = 1	3 ÷ 3 = 1	4 ÷ 4 = 1	5 ÷ 5 = 1
2 ÷ 1 = 2	4 ÷ 2 = 2	6 ÷ 3 = 2	8 ÷ 4 = 2	10 ÷ 5 = 2
3 ÷ 1 = 3	6 ÷ 2 = 3	9 ÷ 3 = 3	12 ÷ 4 = 3	15 ÷ 5 = 3
4 ÷ 1 = 4	8 ÷ 2 = 4	12 ÷ 3 = 4	16 ÷ 4 = 4	20 ÷ 5 = 4
5 ÷ 1 = 5	10 ÷ 2 = 5	15 ÷ 3 = 5	20 ÷ 4 = 5	25 ÷ 5 = 5
6 ÷ 1 = 6	12 ÷ 2 = 6	18 ÷ 3 = 6	24 ÷ 4 = 6	30 ÷ 5 = 6
7 ÷ 1 = 7	14 ÷ 2 = 7	21 ÷ 3 = 7	28 ÷ 4 = 7	35 ÷ 5 = 7
8 ÷ 1 = 8	16 ÷ 2 = 8	24 ÷ 3 = 8	32 ÷ 4 = 8	40 ÷ 5 = 8
9 ÷ 1 = 9	18 ÷ 2 = 9	27 ÷ 3 = 9	36 ÷ 4 = 9	45 ÷ 5 = 9

÷6	÷7	÷8	÷9	÷10
0 ÷ 6 = 0	0 ÷ 7 = 0	0 ÷ 8 = 0	0 ÷ 9 = 0	0 ÷ 10 = 0
6 ÷ 6 = 1	7 ÷ 7 = 1	8 ÷ 8 = 1	9 ÷ 9 = 1	10 ÷ 10 = 1
12 ÷ 6 = 2	14 ÷ 7 = 2	16 ÷ 8 = 2	18 ÷ 9 = 2	20 ÷ 10 = 2
18 ÷ 6 = 3	21 ÷ 7 = 3	24 ÷ 8 = 3	27 ÷ 9 = 3	30 ÷ 10 = 3
24 ÷ 6 = 4	28 ÷ 7 = 4	32 ÷ 8 = 4	36 ÷ 9 = 4	40 ÷ 10 = 4
30 ÷ 6 = 5	35 ÷ 7 = 5	40 ÷ 8 = 5	45 ÷ 9 = 5	50 ÷ 10 = 5
36 ÷ 6 = 6	42 ÷ 7 = 6	48 ÷ 8 = 6	54 ÷ 9 = 6	60 ÷ 10 = 6
42 ÷ 6 = 7	49 ÷ 7 = 7	56 ÷ 8 = 7	63 ÷ 9 = 7	70 ÷ 10 = 7
48 ÷ 6 = 8	56 ÷ 7 = 8	64 ÷ 8 = 8	72 ÷ 9 = 8	80 ÷ 10 = 8
54 ÷ 6 = 9	63 ÷ 7 = 9	72 ÷ 8 = 9	81 ÷ 9 = 9	90 ÷ 10 = 9

Glossary

Absolute value (ab´ sə lüt val´ yü) the distance from zero of a number on a number line (p. 181)

> $|-4|$ is read "the absolute value of negative 4."
> $|-4| = 4$, 4 units from 0.
> $|4| = 4$, 4 units from 0.

Acute (ə kyüt´) an angle less than 90° (p. 316)

Acute triangle (ə kyüt´ trī´ ang gel) a triangle with three angles less than 90° (p. 326)

Addend (əd´ end) number to be added to another (p. 2)

> $4 + 2 = 6$ **The numbers 4 and 2 are addends.**

Addition (ə dish´ ən) the arithmetic operation of combining two or more numbers to find a total (p. 2)

> $3 + 5 = 8$

Adjacent angles (ə jā´ snt ang´ gəlz) two angles that have the same vertex and share a common side (p. 316)

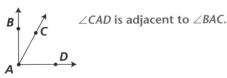

∠CAD is adjacent to ∠BAC.

Algebra (al´ jə brə) the branch of mathematics that uses both letters and numbers to show relations between quantities (p. 2)

Algebraic expression (al´ jə brā´ ik ek spresh´ ən) a mathematical statement that includes at least one operation and variable (p. 22)

> $2x + 5$ $m \cdot 3$

Angle (ang´ gel) a figure made up of two sides or rays with a common endpoint (p. 226)

Area (âr´ ē ə) the number of square units inside a closed region (p. 216)

Arithmetic (ə rith´ mə tik) the study of the properties of numbers using four basic operations—addition, subtraction, multiplication, and division (p. 2)

B

Bar graph (bär graf) a way of comparing information using rectangular bars (p. 344)

Base (bās) the number being multiplied; a factor (p. 210)

a^2

a is the base.

a	hat	e	let	ī	ice	ȯ	order	u̇	put	sh	she		a in about
ā	age	ē	equal	o	hot	oi	oil	ü	rule	th	thin	ə	e in taken
ä	far	ėr	term	ō	open	ou	out	ch	child	ᴛʜ	then		i in pencil
â	care	i	it	ȯ	saw	u	cup	ng	long	zh	measure		o in lemon
													u in circus

Box-and-whiskers plot (boks and wis´ kərz plot) a way to show the spread of data in a set of numbers (p. 358)

C

Circle graph (sėr´ kəl graf) a way to present information using the parts of a circle (p. 346)

Revenue

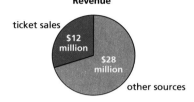

Circumference (sər kum´ fər əns) distance around a circle (p. 40)

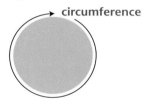

circumference

Common factor (kom´ ən fak´ tər) a number that will divide each of two or more numbers with no remainder (p. 66)

The common factor 9 and 12 is 3.

Compatible numbers (kəm pat´ ə bəl num´ bərs) two numbers that form a basic division fact (p. 18)

$16 \div 2 = 8$ 16 and 2 are compatible numbers.

Complementary angles (kom plə men´ tər ē ang´ gəlz) two angles whose sum of their measures is 90 degrees (p. 318)

60° 30°

45° 45°

Complex fraction (kəm pleks´ frak´ shən) a fraction in which the numerator, the denominator, or both the numerator and the denominator are fractions (p. 136)

$$\frac{\frac{3}{8}}{5} \qquad \frac{10}{\frac{3}{5}} \qquad \frac{\frac{2}{3}}{\frac{1}{2}}$$

Composite number (kəm poz´ it num´ bər) a whole number that is not a prime number (p. 64)

$2 \cdot 2 \cdot 2 \cdot 2 = 16$ 16 is a composite number.

Compounding period (kom pound´ ing pir´ ē əd) the amount of time that the interest rate is calculated (p. 172)

Compound interest (kom´ pound in´ tər ist) interest paid on both the original amount of money plus any interest added to date; compound interest is usually computed on deposits placed into savings accounts (p. 172)

Congruent (kən grü´ ənt) figures that have the same size and shape (p. 328)

Consecutive (kən sek´ yə tiv) following one after the other in order (p. 184)

Constant (kon´ stənt) a number in an expression that does not change, such as *2*, -6, and $\frac{1}{3}$ in an expression such as $2x - 6y + \frac{1}{3}z$ (p. 126)

Coordinate system (kō ôrd´ n it sis´ təm) a way of using number lines to locate points on a plane or in space (p. 286)

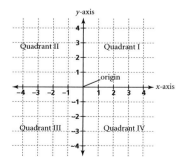

Corresponding angles (kôr ə spon´ ding ang´ gəlz) interior or exterior angles of figures in the same position as those of figures with the same shape (p. 330)

 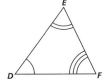

Cross product (krós prod´ əkt) the result of multiplying the denominator of one fraction with the numerator of another (p. 154)

If $\frac{a}{b} = \frac{c}{d}$, then the cross products are $a \cdot d$ and $b \cdot c$

Cube (kyüb) a solid with six square faces (p. 218)

Cylinder (sil´ ən dər) a solid figure with two equal circular bases that are parallel (p. 268)

D

Data (dā´ tə) information given in numbers (p. 344)

Decimal (des´ ə məl) a number that has a decimal point in it (p. 32)

Decimal point (des´ ə məl point) a period that separates digits representing numbers that are one or more from digits representing numbers that are less than one (p. 32)

Denominator (di nom´ ə nā tər) the number below the fraction bar (p. 46)

$\frac{1}{2}$ **2 is the denominator.**

Diagonal (dī ag´ ə nəl) a line segment connecting two vertices that are not next to each other (p. 334)

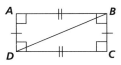

BD is a diagonal of rectangle ABCD.

Diameter (dī am´ ə tər) distance across a circle through the center (p. 40)

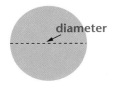

Difference (dif´ ər əns) the result of subtraction (p. 6)

8 − 2 = 6   **6 is the difference.**

Digit (dig´ it) any one of the symbols 0, 1, 2, 3, 4, 5, 6, 7, 8, or 9 (p. 32)

Distributive property (dis trib´ yə tiv prop´ ər tē) numbers within parentheses can be multiplied by the same factor (p. 68)

4(2 + 1) = (4 · 2) + (4 · 1)

Dividend (div´ ə dend) the number that is divided (p. 14)

6 ÷ 3 = 2   **6 is the dividend.**

Divisible (də viz´ ə bəl) able to be divided by a whole number with no remainder (p. 60)

Division (də vizh´ ən) the arithmetic operation of finding how many times a number goes into another number (p. 14)

Divisor (də vī´ zər) the number that is used to divide (p. 14)

10 ÷ 5 = 2   **5 is the divisor.**

a	hat	e	let	ī	ice	ô	order	ù	put	sh	she	ə	a in about
ā	age	ē	equal	o	hot	oi	oil	ü	rule	th	thin		e in taken
ä	far	ėr	term	ō	open	ou	out	ch	child	ᴛʜ	then		i in pencil
â	care	i	it	ȯ	saw	u	cup	ng	long	zh	measure		o in lemon
													u in circus

Equality (i kwol´ ə tē) the state of being equal; shown by the equal sign (p. 276)

$$2 \cdot 2 = 4 \cdot 1$$

Equation (i kwā´ zhən) a mathematical sentence stating that two quantities are equal and written as two expressions separated by an equal sign (p. 130)

$$4n + 4n = 8n$$

Equiangular triangle (ē kwē ang´ gyə lər trī´ ang gəl) a triangle with three equal angles, each measuring 60° (p. 326)

Equilateral triangle (ē kwə lat´ ər əl trī´ ang gəl) a triangle with three equal sides (p. 230)

Equivalent (i kwiv´ ə lənt) the same in value (p. 156)

Equivalent fraction (i kwiv´ ə lənt frak´ shən) a fraction that has the same value as another fraction (p. 46)

$$\frac{4}{6} = \frac{2}{3}$$

Estimate (es´ tə māt) a careful guess; a close or nearly correct answer (p. 10)

Evaluate (i val´ yü āt) to find the numerical value of an algebraic expression (p. 24)

Exponent (ek spō´ nənt) number that tells how many times another number is a factor (p. 38, 210)

2 is the exponent.

$$a^2$$

Expression (ek spresh´ ən) a mathematical statement that usually includes numbers, variables, and symbols (p. 22)

$$10 \div 5 = 2 \qquad 3n + 4 = 10$$

Exterior angle (ek stir´ ē ər ang´ gel) an angle formed by extending one side of a polygon at any vertex (p. 323)

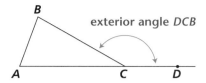

exterior angle DCB

Factor (fak´ tər) the numbers in a multiplication operation (p. 12)

$$4 \cdot 3 = 12 \quad \text{4 and 3 are the factors.}$$

Formula (fôr´ myə lə) a combination of symbols used to state a rule (p. 36)

Fraction (frak´ shən) part of a whole number such as $\frac{1}{2}$ (p. 46)

Frequency (frē´ kwən sē) the number of times an event, value, or characteristic occurs (p. 348)

Frequency table (frē´ kwən sē tā´ bəl) a chart showing the number of of items or number of times something happened (p. 348)

Frequency Table		
Interval	Tally	Frequency
0–9		0
10–19		0
20–29	⊥⊤⊤ l	6

Fundamental Law of Fractions (fun də men´ tl lȯ ov frak´ shənz) the value of a fraction does not change if its numerator and its denominator are multiplied by the same number (p. 90)

$$\frac{2}{3} = \frac{2}{3} \cdot \frac{5}{5} = \frac{10}{15}$$

Fundamental principle of counting (fun də men´ tl prin´ sə pəl ov koun´ ting) a general rule that states if one task can be completed a different ways, and a second task can be completed b different ways, the first task followed by the second task can be completed $a \cdot b$ or ab different ways (p. 362)

G

Geometry (jē om′ ə trē) the study of points, lines, angles, surfaces, and solids (p. 238)

Graph (graf) a diagram showing how one quantity depends on another (p. 224)

Graphing (graf′ ing) showing on a number line the relationship of a set of numbers (p. 276)

$$x = 3$$

Greatest common divisor (GCD) (grāt′ est kom′ ən də vī′ zər) the largest factor that two or more numbers or terms have in common (p. 66)

16: 1, 2, 4, 8, 16   **The GCD of 16**
20: 1, 2, 4, 5, 10, 20   **and 20 is 4.**

Greatest common factor (GCF) (grāt′ est kom′ ən fak′ tər) the largest factor of two or more numbers or terms (p. 67)

10 = 5 • 2   **The GCF of 10**
15 = 5 • 3   **and 15 is 5.**

H

Heptagon (hep′ tə gon) a seven-sided polygon (p. 243)

Hexagon (hek′ sə gon) a six-sided polygon (p. 242)

Horizontal (hôr ə zon′ tl) left to right or parallel to the horizon (p. 286)

Line *M* is horizontal.

Hypotenuse (hī pot′ n üs) the longest side in a right triangle (p. 226)

I

Improper fraction (im prop′ ər frak′ shən) a fraction in which the numerator is greater than or equal to the denominator (p. 86)

$$\frac{2}{2} \qquad \frac{6}{5}$$

Inequality (in i kwol′ ə tē) two quantities that are not the same; shown by the less than, greater than, and unequal to signs (p. 278)

$$5 > 2 \qquad 5 < 7 \qquad 5 \neq 4$$

Integer (in′ tə jər) any positive or negative whole number including zero (p. 180)

$$(\ldots -2, -1, 0, 1, 2, \ldots)$$

Interest (in′ tər ist) the amount of money paid or received for the use of money (p. 50)

Interior angle (in tir′ ē ər ang′ gəl) any angle within a polygon (p. 323)

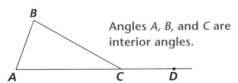

Angles *A, B,* and *C* are interior angles.

Intersection (in tər sek′ shən) a point at which two or more lines cross in a figure (p. 314)

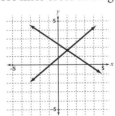

a	hat	e	let	ī	ice	ô	order	ù	put	sh	she	ə	a	in about
ā	age	ē	equal	o	hot	oi	oil	ü	rule	th	thin		e	in taken
ä	far	ėr	term	ō	open	ou	out	ch	child	ŦH	then		i	in pencil
â	care	i	it	ȯ	saw	u	cup	ng	long	zh	measure		o	in lemon
													u	in circus

Interval (in´ tər vəl) set of all numbers between two stated numbers (p. 344)

Inverse (in vėrs´) exactly opposite (p. 6)

Inverse operation (in vėrs´ op ə rā´ shən) an operation that undoes another operation (p. 132)

Irrational number (i rash´ ə nəl num´ bər) a real number such as $\sqrt{2}$ that cannot be written in the form $\frac{a}{b}$ in which a and b are whole numbers and $b \neq 0$ (p. 224)

Irregular polygon (i reg´ yə lər pol´ ē gon) a polygon that is not uniform in shape or size (p. 246)

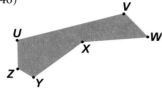

Isosceles triangle (ī sos´ ə lēz trī´ ang gəl) a triangle with two sides of equal length (p. 230)

L

Least common multiple (LCM) (lēst kom´ ən mul´ tə pəl) the smallest number divisible by all numbers in a group (p. 72)

4: 4, 8, *12*, . . .   The LCM of 4 and 6
6: 6, *12*, . . .   is 12.

Linear equation (lin´ ē ər i kwā´ zhən) an equation whose graph is a straight line (p. 292)

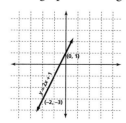

Lower extreme (lō´ ər ek strēm´) the least value of a set of data (p. 358)

{2, 3, 5, 6, 8, 9, 11}   **2 is the lower extreme.**

Lower quartile (lō´ ər kwȯr´ tīl) the median of scores below the median (p. 358)

{2, 3, 5, 6, 8, 9, 11}   **3 is the lower quartile.**

M

Mean (mēn) the sum of the values in a set of data divided by the number of pieces of data in the set (p. 350)

{2, 3, 5, 6, 8, 9, 11}   **6.3 is the mean.**

Measures of central tendency (mezh´ ərz ov sen´ trəl ten´ dən sē) the mean, median, and mode of a set of data (p. 354)

Median (mē´ dē ən) the middle value in an ordered set of data (p. 352)

{2, 3, 5, 6, 8, 9, 11}   **6 is the median.**

Mixed number (mikst num´ bər) an integer and a proper fraction (p. 86)

$$1\frac{3}{4} \qquad 5\frac{1}{2} \qquad 7\frac{2}{3}$$

Mode (mōd) the value or values that occur most often in a set of data (p. 354)

{2, 3, 5, 2}   **2 is the mode.**

Multiplication (mul tə plə kā´ shən) the arithmetic operation that adds a number a given amount of times (p. 12)

$3 \cdot 5 = 15 \qquad 5 + 5 + 5 = 15$

N

Negative integer (neg´ ə tiv in´ tə jər) a whole number less than zero (p. 180)

Numerator (nü´ mə rā tər) the number above the fraction bar (p. 46)

$\frac{1}{2}$ **1 is the numerator.**

Numerical expression (nü mer´ ə kəl ek spresh´ ən) a mathematical sentence that uses operations and numbers (p. 22)

$3 + 2 \quad 6 - 4 \quad 12 \div 3 \quad 5 \cdot 2$

Obtuse (əb tüs′) an angle with a measure between 90 and 180 degrees (p. 316)

Obtuse triangle (əb tüs′ trī′ ang gəl) a triangle with one angle greater than 90° (p. 326)

Octagon (ok′ tə gon) an eight-sided polygon (p. 243)

Open statement (ō′ pən stāt′ mənt) a sentence that is neither true nor false (p. 20)

$$6a = 30 \qquad 30 \div n = 5$$

Operation (op ə rā′ shən) addition, subtraction, multiplication, and division (p. 2)

Opposites (op′ ə zits) numbers the same distance from zero but on different sides of zero on the number line (p. 181)

4 and −4 are opposites.

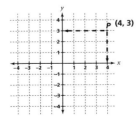

Ordered pair (ôr′ dərd pâr) two real numbers that locate a point in a plane; the x is always first, the y is always second (p. 286)

Order of operations (ô r′ dər ov op ə rā′ shəns) rules that describe the order addition, subtraction, multiplication, and division must be performed (p. 122)

Origin (ôr′ ə jin) the point at which the x-axis and y-axis in the coordinate system intersect (p. 286)

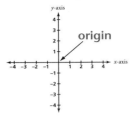

Outcome (out′ kum) a result of a probability experiment (p. 360)

Parallel (par′ ə lel) lines that never meet and are in the same plane (p. 238)

Lines *M* and *N* are parallel.

Parallelogram (par ə lel′ ə gram) a four-sided polygon with two pairs of equal and parallel sides (p. 256)

Pentagon (pen′ tə gon) a five-sided polygon (p. 242)

a	hat	e	let	ī	ice	ô	order	u̇	put	sh	she	ə	a	in about
ā	age	ē	equal	o	hot	oi	oil	ü	rule	th	thin		e	in taken
ä	far	ėr	term	ō	open	ou	out	ch	child	ŦH	then		i	in pencil
â	care	i	it	ȯ	saw	u	cup	ng	long	zh	measure		o	in lemon
													u	in circus

Percent (pər sent´) part per one hundred; hundredths (p. 50)

Perimeter (pə rim´ ə tər) the distance around the outside of a shape (p. 36)

Perpendicular (pėr pən dik´ yə lər) two intersecting lines forming right angles (p. 254)

Lines *M* and *N* are perpendicular.

Pi (π) (pī) ratio of the circumference of a circle to its diameter; about 3.14 (p. 40)

Place value (plās val´ yü) worth of a digit based on its position in a numeral (p. 32)

Polygon (pol´ ē gon) a closed, many-sided figure that is made up of line segments (p. 238)

Positive integer (poz´ ə tiv in´ tə jər) a whole number greater than zero (p. 180)

Power (pou´ ər) the product of multiplying any number by itself once or many times (p. 210)
$$2^1 = 2 \quad 2^2 = 4 \quad 2^3 = 8 \quad 2^4 = 16$$
16 is the fourth power of 2

Power of ten (pou´ ər ov ten) a product of multiplying 10 by itself one or more times (p. 38)
$$10^1 = 10 \qquad 10^2 = 10 \cdot 10 = 100$$
$$10^3 = 10 \cdot 10 \cdot 10 = 1,000$$

Prime factorization (prīm fak tə rə zā´ shən) an expression showing a composite number as a product of its prime factors (p. 72)
$$15 = 3 \cdot 5 \qquad 55 = 5 \cdot 11$$

Prime number (prīm num´ bər) a whole number greater than one that has only 1 and itself as factors (p. 64)
$$7 = 7 \cdot 1$$

Prism (priz´ əm) a solid figure with two parallel bases that are polygons which have the same shape and size (p. 260)

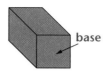
base

Probability (prob ə bil´ ə tē) the chance or likelihood of an event occurring (p. 360)

Product (prod´ əkt) the result of multiplication (p. 12)
$$3 \cdot 4 = 12 \quad \textbf{12 is the product.}$$

Proper fraction (prop´ ər frak´ shən) a fraction in which the numerator is less than the denominator (p. 84)
$$\frac{2}{3} \qquad \frac{3}{4} \qquad \frac{1}{5}$$

Proportion (prə pôr´ shən) an equation made up of two equal ratios (p. 154)
$$\frac{1}{2} = \frac{2}{4}$$

Protractor (prō trak´ tər) a tool used to draw or measure angles (p. 314)

Pyramid (pir´ ə mid) a solid figure with a base that is a polygon and triangular sides (p. 260)

Pythagorean theorem (pə thag ə rē´ ən thē´ ər əm) a formula that states that in a right triangle, the length of the hypotenuse *c* squared is equal to the length of side *a* squared plus the length of side *b* squared (p. 226)
$$c^2 = a^2 + b^2$$

Q

Quadrant (kwäd´ rənt) one of four regions of a coordinate system bounded by the *x*-axis and *y*-axis (p. 286)

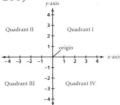

Quadrilateral (kwäd rə lat´ ər əl) a polygon with four sides (p. 239)

Quotient (kwō´ shənt) the result of division (p. 14)

$20 \div 5 = 4$ **4 is the quotient.**

R

Radius (ra´ dē əs) distance from the center of a circle to the edge of the circle (p. 264)

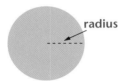

radius

Range (rānj) the difference between the greatest and least values in a set of data (p. 356)

$\{2, 3, 5, 6\}$ $6 - 2 = 4$ **4 is the range.**

Ratio (rā´ shē ō) a comparison of two like quantities using a fraction (p. 152)

$\frac{a}{b}$ also *a:b* or *a* to *b*

Rational expression (rash´ ə nəl ek spresh´ ən) an algebraic expression that can be written like a fraction (p. 140)

$\frac{5 + x}{3x}$

Rational number (rash´ ə nəl num´ bər) any number that can be represented by $\frac{a}{b}$ where a and b are integers and $b \neq 0$ (p. 86)

$2 \quad \frac{1}{3} \quad -3 \quad \frac{-2}{5}$

Ray (rā) part of a line—a ray has one endpoint and extends indefinitely in one direction (p. 314)

ray

Real number (rē´ əl num´ bər) any number on the number line (p. 180)

Reciprocal (ri sip´ rə kəl) the reciprocal of any non-zero number *x* is $\frac{1}{x}$, sometimes called the *multiplicative inverse* of that number (p. 112)

$\frac{1}{2}$ **and 2 are reciprocals.**

Rectangle (rek´ tang gəl) a four-sided polygon with four right angles and the opposite sides equal (p. 239)

Rectangular prism (rek tang´ gyə lər priz´ əm) a solid figure with parallel faces and bases that are rectangles (p. 260)

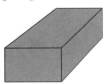

Regular polygon (reg´ yə lər pol´ ē gon) a polygon in which each side and each angle has the same measure (p. 242)

Remainder (ri mān´ dər) amount left over when dividing (p. 14)

Rename (rē nām´) to give a new form that is equal to the original (p. 6)

Repeating decimal (ri pēt´ ing des´ ə məl) a decimal in which one or more digits repeat (p. 48)

$0.3333\ldots = 0.\overline{3}$

a	hat	e	let	ī	ice	ô	order	ù	put	sh	she		a	in about
ā	age	ē	equal	o	hot	oi	oil	ü	rule	th	thin	ə	e	in taken
ä	far	ėr	term	ō	open	ou	out	ch	child	ᴛH	then		i	in pencil
â	care	i	it	ȯ	saw	u	cup	ng	long	zh	measure		o	in lemon
													u	in circus

Rhombus (rom´ bəs) a four-sided polygon with two pairs of parallel and equal sides (p. 239)

Right angle (rīt ang´ gəl) a 90° angle (p. 226)

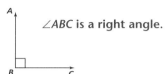

∠ABC is a right angle.

Right triangle (rīt trī´ ang gəl) a three-sided figure, or triangle, with one right, or 90°, angle (p. 226)

Root (rüt) an equal factor of a number (p. 220)
$$\sqrt{25} = 5 \qquad \sqrt[3]{64} = 4$$

Root of the equation (rüt ov ᴛнə i kwā´ zhən) the number substituted for a variable that makes the equation a true statement (p. 130)
$$3 + 6x = 15 \qquad x = 2$$

 S

Scalene triangle (skā lēn´ trī´ ang gəl) a triangle with no equal sides (p. 230)

Scientific notation (sī ən tif´ ik nō tā´ shən) a number written as the product of a number between 1 and 10 and a power of 10 (p. 76)
$$5,432 = 5.432 \cdot 10^3$$

Similar (sim´ ə lər) figures that have the same shape but not the same size (p. 330)

Simplest form (sim´ plest fôrm) a fraction in which the only common factor of the numerator and denominator is 1 (p. 66)
$$\frac{1}{2} \qquad \frac{1}{4} \qquad \frac{2}{3}$$

Simplify (sim´ plə fī) combine like terms (p. 46)
$$2a + 3a = 5a$$

Slope (slōp) the measure of the steepness of a line, slope $= \frac{\text{rise}}{\text{run}}$ (p. 298)

Slope-intercept form (slōp in tər sept´ fôrm) the slope-intercept form of a line in which $m =$ slope and $b = y$-intercept is $y = mx + b$ (p. 304)

Solution (sə lü´ shən) the value of a variable that makes an open statement true (p. 276)

Sphere (sfir) a round solid figure in which all points on the surface are at an equal distance from the center (p. 268)

Square (skwâr) a four-sided shape with sides of equal length and four right angles (p. 216)

Square pyramid (skwâr pir´ ə mid) a solid figure with a square base and triangular sides (p. 260)

Square root (skwâr rüt) a factor of a power of two (p. 220)

$$\sqrt{16} = 4 \qquad 4^2 = 16$$

The square root of 16 is 4.

Statistics (stə tis´ tiks) numerical facts about people, places, or things (p. 344)

Substitute (sub´ stə tüt) to put a number in place of a variable (p. 24)

Subtraction (səb trak´ shən) the arithmetic operation of taking one number away from another (p. 6)

$$10 - 3 = 7$$

Sum (sum) the result of addition (p. 2)

$$6 + 4 = 10 \qquad \text{10 is the sum.}$$

Supplementary angles (sup lə men´ tər ē ang´ gəls) two angles whose sum of their measures is 180 degrees (p. 318)

T

Tally (tal´ ē) a mark of each count (p. 348)

Terms (tėrms) parts of an expression separated by operation signs such as $+$, $-$, $\cdot$, or $\div$ (p. 20)

$$3x + 2x + x \qquad \text{3x, 2x, and x are terms.}$$

Tick (tik) a short line used to mark the sides of a triangle (p. 326)

Trapezoid (trap´ ə zoid) a four-sided polygon with one pair of parallel sides and one pair of sides that are not parallel (p. 256)

Triangle (trī´ ang gəl) a closed figure with three sides (p. 226)

U

Upper extreme (up´ ər ek strēm´) the greatest value of a set of data (p. 358)

$$\{2, 3, 5, 6, 8, 9, 11\} \qquad \text{11 is the upper extreme.}$$

Upper quartile (up´ ər kwȯr´ tīl) the median of scores above the median (p. 358)

$$\{2, 3, 5, 6, 8, 9, 11\} \qquad \text{9 is the upper quartile.}$$

V

Variable (vâr´ ē ə bəl) a letter that represents an unknown number (p. 22)

$$5x \qquad \text{x is the variable.}$$

Vertex (vėr´ teks) a common point to both sides of an angle; the plural of vertex is vertices (p. 314)

Vertical (vėr tə kəl) straight up and down (p. 286)

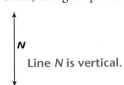

Line N is vertical.

Vertical angles (vėr tə kəl ang´ gəls) pairs of opposite angles formed by intersecting lines. Vertical angles have the same measure. (p. 316)

Angles a and b are vertical angles.

a	hat	e	let	ī	ice	ô	order	ù	put	sh	she		a	in about
ā	age	ē	equal	o	hot	oi	oil	ü	rule	th	thin	ə	e	in taken
ä	far	ėr	term	ō	open	ou	out	ch	child	ᴛʜ	then		i	in pencil
â	care	i	it	ȯ	saw	u	cup	ng	long	zh	measure		o	in lemon
													u	in circus

Volume (vol´ yəm) the number of cubic units that fills the interior of a solid (p. 218)

Whole number (hōl num´ bər) a number such as 0, 1, 2, 3, 4, 5, 6, . . . (p. 2)

x-axis (eks´ ak sis) the horizontal, or left-to-right, axis in a coordinate system (p. 286)

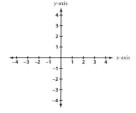

x-intercept (eks´ in tər sept´) the point at which a line crosses or intersects the x-axis (p. 304)

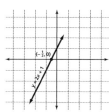

$-\frac{1}{2}$ is the x-intercept.

y-axis (wī´ ak sis) the vertical, or up-and-down, axis in a coordinate system (p. 286)

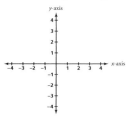

y-intercept (wī´ in tər sept´) the point at which a line crosses or intersects the y-axis (p. 304)

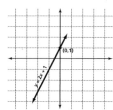

1 is the y-intercept.

Index

I

Improper fractions, 86–89
    defined, 86
Inequality
    defined, 278
    graphing of, 278–81, 284–85
Integers
    absolute value, 180–83
    addition of, 190–93
    comparing, 184–87
    consecutive, 184
    defined, 180
    division of, 202–03
    even and odd, 188–89
    multiplication of, 198–201
    negative and positive, 180–83, 190–203
    and number lines, 180–83
    subtraction of, 194–97
Intercepts
    x, 304
    y, 304
Interest, 50–51
    compound, 172–73
    defined, 50
Interior angles, 322–25
    defined, 323
Intersection
    defined, 314
    points of, 314–15
Interval
    defined, 344
Inverse
    defined, 6
    operations, 132–35
        defined, 132
Irrational numbers, 224–25
    defined, 224
Irregular polygons
    area of, 258–59
    defined, 246
    perimeter of, 246–49
Isosceles triangles, 230–31, 238–39
    defined, 230

L

Least common multiple (LCM), 72–75
    defined, 72
Like denominators, 100–03
Linear equations
    defined, 292
    graphing, 292–97
Lines
    graphing, 296–97
    slope of, 298–303
    slope-intercept form, 304–07
Lower extreme
    defined, 358
Lower quartile
    defined, 358

M

Mean, 350–51
    defined, 350
Measures of central tendency, 350–55
    defined, 354
Median, 352–53
    defined, 352
Mixed numbers
    defined, 86
    dividing, 112–15
    and improper fractions, 86–89
    mutiplying, 110–11
Mode, 354–55
    defined, 354
Multiplication
    of decimals, 38–41
        by powers of ten, 38–39
    defined, 12
    distributive property of, 68–71
    of fractions and mixed numbers, 110–11
    of positive and negative integers, 198–201
    of rational expressions, 144–45
    of terms with exponents, 212–13
    of whole numbers, 12–13

Triangles
    acute, 326–27
    area of, 254–55
    congruent, 328–29
    defined, 226
    equiangular, 326–27
    equilateral, 230–31
    isosceles, 230–31
    naming, 326–27
    obtuse, 326–27
    perimeter of, 36, 238–45
    Pythagorean theorem and, 226–29
    right, 226
    scalene, 230–31
    similar, 330–31

U

Unlike denominators, 104–07
Upper extreme
    defined, 358
Upper quartile
    defined, 358

V

Variables
    defined, 22
    identifying in operations, 22–23
    replacing, 24–25
Vertex
    defined, 314
Vertical
    defined, 286
Vertical angles, 316–17
    defined, 316
Volume, 260–63
    of a cube, 218–19
    of a cylinder, 268–69
    defined, 218
    of a sphere, 268–69

W

Whole numbers
    adding, 2–5
    defined, 2
    dividing, 14–17, 60–63
    estimating, 10–11, 18–19
    multiplying, 12–13
    subtracting, 6–9
Writing About Mathematics, 9, 23, 25, 39, 63, 65, 74, 77, 89, 103, 111, 114, 125, 138, 141, 161, 164, 193, 201, 211, 229, 257, 269, 294, 307, 315, 320, 327, 337, 347, 352

X

x-axis
    defined, 286
x-intercept
    defined, 304

Y

y-axis
    defined, 286
y-intercept
    defined, 304

Photo Credits

Cover, © Brand X Pictures/Alamy; page xviii, © Harald Sund/Image Bank; page 5, © Juan Silva Productions/Image Bank; page 9, © David Young-Wolff/PhotoEdit; page 17, © G. D. T./Image Bank; page 26, © Dennis MacDonald/PhotoEdit; page 30, © Paul Aresu/Taxi; page 47, © Stephen Frisch/Stock Boston; page 51, © David Young-Wolff/PhotoEdit; page 54, © Steve Chenn/Corbis; page 58, © Astrid & Hans Frieder Michler/Science Photo Library/Photo Researchers, Inc.; page 71, © David Young-Wolff/PhotoEdit; page 75, © Addison Geary/Stock Boston; page 79, © Steve Skjold/PhotoEdit; page 82, © Will & Deni McIntyre/Photo Researchers, Inc.; page 99, © Michael Newman/PhotoEdit; page 115, © Mary Kate Denny/PhotoEdit; page 116, © Doug Martin/Stock Boston; page 120, © E. R. Degginger/Color-Pic, Inc.; page 135, Science VU/NASA/Visuals Unlimited; page 143, © David Young-Wolff/PhotoEdit; page 146, © Myrleen Ferguson Cate/PhotoEdit; page 150, © Bonnie Kamin/PhotoEdit; page 165, © Jeff Greenberg/PhotoEdit; page 174, © Howard Grey/Stone; page 178, © W. Geiersperger/Corbis; page 183, © Beverly Factor/Phototake; page 193, © Gerald Corsi/Visuals Unlimited; page 197, © Peter Essick/Aurora & Quanta Productions; page 201, © Corbis; page 204, © Dennis Flaherty/Photo Researchers, Inc.; page 208, © Jim Brandenburg/Minden Pictures; page 217, © Doug Martin/Stock Boston; page 232, © Jim Grace/Photo Researchers, Inc.; page 236, © Mark Gibson/Index Stock Imagery; page 245, © Ronnie Kaufman/Corbis; page 253, © Photri-Microstock; page 263, © Mark E. Gibson/Dembinsky Photo Associates; page 269, © Herrmann/Starke/Corbis; page 270, © Myreen Ferguson Cate/PhotoEdit; page 274, © Mark E. Gibson/Corbis; page 283, © Bob Daemmrich/Stock Boston; page 285, © Jeff Greenberg/Visuals Unlimited; page 308, © Jose Luis Pelaez, Inc./Corbis; page 312, © Jeff Greenberg/PhotoEdit; page 338, © Cary Wolinsky/Stock Boston; page 342, © Rob Crandall/Stock Boston; page 345, © Mark Burnett/Stock Boston; page 357, © Ben Blankenburg/Stock Boston; page 364, © Rob Lewine/Corbis